38th Virginia Infantry

1st Edition

G. Howard Gregory

38th Virginia Infantry

1st Edition

This series is dedicated to the men who served in Virginia Units during the War Between the States. It is the purpose of this series to preserve, as a part of our heritage, the deeds and sacrifices of these men. Your support of this project is greatly appreciated.

Number __730__ of 1,000

G. Howard Gregory

Copyright 1988 H. E. Howard, Inc.

Manufactured in the United States by
H. E. Howard, Inc., Lynchburg, Virginia

Printed by H. E. Howard, Inc.

ISBN-0-930919-58-0

ACKNOWLEDGEMENTS

The 38th Virginia Infantry, C.S.A. has held a special fascination for me since learning that my great-grandfather, John Wilburn Scruggs, served in the 38th from 1861 to 1865. Researching and attempting to document the highlights of the unit's activities and the records of its members has been a most enjoyable challenge and a distinct honor.

Any endeavor of this nature could not be successful without the support and generous assistance of many fine individuals. This project has been extremely fortunate due to the invaluable contributions, guidance and advice of most renown and knowledgeable historians. A definite personal benefit of undertaking such an effort as this is the opportunity to meet and enjoy the fellowship of such wonderful people who share the respect for and desire to preserve our heritage.

I am grateful to Harold Howard, "father" of The Virginia Regimental Histories Series, for his confidence, the opportunity to publish this work, and especially for his friendship.

The single most significant contribution to the history of the 38th has been the daily diary of Colonel George K. Griggs, who methodically recorded the events of each day as he observed them. He would be pleased to know the record of his men, to whom he was so devoted and loyal, has been preserved for posterity. Colonel Griggs' grandson, Mr. James W. Bruce of Birmingham, Alabama, thoughtfully and generously permitted the use of his grandfather's diary. Mr. Archie W. Vipperman of Martinsville was instrumental in locating Mr. Bruce.

F. Lawrence McFall, Jr. of Danville, Lieutenant Commander of the Virginia Division of the Sons of Confederate Veterans (SCV), is the personification of a Southern gentleman and a true friend. His many contributions of information and helpful advice have been of incalcuable worth. Major and Mrs. Neil G. Payne of the Pittsylvania Historical Society painstakingly reviewed the microfilmed Compiled Service Records (CSR) in addition to forwarding many useful tidbits of information. Their cordial Southern hospitality is exceeded only by their deep appreciation for history and desire to preserve our past for future generations.

Gary Lee Hall, of Raleigh, N.C., whose great-grandfather William B. Craddock, served in the 38th, generously donated his time to research and draw the maps for this volume. As you will observe, Gary Lee is both a most knowledgeable historian and an expert cartographer. Dr. Jack I. Hayes, Jr. of Averett College graciously permitted reference to his master's thesis on the 38th.

Roger C. Dodson of Ringgold, who had acquired the microfilmed CSR, generously loaned his records and provided useful information. Bruce A. Flora of Blacksburg did much of the tedious drudgery in transcribing these microfilmed records for print. Past Lieutenant Commander Marvin L. Osborne of the Cabell-Graves Camp, SCV, has carefully copied numerous pension records, which he contributed along with many other pertinent details. Past Commander M. Kenneth Wiles, Robert (Danny) Ricketts, Danny T. Jones and other members of Cabell-Graves Camp No. 1402, SCV at Danville all contributed in one way or another.

No chronicle of the Virginia soldier in The War Between the States would be complete today without the input of Chief Historian Robert K. Krick of the Fredericksburg National Military Park. Bob's advice, leads and careful editing of the manuscript have contributed immeasurably. Lee A. Wallace, Jr. of Falls Church has given welcome advice for which I am grateful. Chief Historian Kathleen R. Georg of Gettysburg National Military Park kindly critiqued the section on "Pickett's Charge." She, John W. Busey of Centreville and David G. Martin of Longstreet House graciously permitted the use of material from their exceptional volume, *Nothing But Glory — Pickett's Division at Gettysburg.* Historian Chris Calkins of Petersburg National Battlefield Park, the acknowledged authority on "the retreat route," reviewed and offered useful comments on that portion. The burial records compiled by Scott W. Hutchison of Richmond and Raymond W. Watkins of Falls Church have provided grave locations for many of the 38th's soldiers.

Dr. James I. Robertson of VPI & SU, Cathy Carlson of the Museum of the Confederacy, Michael Musick of the National Archives, Supt. Jon Montgomery and Historian Ronald G. Wilson of Appomattox Court House National Historical Park, H. Gary Heath, President of the Fauquier Historical Society, Archivist Diane B. Jacob of VMI, Vicki Martin of Lynchburg, Dennis R. Loba of Warrenton, Clarence Warren of Marshall, John E. Divine of Leesburg, H. George Carrison of Awendaw, S.C., Mr. and Mrs. Randall C. Smyth of Hagerstown, Md., William Otey Blair of Frederick, Md., Robert Hardy of Suffolk, Col. Thomas M. Rankin of Silver Spring, Md., Virgil Carrington (Pat) Jones of Centreville, Stuart C. Welch of Richmond, Larry W. Blanks and George Calvin Waldrep III of Nathalie, Freddie L. Hill of Danville, Anna M. Day of Dry Fork, Mary B. Tinsley of Danville, Robert W. Carter of Reidsville, N.C. and Dr. Walter H. Bennett of Ringgold all contributed by supplying information, photographs and old letters or giving advice and guidance as this project progressed.

Exceptionally good fortune has been mine in enjoying the wise counsel of such a distinguished group of historians and fine people. With their support and contributions, no mistakes should be found in this book, but regretfully, I am sure this will not be the case. For any errors, which undoubtedly will appear, and for inadvertently failing to acknowledge other contributors, I alone am responsible. Your kind indulgence and pardon is respectfully sought.

In conclusion, I would be remiss if I failed to express my grateful appreciation to my wife, Linda, for her support, understanding and cooperation. Without these, this undertaking could not have been completed.

G. Howard Gregory

Richmond
September 27, 1988

1861

As the gathering clouds of War continued to darken in the wake of John Brown's Raid, Fort Sumter, and President Lincoln's demand that Virginia furnish troops to subdue her sister states, the citizens of the Old Dominion felt that they had little choice but to secede from the Union and cast their lot with the Confederacy. On April 17, 1861, Virginia adopted an ordinance of secession and preparations for war intensified. Farmers, store clerks, students, lawyers, and able-bodied representatives of practically every other occupation hastily joined the various volunteer military forces of their home state to "repel invasion and protect the citizens of the State in the present emergency". Few doubted that it would be a "shawt wah".

In response to Governor John Letcher's call on May 3, 1861, for volunteer regiments, the companies gathered that were later to form the 38th Virginia Volunteer Infantry Regiment, C.S.A. The initial leaders of the regiment were Colonel Edward C. Edmonds, Lieutenant Colonel Powhatan B. Whittle, and Major Isaac H. Carrington.

Colonel Edward Claxton Edmonds was born January 21, 1835, in Paris (Fauquier County), Virginia, the son of Dr. John Robert and Helen Carter Edmonds. He graduated from the Virginia Military Institute at Lexington on July 5, 1858, where he was Captain of Cadets of Company B and 11th in a class of 19. Following graduation, Edmonds taught mathematics in Staunton for one year before moving to Danville and opening a military academy in association with Major Jesse Jones. Colonel Edmonds who was appointed on June 12, 1861, was killed leading the 38th in "Pickett's Charge" at Gettysburg on July 3, 1863.

Lieutenant Colonel Powhatan Bolling Whittle was born in Mecklenburg County, Virginia, on June 26, 1829, but later moved to Macon, Georgia. In early 1861, he joined Georgia's "Jackson Artillery" as a private, but three months later was elected first lieutenant. As Georgia's Governor Joseph E. Brown would not release the company for service in Virginia, where Whittle realized much of the War would be fought, he resigned his commission. In order to serve in Virginia, he then enlisted as a private in the "Macon Volunteers," who were en route to Fort Norfolk at Norfolk. On June 12, 1861, Governor Letcher commissioned him lieutenant colonel to assist Colonel Edmonds and Major Carrington in raising an infantry regiment in Pittsylvania County. Although severely wounded several times, Whittle served throughout the War.

Major Issac H. Carrington was born March 7, 1827, in Richmond and educated at both the University of North Carolina and the University of Virginia. After "reading law" in 1847 under Pittsylvania County attorney

James M. Whittle, he entered into a law partnership with him. After his appointment on June 12, 1861, Carrington served until May 12, 1862, when he was not re-elected.

Seven of the ten companies that initially would form the 38th Virginia Infantry, also known as "The Pittsylvania Regiment," were organized in various Pittsylvania County communities with one company originating in Halifax County and two in Mecklenburg County. The eleventh company, the "second" Company I, was organized in Norfolk County. Writing to his brother on May 20, 1861, from Pittsylvania Court House (now Chatham), Lt. Col. Whittle reported: "I have been riding over the country ever since my arrival, endeavoring to raise men for our regiment. We are succeeding rather slowly — the men of the region do not seem to enlist as readily as persons in the South. . . . We will go into camp at Danville in a short time, where we will drill the men before being ordered into actual service. This will be better than to be at Richmond, as they have so many soldiers there, and the accomodations are very inferior. . . ."

Company A, which entered Confederate service on May 30, 1861, was organized in State service on August 20, 1860, by Daniel C. Townes of Kentuck, who was its first company commander. Captain Townes served until being killed in action at Gettysburg on July 3, 1863. (His brother, Nathan B. Townes, was Colonel of the 9th Texas Cavalry). Captain Richard J. Joyce was company commander from July, 3, 1863, until his capture on August 25, 1864, at Bermuda Hundred, where he died as a prisoner of war. He was succeeded by Captain Thomas J. Turner, who served until the surrender at Appomattox.

Company B, probably nicknamed the "Pittsylvania Vindicators," was organized at Callands on May 23, 1861, by Dr. John Roy Cabell, a physician, and entered Confederate service on June 4, 1861. Captain Cabell was born in Danville on March 24, 1823, graduated from VMI, married twice, and was the father of five children. One of his brothers was Brigadier General William L. Cabell, who served in the Trans-Mississippi theater. Another brother, Joseph Robert Cabell, was the organizer and first commander of Company E. He resigned his commission on December 10, 1862, due to his failing health and his responsibility for "five small motherless children." Captain William B. Pritchard commanded the company for the remainder of the war. In 1876, Captain Pritchard married Margaret Strother Johnston, the fourth child of General Albert Sidney Johnston. Captain and Mrs. Pritchard moved to Los Angeles and then to San Francisco after the war.

Company C, also known as the "Laurel Grove Riflemen," was organized at Laurel Grove on May 11, 1861, by Captain William B. Simpson and mustered into Confederate service on June 3, 1861. Many of the men in this company had served in the 42nd Virginia Militia. Captain John T. Grubbs was elected company commander on April 29, 1862, when Captain Simp-

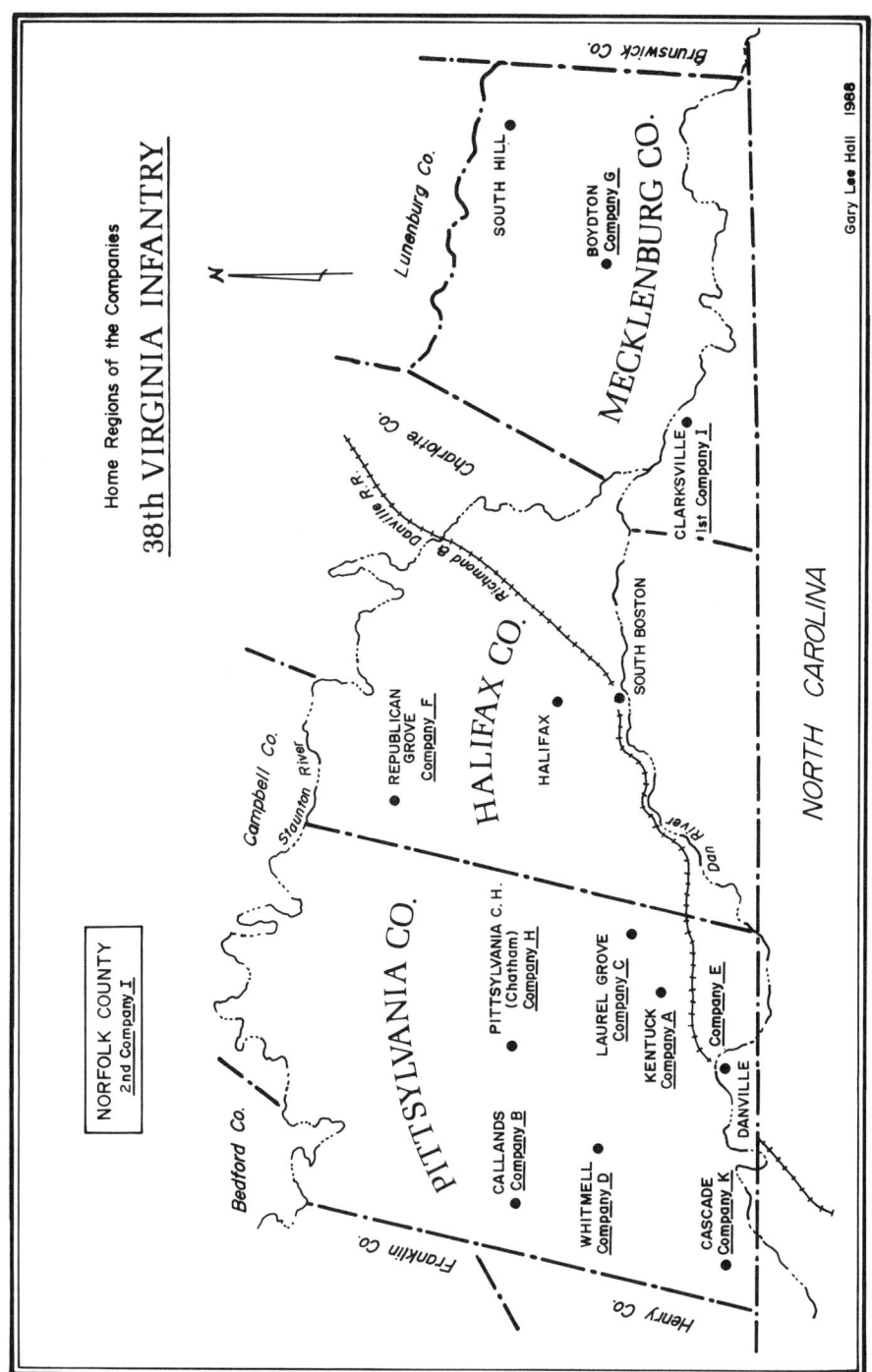

son declined re-election. He served in this capacity until the surrender at Appomattox.

Company D, also known as the "Whitmell Guards," was organized at Whitmell on June 3, 1861, by Captain Ralph C. Herndon, and mustered into Confederate service on June 11, 1861. Captain Herndon was not re-elected and resigned on May 1, 1862. He was succeeded by Captain William H. Badgett, who served until July 17, 1862, when he resigned due to kidney and lung disease. The last company commander was Captain John A. Herndon (brother of Ralph C.) who served until April 1, 1865, when he was captured near Dinwiddie Court House.

Company E, nicknamed the "Cabell Guards," was organized in Danville on May 28, 1861, by Captain Joseph Robert Cabell (brother of Captain John Roy Cabell) and enlisted in Confederate service on June 8, 1861. The Company's motto was "Victory or Death!" Many of the men had been members of the 42nd Virginia Militia. Captain Cabell, a son of General B. W. S. Cabell, was born at "Bridgewater" in Pittsylvania County on May 28, 1840, and educated at Danville Academy and Danville Military Institute. Enlisting as a private in the "Danville Blues," Company A, 18th Virginia Regiment, on April 23, 1861, he was then elected captain of Company E of the 38th Regiment on May 29 and served in that capacity until May 12, 1862, when he was promoted to major. Cabell was promoted to lieutenant colonel on July 3, 1863, and then to Colonel in charge of the 38th on November 15, 1863. On June 24, 1863, he joined and was initiated into Roman Eagle Lodge, No. 122, A. F. & A. M. in Danville and was raised to Master Mason on December 19, 1863. Wounded at Gettysburg, Cabell was killed at the Battle of Chester Station on May 10, 1864, while leading the 38th's charge against the enemy. He was succeeded as company commander by Captain Thomas M. Tyree, who was taken prisoner near Dinwiddie Court House on April 1, 1865.

Company F, nicknamed the "Davis Rifle Guard," was organized at Republican Grove in Halifax County on May 7, 1861, by Captain Jeduthan Carter, Jr., and entered Confederate service on June 4, 1861. Many of the men had been members of the 84th Virginia Militia. Captain Carter, who was detached as a recruiting officer on February 16, 1862, was not re-elected on April 29, 1862. He was succeeded by Captain Lafayette Jennings, who served until his resignation on February 10, 1865. Captain Raleigh T. Daniel, Jr., adjutant of the 5th Kentucky Regiment and an 1853 graduate of VMI, had initially enlisted in the 1st Virginia Infantry. Being on furlough at his home in Richmond, he "volunteered for the fight" and commanded Company F at Malvern Hill in the absence of Captain Jennings, who was recuperating from his wounds sustained at Seven Pines. Captain Daniel was seriously wounded while waving the regimental colors and rallying the company, but survived the war and worked as a lawyer in Richmond, where he died in the Soldiers' Home on February 11, 1919.

Company G, nicknamed the "Mecklenburg Rifles," was organized at Boydton in Mecklenburg County on May 18, 1861, by Captain William Townes, Jr., and entered Confederate service on June 3, 1861. Many of the men had been members of the 98th Virginia Militia. Captain Townes, who was not re-elected on April 29, 1862, was succeeded by Captain Henderson L. Lee, who served until his promotion to major on November 15, 1863. Captain Benjamin J. Hawthorne, who was promoted to the position on that date, was the last commander of Company G.

Company H, nicknamed the "Secession Guards," was organized at Pittsylvania Court House (now Chatham) which was also known as Competition, on June 7, 1861, by Captain Joseph M. Terry, and entered Confederate service on July 2, 1861. Captain Terry resigned on December 13, 1861. Captain Edgar W. Carrington, a graduate of Hampden-Sydney College, was elected to the position, which he held until he was killed in action at Seven Pines on May 31, 1862. Dr. Robert Lewis Dabney, who was a professor of theology at Hampden-Sydney and served on the staff of General Thomas Jonathan "Stonewall" Jackson, wrote a sermon commemorating Captain Carrington's death. After reading this sermon during his daily devotions, General Robert E. Lee wrote his wife on April 12, 1863: "How many noble martyrs have lain down their lives at the altar of their country." Apparently Captain Shields S. Luke was company commander of the "Secession Guards" briefly before also being killed in action at Seven Pines on May 31st. Captain James E. Poindexter served from May 31, 1862, until July 3, 1863, when he was captured at Gettysburg.

The first Company I, nicknamed the "Confederate Guards," was organized by Captain John S. Wood at Clarksville in Mecklenburg County and enlisted in Confederate service on June 20, 1861. After reorganization and the election of Captain William Walter Wood as company commander on April 29, 1862, it was transferred from the regiment and assigned as the second Company G of the 14th Virginia Infantry by Special Order No. 148, A&IGO, dated June 27, 1862.

The second Company I was organized by Captain George Alexander Martin on June 26, 1861, in Norfolk County as Company B, 20th Battalion, Virginia Heavy Artillery, nicknamed the "St. Brides Artillery." It enlisted in Confederate service on July 6, 1861, and was transferred to the 38th infantry on May 3, 1864, by Special Order No. 96, A&IGO, dated April 25, 1864. Captain Martin was promoted to lieutenant colonel on December 2, 1864.

Company K, nicknamed "The Cascade Rifles," was organized at Cascade and mustered into State service on April 24, 1861, probably with a number of men from the 42nd Regiment Virginia Militia. Under the command of Captain George King Griggs, it was mustered into Confederate service on June 3, 1861. The 21-year-old Captain Griggs, a dedicated Chris-than, was a native of Henry County. Having spent two years at Virginia Military Institute, he moved to the Cascade area of Pittsylvania County in early 1861 to marry Miss Sallie B. Boyd. After Captain Griggs' promotion to major the company was commanded by Captain William G. Cabaniss from Aug. 4, 1864 until his retirement on December 17, 1864, due to a severe wound in the jaw. From then until the end of the War, Company K was commanded by Captain James M. Cabaniss and, briefly, by Captain Joseph H. Estes. Although severely wounded several times, Major Griggs was promoted to lieutenant colonel on November 15, 1863, and then to colonel in command of the 38th Regiment from May 16, 1864, until the surrender at Appomattox.

During early June 1861, these ten companies either marched or rode the train from Danville to Richmond. As the preparations continued and the influx of soldiers rapidly swelled the population of the Confederate Capitol, some confusion and difficulty in securing proper provisions for the troops understandably resulted. The companies that were to form the 38th Virginia Infantry were directed to a camp of instruction at Hermitage Fairgrounds or "Camp Lee" (which was later the site of Broad Street Station and today of the Science Museum of Virginia). Here they raised their tents, settled in, and began military drill.

On the weekends the more devout soldiers attended church services and studied their Bibles, while the wilder element spent their free time getting drunk, cursing, and generally carousing. On Sunday, June 9, 1861, an officer in the 38th lamented "Instead of hearing the Word of God preached, I have listened to profanity, but have spent part of the day reading Christ's Holy Word." Various illnesses that would continue to exact a high toll throughout the war soon attacked the men in camp. Like soldiers in every war, the somewhat homesick men eagerly awaited a letter or word from a wife, sweetheart, or the folks at home.

On Friday, June 14, 1861, Colonel John B. Baldwin designated the above ten companies as the 38th Infantry Regiment, Virginia Volunteers, by Special Order No. 192 under the command of the aforementioned Colonel E. C. Edmonds, Lieutenant Colonel P. B. Whittle, and Major Isaac Carrington. Routine military drill continued as the battle commenced against the elements — alternating from very hot and dry weather to heavy thunderstorms with strong winds that blew down most of the tents in camp. Even when in place, the tents leaked terribly. On Saturday, June 22, the men arose nearly covered with sand and dust blown by the strong winds during the night. On Friday, the 28th, during a hard rain, many of the men "pulled off their clothes and ran about in the rain like so many ducks."

At last orders were received to move the 38th to Winchester to join the command of General Joseph E. Johnston. At 8 a.m. on Tuesday, July 9, the men of the regiment marched from Camp Lee to the Virginia Central

Railroad (later the Chesapeake & Ohio) where they boarded a northbound train about 11:30 a.m. After they had travelled about 25 miles, a train from Fredericksburg on the Richmond, Fredericksburg and Potomac Railroad collided with the train transporting the 38th at Hanover Junction (now Doswell). Although a baggage car was derailed, fortunately no one was hurt and after a two-hour delay the trip resumed in the rain. After travelling about 40 more miles, the train arrived late in the afternoon at Gordonsville, where it stopped for two hours.

The trip resumed on the Orange and Alexandria Railroad (later the Southern Railway). The train travelled for about 60 miles through the night until it arrived at Manassas Junction around 2 a.m. on July 10. Here the men of the 38th transferred to the Manassas Gap Railroad (later the Southern Railway) and travelled about 60 miles to Strasburg, arriving at 2 p.m. Due to a heavy rain, Colonel Edmonds ordered the 38th to spend the night at Strasburg.

On July 11 at 6 a.m., the men of the 38th started the 18 mile march to Winchester over a good road in pleasant weather. En route they met many citizens fleeing south to escape the reportedly approaching Yankees. As this was the first march for the regiment, many of the men were exhausted and had to ride on the wagons. Residents along the route of march treated the soldiers kindly, giving them water, bread, and words of encouragement. The regiment arrived in Winchester at 3 p.m.

Here the 38th became one of the five regiments in Brigadier General E. Kirby Smith's Fourth Brigade in the Army of the Shenandoah. Camp was established and drilling began. One of the men in Company A accidentally shot and killed a fellow soldier, so Colonel Edmonds ordered all of the privates to give up their pistols and forbade their carrying them.

Private James Booker of Company D wrote his cousin on July 14: "I dont know how long we'll have to stay here. I am in hopes that we will stay here for some time. We have elegant water and plenty of it and a plenty of good provisions so far and a fine chance of beautyful young ladies and the kindest that I ever saw in my life, and the most beautiful country that I ever saw. They have fine crops over here and not much likely hood of a fight. The yankeys had gone back to Martinsburg and it is thought if we get them we will have to go after them."

This optimism was short-lived as excitement rippled through the camp the next day at the report that 15,000 Union soldiers were advancing south toward Winchester. The men of the 38th struck tents and marched to a position one mile north of town and waited in line of battle. Although the reports persisted through the 16th, the Union forces failed to materialize and the men spent the night laying "on our arms with a blanket and sky for a cover." A hard rain made the night quite disagreeable. Captain Griggs poignantly and prophetically observed in his diary: "I feel rather sad contemplating the great slaughter that would follow from an engagement, but to God we look for success and humbly implore His protection and assistance in making the enemy soon to acknowledge our independence." On July 17 the Regiment returned to camp in Winchester.

As Union General Irvin McDowell slowly moved his 35,000-man army southward from Washington toward Manassas Junction, General Johnston's 11,000-man army started from Winchester toward Manassas Junction to reinforce General P. G. T. Beauregard's 22,000 troops. Colonel J. E. B. Stuart's cavalry successfully screened General Johnston's departure from Winchester from Union General Robert Patterson's 18,000-man army, which had been ordered to hold Johnston at Winchester.

The men of the 38th, one of the last units to depart, marched eastward from Winchester at 5 p.m. on Thursday, July 18, not knowing their destination until their orders were read some two miles east of town. The news of their destination was "received with a shout." The march continued until midnight with the men wading several creeks. The march resumed before sunrise on the 19th. The 38th waded across the Shenandoah River, which was over knee deep, before halting in a field for the night.

Finally, late on Saturday, July 20, the regiment arrived at Piedmont Depot (now Delaplane) on the Manassas Gap Railroad after a march of more than 25 miles. The First Brigade, commanded by Colonel T. J. Jackson, had already rapidly boarded the train pulled by the railroad's one locomotive and continued toward Manassas — this was the first time in history that a railroad was used for the rapid movement of troops to a battlefield. Being near the rear of the line of march, the 38th awaited its turn to board the train, which was shuttling between Piedmont and Manassas Junction. The men were hungry after the long march, followed by this lengthy delay, so Colonel Edmonds ordered a cow killed and it was devoured in less than an hour by the hungry soldiers.

A problem on the railroad — either a minor accident or the deliberate reluctance of the train crew — further delayed the troop movement. As the Battle of First Manassas raged on Sunday, July 21, the 38th spent the day at Piedmont awaiting the train. Some of the men attended church services conducted by a chaplain, the Reverend John S. Cosby.

In the darkness of the early hours of Monday, July 22, the men of the 38th were awakened and boarded the crowded train. After a ride of 34 miles, the regiment arrived at Manassas Junction and then marched eight miles in a hard rain to a campsite near Broad Run. The following day some of the men were detailed to return to Winchester for baggage that had been left behind.

On August 23, 1861, possibly in light of the uniform confusion at First Manassas, the Danville Town Council received a request from Captain

Joseph R. Cabell to furnish uniforms for his Company E. The council recretted that they were unable to make any appropriation as they had been "obliged to furnish, the first companies leaving the town . . . ."

On September 22, the 38th moved its camp about 12 miles to a new site near Centreville. Varied illnesses, including rheumatism, measles, typhus, general debility, and even syphilis took a heavy toll on the regiment. Many of the sick had been left at the "old camp on Broad Run" pending their recovery. During September, 676 men of the regiment were reported sick at various times, with 101 of these suffering from typhus. Six of these died. Some of the sick went back home on furlough to recuperate. The soldiers' immune systems apparently began to strengthen, after prolonged exposure to the filth and poor sanitation experienced in camp. In October, only 25 soldiers were reported with typhus and only a few more were reported sick of other diseases. Those who were able pulled picket duty and drilled as the days and weeks passed and the men grew more accustomed to army life.

Late on Wednesday, October 16, the regiment was ordered to break camp and fall back to a point three miles west of Centreville, when approaching Union troops drove in the pickets. Preparations were made to receive an attack which never materialized.

On Thursday, October 17, the regiment was assigned to Brigadier General C. M. Wilcox's Brigade along with the 9th, 10th, and 11th Alabama Infantry, 19th Mississippi Infantry, and Thomas' Artillery (Va.) This was one of the three brigades in Major General G. W. Smith's Second Division of the Potomac District.

The 38th continued on picket duty near the Fairfax-Loudoun County line while camped on Cub Run. The arrival of sutlers with their supplies somewhat softened the harshness of camp life. On October 30, the regiment, along with other Virginia troops, marched to Centreville, where Governor John Letcher presented state flags to each Virginia regiment. On November 1, the quartermaster issued clothing to the regiment, which was also the recipient of a political speech by Congressional candidate John Goode of Bedford. On November 4, Colonel Edmonds' wife and her sister visited the camp. November 6 was election day and the soldiers could vote for President, Vice President, and Congressman. Picket duty continued and the men were forced to endure the windy, colder nights, snow, and hail without the warmth of a fire. The strong winds blew over some tents, while other soldiers were awakened by the cold rain falling on their faces. Although a devoted Christian himself, on November 7 Captain Griggs paid $2.50 for five pints of whiskey for his men.

In spite of a snow the previous night, the troops were reviewed by Generals Johnston, Beauregard and Smith on November 25. On a clear and warmer November 30, the regiment received orders to send all baggage to

Manassas Junction. Each man could retain only one "outer suit, two under clothing, two blankets, cooking utensils and tents." The bitter cold and rain returned by the next day. On December 3, Generals Johnston and Smith again reviewed the troops.

On December 20, the reported approach of the enemy caused great excitement and the regiment formed in line of battle, but the Yankees failed to materialize. A skirmish did occur 14 miles to the northwest at Dranesville. Christmas Day, 1861, was a clear, beautiful, and quiet day for the men of the 38th. On December 26, the regiment marched to a site one and one-half miles from the stone bridge near the Lewis House in a pine thicket on the battlefield of First Manassas and began building log cabins for their winter quarters. Many soldiers remained in camp sick during the last days of 1861.

1862

The regiment spent January and February of 1862 in winter quarters battling the biting cold, rain, ice, and snow, as well as various diseases, including the mumps. Some of the officers and men were fortunate enough to get leave to visit their loved ones at home, while the remainder of the regiment routinely drilled and pulled occasional picket duty.

As Union General George B. McClellan embarked on his Peninsula Campaign in early March 1862, the Confederate forces encamped near Manassas, including the 38th Regiment, were ordered to move southward toward Richmond to protect the Confederate capital. On Monday, March 10, without knowing their ultimate destination or purpose, the soldiers burned the log huts that had provided their shelter for the past two months and marched toward Gainesville. Here a large quantity of commissary stores and more than 1,000 barrels of flour were destroyed, as the Yankees advanced and occupied Centreville. As the Confederate army continued south toward Orange Courthouse, a portion of the 38th, including Company K, commanded by Captain Griggs, was detached to serve as rear guard of the army.

Leaving Gainesville at 8 a.m. on March 11, the detachment comprised of five companies and accompanied by General J. E. B. Stuart's cavalry, marched about ten miles to a location two miles east of Warrenton by 4 p.m. On March 12, the tired soldiers formed in line of battle and had skirmish drill. The detachment moved slowly toward Warrenton at 9 a.m. on March 14 and again halted before entering the "beautiful village of Warrenton" on the morning of March 15.

By this time the detachment was cut off from the main body of the Confederate army and expected an attack at any time. This did not occur, but the officers did find it necessary to "destroy a great deal of liquor." The troops spent March 15-27 in Warrenton, where they were kindly and cordially received by the citizens and quartered in the Fauquier County Courthouse and the Warren-Green Hotel.

At sunset on March 27, the detachment marched eight miles from Warrenton to the Fauquier White Sulphur Springs where it arrived about midnight. During the morning of March 28, the detachment burned the bridge across the Rappahannock River and marched at 1 p.m. to overtake the army. After covering nine miles, the men made camp for the night at Rixeyville.

At 9 a.m. on March 29, the detachment continued the march in "mud, hail, snow and rain," reaching Culpeper around noon. Early on March 30, the march was resumed through Culpeper and Orange counties, following the Orange and Alexandria Railroad tracks, until the detachment overtook the main body of the army encamped a little more than a mile from Orange Court House. The regiment remained in camp there until 9 p.m. on April 6, when it was marched for six hours until 3 a.m. on April 7 and bivouacked in a thickly wooded area. It then marched back to the old camp site. The constant struggle against disease continued. Many of the men suffered the effects of measles.

Orders were received on April 10 and the regiment departed its camp near Orange Court House at sunset and marched to the nearby railroad. The men entrained and departed at midnight, arriving at Gordonsville at daybreak on April 11, after travelling eight miles. The train rumbled slowly onward toward Richmond, about 60 miles distance, all day and arrived after dark. During the trip, no food was provided for the hungry soldiers, who detrained in Richmond and moved toward Camp Winder.

With orders to move to Yorktown, the regiment departed Richmond aboard the steam ship *West Point* about dark on April 13 and landed at Kings Mill around midnight. From there the regiment marched about five miles to Lebanon Church, within five miles of Yorktown, and encamped in a pine woods. Union troops were about two miles away and firing could be heard. An exchange of shelling continued through the day of April 16. At 5 p.m. Union troops assaulted the entrenched Confederates, but were repelled with losses.

Early on April 17, the regiment was moved to Dam No. 1 on picket duty and then into the "ditches" on the following day, when heavy fire was exchanged. Private Joel P. Tucker of Company F was shot in the chin and later died. The knee-deep water made the 24-hour tour of duty in the ditches or trenches quite disagreeable. After a mostly sleepless night, anticipating an attack, the regiment worked on April 19 improving its breastworks while under continuing harrassing fire from the enemy. Companies I and K returned to the trenches at 8 p.m. in a cold, torrential rain. Heavy musketry fire erupted along the line and continued for some time before it was found to be a false alarm.

Regarding this incident, Private Andrew J. Leftwich of Company D wrote his mother on April 22:

> O you ought to have seen our brave boys shoot the other night when we was on picket. Someone thought he saw or herd somebody and shot and that caused a great many others to shoot. It was very dark and they thought the Yankees was making a charge and it was a false alarm. I shot three times. I have shot a good many times since at them thru the trees but could not see them. I thought I would return the same compliments.

They shoot at us pretty regular. . . . They first day we got here . . . the shots whistled over our heads considerably. Although it was dangerous I was oblige to laugh at the boys doging, I tell you it made me feel rite small too. The first one that came over you ought to have seen the boys bow. Every one that I was looking at had the same motion, they bowed as politely as if they were bowing at ladies and I expect I bowed to. I no I have doged a good many times since from rifle balls. The Yankees shot at us when we was on picket, they are shooting at each other every day on picket, but dont hit often. We are about three or four hundred yards apart and in the woods . . . .

Enemy fire across the swamp continued all day on April 20, but had little effect on the sleepless, weary, wet and cold Confederates. At dark the men were relieved from their tour in the trenches, but returned again at dark on April 21. The rain continued while many men suffered the effects of exposure to the elements, lack of rest, and poor diet. On April 22, the soldiers were again relieved from their duty in the trenches. April 23 was spent working on the fortifications, before going back into the trenches. Captain Griggs kept one third of his men awake while the others dozed fitfully, despite the constant firing of enemy sharpshooters. After a brief respite, the troops returned to the rifle pits, which were nearly full of water, late on April 25. With no tents, his blanket was the only protection the soldier had from the cold and rain which continued throughout the week. Rations for the men were cooked about two miles to the rear and brought to the front. They returned to the trenches again on April 27 for another night.

As authorized by the Confederate government, an election of officers was held on April 29 and resulted in numerous changes in the regiment.

On May 1, which was spent resting, word was received that the 38th was being transferred to General Jubal A. Early's Brigade, which also included the 24th Virginia and 5th and 23rd North Carolina Infantry regiments. On May 2, the regiment started toward Williamsburg, but was ordered back to the breastworks. Heavy artillery fire continued all day on May 3. Finally, at dark the evacuation of Yorktown commenced with the last troops moving out after midnight. Due to the recent heavy rains, the Hampton and Yorktown roads leading toward Williamsburg were quagmires of mud. With General D. H. Hill's Division, including Early's Brigade and a small force of Stuart's cavalry forming the rear guard for the army, the soldiers struggled throughout the night to cover the twelve miles to Williamsburg, where they arrived around 8 a.m. on Sunday, May 4. Wet, cold, and hungry, Early's Brigade, including the 38th, bivouacked about two miles west of Williamsburg.

As the pursuing Union troops led by Stoneman's cavalry engaged Stuart's cavalry around 1 p.m. on May 4, General Johnston decided to fight a delaying action at Fort Magruder, an earthwork located one mile east of Williamsburg and to the north of the junction of the Hampton and Yorktown roads. Five redoubts to the west and seven redoubts to the east of Fort Magruder formed a portion of the line of fortifications that General John B. Magruder had constructed across the Peninsula from the James to Queen's Creek on the York River. Stiff Confederate resistance from Fort Magruder on the afternoon of May 4 brought the Federal pursuit to a halt. Another cold rain during the night added to the soldiers' discomfort. The battle resumed about 6 a.m. on May 5 and intensified during the day, as the fighting spread from the west (right) to the east (left) of the Fort.

Early's Brigade, including the 38th, was ordered back through the mud and cold drizzle, to support General Longstreet at Fort Magruder. After a pause in the rear of the college buildings on the campus of William & Mary until around 3 p.m., Longstreet directed Early to move his brigade through a plowed field to the left rear (northeast) of Fort Magruder and await orders. At this location on the crest of a ridge, the Confederates faced south across a wheatfield about 300 yards wide and toward heavy woods with thick underbrush that bordered a swampy area.

At this location, the men's excitement heightened as they could hear unseen Federal artillery firing toward Fort Magruder from a position about one half mile through the tangled forest. Due to an unexplained oversight by the Confederate high command, the redoubts on the extreme left of the Confederate line had been left vacant on the afternoon of May 5. Union General Winfield Scott Hancock with five regiments and ten guns — about 4000 men — had seized the opportunity to occupy two of the vacant redoubts — the key to the Confederate defenses — and began shelling Fort Magruder. This had little effect, though, due to the lack of support provided by the Federal high command.

Hill and Early conferred and decided to advance across the wheatfield and through the woods with intent to attack the battery from the rear. With extremely scant, if any, reconnaissance of the area, Hill had the troops formed on brigade front to advance from north to south. On the left (east) was the 24th Virginia, which had fought valiantly at Manassas. To the right of the 24th was the 38th Virginia, with the 23rd North Carolina next and the 5th North Carolina on the right (west). Hill positioned himself to lead the North Carolina regiments while Early, astride his horse, led the Virginians from his position in advance of the 24th, his old regiment.

Moments after forming the four regiments in line of battle, Early saw Hill advancing the North Carolina regiments. He started the Virginians forward about 4 p.m. with rifles loaded and bayonets fixed. In the absence of Colonel E. C. Edmonds, the regimental commander, Lt. Colonel P. B. Whittle was in command of the 38th. Neither the regiment nor its commander had experienced the heat of battle before. As the 24th Virginia moved

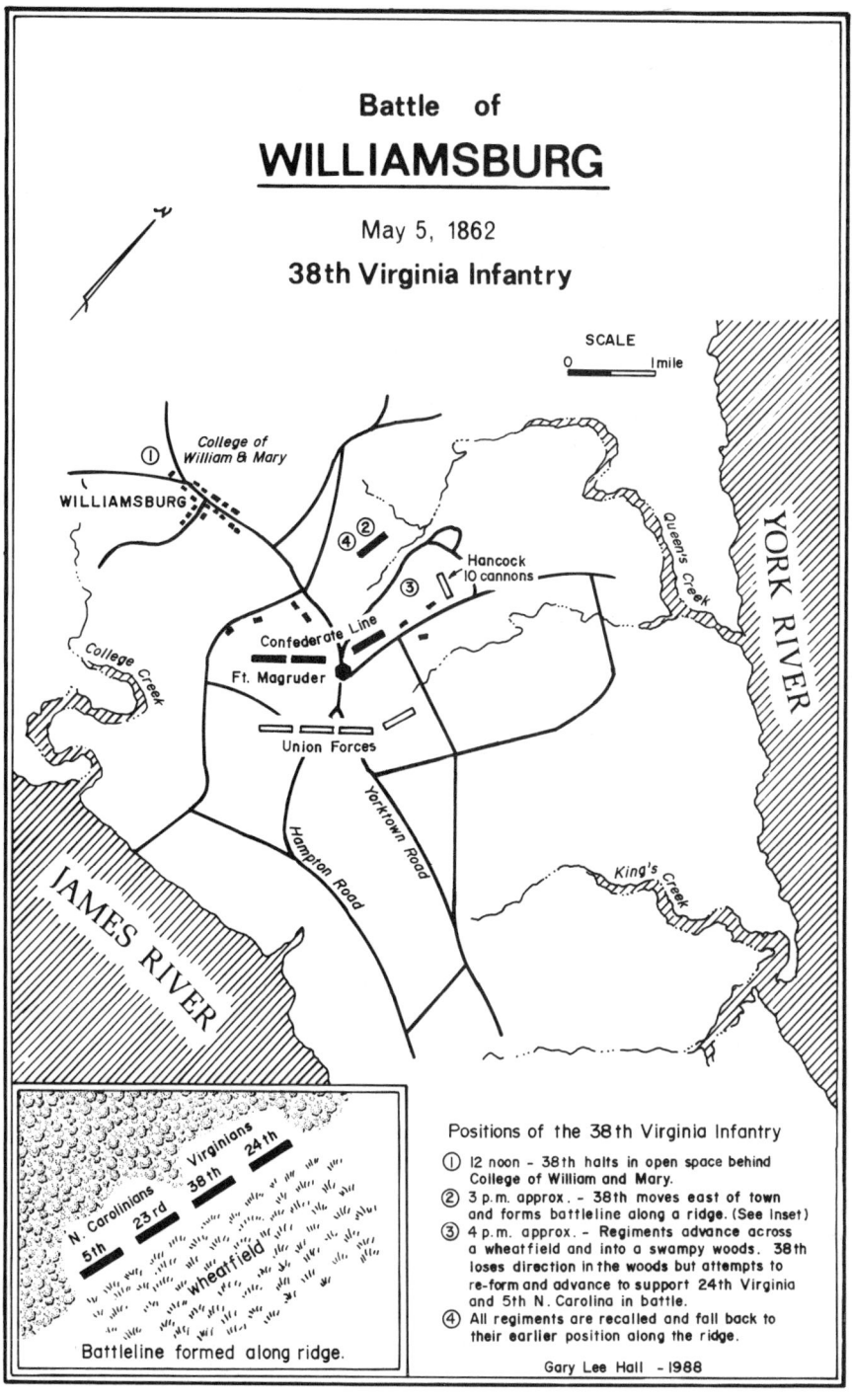

smartly across the wheatfield and into the woods, the 38th lagged and was soon 50 yards behind. Early sent back and ordered the 38th to the double quick, but to no avail as contact between the regiments on the right and left was promptly lost in the woods. The soldiers stumbled and crashed through wet, tangled, dense undergrowth, over and under fallen trees, through a ravine, across a country road, and then uphill into more woods for more than half a mile. The 24th moved considerably ahead of the 38th and the North Carolina regiments, and emerged from the woods along a fence bordering an open field about half a mile east of Fort Magruder. To the left (east), parallel to the line of march of the 24th, and at "most uncomfortably short range" were ten Union guns, heavily supported by infantry, firing on Fort Magruder. As the 38th Virginia groped through the woods toward the firing, Early pivoted the 24th Virginia to the left and ordered it to charge directly toward the guns. Obviously, the lack of reconnaissance and poor planning prior to the impetuous attack resulted in the Confederates rushing needlessly for over half a mile through the heavy woods and then emerging in the open field almost directly in the field of fire of the Union guns.

Both Early and his horse sustained serious wounds, which forced him to turn back just as the 5th North Carolina emerged from the woods about 800 yards west of the guns and at the extreme right of the original line of attack. The 5th North Carolina slowly pivoted to the left and started forward to the right rear of the 24th Virginia to attack the Union guns. After about ten minutes of heavy firing and in the face of the charging 24th Virginia, supported by the 5th North Carolina, the Union troops faltered and began to fall back in confusion.

Meanwhile, General Hill went in search of the missing 23rd North Carolina and 38th Virginia, which had yet to emerge from the woods. He found the 38th "huddled up and in considerable confusion." Lieutenant Colonel Whittle had lost contact with his three left companies and though apparently confused, was attempting to reform and move the 38th by its left flank eastward through the woods toward the sound of the firing. With Hill's assistance, this was accomplished, after which the general located the idle 23rd North Carolina and ordered it also to change front from the south to the east and to form on the left of the 38th. To compound the confusion, under conflicting orders from Early elements of the 38th then emerged from the woods into the open field, as Hill ordered seven companies of the 6th South Carolina to reinforce the Confederate attack. Whittle was wounded in the right thigh while continuing to rally the 38th.

Mindful of the confusion and heavy casualties already suffered by the 24th Virginia, General Hill ordered a retreat, thereby "snatching defeat from the jaws of victory." The 24th and elements of the 38th moved quickly to the left and the sheltering cover of the woods, sustaining few additional casualties. Unfortunately, the practically unscatched 5th North Carolina then had to retrace its steps across the open field under the murderous fire of the Union cannons, for which it paid a terrible price in killed and wounded.

Of the 544 men and officers comprising the 38th Virginia Infantry at the Battle of Williamsburg, none were reported killed, two were captured, and seven were wounded in addition to Lt. Col. Whittle, the only officer wounded. In comparison, the 24th Virginia reported a total of 190 killed, wounded, and missing. The brigade moved back to the wheatfield from which the attack had started and "remained in line of battle all night, without fire, during a cold and wet rain."

Unquestionably, the 38th's "baptismal under fire" was inglorious at best, but responsibility is justly placed on the brigade (Early) and division (Hill) commanders for needlessly attacking with no reconnaissance whatsoever. To compound the tragic losses, unknown to the Confederates General Hancock was preparing to retire from his position just as the attack commenced.

The regiment continued to fall back toward Richmond with the army, leaving Williamsburg around 1 a.m. on May 6. The slow march continued May 7-9 with only "course, parched corn — one ear a day to the man" to eat before the regiment camped on the Chickahominy River on May 10.

Due to his failure to be reelected, Major Isaac Carrington was replaced by Captain Joseph R. Cabell on May 12. Captain Griggs noted in his diary: "the Army is very despondent and everything looks gloomy;" possibly this was due partially to their half-rations and the continuing rain. After resting in camp and drilling for several days, the regiment marched four miles on May 15, crossing the Chickahominy. The march continued in a hard rain on May 16, with the regiment halting nine miles from Richmond and anticipating a "great battle." May 17 proved a beautiful day and the march continued until a halt was called within three miles of Richmond. McClellan's pursuing Army of the Potomac was about six miles from the capital. May 18 found the regiment bivouacked in "thick undergrowth" about one mile from Rocketts, where it remained for several days with various elements on picket duty.

On May 24, the 38th was transferred to the brigade of General Samuel Garland, Jr., "to the pleasure of all," as Captain Griggs noted. Garland, a well-educated attorney prior to the War, was a native of Lynchburg and a graduate of VMI and the University of Virginia. The 38th had had quite enough of General Jubal A. Early.

Garland's Brigade went on picket duty on the Williamsburg Road about one-half mile from the Army of the Potomac on May 28. Minor skirmishing continued on May 29 and 30. By that time, McClellan had gathered all of his Army of the Potomac, except for one corps, south of the Chickahominy near Fair Oaks and Seven Pines, about six miles east of Richmond.

As the Union troops began forming to advance "on to Richmond," the Confederates planned a frontal assault on the Fourth Federal Corps to divide and rout the invaders before their ranks could be consolidated. Toward this objective, Hill's division was to move eastward along the Williamsburg Road toward the Union-held Casey's Redoubt in front of Seven Pines as Longstreet's division moved southeastward toward Fair Oaks and Seven Pines along the Nine Mile Road early on May 31.

For various reasons the attack at Seven Pines did not commence until around 1 p.m. Garland's Brigade, composed (left to right) of the 2nd Florida, 24th Virginia, 23rd North Carolina, 38th Virginia and 5th North Carolina regiments, advanced on the left (north side) of the Williamsburg Road and was supported by Featherston's Brigade (commanded by Colonel G. B. Anderson), about one-quarter mile to the rear. Rodes' Brigade advanced on the right of the highway and somewhat to the rear of the van, supported by Rains' Brigade. Garland's and Featherston's brigades were soon "hotly engaged" in the thick and tangled undergrowth in the forest against Union infantry and artillery. As the Federals "threw their deadly missiles thick and fast," the Confederates "moved steadily forward, driving the enemy from his works" and capturing eight guns, camp equipment, and supplies.

The 38th charged through miry swamps with pools of water hip-deep in places so that wounded men faced the real prospect of drowning. The charging Virginians broke out of the swampy woods to find the opposing Federals in strength behind an abatis and fence. As the battle grew furious, lines were confused and overlapped. Many officers and men fell, but gradually the Union troops faltered. Colonel Edmonds' horse was shot from under him and he was "struck with a fragment of spent shell, causing a painful contusion, yet he left the field only for a short space, and returned to his command, which he led in the most handsome manner." Lieutenant Colonel Whittle "had his horse shot three times, and being dismounted, fought valiantly forward on foot..." Major Cabell "also had his horse shot under him, and charging considerably in advance of his regiment, was the second man to place his hand upon a piece of the enemy's artillery and claim it as our own. The first man was an officer of the Second Florida, killed soon afterward...." Captain Edgar W. Carrington of Company H was killed. Captain Griggs of Company K captured the regimental colors of the 104th Pennsylvania Volunteers, although a shot grazed the top of his head and another penetrated his coat.

Late in the battle, with its ammunition exhausted, General Garland ordered the 38th to fall back to re-supply and hold near the position from which the advance had begun. The 38th entered the Battle of Seven Pines

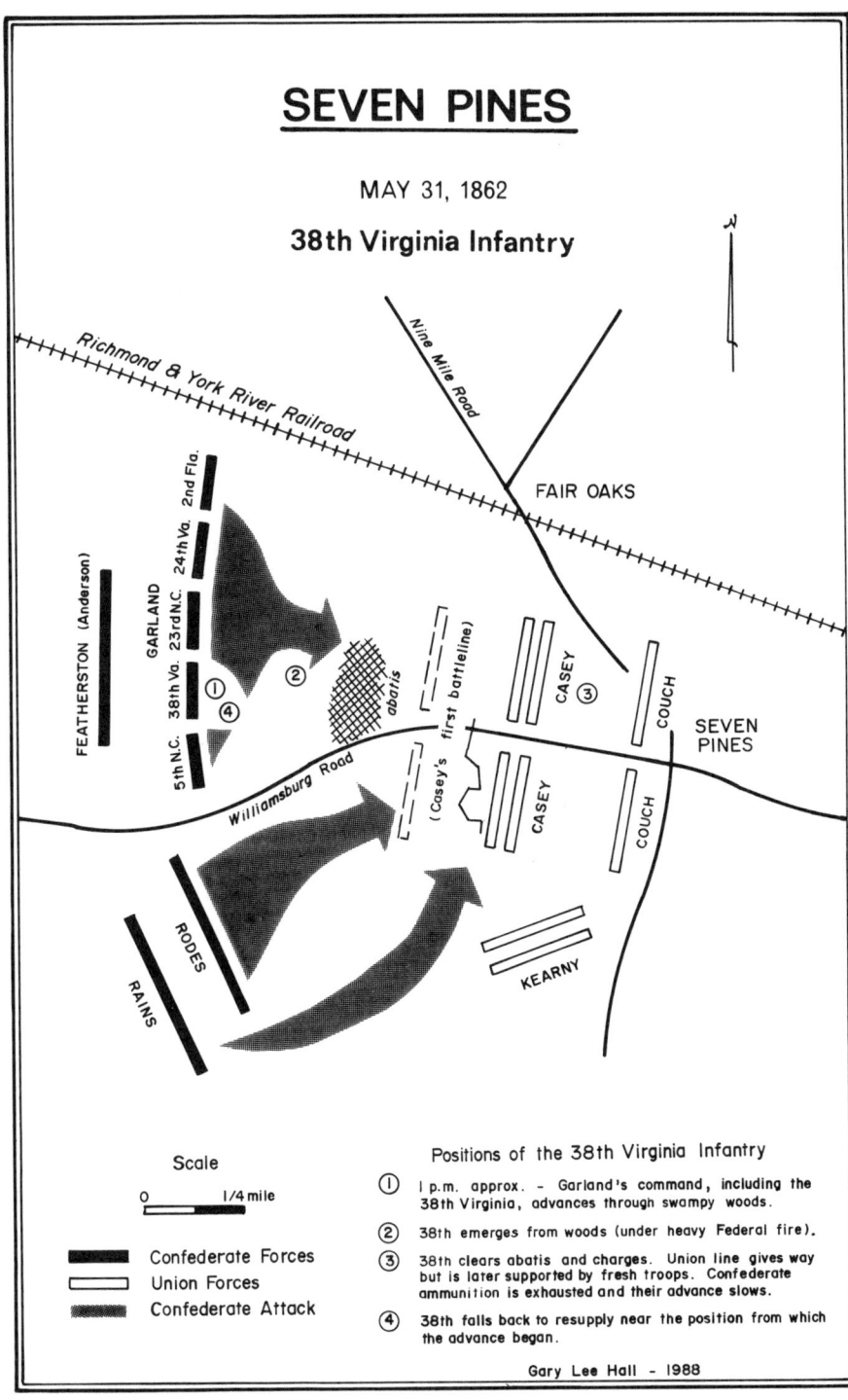

with approximately 350 officers and men, of whom 147 were casualties, including 16 killed, 117 wounded with 14 missing in action — for a casualty rate of 42%

The brigade remained in camp near Seven Pines, often anticipating an attack, from May 31 until late June. On June 5, Generals D. H. Hill and Garland made short speeches to the brigade in formation and a chaplain was appointed for the 38th Regiment. Rains from June 3-9 continued to make camp life uncomfortable as the men drilled and dug rifle pits. On June 14, "Williamsburg" and "Seven Pines" were placed on the 38th's flag "for good conduct and bravery at those places." On June 17, the 38th was transferred to General William Mahone's Brigade very briefly, but before it could join him at dark that day, the order was countermanded. Orders were received to report to Brigadier General Lewis A. Armistead's Brigade of Major General Benjamin Huger's division, which was done on June 18. The 38th, along with the 9th, 14th, 53rd, and 57th Virginia regiments, was to remain in this brigade for the remainder of the War. Intermittent skirmishing continued on the front as elements of the 38th pulled picket duty south of the Williamsburg Road and continued digging rifle pits until June 25. At this time, the 38th reported 389 men present and 451 absent.

Upon assuming command of the Army on June 1, General Robert E. Lee planned to concentrate most of his army of 85,000 men north of the Chickahominy River to annihilate General FitzJohn Porter's isolated Federal Fourth Corps there. To protect Richmond from McClellan's troops south of the Chickahominy, Lee detailed several brigades, including Armistead's with the 38th, under General John B. Magruder. This brigade occupied rifle pits at the eastern edge of the woods between the Richmond & York River Railroad (later the Southern Railway) and the Williamsburg Road, about five miles east of Richmond. The Confederates faced across an open field three-quarters of a mile wide to another belt of woods where the Union troops were entrenched.

At 10 a.m. on June 25, McClellan advanced in force in an attempt to break through to Richmond, but was repulsed. Having been ordered forward at 9 a.m., the 38th, along with the 14th Virginia, was in support of the 53rd Virginia, who along with the 9th Virginia and 5th Battalion, served as advance pickets during the engagement known as King's School House or Oak Grove. Later in the day, the 38th and 14th regiments occupied the advance line with the aforementioned regiments in support.

From June 25 to 29, the 38th alternated between picket duty and manning the rifle pits. Another enemy advance was repulsed on June 27 late in the afternoon. Heavy skirmishing and cannonading continued during the period. At noon on June 29, the brigade moved forward and entered the Union earthworks at Seven Pines, as McClellan's forces retreated down the Peninsula. On June 30, Armistead's Brigade, including the 38th, moved southeast down the Charles City Road with Mahone's Brigade in the van to flank the retreating Yankees, as skirmishing and artillery exchanges continued.

Around 3 a.m. on July 1, General Huger ordered Armistead's (with the 38th in the lead) and Wright's brigades to advance through swamps and thick woods to the right of the Charles City Road from their position between the White Oak Swamp and P. Williams' farm and on to the Long Bridge Road. Here General Armistead reported to General Lee and was ordered to move toward Willis' Church on the Quaker Road. Proceeding in that direction, around 10 a.m. Armistead learned that the Yankees were in close proximity.

Around noon, Armistead moved his brigade into a ravine north of the Crew farm and "immediately threw out the necessary pickets and skirmishers . . . ." — about 50 men under the command of Major Cabell — "to watch and report the movements of the enemy."

Yankee soldiers, supported by about 40 pieces of artillery, were in force, around the Crew farm on Malvern Hill. In a reconnaissance of the area, Colonel Edmonds of the 38th drew a sketch of the Federal position for General Armistead, who forwarded it to General Lee. Armistead determined that a hill in front of the ravine occupied by his brigade offered a good position for artillery to challenge the Federals. This was sent for, but batteries under Captains C. F. Grimes and W. J. Pegram arrived in piecemeal fashion and were systematically knocked out by the superior Federal artillery fire, which had commenced around 1 p.m.

Shortly after 3 p.m., Federal skirmishers advanced in force and Armistead ordered the 38th and elements of the 14th and 53rd Virginia regiments under Colonel Edmonds' command "to drive them back, which they did in handsome style," with the 38th leading the charge on the right. Brimming over with excited enthusiasm, these units advanced nearly three quarters of a mile too far into "no man's land" and found themselves pinned down by a galling "storm of bullets, cannister, grape, and shell, with occasional shells from . . . the gunboats." Fortunately, a "wave of the ground" offered some shelter from the enemy fire and the men huddled in its protection for about three hours awaiting orders. Colonel Edmonds sent Major Cabell to General Armistead requesting orders. Armistead instructed Cabell that the men should hold their position and await reinforcements.

At last reinforcements did arrive when the "gallant" General Wright "with hat off and glittering blade" led his brigade to the support of the 38th and its comrades. "New life was infused among those wearied with watching and waiting; every man was at his post; loud shouts of welcome rent the air; all sprang to their feet, feeling certain of victory with such a support," reported Colonel Edmonds, who then "gave the order to charge." The 38th, followed closely by Wright's Brigade, did charge until the galling

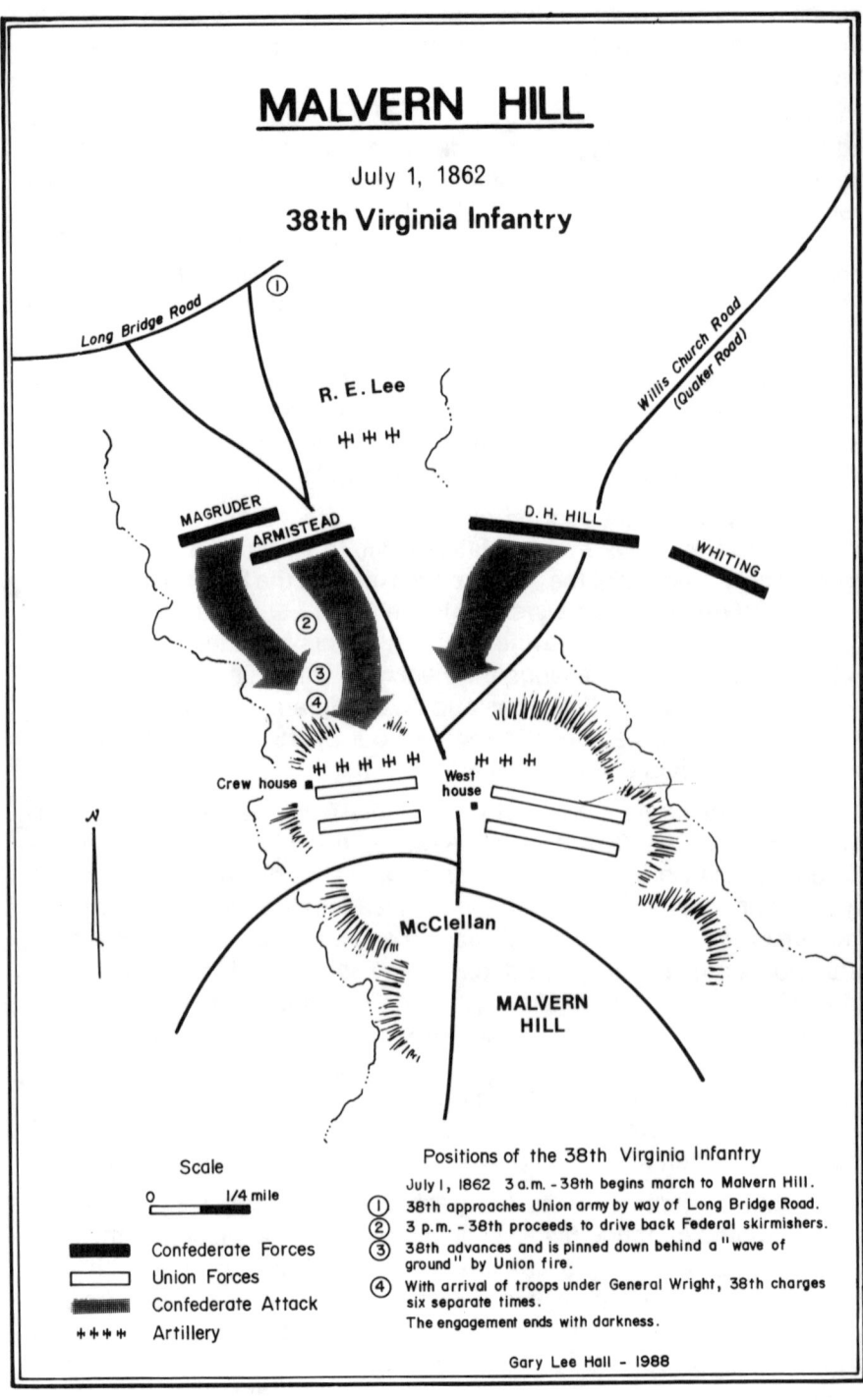

fire of musketry and artillery forced a momentary pause. Six times the Virginians charged the Union batteries and six times they were forced back to "the cover of the brow of the hill." Color Sergeant Luke P. H. Tarpley and Color Corporal Cornelius Gilbert of Company D and Private Churchwell Parker of Company F each fell mortally wounded "while bearing the colors in advance of the regiment during the charges. . . ." Corporal Linnaeus D. Watkins of Company E, Corporal John R. Bullington of Company K, and Private Christopher C. Gregory of Company C "were severely wounded each in turn as they grasped the colors." Lieutenant Colonel Whittle then seized the colors and charged forward considerably in advance of the regiment until shot through the left arm, which he subsequently lost. Captain R. T. Daniel, Jr., temporarily commanding Company F, then "grasped the colors and coolly and calmly waving them, appeared not to be moving a muscle save the motion of his arm" as he rallied his company before being "pierced with three balls. As he fell he drove the staff into the ground, still holding on to it until taken from him by Colonel Edmonds, in whose hands the staff was soon after shot with grape and literally shivered into fragments." Color Corporal William M. Bohannon then bore the colors from the field upon the bayonet of his musket. Later examination revealed that the 38th's colors had been pierced in 50 places.

Darkness brought an end to the battle and its carnage. The 38th had suffered severely in the Battle of Malvern Hill or Crew's Farm with 11 killed, 72 wounded and 11 missing. Lieutenant Colonel Whittle was confined to bed for nearly eight months recuperating from the loss of his arm.

McClellan retreated during the night to Harrison's Landing near Westover, under the protection of the gunboats on the James River. The route of the Federal retreat was littered with rifles and the various implements of war. Heavy rain on July 2 hampered any possible prompt pursuit of the Union forces. The 38th remained in the vicinity of Malvern Hill and Harrison's Landing resting and collecting property from the battlefield.

On July 8, the regiment marched toward Richmond. At 6 a.m. on July 11, the 38th crossed the James River on a pontoon bridge and camped north of Drewry's Bluff near Falling Creek, five miles south of Richmond. Because of displeasure with his recent performance at Seven Pines and Malvern Hill, General Huger was relieved and Major General R. H. Anderson assumed command of the division. The men rested in camp, drilled, went on leave, or received visitors from home through August 15.

On the following day, the regiment was ordered to march to Richmond, where it boarded a train on the Virginia Central Railroad and moved to Louisa Court House, arriving during the night. On August 17, the troops bivouacked about a half mile northwest of Louisa, where they remained until 9 a.m. on August 19. At that time they began a hot, dusty 15-mile march to the vicinity of Orange Court House. The trek resumed in "very oppressive heat" at 8 a.m. on August 20 and the regiment bivouacked that night on the Rapidan River near Clark's Mountain, after travelling about eight miles. The march continued on August 21 to Stevensburg in Culpeper County. The 38th left Stevensburg early on August 22 and trudged onward until 11 p.m., "passing over some fine land, now desolate from the ravages of war," as Captain Griggs observed. On a rainy August 23, the men were awakened, "by the booming of cannon" and the march continued. On August 24, the regiment halted at Jeffersonton, near the northern tip of Culpeper County, as skirmishing and cannonading across the Rappahannock River continued. Captain Griggs noted that the Confederates had "taken [a] good many prisoners."

On August 25, the regiment went on picket duty along the Rappahannock, opposite the enemy and near the Fauquier White Sulphur Springs resort, which was destroyed in the crossfire. At sunset on August 26, the 38th Virginia, near the rear of Anderson's division, which was last in marching order, left the vicinity of the Springs and plodded through the night, wading the Rappahannock River before stopping to rest at daybreak. The "very hot" march continued all day on August 27 with the regiment bivouacking at dark west of Salem (now Marshall) on the Manassas Gap Railroad, having traveled more than 20 miles from The Springs. The march resumed at daybreak on August 28 with the regiment passing through Salem and then halting until 3 p.m. before moving on through White Plains (now The Plains). Many "roasting ears" of corn were eaten along the way. There were numerous stragglers on the march, which continued on August 29 with the sound of heavy cannonading to the front from the Battle of Second Manassas, which was already in progress. The regiment passed through Thoroughfare Gap about dark with Anderson's division near the rear of Longstreet's corps. Anderson's division inadvertently almost stumbled into the Union lines near Manassas before discreetly retreating to safety.

The tired and weary 38th reached the vicinity of Groveton at daybreak on August 30. The men slept about an hour before being formed in line of battle in the rear of Longstreet's corps across the Warrenton Turnpike about one-half mile west of Groveton. In midafternoon, the final phase of Second Manassas commenced as the divisions of Major Generals Fitz John Porter and Irvin McDowell of Pope's army surged toward Jackson's entrenched troops on the "unfinished railroad bed." As Longstreet crashed into the Union left flank and rolled it up, "Anderson's division [with the 38th] being in reserve moved from point to point until late in the evening, [when it was] ordered on extreme right where [the troops] went in quick time and occupied the right flank."

As the Yankees fled once more across Bull Run toward Centreville and the safety of the Washington fortifications, nightfall and rain brought an end to the bloodshed. Due to its late arrival on the field and the support position it occupied, the 38th's casualties at Second Manassas were light. Armistead's Brigade reported only two killed and eighteen wounded. The rain continued on August 31 as the 38th remained on the Manassas battlefield.

On September 1, the 38th, positioned near the rear of the army, advanced in the rain on the Little River Turnpike toward Fairfax before bivouacking in a wooded area. The regiment marched at 8 a.m. on September 2 and halted at noon about five miles west of Fairfax Court House to cook rations.

Even before the Confederate victory at Second Manassas, Southern newspapers had discussed, and government and military leaders had considered, the option of carrying the war to Northern soil. After August 30, this idea seemed even more logical militarily and politically. Militarily, moving the Army of Northern Virginia into Maryland and beyond would serve the multiple purposes of drawing the Federal army from its strong fortifications around Washington and simultaneously easing the fear of a Federal advance on Richmond, while permitting the Southern farmers to harvest their crops in peace. Politically, any Southern sentiment in Maryland would be fanned; and internationally, France and England would be duly impressed by such a Confederate movement. On September 3, Lee decided and started his powerful, if hungry and ragged, Army of Northern Virginia north through Loudoun County.

At 1 p.m. on that day, the 38th left Fairfax and marched about eight miles northwest to Frying Pan where it camped for the night "in an old field." Some of the men "shot a hog and cooked up rations." At 7 a.m. on September 4, the march northward resumed and covered about 12 miles before halting at dark three miles south of Leesburg. Continuing to march near the rear of the army, late on September 5 the 38th passed through Leesburg, where the soldiers were "cheered loudly by the ladies." The regiment bivouacked at midnight six miles north of Leesburg.

About 2:15 p.m. on September 6, a beautifully clear and cool day, Anderson's division, including the 38th Virginia, waded the Potomac River at Conrad's Ferry (about 500 yards below today's White Ferry) and stepped on to "the enemies' soil" in Montgomery County, Maryland. Captain Griggs recorded this observation and prayer: "It was a beautiful scene — train of wagons, column of infantry and artillery all crossing over at the same time . . . . oh God, grant us success and make our foes to acknowledge our independence so that peace may be restored which is all we ask." Straggling and desertion had become increasingly serious problems for the army. In an attempt to counter these "and prevent depredations upon the community," Lee designated Armistead as provost marshal for the army. The northward movement continued all day on September 7. The troops waded the

Monocacy River twice before bivouacking at Buckeystown, about eight miles upstream from the Potomac. September 8 found the 38th crossing the Monocacy for the third time, giving the men an opportunity to bathe in the river before camping for the night near Frederick City. The problem of straggling and desertion continued.

On September 9, Lee counseled with Jackson and Longstreet. Over the latter's objections, Lee determined to divide his forces. A portion of the army would capture the Union garrison at Harper's Ferry, while the main body moved on toward Hagerstown. Harper's Ferry was strategically quite important and yet quite vulnerable. Securing Harper's Ferry would ensure the safety of Lee's lifeline back to the Shenandoah Valley. Lee assigned McLaws' and Anderson's (including the 38th) divisions to seize Maryland Heights to the north of Harper's Ferry, while Brigadier General John G. Walker's division held the Loudoun Heights to the east and Jackson secured the southern approaches on Bolivar Heights. After capturing Harper's Ferry on September 12, the army would quickly reunite at Hagerstown or Boonsboro for the advance northward. These plans were detailed in Lee's Special Orders No. 191 issued on September 9. In one of the most costly and very nearly disastrous misfortunes suffered by the Confederacy, an unknown officer on D. H. Hill's staff used a copy of these orders as a wrapping for three cigars. This package, which he promptly lost, was recovered shortly after noon on September 13 by a Union enlisted man, who immediately forwarded the invaluable document to McClellan.

At 1 p.m. on September 10, the 38th Virginia left Frederick with Anderson's and McLaws' divisions for the approximately 20-mile march to Harper's Ferry via Burkittsville, halting around midnight near South Mountain. The advance resumed at 2 p.m. on September 11 and moved slowly forward into Pleasant Valley with Armistead's Brigade, including the 38th, serving as rear guard. On September 12, the regiment, now in the lead, passed through Brownsville and bivouacked at Weverton, three miles from Harper's Ferry, after skirmishing with Union pickets. Moving forward early on September 13, the 38th was engaged as skirmishers and fought the enemy all day, driving him from Maryland Heights by 4:30 p.m.

On a cloudy and cool Sunday, September 14, as McClellan's troops advanced toward Turner's Gap and broke through Crampton's Gap of South Mountain, Captain Griggs recorded: "Heavy fighting in our rear. The enemy drove our force from opposite mountain.... I was on picket with my company on top of Maryland Heights. We opened artillery on Ferry from the Heights at same time Jackson was shelling from opposite side. The scenery was grand. We blew up some of the enemies' caissons. The roar and echo of artillery among the mountains was awful. Everything was calculated to inspire one's awe. Everyone is anxious to hear of the surrender of the Town. Our situation is becoming one of peril. While we have surrounded the Ferry, our division is also surrounded without any means of escape except by the Ferry." The Confederates resumed cannonading before daybreak on September 15 and by 10 a.m., the Federal garrison at Harper's Ferry unconditionally surrendered more than 11,000 men and 73 guns.

On September 16, the 38th with Anderson's division "crossed over [the Potomac] into old Virginia," noted Captain Griggs, who felt "thankful and free [to] set my foot on her dear old soil." After getting some scant provisions in Harper's Ferry, the regiment marched about three miles and rested near Halltown until 3 p.m., when orders were received to move toward Sharpsburg, Maryland, where Lee's army was engaging the advancing Union troops. The Confederates started toward Sharpsburg, but halted a couple of miles from Shepherdstown. Here a courier found McLaws and delivered Lee's order for his troops to hasten to the front. The march resumed after midnight and the 38th, near the rear of the column, recrossed the Potomac at Shepherdstown, at 8 a.m. on September 17.

As the 38th hurried forward, the men could hear the Battle of Sharpsburg raging to their front. Soon they met the wounded streaming toward the rear. Around noon, the 38th (with Armistead's Brigade) was "drawn up in line [of] battle" supporting McLaws' division, which was already heavily engaged, west of the Hagerstown Road in the West Wood near the Dunker Church toward the left of the Confederate line. Captain Griggs, who had "never heard such cannonading or saw such destruction by it," was slightly wounded by the concussion of a shell and forced to retire around 3 p.m. As the fighting continued, the 38th held its position, suffering only light casualties, until nightfall and the end of the war's "bloodiest day."

A rainy September 18 found the opposing forces warily facing each other as they buried their dead and cared for their wounded. With neither side anxious to resume the general engagement, Lee ordered his Army of Northern Virginia back to the Old Dominion and it recrossed the Potomac at Boteler's Ford, about a mile downstream from Shepherdstown, early on September 19.

To thwart a Federal pursuit, Lee ordered his chief of artillery, General William Nelson Pendleton, with 44 guns to guard Boteler's Ford. The brigades of Armistead and A. R. Lawton, totalling only 600 men, were detailed to support Pendleton and his artillery. With Armistead having been slightly wounded early in the day at Sharpsburg, Colonel James Gregory Hodges of the 14th Virginia Infantry had assumed command of the brigade. At 10 a.m. the Yankees commenced shelling this Confederate rear guard, as the main body of the Southern army continued southward a short distance to safety and then stopped to rest for the night. Due to Pendleton's inexperience in such an operation and the newness of the acting brigade commanders, the relatively few infantrymen assigned the task of supporting the artillery detachment (how few even Pendleton did not realize), and the exhaustion of much of the artillery ammunition, after dark the Union troops forced the ford upstream and routed the Confederate detachment. Concerning Armistead's and Lawton's infantrymen, Pendleton later wrote: "worn as were these men, their state of disorder . . . was not, justly, to be met with harshness." He hastened to report this state of affairs to Lee after midnight, including his erroneous belief that all 44 guns of the artillery reserve had been captured.

After retreating all night, the 38th Virginia stopped at daybreak on September 20 for breakfast. Captain Griggs "went to sleep while standing up . . . . nearly worn out for the want [of] rest." Meanwhile, Jackson dispatched A. P. Hill to return and drive the Union forces back across the river. This was quickly accomplished with moderate Federal losses. The Confederate march resumed toward Martinsburg, as McClellan abandoned any further attempt at pursuit. In the entire Maryland campaign, the 38th had suffered only two killed and fourteen wounded.

The regiment remained in camp in at least two different locations in the vicinity of Martinsburg through September 26. The only excitement occurred on September 25 when "some of the boys killed an old skunk for [an] opossum which perfumed the camp. [We can] hardly stay in it."

From its camp near Martinsburg, the regiment marched south for about 18 miles on September 27-28 to a new camp site about five miles north of Winchester near Clearbrook at the Quaker's Hopewell Church (built in 1759 and still standing in 1988). September 29 through October 29 was spent in camp there. The men were occupied with company and brigade drill, repairing equipment, going on furlough, and at least some of them attended worship service. Many of these were converted, accepting Jesus Christ as their personal Saviour.

Private James Booker of Company D wrote his cousin on September 30:

"Now they are giving us any quantity of fresh beef and fresh hog meat [except] salt . . . . Our old members has kept up finely considering the exposure. We have to waid every stream we come to that has no bridge across it. We have waided the Potomac three times. We have not aloud time to take off our clothings to cross creeks and rivers. We have to get in just as we are, and then march with our wet clothing on . . . ."

Longstreet, accompanied by two members of the British Parliament, reviewed the division on October 13. About 10,000 men were in the line, but "orders forbade the barefooted men from going out." On October 16, Colonel Edmonds was put under arrest for complaining at brigade headquarters about the lack of salt for his men. Generals Lee, Longstreet, and Wilcox reviewed the corps on October 20.

At 8:30 a.m. on October 30, the regiment began a "very hard march" southward, covering about 25 miles before halting for the night three miles north of Front Royal. There were numerous complaints of sore feet and many men "gave out" on the march, which resumed at 9 a.m. on October 31. That day the regiment covered about 14 miles, wading the Shenandoah River and crossing the Blue Ridge at Chester Gap before halting at dark at Flint Hill. Still not knowing their destination, the men moved out again early on November 1 and covered about 15 miles, passing Gaines' Cross Roads (now Ben Venue) and crossing the Rappahannock River bridge before halting about ten miles north of Culpeper. Resuming at 8:45 a.m. on November 2, the march halted at 3 p.m. one mile north of Culpeper. Many of the soldiers (33 in Company K alone) were barefooted and their feet were "much blistered." The men rested in camp there until November 20.

On November 6, Armistead's Brigade was transferred to Major General George E. Pickett's division of Longstreet's corps. Snow and very cold weather on November 7 compounded the problems faced by the poorly clothed and ill-shod soldiers. In a compassionate but ill-advised attempt to alleviate the suffering of his men, the city-bred Armistead determined to have mocassins made for them from the "green" hides of slaughtered beef cattle that he saw piled in a field. He had the uncured hides cut into strips and two strips issued to each man with instructions to turn the fur side inward and make mocassins. A soldier wrote home that his home-made shoes "stink very bad" and that he had to use a bush to "keep the flies off." Only possibly in jest, he continued that the rawhide shoes met their end when "some of the boys boiled them and eat them." From November 8-10, the regiment pulled picket duty on the road about four miles north of Culpeper, where cannonading could be heard to the north.

In mid-November, Union General Ambrose E. Burnside, after reluctantly accepting command of the Army of the Potomac, moved southeast from his camp at Warrenton toward Richmond. His unusual winter offensive ground to a halt on Falmouth Heights overlooking Fredericksburg while waiting for pontoon bridges to cross the Rappahannock River there. To intercept the Yankee advance, Lee started Longstreet's corps from its camp near Culpeper. The 38th marched at 7 a.m. on November 20 on muddy roads in rainy, disagreeable weather. At sunset on November 22, the regiment camped ten miles west of Fredericksburg. At 2 p.m. on November 23, the 38th halted within two miles of Fredericksburg and began picket duty, drilling, and inspections while facing the Union troops across the river. On November 29, Lt. J. W. Millner of Company K was placed under arrest for "firing his pistol in camp." The stalemate continued in early December as the men battled biting cold and snow, which was several inches deep on December 5, without tents.

The slumbering Confederates were awakened by cannon fire early on

December 11 as the Yankees attempted to position their pontoon bridges, which had finally arrived, for a crossing. Thwarted in these attempts by Barksdale's Mississippi sharpshooters, the Union artillery unleashed a terrible barrage on the town at 1 p.m. Finally late in the day with Confederate preparations completed, Longstreet ordered Barksdale to withdraw in the face of a Federal bridgehead assault — the first of its type in history. The Federals completed their pontoon bridges and streamed across the river during the night and on the following day when, acting as an undisciplined mob, they sacked the town of Fredericksburg.

Artillery fire and minor skirmishing resumed at 9:30 a.m. on December 12 with the 38th Virginia in the center of the defensive line not far from the foot of "Lee's Hill." While on picket duty and deployed as skirmishers there, the regiment saw little action, but suffered during the extremely cold night on the hard frozen ground without the comforting warmth of camp fires.

Shortly after 10 a.m. on Saturday, December 13, the enveloping fog burned off the plains about Fredericksburg and Burnside launched his attack in earnest. From the 38th's position less than two miles southwest of Marye's Heights, Captain Griggs noted: "the enemy advancing on our right and left, moving up their heavy columns in grand style, but it was only to meet with defeat. We drove them back with great slaughter. I could see a large portion of the field and [it] was quite exciting to witness the gallantry of our troops." Late in the evening, after the virtual massacre of more than 12,000 Union soldiers, Burnside called off his ill-advised and ill-fated attack and moved his troops back to the relative safety of Fredericksburg.

Some skirmishing between opposing pickets occurred on December 14, before the 38th Virginia was relieved from picket duty that night. The Union army "sent in flag of truce 3 times before [it was] accepted to bury their dead." Cannonading and skirmishing continued on December 15. The following day the Union army retreated across the Rappahannock and the 38th went into camp in the evening. A reported advance of the enemy on December 19 proved false and the 38th's orders "to march at moment's notice" were countermanded. The men spent most of their time drilling, standing inspections, pulling picket duty, and battling the bitter cold. While on picket duty on the river bank on December 23, Captain Griggs noted: "Several Yankees crossed over on boat & exchanged papers, coffee, & etc." Christmas Day was foggy, cloudy and warm and "remarkably dull in camp" — undoubtedly an unusually lonely day for the homesick soldiers whose thoughts wandered back to happier Christmas days among loved ones. The 38th marched at 9:30 a.m. on December 27 for approximately eight miles on Telegraph Road to a bivouac in a pine forest within three miles of Guinea Station on the R. F. & P. Railroad. The men began constructing crude shanties for their winter quarters there. A dress parade was held on December 28, followed by company and brigade drill on December 29. The bitterly cold last day of 1862 was occupied with a muster and inspection in the fresh-fallen snow.

1863

New Year's Day dawned beautiful and clear. After inspection and drill, some soldiers were fortunate enough to be granted furloughs to go home. Those not so fortunate remained in camp improving their quarters, drilling, standing inspections, and, as always, battling the elements. At 8 a.m. on January 27, Pickett's division marched from its camp over muddy roads to a section of unfinished railroad near the Plank Road about five miles from Fredericksburg to "throw up fortifications" against an anticipated Federal advance. Unable to do so, apparently because of snow thirteen inches deep, which also thwarted Burnside's "Mud March," the division started at 9 a.m. on January 29 on a hard march back to its original camp near Guinea's Station, arriving at sunset. That bitterly cold night Captain Griggs and many others "slept outdoors [with] nothing but a blanket and the heavens for a cover." To relieve the tedious monotony and boredom of camp life, the soldiers of Toombs', Corse's, and Armistead's brigades entertained themselves with a gigantic snowball fight on January 31.

Early February found the regiment building breast works and battling smallpox, in addition to more snow and the biting cold. "A band [of] Confederate minstrals who perform at night for the gratification of soldiers" was organized in the division. In mid-February, the Federal Ninth Corps moved down the Potomac by ship toward Hampton Roads. Its ultimate destination — whether Richmond, Wilmington, Savannah or elsewhere — was unknown. To protect Richmond, Lee dispatched Pickett's division (with Hood's to follow), thereby granting Longstreet a semi-independent command in eastern Virginia. On February 14, the 38th broke camp and moved through Richmond en route to Chester Station, where it arrived on February 17. From there the movement continued on to Petersburg, where the regiment arrived on March 1, going into camp about three miles east of the city.

March continued as uneventful as February with routine inspections and drills. As the heavy snows continued, on March 21 the Confederates had another large snowball battle, resulting in a "great many black eyes." At 3 p.m. on March 26, the regiment marched southeastward toward Ivor Station, 33 miles away on the Norfolk & Petersburg Railroad (later Norfolk & Western Rwy.). The march covered 20 miles between 7 a.m. and 4 p.m. on March 27, with the men wading many streams and swamps "more than knee deep." At 3 p.m. on March 28, the march halted two miles from Ivor and then resumed for a short distance on March 30, before the regiment went into camp near Ivor "in [a] beautiful grove on [the] side of [the] road."

At 8 a.m. on a hot and dusty April 9, the 38th Virginia marched toward Franklin depot, 15 miles to the south, where it arrived the following day. The march resumed at 6 a.m. on April 11 with the 38th crossing the Blackwater River at South Quay at 10 a.m. and continuing toward Suffolk, after leaving the wagons and sick personnel behind.

After camping for the night, the advance resumed at 4 a.m. on April 12 and after covering about two miles, Captain Griggs with his Company K "was ordered... forward in front of the brigade. [It] had not gone far before... [engaging] the enemy's cavalry and [driving] them several miles, exchanging good many shots." Griggs continued: "No body hurt on our side. We went in about 3 miles [of] Suffolk and finding the road blockaded, marched back some 3 miles to receive orders. [We] did not wait long before [we] received orders to march on the same road forward and I had again to drive the enemy's cavalry. We halted about 4 p.m. about 3 miles from Suffolk, my company remaining in front as pickets. [It is] very hot and dusty and I am very much exhausted." On April 13, the 38th drove the Union pickets "to within a mile of Suffolk." Company K was held in reserve as heavy skirmishing continued all day. Captain Griggs "expected every moment to be ordered to charge the outer works of the Town, but were not." Major Joseph R. Cabell felt the city could have been taken easily, but with no orders to advance, a golden opportunity was lost.

Late in the day, Lieutenant William G. Cabaniss with ten privates from Company K was dispatched on a secret mission to steal about six miles from the Confederate lines south of Suffolk, cross the Dismal Swamp, and destroy the railroad track east of Suffolk. Heavily posted Union pickets at the point they were to cross the swamp thwarted their plan and the men returned to camp on April 15 without accomplishing the mission. A lady was shot by the enemy on April 14 between the picket lines when she left her home to seek a place of safety, as the fighting continued.

From April 14 to May 3, the regiment remained on picket duty about a mile south of Suffolk, where "the ladies... seem very much rejoiced to see us," as intermittent skirmishing and cannonading continued. On April 24, the 38th quickly responded, traveling four miles in single file through the swamps from 5 p.m. to 9 p.m., to reinforce the 57th Virginia which was under a heavy Federal assault on the White Marsh Road. Lieutenant Colonel Whittle returned to the regiment on April 29 after recuperating from the loss of his left arm at Malvern Hill.

Longstreet's objective of protecting the capital and replenishing supplies had been accomplished. He could now withdraw Hood's and Pickett's divisions to move northward to reunite with the remainder of the army then locked in the Battle of Chancellorsville. Here Lee won one of his greatest victories, but lost his "right arm" with the mortal wounding of the lengendary "Stonewall" late on May 2.

At dark on May 3, the 38th Virginia broke camp and began a muddy 27-mile march to Franklin Depot, where it arrived at mid-day on May 4. The regiment marched from 8 a.m. to 4 p.m. on May 5, halting at Jerusalem (now Courtland) after traveling about eight miles. Resuming the march at 7 a.m. on May 6, the men "had to wade water nearly all day" and some "marched all day barefooted" in the rain for about 10 miles, before halting on the Jerusalem Plank Road, still about 27 miles from Petersburg. The regiment, now in the "van guard for the army," covered about 20 miles in the rain on May 7 from 8 a.m. to 5 p.m. On May 8, the 38th marched about nine miles and camped two miles north of Petersburg. The march from 8 a.m. to 3 p.m. on the following day brought the regiment to a camp site on Falling Creek, seven miles south of Richmond. On May 11, some of the men "went to Richmond on 12 hours leave" where "every body looked sad and all businesses [were] closed for the day in honor to the remains of... Lt. Genl. T. J. Jackson [whose] remains... [were] brought today in [to] the City" after his death on May 10 at 3:15 p.m. near Guinea Station.

On May 13 the 38th Virginia moved to its old camp site from the previous August on Falling Creek north of Drewry's Bluff. Several thousand Union prisoners who had been captured near Chancellorsville passed by the camp on May 13 and 14 en route to City Point for exchange. At 2 p.m. on May 15, the 38th departed its camp site and moved to within a mile of Richmond. Marching at 6 a.m. on May 16, it passed through Richmond and continued on the Brook Turnpike for 10 miles before halting for the night. May 17's march of about 10 miles brought the 38th to within two miles of Hanover Junction (now Doswell) where camp was established near Taylorsville and the North Anna River for the next 16 days. On May 27 the soldiers were subjected to political campaign speeches from the Pittsylvania County candidates for the State Senate and House of Delegates, but there was "no excitement." General Pickett reviewed Armistead's Brigade on May 29. The remainder of this time was spent in company and brigade drill, standing inspection, fishing in the North Anna River, attending worship sevices, etc.

The Pittsylvanians marched early on June 2 to Hanover Court House where Company K was detailed to guard the bridge over the Pamunkey River. Responding to a report of Union troops in King & Queen County, the regiment with the brigade left Hanover Court House at 4 a.m. on June 3 and marched about 18 hot and dusty miles, crossing the Mattaponi River, before halting at 4 p.m. two miles from New Town. Finding no enemy there on June 4, the tired soldiers marched all day on June 5 to Reedy Mills on the Mattaponi River in King William County. At 1 a.m. on June 6, the troops marched to within five miles of Aylett before being ordered back to Hanover Junction, where they arrived at 1 p.m. after "a pretty hard march... over some beautiful country."

On June 7 the 38th Virginia left Hanover Junction and trudged about nine miles to Hanover Court House, arriving at noon. Departing early on June 8 for Culpeper Court House, the troops covered well over 20 miles before camping for the night two miles northwest of New Market. The march continued from 6 a.m. to 4:30 p.m. on June 9. On June 10, the Pittsylvanians crossed the Rapidan River at Sommerville Ford and then halted about eight miles south of Culpeper. On June 11 the 38th moved to a camp site three miles south of Culpeper, where it remained until June 15. On that day with "3 days rations cooked [and] 10 days on wagons," the regiment moved north with Company K in the vanguard, halting for the night three miles north of Culpeper "on the road to Flint Hill." Resuming the advance at 5 a.m. on June 16, the regiment covered about 20 miles, serving as rear guard, before halting at Gaines' Cross Roads. In the oppressive heat and dust, a "great many fainted from exhaustion." The regiment moved again at 5 a.m. on June 17 and trudged another approximately 20 miles in the stifling heat before halting for the night two miles south of Piedmont (now Delaplane). Eight men in Company K alone "gave out from [the] effect [of the] heat." June 18 started with another 5 a.m. march which covered about eight miles before halting at Paris, near Ashby's Gap, at 11 a.m. On June 19 the regiment marched more than ten miles to Snicker's Gap, where it crossed the Blue Ridge and halted at dark after skirmishing with Union cavalry during the day. The regiment was ordered to ford the Shenandoah River on June 20, but was turned back shortly after noon because heavy rains the previous night had swollen the river. Finally, late in the afternoon, the men successfully waded across the "muddy and swift and waist deep" river at Castleman's Ferry "with some difficulty," by marching "four deep and hold[ing] to each other . . . to prevent being washed down." The regiment rested near Berryville from June 21 until June 24 in position to support Stuart's cavalry, if needed, which was battling Union cavalry at Aldie and Upperville. The march resumed at 3 a.m. "with 3 days rations" and passed through Berryville and country "ruined by the enemy" before halting at 4:30 p.m. at Bunker Hill, West Virginia.

The soldiers were back on their feet at 4 a.m. on June 25 and moving farther north, passing through Martinsburg and then wading the Potomac River at Williamsport before halting for the night two miles north of the town at 6 p.m. Here the men received Lee's order "forbidding the destroying of private property." The troops moved again at 4 a.m. on June 26 and covered more than 20 miles, passing through Hagerstown and on into Pennsylvania at Middleburg, before halting for the night at Greencastle. Captain Griggs observed, "the citizens are generally very much frightened at our invasion of their soil."

A "muddy and hard" march commencing early on June 27 covered about 12 miles and brought the 38th to a site two miles north of Chambersburg on the York Road. Along the way, the soldiers "did not stay in [the] road, but marched through fields, making a road [and] trod down a great deal [of] wheat" in the "fine grain and grass country."

Writing to his wife from Chambersburg, Private Joseph T. Payne of Company C observed:

> I cant no how long it will be before we will get to verginia if we ever do. This is great country evry thing to eat is plenty and at low prises and there is a great crop of corn and wheat at this time and the people is very kind to us but I think it is thru fere for I dont think they have eny love for us. Our people are taking a great many horses and beef cattle and a great many other things. I never wanted to cross the potomac and if it hadnt of binn for beeing punish for it I never would of crost it but general lee says that if we will follow him thrue he will bring pece out with him ... I hope it will be God's will that I may live to see you all again in this world. But parting in this world is but a small item to the thorts of parting in the world to come. So I want us to try and be prepared to meat in the world to come to part no more.

Less than a month later, while a prisoner of war, Payne died of wounds received at Gettysburg.

Very early on June 28 the regiment marched to Scotland on the Cumberland Valley Railroad where it was detailed to guard commissary stores. The 38th moved back through Chambersburg and camped with the division south of town on June 29. Here a muster and inspection was held in the rain on June 30 with a preaching service in the evening.

On the same day, Private James Booker of Company D wrote his cousin:

> We have quite a nice time since we have bin [in] Pennsylvania in the way of something to eat. We can get plenty of milk and butter and apple butter that is verry good. The citizens in this country all seem to be afraid of us. They treat us verry kind though I believe it is done through fear. The most of our Virginia boys treat them verry kind though there is some [of] our extreams southern troops has treated the people badley. I am sorry thay do so. It is against Gen Lees orders to interrupt private property. This is a verry flourishing looking country. The crops all look fine. It has never felt the affect of the war. Though I guess if we stay here long, it will tell the affect of it. Our Quarter Masters and Commisarys has goten a great many necesarys for our army since we have bin this state.

> "Thare is but verry few people that charges us eney thing for milk or butter. I beleave thay had asoon give us such things as to take our money and they are afraid to refuse us while thay

have such things. The people in this country are verry much split up about the war. Thay dont unite like our people do. I dont think this war can last much longer, if it does I beleave the North will have war with its self. The Dimocrat say thay will not take sides with the abolitionist. Thay say we are fighting for our rights and the abolitionist are fighting for money, and I beleave the Dimocrats will raise against them if the war last much longer.

I am staying at a private home guarding the mans property. He boards me free while I stay with him. I am fairing finely . . . .

On July 1, 1863, other segments of the Confederate army collided with Union forces at Gettysburg, Pennsylvania. Union Major General George Gordon Meade had assumed command of the Army of the Potomac only two days earlier. Meanwhile, the 38th Virginia had three drills at its campsite south of Chambersburg, both for routine practice and to prevent the troops from roaming the countryside. Beginning to realize the strength of the opposing Federal forces, Lee ordered his remaining troops to the front. At 2 a.m. on July 2, the 38th with Pickett's division broke camp and moved back through Chambersburg for the third time and on toward Gettysburg on the Gettysburg-Chambersburg Turnpike. Bringing up the rear, the Pittsylvanians traveled about 25 miles on this forced march during which they were often "fired on while crossing [South] mountain by bushwhackers," who were probably civilians or local militia units. The division halted three miles west of Gettysburg, south of the Chambersburg Pike in the woods near Marsh Creek at 3:30 p.m. The troops could hear the battle raging to their front. As Pickett's men would be of little assistance so late in the day, Lee ordered the division to rest in preparation for the morrow.

At 3 a.m. on a fateful July 3, 1863, the 38th Virginia was ordered forward with Pickett's division to the center of the Confederate line behind Seminary Ridge nearly two miles southwest of Gettysburg. The division moved about five miles, most of the way on the farm roads, and deployed in position after daybreak. Here the troops rested during a light shower in the morning, protected from the enemy somewhat by the brow of a ridge and a small strip of trees. The day grew hotter as the temperature hovered around 87 degrees, but the men of the 38th were fortunately positioned in the northern portion of Spandler's Woods, where shade provided some relief.

After being repulsed on Culp's Hill and the Round Tops on July 2, Lee was confident that a third assault by his "invincible army" would be victorious. Over Longstreet's strenuous objection, he determined to assault the center of the Federal line, concentrating the attack toward a grove of oak trees — "the copse of trees" — conspicuous on Cemetery Ridge. As they were the freshest troops on the field, Lee chose Pickett's division, supported by Pettigrew's (Heth's) and Trimble's divisions — totaling approximately 10,500 men — to spearhead the assault.

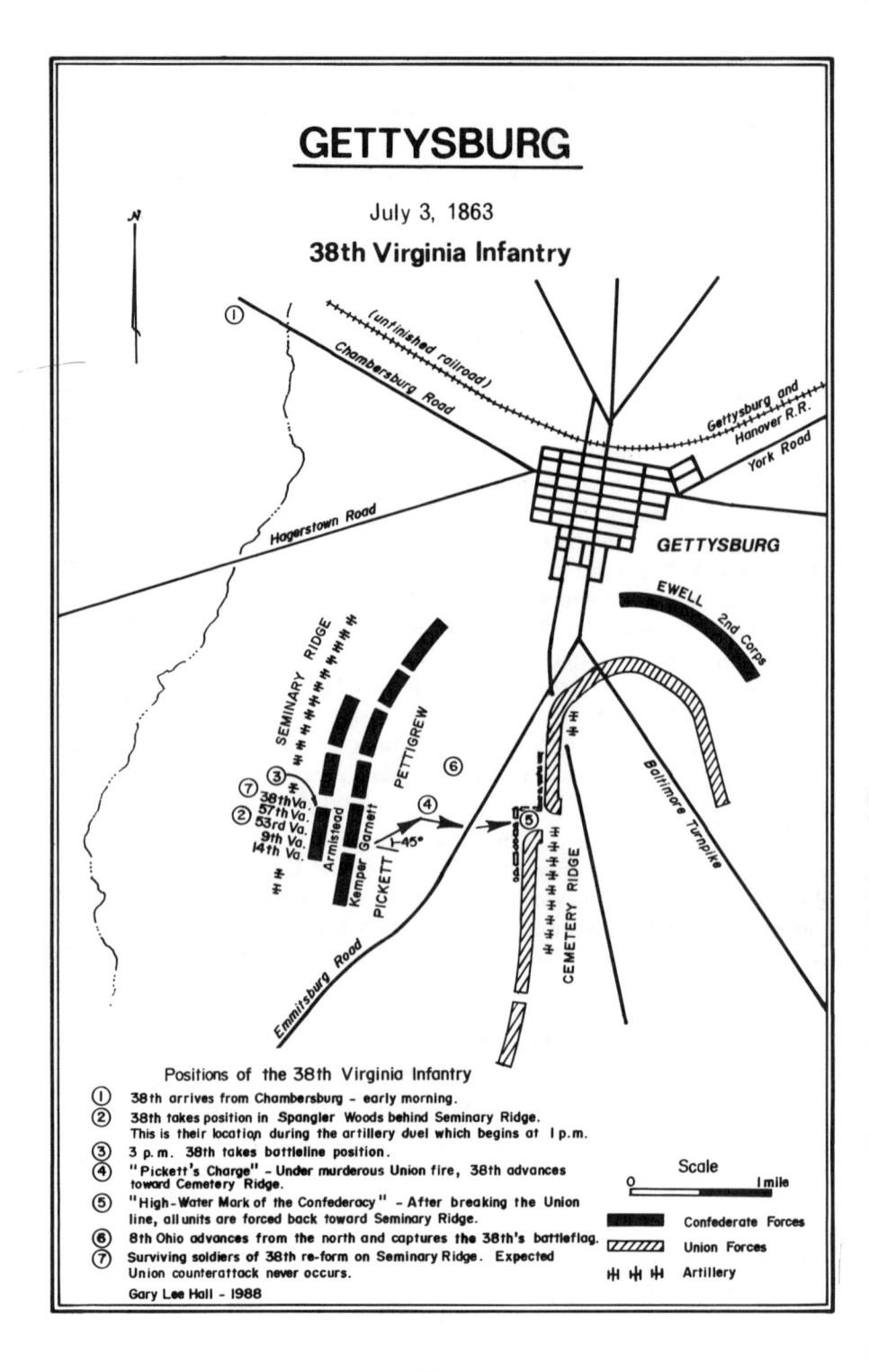

GETTYSBURG

July 3, 1863
38th Virginia Infantry

Positions of the 38th Virginia Infantry

1. 38th arrives from Chambersburg - early morning.
2. 38th takes position in Spangler Woods behind Seminary Ridge. This is their location during the artillery duel which begins at 1 p.m.
3. 3 p.m. 38th takes battleline position.
4. "Pickett's Charge" - Under murderous Union fire, 38th advances toward Cemetery Ridge.
5. "High-Water Mark of the Confederacy" - After breaking the Union line, all units are forced back toward Seminary Ridge.
6. 8th Ohio advances from the north and captures the 38th's battleflag.
7. Surviving soldiers of 38th re-form on Seminary Ridge. Expected Union counterattack never occurs.

Gary Lee Hall - 1988

At 1:00 p.m. more than 120 Confederate cannon, commanded by 28-year-old Colonel E. Porter Alexander, unleashed a terrible bombardment concentrated against the Union center near the angle of a stone wall and "the copse of trees" Yankee artillerymen responded in kind and for about an hour and a half the "very earth seemed to shake and the hills to reel as the terrible thunder re-echoed among them." Billowing smoke and dust promptly obscured the targets and consequently most of the Confederate shells overshot the Union lines on Cemetery Ridge, falling into rear areas. The same was true on Seminary Ridge as Union shells sailed beyond the Southern artillery line and fell amongst the Confederate infantry who hugged the ground for protection and concealment. Both sides suffered heavily from the exploding shells and shrapnel. Pickett's division alone counted several hundred casualties. Due to its relatively well-covered position on Armistead's extreme left in Spangler's Woods, the 38th sustained comparatively few losses.

About 2:30 p.m., as his ammunition ran low, Alexander observed some of the Federal batteries withdrawing from Cemetery Ridge and erroneously concluded that they had been driven off. He ceased firing and sent a note to Pickett advising him of this.

Pickett approached Longstreet and inquired, "General, shall I advance?" Receiving only an affirmative, possibly "tear-choked," nod from Longstreet, Pickett responded, "I shall lead my division forward, sir." He then ordered the advance of his three brigades — totaling about 6300 men — under Armistead, Garnett and Kemper.

All unnecessary equipment such as knapsacks, blankets, and cooking gear was left behind the brigade's position to prevent their impeding the advance. Calling his brigade to attention, Armisted inquired of Color Sergeant Leander C. Blackburn of the 53rd Virginia, "Sergeant, are you going to plant those colors on the enemy's works today?" and pointed toward the enemy's lines on Cemetery Ridge. Blackburn responded, "Yes, General, if mortal man can do it!" The general then took out a small flask and shared it with the sergeant. Thirty minutes later both men were captured and dying. Pacing in front of his brigade, Armistead in his loud commanding voice reminded the troops of Sergeant Blackburn's resolve and continued, "Men, remember what you are fighting for! Remember your homes, your fire sides, your wives, your mothers, your sisters and your sweethearts!" As the division was formed, Pickett exhorted those within hearing: "Up, men, and to your posts! Don't forget today that you are from Old Virginia!" Armistead then moved out about twenty paces in front of Sergeant Blackburn with the colors of the 53rd Virginia, his battalion of direction, and led his brave brigade forward into glory.

Emerging from the woods on Seminary Ridge at about 3 p.m., the Virginians with loaded muskets and fixed bayonets moved steadily forward in line of battle with James L. Kemper's Brigade on the right, Richard B. Garnett's on the left and Armistead's Brigade, largest of the three, behind Garnett's and the extreme left of Kemper's Brigade. From left to right of the brigade, the 38th, 57th, 53rd, 9th, and 14th Virginia regiments advanced silently under instructions to neither shoot nor yell until ordered to do so. To the immediate left of the 38th was Pettigrew's (Heth's) division. Forty years later, Captain James E. Poindexter of Company H recalled: "Before us, one hundred and fifty yards away, moving on like waves of the sea, marched Garnett and Kemper, their battle flags flashing in the sun light.... Marching in perfect order, with disciplined tread, [we] followed where they led." The defending Federals on Cemetery Ridge found the sight of the advancing Confederate line — nearly a mile in length — with glittering bayonets and muskets and battle flags whipping in the hot, humid breeze an awe-inspiring one as they prepared to meet the onslaught of the assault.

Pickett's division advanced nearly 500 yards straight toward the Emmitsburg Road. The division then obliqued to the left at an angle of about 45 degrees for almost 300 yards, before realigning and continuing 200 yards farther to close with Pettigrew's right flank (Col. Birkett D. Fry's Brigade) as they approached the Emmitsburg Road. The Confederates came under murderous enfilading fire from Union artillery on the right near Little Round Top and on Cemetery Ridge. Captain Poindexter saw "men fall at every step... like grass before the scythe." The advance continued in the face of combined canister and musketry toward "the copse of trees." With gaping holes blasted in the lines, the resolute, heroic Confederates closed gaps and pressed forward with deliberate parade-ground precision. Kemper's and Garnett's brigades began exchanging fire with the Federals. Armistead's Brigade, with muskets at shoulder arms, continued forward behind Garnett's and the left of Kemper's brigades, whose formation was now steadily deteriorating.

At the Emmitsburg Road, which was bordered on either side by a five-rail chestnut fence, one veteran later recalled "the moments of anxious suspense and the length of time it seemed to climb up to the top of the fence, tumble over it, and fall flat into the bed of the road. All the while, the bullets continued to bury themselves into the bodies of the victims and the sturdy chestnut rails.... [the men of] Armistead's brigade remained within the roadbed but a few seconds before leaping again atop the five-rail fences that enclosed the roadway, leaving behind scores of dead and wounded comrades in the dust of the road."

Fifty years later, Sergeant Patrick DeLacy of the 143rd Pennsylvania Volunteers recalled of Pickett's Charge:

> We have been hearing about their valor and their courage. Now we are going to see them put to the iron test. We are firing as fast as we can and fairly riddling one of the detachments of that

magnificent line. We keep pelting at this force. I can see no end to the right nor left to the line that is coming. Skilled troops on parade could not hold an alignment of line better. It is a picture that makes man wonder at men being able to hold together in form amidst such terrible havoc in their ranks. There is praise for those men, from the boys in blue. One says "great" and "fine" without even a thought of pity for the deaths that are coming to those brave men as they advance by order of their commanders. Men are being mowed down with every step. And men are stepping into their places. There is no dismay, no discouragement, no wavering. It grows in magnificence as death's sting waxes stronger. Now they are in double quick stride. And we answer their spurt with more shot and shell.

Still about 200 yards from the Union lines, the advancing Confederates received a tremendous volley of musketry and cannon fire and "underwent an instantaneous transformation," observed a Federal officer. "Arms, heads, blankets, guns and knapsacks were tossed into the clear air. A moan went up from the field distinctly to be heard amid the storm of battle." The terrible flanking fire from Ohio and New York troops to the north and Vermont troops to the south as well as the maelstrom of musketry and canister from the Union center staggered the advancing Confederates. They gradually herded toward the center, but continued the assault toward the 69th, 71st and 72nd Pennsylvania regiments at The Angle. Nearing the wall, Kemper rode back and shouted: "Armistead, hurry up, my men can stand no more! I am going to charge those heights and carry them and I want you to support me!" Armistead responded: "I'll do it! Look at my line! It never looked better on dress parade!" Placing his slouch hat on the tip of his sword, Armistead waved it toward the enemy and commanded, "Forward double quick!" The sharp saber soon penetrated the hat which slipped down the blade to the hilt, but Armistead continued waving it and urging his men onward.

Around 3:30 p.m. — after advancing nearly a mile in about 20 minutes — with Kemper greviously wounded, Garnett dead and most of the regimental officers wounded or dead, Armistead pushed forward to rally his faltering brigade, waving them onward with his hat still on the blade of his sword. Surveying the desperate situation and receiving enemy fire from three sides, Armistead turned to Lieutenant Colonel Rawley W. Martin, commanding the 53rd Virginia and urged: "Martin, we can't stay here; we must go over that wall!" "Then we'll go forward," responded Martin, "Forward the colors!" Replacing his hat on his sword tip, Armistead shouted: "Give them cold steel, boys!" and surged over the stone wall, followed by about 150 to 300 Virginians emitting a spine-tingling Rebel yell. While some Confederates crouched at the stone wall, the charge routed the 71st Pennsylvania and continued about 150 feet toward the abandoned ordnance rifles of Alonzo H. Cushing's Battery A of the 4th U. S. Artillery. Just as he touched the barrel of one of the guns and urged his men to turn the guns on the Yankees, Armistead was shot in the arm and below the knee and fell mortally wounded. Other elements of Gibbon's Division held firm at the crest of the ridge, as the 19th Massachusetts and 42nd New York regiments of Hall's Brigade swung right to enfilade the charging Confederates. These units along with Captain Andrew Cowan's artillery and others unleashed a merciless fusillade, finally thwarting "Pickett's Charge" at the "high water mark of the Confederacy."

Indescribably fierce hand-to-hand fighting with point-blank firing ensued in the dense smoke and dust in and around "the copse of trees." "Foot to foot, body to body and man to man they struggled, pushed and strived and killed. The mass of wounded and heaps of dead entangled the feet of the contestants, and, underneath the trampling mass, wounded men who could no longer stand, struggled, fought, shouted and killed — hatless, coatless, drowned in sweat, black with powder, red with blood, with fiendish yells and strange oaths, they blindly plied the work of slaughter," recalled a Massachusetts soldier. "Valor could do no more." With no reinforcements and flanked on three sides, the Confederates could not hold the position for which they had so courageously and valiantly fought.

Gradually the few surviving Virginians who had avoided capture began streaming back from Cemetery Ridge across the Emmitsburg Road toward the safety of their own lines. Although the colors of the 9th, 14th, 53rd and 57th Virginia regiments had been captured near the Angle, the colors of the 38th started back toward Seminary Ridge. The color bearer of the 38th was cut off by a flanking movement from the north by the 8th Ohio. The 38th's colors, stained by the blood of her defenders, were captured by Sergeant Daniel Miller of Company G of the 8th Ohio, for which he received the customary Congressional Medal of Honor. Although terribly shaken, the victorious Union troops continued throwing shot and shell into the retreating remnants of Pickett's valiant division, but refused to mount an active pursuit as Meade had his men prepare for a second attack which never came.

Like the other units in "Pickett's Charge," the 38th had paid a terrible price. Colonel Edmonds and Captain Daniel C. Townes of Company A lay dead on the field. Lieutenant Colonel Whittle was wounded in the right arm and shoulder and left thigh, while Captain Lafayette Jennings of Company F had his upper jaw fractured by grape shot and Captain Henderson L. Lee of Company G was shot in the upper arm. Captain Griggs of Company K received a severe flesh wound in his right thigh from a minie ball. Captain James E. Poindexter of Company H was captured and remained a prisoner of war until his exchange on March 22, 1865. The 38th had entered the battle with approximately 484 officers and men. Of these 40 were killed on the battlefield (8%); 51 were wounded (10%); and 103 were captured (21%), of whom at least 61 were also wounded. About 40% of the men of the 38th were casualties.

From the vicinity of Cordori farm east of the Emmittsburg Road, Pickett had observed the decimation of nearly half of his division — about 2700 men — as Lee watched the debacle from near Spangler's Woods, about where the Virginia Monument stands today. Pickett met the survivors as they trickled back. A few minutes later Lee instructed Pickett to ready his division for a possible Union counterattack. Bursting into tears, Pickett responded: "General Lee, I have no division now." Lee responded, "General Pickett, your men have done all that men could do; the fault is entirely my own." Until his dying day, Pickett blamed Lee for the annihilation of his division on that awful July 3 afternoon.

Later, after surviving "one of the most terrible ordeals of my life," Captain Griggs recorded:

> The troops remained under partial shelter by a small strip of woods until the order of advance, when they moved forward as steadily as when on drill . . . . Thirty-eighth charged the enemy across a wide plain — they being sheltered behind a rock fence, earthworks, & etc. — and though unprotected and having to climb two high fences, the enemy throwing shell, grape & all kind of missles of death at us, we moved steadily forward, driving the enemy from his strong position, capturing all his guns, but only for a moment; we had lost too many to hold our trophies and having no reinforcement, and the enemy in strong force on our flanks and rear, the few surviving men cut their way back. The loss was irreparable to the regiment as well as division . . . . Never did men more than these on that day.

As Lee comforted the returning survivors and braced for a possible counterattack, most of the approximately fifty seriously wounded survivors of the 38th and other Confederates who had avoided capture continued west of Seminary Ridge to Pitzer's Run, where some bathed their wounds, "making its clear water run red," while others sought to "quench their burning thirsts." They then continued on to Pickett's Division Hospital at Bream's Mill and on John Curren's Farm on Marsh Creek.

As Lee now had no choice but to return to Virginia, most of those who were able to travel, including Captain Griggs who was on crutches, boarded (or walked with) the 17-mile-long wagon train under General John D. Imboden. This "train of misery" departed at 4 p.m. on July 4 from Cashtown on the Chambersburg Pike (US Rte. 30 today) en route to Williamsport. East of Chambersburg, the wagon train turned south on the Pine Stump or Walnut Bottom Road and traveled through New Franklin, Marion, and Greencastle.

Torrential rain and a tremendous thunderstorm partially drowned the screams of agony as the mangled victims of battle were tossed and jostled about on the often bare floorboards of wagons without springs, bouncing over the terribly rough and rutted roadway. Harrassment by Yankee cavalry and attacks to disable individual wagons by civilians in Greencastle added to the misery of the drenched invalids. Those who died were buried in unmarked graves along the way. The wagon train reached Williamsport around 3 p.m. on July 6, but took until July 14 to ferry all the wagons across the rain-swollen Potomac on two rickety ferry boats. Those unfortunate victims unable to travel with the wagon train were unavoidably left in the hospitals to await death or capture by Union forces.

The 61 captured Pittsylvanians who were seriously wounded received some medical attention in Union field hospitals and at Fort McHenry before being incarcerated in Yankee prison camps. Most of the 42 members of the 38th Virginia and other Confederates captured on the field without serious injury were moved to Westminster, Maryland, after midnight early on July 4. Here they remained until the afternoon of July 5, when they were placed on trains for Baltimore and then forwarded to Fort Delaware prison camp on an island in the Delaware River on July 6. The majority of the 40 Pittsylvanians and other heroic Confederates who died on the battlefield were hastily buried in unmarked graves by Union burial details.

While holding his line on Seminary Ridge on July 4, Lee reluctantly assigned Pickett's division with the 38th the undesirable task of escorting about 3400 Yankee prisoners of war back to Virginia. Moving southwest on the Fairfield Road (Rte. 116 today) and connecting roads through Monterey Gap, following a route shorter than Imboden's, the division moved with Longstreet's corps in the center of the line of march. Yankee cavalry under General Judson Kilpatrick attacked the column in Monterey Gap around midnight, but were driven off. Pickett's division reached Williamsport with the prisoners on July 7.

The Confederates threw up elaborate earthworks nine miles long with the 38th Virginia and Longstreet's corps on the extreme right of the line on the Potomac at Falling Waters, three miles below Williamsport. Heavy rains continued. Fortunately, no major attack materialized, although there were clashes with Yankee cavalry. The 38th crossed the Potomac on a temporary pontoon bridge on July 13 and turned its prisoners over to Imboden.

The march continued south up the Valley on the Valley Turnpike (U.S. Route 11 today) through Martinsburg and Winchester before crossing the Blue Ridge Mountains via Front Royal. All along the route, churches, private homes and any other suitable buildings became hospitals for the gravely wounded. Since Armistead's capture and death, Colonel William R. Aylett of the 53rd Virginia had been in command of the brigade. With the death of Colonel Edmonds, P. B. Whittle was promoted to colonel to com-

switched to the Atlantic & North Carolina Railroad at Goldsboro and reached Kinston at 11 p.m., after traveling about 110 miles "over a poor and destitute looking country." October 8 found the 38th encamping "about two miles from Kinston [in] a low, sandy, dismal looking region" which the troops did "not like ... at all." Winter quarters were assigned on October 9. A portion of the 38th went on picket duty about four miles below Kinston on October 10 and 11 and was relieved by the 57th Virginia at 1 p.m. on October 12. On a rainy October 14, the men began constructing crude huts, some even with floors and chimneys, for their winter quarters. Except for work on the winter quarters and routine camp life, all was quiet until October 31, when the 38th received marching orders.

The brigade, except for the 53rd Virginia, departed Kinston at 1 p.m. on November 1 and moved back to Weldon in anticipation of an enemy raid which failed to materialize. The troops of the 38th then continued on to Petersburg and Hanover Junction with high hopes of reuniting with the Army of Northern Virginia. To their great disappointment, the 38th returned on November 11 to its campsite near Kinston for the winter.

Due to the wounds he had received at Gettysburg, Colonel Whittle applied for and was relieved from active duty on November 15 and assigned as a judge of the military court of A. P. Hill's Third Corps. Lieutenant Colonel Cabell was promoted to colonel commanding the 38th and Major Griggs to lieutenant colonel, although he served as a judge on a military court in Goldsboro and Kinston from November 1, 1863, to January 29, 1864.

Undoubtedly expressing the sentiments of his comrades in arms as well as of the common soldier in every war, on December 22 John Booker of Company D wrote his cousin: "Christmas is close by and I see no chance for me or James to get home .... if the officers would do rite, we would get [a furlough], but if they can get home when ever they please, they dont care for us. I beleave Capt. Herndon ... is just too lazy to write one. Capt. Herndon expects to get another furlough soon after Christmas to go home, but if I had it in my power, he would not get one till the last man in his company get one. We are here now doing nothing in the world not even picket duty ... this is a rich mans war and a poor mans fight." In all probability, those soldiers not fortunate enough to get a furlough home spent a quiet and melancholy Christmas Day in camp.

Describing living conditions in camp, Corporal Linnaeus D. Watkins of Company E wrote to his sister on December 27: "We are as comfortable fixed up as any men in the army — good beds make out of boards up off the floor — good stools to set on — splendid log houses. And can buy any thing to eat we want — sweet potatoes 4 dollars a bushel, bacon from one dollar to one and a half, eggs one dollar and a quarter, corn meal three to four dollars a bushel] ... flour cant be bought at enny price a tall."

On December 31, the 38th started toward Greenville, N.C., on muddy roads in the rain in response to a Federal advance against the 57th Virginia Regiment there. Fortunately, the enemy withdrew when within five miles of Greenville and the 38th returned to camp.

As of March 31, Barton's Brigade was assigned to the Department of Richmond, commanded by Major General Arnold Elzey. April 8 was observed as a day of "fasting, humiliation and prayer" by order of President Davis. Most of the time was spent drilling, improving winter quarters, attending worship services, pulling picket duty, or on furlough home. Unfortunately the boredom of camp life contributed to personal conflicts as evidenced on April 2 by Private John Q. Adams throwing a bayonet into Private Joel Harris' arm. Both men were members of Company K. Heavy snows and a severe shortage of food added to the men's discomfort. The 38th remained encamped near Richmond until May 3 when the "second" Company I, commanded by Captain George A. Martin, joined the regiment.

On that day the 38th Virginia departed its campsite at 8 a.m. with only two wagons and marched north on the Brook Turnpike (approximately parallel to and just east of today's U.S. Rte. 1) before halting at 4 p.m. Resuming the march at sunrise the following day, the regiment halted near Hanover Junction at 2 p.m., having covered more than 25 miles. On May 5, a portion of the 38th was assigned picket duty guarding one of the railroad bridges over the South Anna River. The detachment rejoined the brigade near Taylorsville the following day.

At 2 a.m. on May 7, the 38th marched to the R. F. & P. railroad depot at Taylorsville and boarded a train for Richmond. Upon arrival there, the troops transferred to a steamer and sailed down the James River about eight miles to Drewry's Bluff, where they debarked and marched southwest about five miles to the vicinity of Chester Station on the Richmond & Petersburg Railroad (later the Seaboard Coast Line). This movement was necessitated by the menace posed to Richmond by Union General Benjamin F. Butler's 20,000-man Army of the James, which had landed at Bermuda Hundred on the James River and begun to advance. Upon arrival at Drewry's Bluff, the brigade came under the command of Major General Robert Ransom, Jr. Ransom already commanded Gracie's, Hoke's and Kemper's brigades in the Department of North Carolina and Southern Virginia under General P. G. T. Beauregard.

The 38th Virginia held its position manning a second line of breastworks near Chester Station on May 8 and 9. On May 10 at 6:30 a.m., Ransom sent Barton's Brigade south along the Richmond-Petersburg Turnpike to reconnoiter Butler's exact position. The 38th was east of the turnpike and on the left of the brigade. According to Lt. Col. Griggs:

> About 9 o'clock a.m., the signal for advance was given, the regiment moved forward and soon engaged the enemy's skirmishers, driving them upon their line of battle. At this point I found my left entirely unprotected and the enemy upon a line with my own. I immediately reported the fact to Colonel Cabell and one of General Barton's staff and deployed my left, Com-

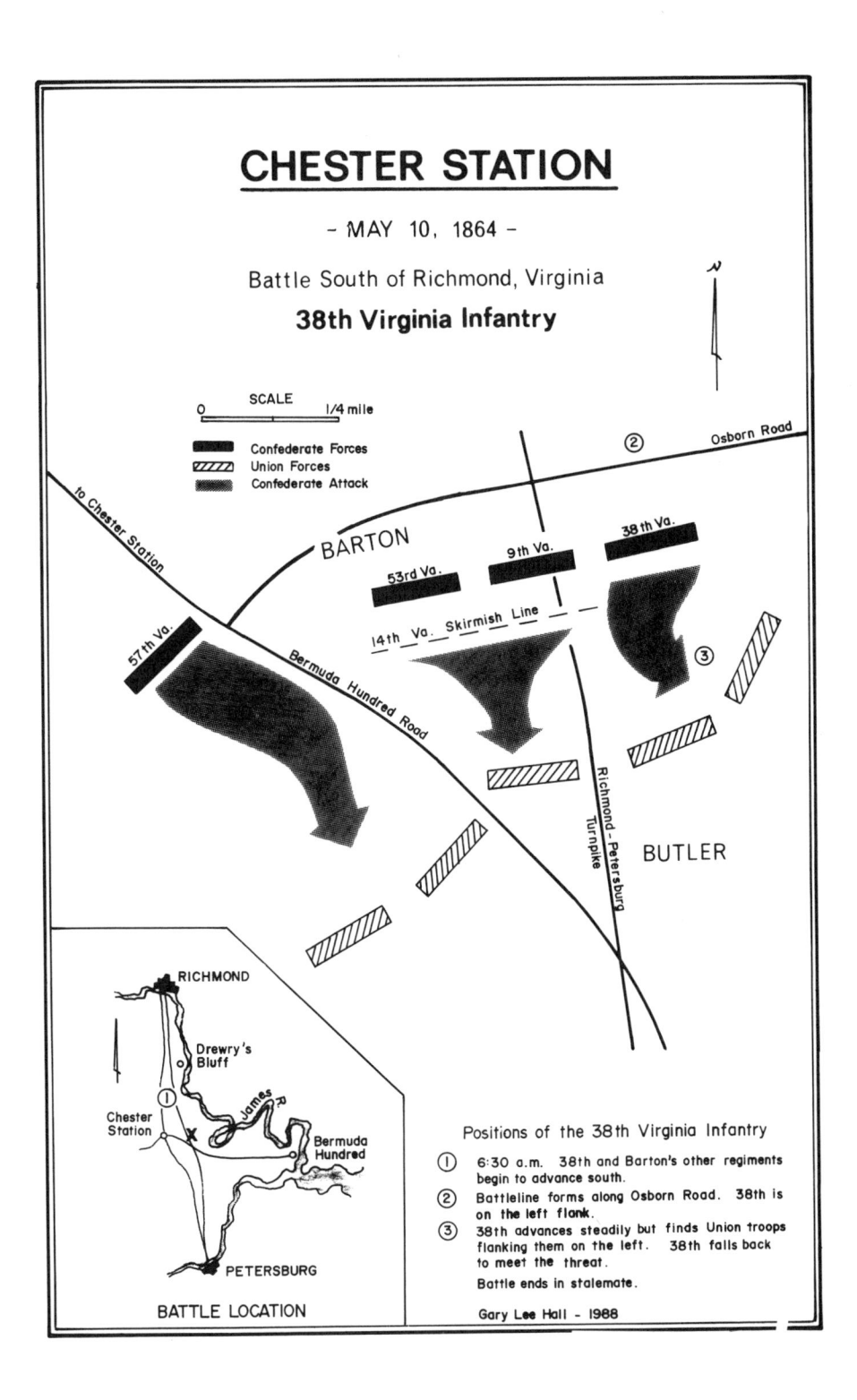

CHESTER STATION

– MAY 10, 1864 –

Battle South of Richmond, Virginia

38th Virginia Infantry

SCALE 0 — 1/4 mile

- ▮ Confederate Forces
- ▨ Union Forces
- ▮ Confederate Attack

N

② Osborn Road

BARTON

53rd Va.   9th Va.   38th Va.

14th Va. Skirmish Line

57th Va.

Bermuda Hundred Road

to Chester Station

③

Richmond-Petersburg Turnpike

BUTLER

BATTLE LOCATION

RICHMOND
Drewry's Bluff
James
Chester Station
Bermuda Hundred
PETERSBURG

Positions of the 38th Virginia Infantry

① 6:30 a.m. 38th and Barton's other regiments begin to advance south.
② Battleline forms along Osborn Road. 38th is on the left flank.
③ 38th advances steadily but finds Union troops flanking them on the left. 38th falls back to meet the threat.
Battle ends in stalemate.

Gary Lee Hall - 1988

51

mond for Barton's restoration to his rightful place of command. Their petition referred to "his gallantry and coolness" at Chester Station, where "he was always in the thickest of the fray, leading his officers and men where necessary, and when the enemy were driven from their gun, he was the first to take possession of it." For whatever reason, the Confederate government failed to act favorably on the petition and Barton never regained his command.

On a rainy May 12 at 2 a.m., the 38th marched to Drewry's Bluff and then moved by boat to Richmond in anticipation of a Union cavalry raid. Upon arrival, the regiment marched to trenches on the Mechanicsville Turnpike, then to Meadow Bridge Road and to Brook Turnpike, before returning to the Mechanicsville Turnpike after "a great deal of unnecessary marching." The raid did not materialize and Colonel Griggs observed, "a great want of generalship has been displayed by those in command." May 13 and 14 were spent likewise moving from position to position near the York River Railroad. On May 15, the troops marched to Rocketts and boarded a steamer to return to Drewry's Bluff, where they arrived and bivouacked around midnight.

After resting about an hour and a half, the weary Pittsylvanians were formed in line of battle early on May 16 east of the Richmond-Petersburg Turnpike on the left of the Confederate line in a dense fog. Ransom ordered Barton's (Fry's) Brigade to support Hoke's Brigade as the Confederates again faced Butler. Receiving Ransom's order to advance, Hoke moved his brigade to the right, leaving the 38th, positioned between the 9th and 57th Virginia regiments, completely exposed to the front. The Confederates advanced after 4 a.m. over heavy abatis and across a wide field with visibility limited to 40 paces. "Laboring under the delusion that General Hoke's brigade was in our front," many men hesitated to fire and "were shot down without firing a gun." Colonel Griggs continued: "it was not until when within twenty paces of the enemy's works, which were yet invisible, that a fire was made, when, with much reduced ranks, only a few of the right and many of the left wing entered the enemy's works, capturing many prisoners," including Union Brigadier General C. A. Heckman. Colonel Griggs received a severe wound to his left thigh and was taken to Howard's Grove Hospital, northeast of Richmond. The 38th lost 23 killed and 77 wounded at Drewry's Bluff. As a result of this action, Butler was neatly "bottled" at Bermuda Hundred, posing little further threat to the Confederacy.

In the meantime, General U. S. Grant had continued to press Lee at the Wilderness and then at Spotsylvania Court House. On May 18, the 38th Virginia entrained on the R. F. & P. Railroad and was transported about 38 miles north to Milford Station in Caroline County. From Milford, the Pittsylvanians marched about 15 miles northwest toward Spotsylvania Court

House to join Lee. Finding Lee falling back, the troops "returned to Hanover Courthouse on May 20, having marched two days and nights on short rations, and but little rest." While resting at Hanover Court House on May 29, the regiment was reunited with Pickett's division "to the great joy of all."

The 38th remained in the Hanover Courthouse — Mechanicsville — Richmond vicinity for the next couple of weeks. Throughout the bitter fighting around Cold Harbor, Fry's Brigade held a stretch of line along a road (now Va. Rte. 633 between Rte. 615 and Rte. 635) as the middle element of Pickett's division, supporting Frank Huger's artillery battalion.

On June 17 as Grant crossed to the south of the James River and began the siege of Petersburg, the 38th participated in a skirmish with Union troops near Bermuda Hundred. One Pittsylvanian was killed and one wounded, but the enemy's pickets were completely dispersed. The regiment continued to assist in holding the defensive positions around Richmond and engaged in minor skirmishing during June, July and August. The pickets were often within talking distance of the enemy. Having sufficiently recuperated from his wound, Colonel Griggs resumed command of the regiment on August 1.

At Bermuda Hundred on August 25 at 3:30 a.m., the 38th Virginia with the division was called up and advanced the picket line around dawn in a spirited skirmish. The enemy was driven from his rifle pits and some prisoners were captured, before the Confederates returned to their original position, "leaving the field between the lines and the lines themselves about as they were before the attack." The Pittsylvanians suffered 14 casualties. Captain W. G. Cabaniss of Company K was severely wounded in the mouth and jaw and subsequently retired from the Army. Captain Richard J. Joyce of Company A was mortally wounded.

More than forty years later, First Lieutenant John Wainwright of the 97th Pennsylvania Infantry recalled being directed to relieve the Union pickets after this attack. After placing his men along their two hundred yards of front around 9 a.m., Wainwright was on the extreme left of his line

> on a knoll amongst some bushes and slashed timber which afforded only fair protection, where I was kept down close to the ground all day by the wicked sharp shooters [of the 38th], nevertheless, I could see the entire field which was open ground on my front between the lines. The August sun rose hotter and hotter and the fire of the sharp shooters from several points was hotter still, but during that hot August day, I observed out between the Union and Confederate lines over which the latter had charged that morning a moving object which I found to be a man in distress, half rising to his feet, stumbling a step or two, and then falling to the ground to lie there awhile in the burning sun

November 10, the Pittsylvanians could hear "great rejoicing in [the] enemies' camp," apparently due to the re-election of Abraham Lincoln, followed by "heavy shelling in [the] direction [of] Petersburg." November 15 "by request of the President [was] kept as [a] day of Thanksgiving and prayer [with] all duties suspended." During the night of November 17, the 38th with the 9th and 18th Virginia regiments and three regiments of Hunton's Brigade charged and captured the Union line, killing four and capturing thirty-seven Yankees, including a captain and a lieutenant, as well as twenty-two guns and 18 sets of accoutrements. The only casualties to the 38th were Pvt. George J. Robertson of Company D, who was shot in the left thigh, and Pvt. William H. Barker of Co. C, who was captured. The Confederate line was thus established "much nearer the enemy."

Private Moses Barker wrote his wife on November 23:

> The Beast (I mean Butler) has been quite mad with us for on the night of the 17th we captured his pickett in line front of the 38th, 9th, and 18th Regiments and took nearly all the pickets prisoner. Some of them were killed and a few escaped, but they were so completely surprised that they had little chance to fight or run off either.... I had one hard time last Friday night and Saturday (November 18 and 19) on picket. I was just posted on vidett amid rain and mud and had not walked half the length of my beat before the minie balls was flying around me. We pickets that were on vidett at the time got into our pits with our reliefs and commenced firing and were fired upon... we had no where to stand, sit or lay down, but right in the mud and water.... On Saturday morning the Yanks commenced shelling us furiously and kept it up until late in the evening, and then we had to lay in our pits and the rain coming down and the bumbs flying and bursting, and we bumbed them back.

Colonel Griggs noted: "Much indiginity (was) felt among" the Pittsylvanians when they found "Negro troops" in their front on November 27, resulting in an increase in the exchange of gunfire on November 28 and 29. By December 1, there were "no Negroes in our front [and] no picket firing," but "two of the enemy deserted to our lines." The Negro pickets returned on December 2 and the exchange of gunfire resumed.

On December 7, Moses Barker wrote to his wife regarding a soldier who ran in battle and was apparently given a death sentence which was commuted:

> He was marched... in front of the Regt.... [with] a chain and large heavy ball fastened to his leg — holding the chain and ball up with his hands and a plank [strapped] to his back with the word 'coward' on it. This man run in battle or rather did not go into it... or went home. He was to of been shot the next day, and

his grave was dug, or rather [a] hole to of thrown him in about two feet deep. I have seen the grave today and I have seen him today at work with his chain and ball and plank as described above, and I was sorry for him. Perhaps that man has a wife that wrote to him not to go in battle. I know of more than one woman that has wrote to their husbands not go in battle, but I want tell who they are, but they ought not to . . . .

On December 15, Colonel Griggs noted the establishment of brigade and regimental badges as follows: Brigade — red shield; 9th Virginia — blue shield; 14th Virginia — black shield; 38th Virginia — blue heart; 53rd Virginia — blue circle; and 57th Virginia — black shield. On Sunday, December 21, Steuart's Brigade was inspected by Major Giles B. Cooke of Lee's staff.

Christmas Day 1864, the last for the Confederacy, was a quiet and uneventful day in camp for the men of the 38th Virginia.

> has in keeping the welfare of nations;
>
> IV. that this resolution be published in the Richmond daily and Danville papers.

January faded into February with the 38th Virginia manning the trenches on the Howlett Line at a location between Chester Station and Bermuda Hundred. The soldiers wearily continued the struggle against hunger, penetrating cold, snow, ice, boredom, occasional sniping from enemy pickets, and small skirmishes. They heard the Yankees fire salutes on February 21 celebrating the fall of Charleston and on February 24 for the fall of Wilmington.

The number of desertions continued to increase with some of the men joining the enemy and others just going home to aid their loved ones against the ravages caused by the war. These desertions occurred in spite of the fateful consequences faced by those deserters who were apprehended and convicted of their crime. On February 11, Private Moses Barker wrote his wife:

> I witnessed an awful sight yesterday. I was summonsed as a detail to witness the execution of the sentence of death . . . against Mr. Baise of Co. E 38th Va. Regt. [according to the Compiled Service Records, this apparently was Pvt. David E. Bays of Co. E who was listed as confined in the Provost Guardhouse for desertion prior to Dec. 31, 1864] and saw him shot to death. He was brought to the place of execution by guards and accompanied by the Rev. Mr. Cridlin. (The details from the various companies of the Brigade being already formed in three forths of a hollow square.) He took his stand by the stake and as soon as his sentence was read, Mr. Cridlin, standing close to him, come to his knees and he done the same after prayer by Mr. Cridlin (our chaplain), he went to Baise and shook hands with him. He was then tied to the stake, and soon was in Eternity. He professed hope of being better off. . . .

Pickett's division, including the 38th, was relieved from the trenches on the Howlett Line on March 4 and replaced by General William Mahone's division. After brigade and division reviews on March 6 and 7 respectively, the 38th marched about eight miles to a camp site within two miles of Richmond late on March 7.

In response to unconfirmed reports of Union cavalry under General Philip H. Sheridan operating in the vicinity of Farmville, the regiment broke camp at 7 a.m. on March 10. Along with the 53rd and 57th regiments, the 38th boarded a train in Manchester and proceeded about 50 miles to Burkeville Junction on the Richmond & Danville Railroad (later the Southern Railway), arriving at 4 p.m. After a halt there, the trip resumed at 9 p.m. on the South Side Railroad (later the Norfolk & Western Railway) with the troops travelling about 17 miles and crossing High Bridge en route to

Farmville, where they camped briefly.

Finding no Sheridan, the Pittsylvanians returned to Richmond by train on March 12. While on the train near Richmond on March 13, Griggs noted a "good many men and officers drunk" and placed Capt. John T. Grubbs of Co. C under arrest for drunkeness and disobedience of orders.

The men paused at Manchester on March 14 and cooked three days' rations. Still in pursuit of Sheridan, they then marched through Richmond and boarded a train at the Virginia Central Railroad depot and traveled north about 10 miles to Atlee's Station, arriving in the night. Detraining there, the troops marched cross country toward Ashland on March 15 and reported minor skirmishing. They were occupied marching and counter-marching over muddy, swampy roads near Ashland on March 16, before reaching New Hundley Ford on the Pamunkey River and then bivouacking about a mile away late on March 17. The regiment marched all the following day and camped that night on the Mechanicsville Turnpike about two miles north of Richmond. Leaving this camp site at 3 a.m. on March 19, the Pittsylvanians trudged to the outer defenses of Richmond on the Charles City Road and then moved back to a point on Nine Mile Road about three miles from the city and went into camp.

After an inspection at 8 a.m. on March 21, the division was reviewed at noon in a hard rain by Longstreet, Secretary of War John C. Breckinridge, Governor William Smith, and "many ladies." March 22 thru 24 was spent in camp drilling. Leaving its camp site at 7 p.m. on March 24, the 38th moved by train back to Richmond and then marched south on the Richmond & Petersburg Turnpike. The Pittsylvanians passed through Petersburg around 7 a.m. on March 26 and halted at Battery No. 45, south of the city, where they "commenced throwing up fortifications." As this work continued on March 28, Lee passed by the position.

As Sheridan's cavalry moved to threaten Lee's right and the South Side and Richmond & Danville railroads, Lee and Longstreet determined to send a combined cavalry, infantry, and artillery force to meet this critical threat. Pickett's division of infantry was chosen for this mission along with Fitz Lee's cavalry. At 4:30 p.m. on March 29, the 38th marched to Sutherland Station on the South Side Railroad and then marched all the following day in the rain to Five Forks, where it halted at 8 p.m. The 38th, serving as rear guard for the division, skirmished with the enemy most of the day. Moving toward Dinwiddie Court House at 8 a.m. on March 31, Fitz Lee's cavalry engaged Union cavalry about 2 p.m. and drove them until dark. Pickett's division was able to force its way across Chamberlain's Bed at Danse's Ford and secured a position across Adams Road, although the 38th with Steuart's Brigade was not actively engaged. Sheridan's forces were driven back almost to Dinwiddie Court House and sustained 450 casualties.

During the night of March 31, Union infantry reinforcements swelled

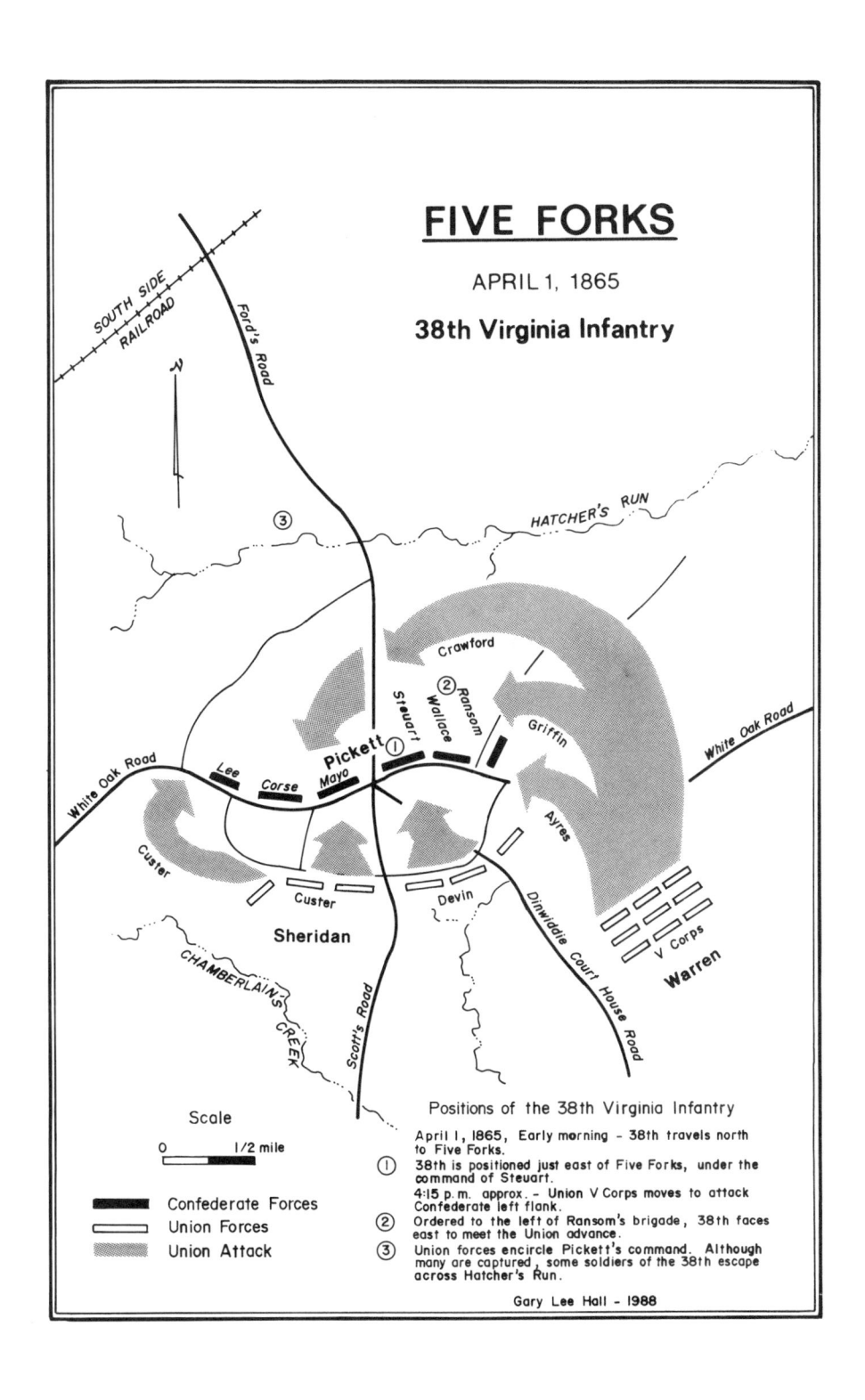

FIVE FORKS

APRIL 1, 1865

38th Virginia Infantry

Scale

0 — 1/2 mile

- Confederate Forces
- Union Forces
- Union Attack

Positions of the 38th Virginia Infantry

April 1, 1865, Early morning - 38th travels north to Five Forks.

① 38th is positioned just east of Five Forks, under the command of Steuart.

4:15 p.m. approx. - Union V Corps moves to attack Confederate left flank.

② Ordered to the left of Ransom's brigade, 38th faces east to meet the Union advance.

③ Union forces encircle Pickett's command. Although many are captured, some soldiers of the 38th escape across Hatcher's Run.

Gary Lee Hall - 1988

Sheridan's force to about 25,000 men opposing Pickett's 12,600. At 4:30 a.m. on April 1, Pickett began to fall back toward Five Forks, harassed by Custer's cavalry. Lee telegraphed Pickett urging him to: "Hold Five Forks at all hazards. Protect road to Ford's Depot and prevent Union forces from striking the South Side Railroad. Regret exceedingly your forced withdrawal, and your inability to hold the advantage you had gained." Lee realized that the loss of Five Forks would permit the Yankees to reach and sever the South Side Railroad and the wagon roads to the west. Such a disaster would spell doom for Petersburg and, consequently, Richmond.

Reaching Five Forks, Steuart's Brigade, including the 38th, "proceeded to throw up rifle pits along" the north side of the White Oak Road (SR 613) from Ford's Road (SR 627) for about one-third mile to the East. (The 1988 state highway route numbers — for example: SR 613 — will be used in this narrative to assist in following the retreat route from Five Forks to Appomattox.) Steuart's Brigade occupied the center of Pickett's five-brigade front to the east of the Forks. Meanwhile, Generals Pickett, Fitz Lee and Tom Rosser met more than a mile to the rear and leisurely proceeded to enjoy a shad bake.

Federal cavalry and infantry attacked in force in the afternoon and rolled back Ransom's and Wallace's brigades on Steuart's left. Colonel Griggs later recorded:

> Early in the action the Thirty-eighth was ordered from [the] brigade, and to go to the left of Brigadier-General Ransom, which [it] did at a double quick. Finding no troops but a few cavalrymen, who left to join (they said) their command, [Griggs] deployed the [38th] into single file, and opened a destructive fire upon the enemy, who were marching in view, to the rear of their line of battle, in three columns to our left. Colonel Griggs dispatched a courier to brigade and division headquarters to report this movement of the enemy, and continued to deploy his regiment and fire upon the enemy, and kept his front in check; but there being no troops on his [Griggs'] left, the enemy's column soon passed to the rear of his line and opened upon his front and rear. Many of the men having expended all their ammunition, and the enemy rapidly closing all means of escape, the few men left were ordered to retire. After cutting through the lines of the enemy, Colonel Griggs reported in person to General Pickett the condition he was in. The general replied, "He knew it, but could not help it — had done all he could." The regiment fought odds of about ten to one, in full view of the enemy, where each private could see for himself the odds against him. Yet there seemed no unusual excitement or fear among them, and some were seen to club their muskets after they had fired their last round of ammunition.

The death knell of the Confederacy had sounded.

Pickett and Fitz Lee, with 8,000 survivors of their commands, including those from the 38th, retreated to the north during the night, covering about nine miles and following the paths of today's State Routes 627 and 611 to Exeter Mills on the Appomattox River. Shortly after daybreak on April 2, they attempted to cross the rain-swollen river there, but the high water turned them back. The men moved up stream on the south side of the Appomattox for about 12 miles and attempted another crossing at Deep Creek bridge, but failed again and halted there for the night. Here they received word of the evacuation of Richmond. Moving out at 11 a.m. on April 3, the weary soldiers finally were able to cross Deep Creek about 20 miles west of Petersburg and halted nearby for the night. The retreat resumed at 8 a.m. on April 4. About seven miles east of Amelia Court House at Tabernacle Church near Beaverpond Creek (SR 153), the beleaguered troops formed in line of battle and drove off Union cavalry under General Wesley Merritt, who was attempting to reach Amelia Court House.

Marching again at 4 a.m. on April 5, the exhausted Confederates reached Amelia Court House and were bitterly disappointed at the absence of expected rations. The bone-tired troops rested during the day as Lee appealed to the local citizenry for food, but to no avail. This delay allowed time for Sheridan's cavalry to reach Jetersville on the Richmond and Danville Railroad, eight miles southwest of Amelia Court House, and hastily construct earthworks. This effectively blocked Lee's intended route to Danville and thence to unite with General Joseph E. Johnston's Army of Tennessee, which was then in North Carolina and retreating from Sheridan. Lee chose to veer west toward Farmville, intending to obtain rations there and then cut south to Keysville to resume the retreat to Danville. Still with only parched corn, intended for horse feed, to appease their ravenous hunger, the haggard soldiers crossed the Richmond and Danville tracks and trudged through the night of April 5 toward Amelia Springs. Harassed by Union cavalry, the retreat continued in the early hours of April 6 along today's Route 617 through Deatonsville and paused at Holt's (Hott's) Corner (intersection of SR 617 and 618) to stave off a cavalry attack, before continuing past the Hillsman House and across Little Sayler's (Sailor's) Creek.

At Marshall's Cross Roads (intersection of SR 617 and 620) in the early afternoon of April 6, Federal cavalry fell on Pickett's and Bushrod Johnson's divisions. The embattled Confederates "formed line of battle across an open field, and held it for several hours against repeated charges of Sheridan's dismounted cavalry." Here on Sayler's Creek battlefield, the 38th fought its last battle "with as much determination as on any previous field." Referring to the attacking Union soldiers, Colonel Griggs noted:

> We repulsed him in front but he turned our flank and in our rear with large numbers, overpowering and capturing most of the

Division. I made with my regt. the last effort to check the enemy but [was] powerless to do so and barely escaped being captured myself.

Colonel John Hughey of Company L of the 2nd Ohio Cavalry captured the 38th's regimental colors. This was the second time the colors were lost during the War. Corporal Hughey later received the customary Congressional Medal of Honor for this capture. Generals Richard Ewell, Eppa Hunton and Montgomery Corse were all captured at this debacle.

As human beings tend to observe events differently, especially at times of extreme stress, it is not surprising that some criticism was directed at Pickett's division. General Henry A. Wise noted: "We had hardly formed . . . before Pickett's whole command stampeded." To the contrary, Major Walter H. Harrison, Inspector General and later historian for Pickett's division, observed: ". . . those men behaved as well on that last battle-field as they had ever done in their first flush of glory. . . ."

The 38th's survivors passed through Rice's Depot and reached Farmville late during the night of April 6-7, covering about eight miles from the site of the battle at Sayler's Creek. After a brief rest, they moved north out of Farmville on April 7 along today's State Route 45 for two and a half miles before turning west and continuing on through New Store on today's State Route 636. Colonel Griggs was in command of the brigade. The regiment trudged on at 5 a.m. on April 8 and travelled unmolested all day before turning west on the Richmond-Lynchburg Stage Road (SR 2307, 626, and 24). Considering the physical and mental state of the soldiers, the stragglers and discarded weapons noticed along the way by some observers were understandable. A halt was finally called around 4 p.m. near New Hope Baptist Church (at today's Vera on SR 24). The exhausted soldiers dug earthworks in preparation for an attack. These earthworks ran roughly north-south and bisected the Richmond - Lynchburg Stage Road (SR 24) about one quarter mile west of New Hope Baptist Church. The 38th and the other remnants of Pickett's division occupied these trenches adjacent to the Stage Road on the north side.

Early on April 9, as the fog burned off, Lee attempted to push through Appomattox Court House to the west, but found Federal cavalry, closely supported by infantry, blocking the route. The last casualties in either army were inflicted that morning at the Battle of Appomattox Court House. The 38th left its earthworks near the rear of the army at 9 a.m. and marched a mile west before halting near "Pleasant Retreat" about two miles east of Appomattox Court House. Lee now fully realized that his once proud and formidable, but now starving, exhausted, and ragged Army of Northern Virginia was in a Federal vice grip — blocked to both front and rear — and outnumbered at least two to one by the best-equipped and best-supplied army in the world. To his staff, Lee admitted: "Then there is nothing left me but to go and see General Grant, and I would rather die a thousand deaths." Lee did this and around 3 p.m. on that fateful Palm Sunday, "after four years of arduous service, marked by unsurpassed courage and fortitude, the Army of Northern Virginia [was] compelled to yield to overwhelming numbers and resources."

April 10 and 11 were spent in camp. Colonel Griggs prepared a list of his soldiers to be paroled and the hungry men received welcome rations from the Confederate supplies captured by the U.S. Army at Appomattox Depot. The 38th counted 13 officers, 9 sergeants and 51 privates for parole on April 12.

At daybreak on April 13, the men broke camp for the last time, bade their farewells, and started the long trek home. Most of those returning to Pittsylvania County travelled through Concord and Campbell Court House (now Rustburg), then crossed the Staunton River at Dew's Ferry as Ward's Bridge (about a mile upstream near today's Altavista) had been burned. By late on April 14, many Pittsylvanians were reunited with their loved ones at home. The prisoners of war who remained captive in Yankee prisons returned home in June and July. We can only imagine the agony of the families of those who had made the supreme sacrifice and "just never came home."

The experiences of the men of the 38th Virginia Infantry were typical of others in the Army of Northern Virginia. There had been the extraordinary bravery and devotion to duty at Seven Pines, Malvern Hill, Gettysburg and Five Forks. Yet charges of "confusion," "demoralization," and "stampeding" before the enemy, were leveled at Williamsburg, Boteler's Ford, Chester Station and Sayler's Creek. Considering the human frailities of the men of the 38th, of their leaders, and of their critics, we can understand and appreciate their lack of perfection at all times in all circumstances. By the same token, their patriotism, devotion to duty, and great courage in the most difficult and trying of circumstances is a tremendous source of pride and inspiration. Thse brave soldiers, like Americans in every war, answered the call to duty and fought to the last for their country and for a cause they perceived as just and true.

Soon many of the survivors of the 38th were again farming the Pittsylvania County fields, untouched by the harsh realities of four years of war, and raising their families. The twentieth century gradually took its toll under the last survivor of the 38th answered the "final roll call" and the 38th Virginia Volunteer Infantry became a proud and glorious memory.

Colonel P. B. Whittle

G. K. Griggs, colonel, 1865.

Pvt. John Wilburn Scruggs, Co. H and wife, Nannie Jane Hamlet Scruggs.

Courtesy: Marvin Osborne, Danville, Va.

Pvt. William Bryon Slayton, Co. D and wife Sarah Thomas

Courtesy: Clarence J. Warren, Marshall, Va.

Lt. James P. Warren, Co. B

Pvt. Reuben B. Ricketts, Co. E and wife Jane Richardson

Lt. John Coles, Jr., Co. H

Pvt. Felix Shelborne Dodson, Co. A

Flag of the 38th, probably the one captured at Saylers Creek 4/6/65. Note that portions of flag have been reconstructed.

George A. Harville, Pvt., Co. K

Pvt. James Allen Oakes, Co. B

Pvt. Thomas B. Coleman, Co. G

Pvt. John Ward Reynolds, Co. B

INTRODUCTION TO THE ROSTER

This roster includes the names of 1,656 soldiers who served in the 38th Regiment of Virginia Volunteer Infantry. The primary source for this information was the Compiled Military Service Records file for the 38th Virginia Infantry which is catalogued in Microcopy No. 324, Roll nos. 840-849, of the War Department Collection of Confederate Records in the National Archives, Washington, D.C. The microfilmed Compiled Service Records (CSR) are also available at the Virginia State Archives in Richmond and at Virginia Polytechnic Institute & State University (VPI & SU) in Blacksburg. These records consist of jacket-envelopes containing cards, which list the soldier's name, rank, organization, service data and occasionally his physical description, extracted from the original muster rolls, payrolls, rosters, hospital and prison registers, parole records and other pertinent data relating to the soldier's service.

The muster rolls, which form the foundation of the Compiled Service Records (CSR), were normally recorded by the adjutant every two months near the end of the month. They reflected each soldier's status as of that particular day for pay roll purposes. For example, a soldier who had been absent sick for several weeks, but was present in camp on the day the muster roll was recorded, would be listed as "present", probably with no mention of his recent absence. Conversely, a soldier who had dutifully served until being taken ill and hospitalized the day before the muster roll, would be listed "absent sick". This explains the frequent notation of a given event as "prior to" a certain date. We must also remember the tendency of the record keepers of that day to spell a word or name just the way it sounded, so Chisholm became Chism, or Meaks might be Meeks, for example. For the reader researching an ancestor or a particular soldier, occasionally some additional information, not included here, may be located by reviewing that soldier's file in the CSR. Such information will probably be of minor significance — a clothing or supply receipt, for example. Occasionally information contained in the Compiled Service Records is self-contradictory. In those instances, the notation "CSR also states . . ." is made and the reader is left to determine the true facts.

The names of many soldiers are accompanied by the notation "Postwar record only". This indicates that the individual's name does not appear in the CSR, probably for one of the reasons explained below. In most of these cases, that individual later applied for a pension due to his service in the 38th. The applicant swore under oath that he had served in the regiment and his application was supported by the sworn affadavit of two known veterans who stated they had served in the 38th with the applicant.

Before harshly judging a soldier for being AWOL, we must remember the circumstances they faced in the context of the time. Often a soldier would receive a letter from his wife begging him to come home to harvest the crops or perform a similar duty for the well-being of his family. Usually the wife had sole responsibility for the care of the children and maintenance of the home. It is difficult to fault a man for tending to the vital needs of his family and then returning to his assigned duties to shoulder his responsibilities to his country.

When a Confederate soldier is recorded as being taken prisoner or even deserting to the Union troops, this information was usually recorded by a Union soldier. Often the Yankees in unfamiliar surroundings did not know their precise position, so their recorded locations must be viewed with some skepticism. For example, a Confederate POW at Five Forks also might be shown as being captured at Petersburg, Dinwiddie Court House, White Oak Road, or the South Side Railroad, depending upon the Yankee's perception of his location on that day. The date of the capture or desertion when considered with the unit's location at the time is probably a more accurate indication of where the event actually occurred. We must remember also that the soldier could have been wounded or fell behind on the march and then was captured by the advancing enemy. Please bear in mind that the soldiers listed as "Paroled at Appomattox on 4/9/65" actually were not paroled until April 12, 1865, but the CSR reflects the former and no change was made in this record.

Captured Confederates were held in various Union prison camps. Most POWs from the 38th were held in one or more of the following camps:

City Point	a POW depot & exchange point at the confluence of the Appomattox & James Rivers, site of Hopewell, Va. today
Elmira	on the Chemung River near Elmira, NY
Fort Delaware	an island in the Delaware River
Fort McHenry	Baltimore, Md.
Hart's Island	New York harbor
Johnson's Island	in Sandusky Bay of Lake Erie in Ohio
Libby Prison	at Cary & 20th Streets in Richmond.
Old Capitol Prison	at 1st & East Capitol Streets in Washington, D.C., the site of the U.S. Supreme Court building today.
Point Lookout	on a peninsula between the Chesapeake Bay & the Potomac River in Maryland.

Salisbury, N.C. . . . . prison for Union POWs & Confederate deserters or prisoners being court-martialed.

Regretfully, the extant records of the Confederate soldiers' service are extremely fragmentary and sketchy, at best. The records were probably never as detailed and complete as we would like. A large portion of even these was lost in the chaos of the evacuation and burning of Richmond.

The information contained in the Compiled Service Records is supplemented in this roster whenever possible by other reliable information from cemetery records, family Bibles, genealogies, local histories, newspaper obituaries, pension and census records. The format for the roster following the soldier's name is all known information in chronological order beginning with his date and place of birth, enlistment data, service record, postwar activities, date and place of death and place of burial. In addition to the more commonly accepted abbreviations, the following are utilized in the roster in the interest of conserving space:

AWOL — Absent without leave
B. — Born
Bur. — Buried
Cem. — Cemetery
C.H. — Court House
CSR — Compiled Service Records
D. — Died
enl. — Enlisted or enrolled
g.s.w. — Gun shot wound
KIA — Killed in action
MWIA — Mortally wounded in action
Occ. — Occupation
Prom. — Promoted
Vulnus selopiticum or v.s. — Gun shot wound (medical term)
WIA — Wounded in action

As you turn the pages and meet the soldiers of the 38th Virginia Infantry, think of them not as merely a list of names followed by small print, but rather as flesh and blood human beings like you and me. They were mostly good men with parents, wives, sweethearts, children, and friends who loved them. They experienced the deepest emotions and suffered the severest illnesses and wounds in an environment brutal beyond our comprehension. They lived, served, and often died, in the most turbulent period of our Nation's history. We are fortunate to inherit the legacy of such men.

38th Virginia Infantry

ABBOTT, DAVID J.: enl. 3/6/62 in Appomattox Co.; 2nd Co. I. Cpl. to Sgt. prior to 12/31/64. Present 8/31/64 (1st muster roll dated) until POW at Five Forks on 4/1/65. Arrived at Pt. Lookout, Md. from City Pt., Va. on 4/6/65. Released from Pt. Lookout, 6/23/65. Resident of Appomattox Co.; dk. complex., brown hair, blue eyes, 6'¼".

ABBOTT, GEORGE W.: enl. 7/2/61, at Pittsylvania C.H., Sgt. in Co. H. Died near Centreville on 8/15/61 of typhoid fever.

ABBOTT, WILLIAM H.: enl. 7/2/61 at Pittsylvania CH; Pvt.; in Co. H. Prom. to Cpl. by 12/1/61. Present until sent to Richmond Hosp. 12/5/61, with rheumatism. Returned to duty 2/19/62, but sent back to Richmond Hosp. 2/27/62. Discharged 9/5/62, at Leesburg for being over age 35.

ABSALOM, J. T.: Pvt.; 1st Co. I. Postwar record only.

ADAMS, ABRAM: Pvt.; Co. K. Postwar record only.

ADAMS, GEORGE W.: Pvt.; Co. D. Hospitalized 4/1/62 and died 4/14/62, at Richmond; no cause given.

ADAMS, JAMES M.: b. Pittsylvania Co.; enl. 5/30/61 at Laurel Grove; Sgt.; Co. C. Present until received Surgeon's discharge 12/1/61, due to pulmonary tuberculosis. Age 32, lt. complex., gray eyes, brown hair, farmer.

ADAMS, JAMES M.: enl. 3/1/62 at Cascade; Pvt.; Co. K. Admitted Danville G.H. 5/28/62. Present until POW at Gettysburg 7/3/63. Sent to Fort McHenry, Fort Delaware and then to Pt. Lookout on 10/26/63. Joined U.S. service and released from Pt. Lookout on 1/24/64. CSR also states: hospitalized Richmond G.H. #9 4/8/64.

ADAMS, JAMES W.: enl. 6/20/61, at Hermitage Fairgrounds in Richmond; Pvt.; Co. F. Detailed as company cook prior to 7/1/63. Present through last muster roll dated 2/25/65.

ADAMS, JESSE: enl. 3/1/64 near Richmond; Pvt.; Co. F. Present through only muster roll dated 4/4/64.

ADAMS, JOHN: Pvt.; Co. A. Died in Richmond prior to 5/62.

ADAMS, JOHN Q.: enl. 6/2/61 at Cascade; Pvt. in Co. K. Present until hospitalized in Danville 12/31/61 with pneumonia. Returned to duty. Hospitalized in Chimborazo 6/26/62, with diarrhea and then Danville G.H. 8/6/62, with debility. Returned to duty 8/10/62. Due to personal conflict, threw bayonet into Pvt. Joel Harris' arm on 4/2/64. Promoted to 5th Sgt. prior to 8/31/64. Present thru last recorded roll on 2/25/65.

ADAMS, JOHN S.: enl. 3/5/62; Pvt. in Co. A. Died unmarried in Richmond 5/8/62. Son of James Adams. Bur. Oakwood Cem., Richmond.

ADAMS, NATHAN: Born in Pittsylvania Co.; enl. 6/8/61 at Danville; Sgt. in Co. E. Present until received Surgeon's discharge on 12/1/61, due to kidney disease. Age 41, 6'4", fair complex., grey eyes, lt. hair, farmer.

ADAMS, ROBERT A.: Born 3/17/19; enl. 5/30/61, at Laurel Grove in Co. C. Present until hospitalized in Richmond G.H. #18 on 3/2/62, with chronic diarrhea. Admitted Chimborazo on 4/24/62, with debility and returned to duty 5/3/62. Discharged 8/25/62, due to being over age and having served his term. 5'11", fair complx., blue eyes, dk. hair, farmer. Died 10/31/92. Bur. Leemont Cem., Danville.

ADAMS, ROBERT L.: enl. 5/18/61, at Boydton; Pvt.; in Co. G. Present until WIA at Seven Pines on 5/31/62. Returned to duty on 3/26/63. Present until MIA at Chester Station on 5/10/64.

ADAMS, ROBERT R.: b. Campbell Co.; enl. 6/4/61 at Republican Grove; Pvt. in Co. F. Present until sent to Richmond G.H. on 10/22/61. Given medical discharge on 12/1/61 due to badly cut finger. Age 43, 5'10", lt. complex., dk. eyes and hair, farmer.

ADAMS, R. W.: enl. 10/10/64 at Danville; Pvt.; in Co. C. Present thru last recorded muster roll 2/25/65.

ADAMS, SAMUEL H.: enl. 7/2/61, at Pittsylvania C.H.; Pvt.; Co. H. Promoted to Cpl. Died on 8/15/61, of typhoid fever.

ADAMS, THOMAS J.: Son of Joshua Adams of Halifax Co. enl. 6/4/61 at Republican Grove; Pvt.; Co F. Present until died near Richmond on 6/23/62.

ADAMS, WILLIAM N.: enl. 10/14/64 at Danville; Pvt.; Co. K. Present until admitted Chimborazo on 3/5/65, with debility. Paroled 5/5/65.

ADAMS, WILLIAM R.: enl. 6/2/61 at Cascade; Pvt.; Co. K. Present until died at Leesburg in 9/62.

ADKERSON, JOHN Q.: enl. 5/24/61 at Whitmell; Pvt.; Co. D. Present until KIA at Battle of Crew's Farm, Malvern Hill, on 7/1/62.

ADKINS, BARTLETT E.: enl. 7/10/61 at Winchester; Pvt.; Co. B. WIA at Seven Pines on 5/31/62. 25 yrs. old in 1862. Present until POW at Gettysburg on 7/3/63. Sent to Ft. McHenry, then to Ft. Delaware and to Pt. Lookout on 10/27/63. Took oath and released on 3/14/64.

ADKINS, BOOKER: enl. 7/10/61, at Winchester; Pvt.; Co. B. Present until received medical discharge on 11/1/61, for chronic rheumatism.

ADKINS, CALEB: enl. 3/11/62 at Callands; Pvt.; Co. B. Present until deserted in 9/62. Voluntarily returned on 3/29/64. WIA at Drewry's Bluff on 5/16/64 and admitted to Chimborazo with wound to collar bone.

ADKINS, COLEMAN D.: Pvt.; Co. H. Deserted in 10/64. Postwar record only.

ADKINS, DOCTOR L.: Co. B. Died at Winchester on 7/25/61.

ADKINS, EDWARD J.: enl. 3/11/62 at Danville; Pvt.; Co. E. Present until confined in Provost Guardhouse for desertion prior to 12/31/64. Returned to duty and POW at Five Forks on 4/1/65. Sent to City Point and then to Pt. Lookout on 4/5/65. Released there 6/23/65.

ADKINS, GREEN BERRY: enl. 6/4/61, at Callands; Pvt.; Co. B. Admitted Chimborazo 3/21/62, with typhoid fever. Trans. to Farmville on 5/7/62. Present until deserted 12/62. Volunarily returned 3/29/64. Present thru last roll dated 1/1/65. Died 5/20/30, age 88. Bur. in family cem. near Sandy River.

ADKINS, HENRY: enl. 6/11/61, at Callands; Pvt.; Co. B. Slightly WIA at Malvern Hill on 7/1/62. Present until deserted 10/5/63. Voluntarily returned 3/29/64. Present until POW at Five Forks on 4/1/65. Sent to City Point and then to Hart's Island, NY Harbor on 4/7/65. Released there on 6/20/65. Res. of Patrick Co., lt. complex., lt. hair, blue eyes, 6'1½".

ADKINS, JAMES: enl. 3/11/62, at Danville; Pvt.; Co. B. Present until sick in hosp. 5-7/62. Returned prior to 6/30/63. POW at unknown date and place. Sent to Pt. Lookout and took oath of allegiance there 6/23/65. Res. of Pittsylvania Co., lt. complex., dk. brown hair, grey eyes, 6'1¾".

ADKINS, JAMES C.: enl. 7/2/61, at Pittsylvania CH; Pvt.; Co. H. Present until admitted to Chimborazo on 4/19/62, with erysipelas and returned to duty 4/28/62. Present until admitted to Chimborazo #2 on 5/16/62, with debility. Trans. to Lynchburg Hosp. on 5/22/62 and then admitted to Farmville G.H. on 5/23/62 with diarrhea. Discharged 11/6/62.

ADKINS, JOHN O.: Born Pittsylvania Co.; enl. 6/8/61 at Danville; Pvt.; Co. E. Present until WIA at Seven Pines 5/31/62 and admitted to Chimborazo 6/2/62 with gunshot flesh wound of hand. Admitted Chimborazo 9/1/62 with rheumatism. Returned to duty prior to being MWIA at Gettysburg 7/3/63. Died at Pickett's Division Hosp. and bur. at Bream's Mill on the hill; disinterred to Richmond 1872 with 33 others in 3 large boxes marked "P. Curns").

ADKINS, JOHN W.: Pvt.; Co. B. Present until admitted to Richmond G.H. #18 by 5/2/62, with measles. Died in Lynchburg G.H. 5/10/62 with pneumonia. Bur. Lynchburg Cem.

ADKINS, LEWIS: enl. 5/22/64 at Richmond; Pvt.; Co. B. Present thru last roll dated 1/1/65.

ADKINS, OBADIAH L. (or D.): enl. 6/8/61 at Danville; Pvt.; Co. E. Present until absent in 4/63, due to wound. Returned prior to 4/1/64. Confined in Provost Guardhouse for desertion prior to 12/31/64.

ADKINS, RICHARD: enl. 6/4/61 at Callands; Pvt.; Co. B. Admitted Farmville G.H. 5/7/62 with catarrh. Present until WIA and POW at Gettysburg on 7/3/63. Sent to Ft. Delaware on 7/7/63 and Pt. Lookout on 10/26/63 and probably died there.

ADKINS, WHITMELL T.: enl. 6/4/61 at Callands; Sgt.; Co. B. Promoted to 2nd Lt. on 12/22/62. Detailed to arrest deserters in Mecklenburg, Co. prior to 9/16/63. Present until POW at White Oak Road 3/30/65. Held at Old Capitol Prison, Washington, D.C. 4/3-9/65. Sent to Sandusky, Ohio and then to Johnson's Island. Released there 6/4/65, after taking oath. Res. of Washington, D.C., age 24, florid complex., lt. hair, blue eyes, 5'10".

ADKINS, WILLIAM THOMAS: Born 5/22/46. Co. B. Postwar record only. Died 4/2/13. Bur. off Rt. 800 at Climax.

ALDERSON, JAMES A.: enl. 5/30/61 at Laurel Grove; Pvt.; Co. C. Present until admitted to Camp Winder G.H. at Richmond 5/7/62, with measles. Returned to duty 5/19/62. Present until admitted to Chimborazo Hosp. on 2/19/63, with chronic rhematism. Trans. to Danville G.H. 3/14/63. Returned to duty by 5/18/63. Slightly WIA four times at Gettysburg 7/3/63. 25 yrs. old in 1863. Stunned by explosion of shell at Chester Station on 5/10/64 and sent to Chimborazo Hosp. on 5/11/64. Trans. to Lynchburg 5/21/64. POW at Southside RR on 4/2/65. Sent to City Point and there to Pt. Lookout 4/13/65. Released there 6/23/65. Res. of Pittsylvania Co. Lt. complex., lt. brown hair, grey eyes, 5'5¼", farmer.

ALDERSON, JAMES M.: Pvt.; Co. C. Present until admitted to Richmond Hosp. 5-7/62. Deserted 9/62.

ALDERSON, JOHN C.: enl. 5/30/61 at Laurel Grove; Pvt.; Co. C. Sick or wounded in hosp. 9/62. Present until paroled at Appomattox CH 4/9/65.

ALDERSON, THOMAS M.: enl. 3/18/62 at Laurel Grove; Pvt.; Co. C. Present until admitted to Chimborazo #5 5/10/62 with mumps. Returned to duty 5/29/62. Severely WIA in leg at Seven Pines 5/31/62 and sent to Danville G.H. 6/4/62. Returned to duty 8/13/62. POW at Petersburg 4/2/65. Sent to City Point and then to Pt. Lookout where arrived 4/4/65. Released there 6/23/65. Res. of Pittsylvania Co., lt. complex., brown hair, grey eyes, 5'5¼".

ALDERSON, WILLIAM H.: enl. 3/15 or 18/62 at Laurel Grove; Pvt.; Co. C. Sent to hosp. in Richmond 4/17/62 and then trans. to Camp Winder 5/18/62. CSR also lists him as deserter from day of enlistment until 12/1/62. Court martialed and confined in E.D.M. Prison. Sent to G.H. #13 3/16/64, with gastraligia. Sent to Castle Thunder 3/19/64. Pardoned by President 8/3/64, for volunteering to defend Richmond in Winder Legion against Sheridan's Raid. Returned to duty prior to 12/31/64. Deserted 1/12/65 and "will be found near Laurel Grove."

ALEXANDER, CHARLES: enl. 3/10/62 at Clarksville; Pvt.; 1st Co. I. Present until discharged 5/12/62. Apparently commissioned 2 Lt. in Provisional Army to date from 4/21/62.

ALGOOD, JOHN D.: enl. 5/18/61 at Boydtown; Pvt.; Co. G. Present until granted 30 day furlough at home 2/12/62. Returned to duty but died 7/26/62, at Falling Creek.

ALGOOD, WILLIAM T.: enl. 2/4/63, in Mecklenburg Co.; Pvt.; Co. G. Present until deserted 12/7/64.

ALLEN, FERDINAND R.: enl. 6/4/61 at Callands; Pvt.; Co. B. Admitted Chimborazo Hosp. 2/16/62 with rheumatism. Admitted Farmville G.H. 5/7/62 with catarrh. 22 years old in 1862. Present thru last recorded roll dated 5/19/63. WIA (gun shot in left hip) at Gettysburg on 7/3/63.

ALLEN, GREEN W.: enl. 8/15/64 in Pittsylvania Co.; Pvt.; Co. B. Present until admitted to Chimborazo 3/5/65, with chronic rheumatism.

ALLEN, HENRY CLAY: Born in Pittsylvania Co. 11/4/44; son of James Green Allen and Lavicia Forrest Vaden; enl. 3/13/62 at Kentuck; Pvt.; Co. A. Present until WIA at Malvern Hill 7/1/62. Sent to Danville G.H. on 8/6/62, with chronic diarrhea and returned to duty 11/13/62. Captured 2 Union soldiers at Chester Station 5/10/64. Admitted to Howard's Grove Hosp., Richmond 5/17/64 with wound to right thigh, probably received at Drewry's Bluff on 5/16/64. Married Elizabeth Taylor on 11/7/67 and fathered 9 children; later married Ora Graves. Tobacco farmer near Spring Garden. Elected Va. House of Delegates as Democrat in 1897. Died at home of heart disease 6/5/25.

ALLEN, JAMES WILLIAM: Born 1/24/38, at Callands; enl. 3/10/62 at Callands; Pvt.; Co. B. Present until admitted to Chimborazo Hosp. 5/16/64 with abdominal wound, probably received at Drewry's Bluff. Trans. to Danville G.H. 5/22/64 and returned to duty 6/21/64. Prom. to Cpl. 9/1/64 and to Sgt. 12/1/64. POW at Five Forks on 4/1/65. Sent to City Point and then to Hart's Island, NY Harbor on 4/7/65. Released there 6/20/65. Lt. complex. and hair, blue eyes, 5'7½". Farmer at Callands. Died 1/20/13.

ALLEN, JOHN R.: enl. 7/6/61, in Norfolk Co.; Pvt., 2nd Co. I. Admitted Chimborazo Hosp. 5/16/62 with wound of right knee, probably received at Drewry's Bluff. Present until deserted to the enemy 12/30/64. Took oath 1/2/65, at Bermuda Hundred and sent to Norfolk.

ALLEN, OTEY F.: Pvt.; Co. B. In hosp. 4-7/62. Died at Chimborazo Hosp. prior to 4/8/63.

ALLEN, R. GEORGE: enl. 4/16/64 at Richmond, conscript; musician in Co. E. Absent from enlistment on detached duty with Brigade Band as of 2/25/65.

ALLEN, THOMPSON C.: enl. 6/10/63 in Pittsylvania Co.; Pvt.; Co. D. Trans. from Co. D, 30th Va. Battalion Cavalry in exchange for T. M. Carter 11/64. Present until deserted 1/28/65, to Pittsylvania Co.

ALLEN, WILLIAM: enl. 6/4/61 at Callands; Pvt.; Co. B. Present until admitted Farmville G.H. 5/7/62 with diarrhea. Admitted Chimborazo Hosp. 6/26/62, with debility. KIA at Sharpsburg 9/17/62.

ANDERSON, A. J. B.: enl. in 1861, Pvt.; 1st Co. I. Served 4 years. Postwar record only.

ANDERSON, ALFRED: Born 3/29/27. enl. 6/7/61 at Richmond; Pvt.; Co. C. Elected 2nd Lt. on 4/29/62. Prom. to 1st Lt. 5/31/62. Resigned 9/10/62. Died 3/28/07 Pitts. Co.

ANDERSON, GEORGE W.: enl. 10/14/64 at Danville; Pvt.; Co. A. Present until POW at White Oak Road 4/1/65. Sent to City Point and then to Pt. Lookout 4/5/65. Released there 6/23/65. Res. of Pittsylvania Co., dk. complex., blk. hair, hazel eyes, 5'7".

ANDERSON, JAMES R.: enl. 6/2/61 at Cascade; Pvt.; Co. K. Prom. to 3rd Cpl. by 4/1/64 and then to 3rd Sgt. by 8/31/64. Present until POW at Farmville (Saylers Creek?) 4/6/65. Held at Newport News and took oath there 7/1/65. Res. of Pittsylvania Co., dk. complex. and hair, blue eyes, 5'9".

ANDREWS, JOSEPH: enl. 2/27/62 at Republican Grove; Pvt.; Co. F. Present until sent to Chimborazo Hosp. 4/24/62. Died there 6/10/62 of measles and bronchitis. Son of William A. Andrews.

ANGLEA, ALLEN C.: Born Pittsylvania Co., son of Allen C. Anglea; enl. 6/8/61 at Danville; Sgt.; Co. E. Prom. 4th Sgt. to 3rd Sgt. by 8/30/61. Present until KIA at Chester Station 5/10/64.

ANGLEA, SAMUEL R.: enl. 2/20/62 at Cascade; Pvt.; Co. K. Present until admitted Chimborazo Hosp. 7/8/62 with Icleus. Trans. to Danville Hosp. 7/22/62. Assigned as Brigade mail carrier on 8/31/62. Present until POW at Five Forks 4/1/65. Sent to City Point and then to Pt. Lookout where he arrived 4/6/65. Released there 6/23/65. Res. of Pittsylvania Co., fair complex., dk. brown hair, hazel eyes, 5'10¼".

ANGLEA, THOMAS B.: enl. 3/5/62, at Cascade; Pvt.; Co. K. Present until admitted to Chimborazo Hosp. 4/30/62 and then trans. to Danville Hosp. 5/27/62 with debility. Returned to duty 6/10/62.

ANGLIN, J. H.: Pvt.; Co. D. Present until WIA, g.s.w. to right arm, at Gettysburg 7/3/63 and POW there on 7/4/63. Received at Fort Delaware 7/7-12/63. Died there 10/8/63. Bur. Finn's Pt. Nat'l. Cem., N.J.

ANGLIN, SAMUEL H.: enl. 3/1/62 at Whitwell; Pvt.; Co. D. Present until WIA on Chickahominy (Seven Pines?) 5/31/62. Returned to duty until POW at Chester Station 5/10/64. Sent to Ft. Monroe and then to Pt. Lookout 5/13/64. Joined U.S. service and released there 5/20/64.

ANTHONY, PHILLIP S. P.: enl. 6/2/61 at Cascade; Pvt.; Co. K. Prom. to 3rd Cpl. by 12/8/62 and then to 3rd Sgt. by 7/3/63. Present until POW at Gettysburg 7/3/63. Sent to Fort McHenry 7/6/63, to Ft. Delaware 7/7-12/63 and to Pt. Lookout on 10/26/63. Died of pneumonia and bur. there 2/11/65.

ARNN, ISAAC CLAY: Born 12/31/44; enl. 6/4/61 at Callands; Pvt.; Co. B. Present until sent to Chimborazo 10/61. Given medical discharge 11/8/61, due to typhoid fever and debility. Reenlisted in 2nd Co. E, 6th Va. Cavalry 12/25/62 at Camp Ashby. Died 4/13/24. Bur. Arnn family cem., Callands.

ARNN, JOHN: Pvt.; Co. A. Postwar record only.

ARNOLD, BERY L.: Sgt.; Co G. Received medical discharge 9/17/61, due to hernia.

ARTHUR, HENRY: Pvt.; Co. H. Postwar record only.

ARTHUR, JOHN: enl. 6/4/61 at Callands; Pvt.; Co. B. Present until MWIA at Malvern Hill 7/1/62. Died in Chimborazo Hosp. 7/30/62, due to compound fracture of thigh which led to gangrene.

ARTHUR, L. BERRY: enl. 3/17 or 19/62, at Lynchburg; Pvt.; Co. H. Convalescent in Chimborazo Hosp. 5/12/62. Present thru 12/31/64. Absent on furlough on last muster roll 2/26/65. In Danville Hosp. 4/5/65.

ASHBY, HENRY S.: Born Pittsylvania Co.; enl. 1/1/62 at Manassas; Pvt.; Co. E. Present until absent sick in Richmond G.H. #18 4-26-7/12/62. Returned to duty by 6/30/63. KIA at Drewry's Bluff 5/16/64.

ASHBY, WILLIAM F.: enl. 11/1/61 at Danville; musician/Pvt.; Co. E. Admitted Chimborazo Hosp. 4/24/62 with mumps. Present until paroled at Appomattox C.H. on 4/9/65.

ATKINSON, J. C.: Pvt.; Co. H. Deserted and captured by U.S. forces 1/10/65. Sent to Washington, D.C. on 1/14/65. Took oath and sent to Philadelphia on 1/16/65.

AUSTIN, JOSEPH H.: enl. 1/6/62 at Cascade; Pvt.; Co. K. Present until paroled at Appomattox C.H. 4/9/65.

AVERETT, JAMES G.: enl. 3/8/62 at Clarksville; Pvt.; 1st Co. I. Present on only roll dated 7/17/62.

AVERETT, JOHN TAYLOR: Born 12/24/27. enl. 5/30/61 at Kentuck; 2nd Lt.; Co. A. Prom. to Capt. 5/30/61 and to A.Q.M./F.&S. 7/1/61. Detailed as Quartermaster on 6/23/61. Relieved 9/25/64. Co-founder of Averett College in Danville. Died 1898 Danville.

AYCOCK, AUSTIN C.: enl. 2/27/62 at Boydton; Pvt.; Co. G. Detailed as litter bearer with medical dept. of regt. 5-6/62.

BADGETT, WILLIAM H.: enl. 5/24/61 at Whitmell; Pvt.; Co. D. Appointed 2nd Lt. 6/3/61. Prom. to Capt. 5/1/62. Present until sick in hosp. 5/26/62. Resigned 7/17/62 on Surgeon's certificate due to disease of lungs and kidneys.

BAGBY, JESSE P.: Born in Powhatan Co. Schoolmaster. Age 38; enl. 5/18/61 in Mecklenburg Co.; Pvt.; Co. G. Medically discharged 10/2/61 due to bronchitis. Dk. complex., black eyes and hair, 5'9".

BAIRD, HENRY R.: enl. 3/1/62 at Danville; Pvt.; Co. E. Absent on leave 3/62. Absent sick 4-9/20/62, when he died in Richmond G.H. #20 of typhoid fever.

BAKER, JOHN: Pvt.; Co. K. Sent to hosp. 7/62. Deserted and dropped from roll 9/62.

BALL, LEWIS J.: enl. 6/8/61 at Danville; Pvt.; Co. E. Present until admitted to Richmond G.H. #18 3/30/62 with dropsy. Returned to duty 5/7/62. Discharged by 9/62, under Conscript Act.

BALLS, JOHN R.: enl. 3/1/62 in Norfolk Co.; Pvt.; 2nd Co. I. Admitted Richmond G.H. #9 5/16/64, probably due to WIA at Drewry's Bluff. Died of battle wounds 7/16/64.

BANKS, HARTWELL R.: enl. 3/12/62 at Boydton. Pvt.; Co. G. Present until admitted Richmond G.H. #3 4/28/62. Died there on 6/1/62 with typhoid fever.

BARBER, DANIEL C.: enl. 6/8/61 at Danville; Pvt.; Co. E. Present until assigned to detached service as teamster 6/30/63. Served in this capacity thru 2/25/65. Paroled at Appomattox C.H. 4/9/65.

BARBER, JAMES A.: enl. 5/24/61 at Whitmell; Pvt.; Co. D. KIA at Gettysburg 7/3/63.

BARBER, THOMAS L.: enl. 3/14/62 at Danville; Pvt.; Co. E. Present until POW at Dinwiddie C.H. 4/2/65. Sent to City Point and then to Pt. Lookout 4/4/65. Released there 6/23/65. Res. of Pittsylvania Co., dk. complex. and hair, grey eyes, 5'7". Thos. Barber of Co. also listed as paroled at Appomattox C.H. on 4/9/65.

BARBOUR, WILLIAM T.: enl. 3/3/62 at Boydton; Pvt.; Co. G. Absent sick 3-7/62. Admitted Richmond G.H. #6 12/15/62 and died there on 1/6/63 of pneumonia.

BARCROFT (possibly BRANCROFT), EDWARD: enl. 2/26/62 in Norfolk Co.; Pvt.; 2nd Co. I. Present until paroled at Appomattox 4/9/65.

BARKER, CLARK H.: Age 22; enl. 5/30/61 at Kentuck; Pvt.; Co. A. Absent on furlough 8/31/61. Admitted Richmond G.H. #21 on 11/26/62, with smallpox. Trans. to Howard's Grove Hosp. 12/16/62 with rheumatism. Admitted Danville G.H. 5/4/63 with debility and returned to duty 5/19/63. POW at Gettysburg 7/4/63 while serving as Nurse in hosp. there. Sent to Ft. McHenry 7/6/63; to Ft. Delaware 7-12/63; and to Pt. Lookout 10/27/63. Exch. 2/10/65. On furlough 2/25/65, but returned in time to be POW at Petersburg 4/2/64. Sent to City Point and then to Pt. Lookout 4/4/65. Released there 6/24/65. Res. of Danville, dk. complex., dk. brown hair, blue eyes, 5'11¾".

BARKER, FRANCIS MARION: Born 7/19/45. enl. 5/30/61 at Kentuck; Pvt.; Co. A. Present until MWIA at Seven Pines 5/31/62. Died of these wounds in Richmond 6/17/62.

BARKER, HENDERSON S.: enl. 4/6/64, in Henry Co.; Pvt.; Co. D. Conscript. In custody of Provost Guard for desertion 7/7/64 and remained so through last roll dated 2/25/65. Paroled as POW 5/8/65.

BARKER, HENRY FINCH: Born 3/21/41; son of William and Nancy Barker; enl. 5/30/61, at Kentuck; Pvt.; Co. A. Present until "left sick at old camp" prior to 10/61. Died 12/12/62 in Richmond due to smallpox.

BARKER, JAMES M.: enl. 4/6/64 in Henry Co.; Pvt.; Co. E. Conscript. Absent 12/31/64 in Salisbury, N.C. undergoing sentencing of general court martial for desertion. Absence continued thru last roll dated 2/25/65.

BARKER, JOSIAH: enl. 3/19/62, at Laurel Grove; Pvt.; Co. C. Absent in Danville G.H. 5/15/62, for debility, but returned to duty 11/7/62. POW at Gettysburg 7/4/63. Sent to Baltimore and then to Pt. Lookout 8/21/63. Exchanged 3/17/64 suffering from swelling of the right leg. Returned to duty as Provost Guard at Danville 9/30/64. Admitted Danville Hosp. on 2/14/65 with syphilis primitiva, but returned to duty by 3/14/65.

BARKER, MOSES: Born 6/17/25; son of William and Nancy Barker; enl. by 6/14/61 at Danville; Pvt.; Co. A. Present until POW at Dinwiddie C.H. 4/2/65. Sent to City Point and then to Pt. Lookout 4/4/65. Died and buried there 6/23/65.

BARKER, SPIAS: enl. 5/30/61 at Laurel Grove; Pvt.; Co. C. Present until detached as regimental teamster 12/20/61. Admitted Richmond G.H. #18 3/2/62, with chronic rheumatism. Admitted Danville G.H. 6/12/62, wounded. Discharged 9/5/62, due to being over age.

BARKER, STEPHEN Y.: enl. 5/30/61 at Laurel Grove; Pvt.; Co. C. Absent on furlough 8/18/61. WIA, thigh, at Seven Pines 5/31/62. Admitted to Danville G.H. 9/16/62, wounded, but returned to duty by 11/18/62. AWOL 8/64.

BARKER, TOLBERT B.: Carpenter; enl. 2/8/64 at Kinston, N.C. WIA (flesh wound of left hand caused by ram rod). at Chester Station 5/10/64. Admitted to Chimborazo 5/11/64 and died there 9/24/64 of continued fever. Probably bur. Oakwood Cem., Richmond. Widow: Margaret Barker.

BARKER, WILLIAM D.: Born 6/20/27; son of William and Nancy Barker; enl. 5/30/61 at Kentuck; Pvt.; Co. A. Present until "left sick at old camp" in 10/61. Died at Warrenton 2/26/62 due to typhoid fever.

BARKER, WILLIAM H.: Pvt.; Co. B. Discharged from hosp. at Culpeper 11/16/61.

BARKER, WILLIAM H.: enl. 5/30/61 at Laurel Grove; Pvt.; Co. C. Present until detailed as teamster 3/12/62. Admitted Danville hosp. 9/1-12/12/62 with debility. POW at Gettysburg 7/4/63. Sent to Ft. McHenry and then to Ft. Delaware 7/7-12/63 and then to Pt. Lookout 10/27/63. Exchanged there 3/17/64 and returned by 8/64. POW again at Bermuda Hundred 11/17/64. Sent to City Point and then to Pt. Lookout 11/24/64. Took oath of allegiance and released there 6/23/85. Res. of Pittsylvania Co., lt. complex., brown hair, grey eyes, 5'9".

BARKER, WILLIAM M.: enl. 6/10/61 at Callands; Pvt.; Co. B. Discharged 11/1/61 by order of Gen. Johnston.

BARKSDALE, JOHN H.: enl. 6/15/61 at Whitmell; Pvt.; Co. D. Present until sent to Chimborazo Hosp. 10/61. Received medical discharge on 11/18/61, due to varix and rheumatism.

BARLEY, ADOLPHUS: enl. 6/4/61 at Republican Grove; Pvt.; Co. F. Present until wounded and sent to hosp. 7/8/62. Returned to duty, but between 11/1/62 and 11/1/63, 85 days pay was deducted for being AWOL. Admitted Chimborazo Hosp. on 5/17/64, with hip wound (possibly received at Drewry's Bluff) and transferred to Danville hosp. 5/26/64. Present until AWOL 2/19/65.

BARNES, WILLIAM H.: enl. 3/12/62 at Norfolk Co.; Pvt.; 2nd Co. I. Present until absent in Richmond hosp. 5/21/64 but returned to duty 12/12/64. Admitted Chimborazo Hosp. 3/5/65, with chronic rheumatism. POW there 4/3/65. Held in Libby Prison in Richmond and sent to Newport News 4/24/65. Took oath 6/16/65. Res. of Norfolk, Va., dk. complex., dk. hair, hazel eyes, 5'10".

BARTON, JOHN M.: Pvt.; Co. C. Postwar record only.

BATEMAN, R. R.: Pvt.; Co. K. Paroled 5/1/65.

BATES, JORDAN: enl. 3/10/62 at Callands. Pvt.; Co. B. Present until WIA (gunshot to right thigh and grapeshot in left side) and POW at Gettysburg 7/3/63. Sent to Ft. McHenry 7/6/63, then to Ft. Delaware 7/7-12/63 and then finally to Pt. Lookout 10/27/63. Exchanged there 2/18-21/65. Name appears on muster roll of paroled and exchanged prisoners at Camp Lee, near Richmond 3/1/65. Alive at Red Eye 4/19/98.

BATES, NATHANIEL: enl. 6/4/61 at Republican Grove; Pvt.; Co. F. Present until admitted to Chimborazo Hosp. 10/27/61 with typhoid fever, then returned to duty. Admitted to Chimborazo Hosp. 6/2/62, with shell wound to head (possibly from Seven Pines) and again returned to duty. WIA (gunshot wound in left side and thigh) and then POW at Gettysburg 7/4/63. Treated at U.S. XII Corps. Hosp. Sent to Ft. McHenry 7/6/63 and then to Ft. Delaware 7/7-12/63. Paroled there 7/30/63.

BATES, THOMAS: Born Hanover Co.; enl. 6/4/61 at Republican Grove; Pvt.; Co. F. Present until admitted Manassas G.H. 1/2-3/62. Returned to duty and sent from camp at Falling Creek to Halifax Co. to arrest stragglers 7/13/62; WIA at Gettysburg 7/3/63; admitted Charlottesville Hosp. 7/12/63. Returned to duty 8/31/64. Deserted 12/16/64 but returned by 2/25/65. Lived in Halifax Co. and Camp Lee Soldiers' Home, Richmond. Died 3/17/15 at age 79. Bur. Hollywood Cem. (East Sec.), Richmond.

BAUGH, ROBERT S.: enl. 8/1/63 at Danville; Pvt.; Co. E. AWOL as of 12/31/64; but present 2/25/65. Paroled at Appomattox C.H. 4/9/65.

BAYS, DAVID E.: enl. 6/8/61 at Danville; Pvt.; Co. E. Admitted Richmond G.H. #13 4/28/63 with contusion. Confined in Provost Guardhouse for desertion prior to 12/31/64. Probably shot to death by firing squad before the brigade 2/10/65.

BEALES, JOHN: enl. 7/6/61 in Norfolk Co.; Pvt.; 2nd Co. I. AWOL 3/1-5/8/63. Deserted and taken prisoner by U.S. troops 7/16/64. Held at Bermuda Hundred and then sent to Norfolk. Released there 7/21/64. Res. of Norfolk, brown eyes, black hair, dk. complex., 5'10¼".

BEAVERS, JED C.: enl. 10/14/64 at Danville; Cpl.; Co. D. Present until POW at White Oak Road 4/1/65. Sent to City Point and then to Pt. Lookout 4/5/65. Released there 6/24/65. Res. of Danville, fair complex., lt. hair, blue eyes, 5'8¾".

BEECHER, JOHN: Pvt.; 1st Co. I. Postwar record only.

BELCHER, JAMES: enl. 6/20/61 at Clarksville; Pvt.; 1st Co. I. Present until detailed as cook 6/62.

BELCHER, JOHN: enl. 3/22/62 at Clarksville; Pvt.; 1st Co. I. Discharged 4/12/62.

BENNETT, CHARLES DODSON: Born 10/14/40; enl. 5/30/61 at Kentuck; Pvt.; Co. A. Present until admitted to CSA Hosp., Farmville 4/18/63 and returned to duty 4/25/63. WIA at Gettysburg 7/3/63. Admitted to Chimborazo Hosp. 7/13/63 for wound. Prom. to 4th Cpl. by 4/1/64 to 3rd Cpl. by 10/21/64 and to 2nd Cpl. by 1/7/65. Died 2/21/10. Bur. in Bennett Farm. Cem., Ringgold, Va.

BENNETT, JOEL LEWIS: enl. 5/30/61 at Kentuck; Pvt.; Co. A. Present until admitted Richmond G.H. 3/2/62 with paralysis; detailed to go home with brother 3/21/62. Admitted Richmond G.H. 5/17/64 with severe wounds to both thighs (probably sustained at Drewry's Bluff 5/16/64). Given wounded furlough prior to 10/12/64. Assigned light duty by order of Medical Examiners Board 12/8/64. Detailed to Lynchburg 2/25/65 and paroled there 4/13/65. Age 29.

BENNETT, J. SAMUEL: enl. 1/1/63 at Kentuck; Pvt.; Co. A. WIA at Gettysburg 7/3/63. Present until admitted Chimborazo Hosp. 7/13/63 with wound. Served as Co. Cook. Ordered to light duty by Medical Examiners Board and assigned as Brigade mail carrier. Paroled at Appomattox C.H. 4/9/65.

BENNETT, THOMAS C.: enl. 5/30/61 at Kentucky; Pvt.; Co. A. Detailed as nurse 2/62. Died in Richmond G.H. #18 3/21/62, due to debility.

BENTLEY, GEORGE W.: enl. 3/13/62 at Kentuck; Pvt.; Co. A. Present until in hosp. in Richmond 5/62, until his death 7/15/62. Widow: Elizabeth Bentley.

BENTLEY, LEON W.: Pvt.; Co. A. Postwar record only.

BERGER, JAMES H.: enl. 7/4/61 at Callands; Cpl.; Co. B. Prom. to 2nd Sgt. 4/5/63. Present until WIA (shot in right elbow) at Gettysburg 7/3/63. POW there 7/5/63. Sent to DeCamp G.H., Davids Island, N.Y. Harbor and paroled there 10/22/63. Admitted Richmond G.H. 10/28/63. Application for retirement approved due to permanent injury from Gettysburg wound 10/14/64. (CSR also states: Detailed to duty in Richmond Hosp. 12/10/64.

BETTERTON, BENJAMIN F.: enl. 6/4/61 at Republican Grove; Pvt.; Co. F. Admitted Lynchburg G.H. 2/27/62. Admitted Richmond G.H. 10/28/62 with debility. Present until POW at Five Forks on 4/1/65. Sent to City Point and then to Pt. Lookout 4/6/65. Released there 6/23/65. Res. of Halifax Co., lt. complex., brown hair, grey eyes, 5'7".

BETTERTON, JAMES W.: enl. 6/4/61 at Republican Grove; Pvt.; Co. F. Present until admitted Chimborazo Hosp. 12/3/61 with hernia. Returned to duty 4/15/62. Detailed as Division Wagoner prior to 7/1/63. Paroled 4/18/65.

BEVILL, CHARLES D.: enl. 2/4/63 in Mecklenburg Co.; Pvt.; Co. G. Present thru last muster roll dated 2/65. Bur. Liberty Bapt. Ch. cem., Rt. 677 in Mecklenburg Co. Tombstone inscribed: "Co. B, 38th Va. Inf."

BEVILLE, J. T.: Pvt.; Co. G. Admitted Chimborazo Hosp. 2/26/65.

BIGBY, J. P.: Pvt.; Co. G. Disabled and discharged. Postwar record only.

BILLINGS, JOHN R.: enl. 6/2/61 at Cascade. Pvt.; Co. K. Present until WIA at Seven Pines on 5/31/62. Prom. to 1st Cpl. by 4/1/64, and to 4th Sgt. by 8/31/64. POW at Farmville (Saylers Creek?) 4/6/65. Sent to City Point and then to Newport News 4/14/65.

BINGHAM, C. F.: enl. 3/6/62 in Appomattox Co. Pvt.; 2nd Co. I. Present until admitted to Chimborazo Hosp. 3/5/65, with double hernia.

BLACKSTOCK, JOHN MONROE: enl. 6/20/61 at Hermitage Camp; Pvt.; Co. F. Died in camp near Broad Run 8/30/61 of typhoid fever. Son of John Blackstock of Halifax Co.

BLACKWELL, MOORE CARTER: Born 1833. enl. 10/12/62 at Winchester. Appointed Commissary Sgt. prior to 8/31/64. Present until POW. Paroled at Winchester on 4/23/65 at age 31. Lt. complex., sandy hair, blue eyes, 5'11". Died 1917.

BLAIR, DRURY A.: enl. 5/24/61 at Whitmell; Pvt.; Co. D. Present until discharged 8/12/61, due to chronic bronchitis.

BLAIR, GEORGE W.: b. 6/15/40. enl. 6/4/61 at Callands; Pvt.; Co. B. 21 yrs. old in 1862. Present until POW at Gettysburg 7/4/63. Sent to Ft. McHenry on 7/6/63 to Ft. Delaware from 7/7-12/63 to Pt. Lookout 10/26/63. Prom. to S. Sgt. 12/22/63. Exch. there 2/20 or 21/65. At Camp Lee 3/1/65. KIA at Five Forks 4/1/65.

BLAIR, SUTER F.: b. 3/20/43 in Pittsylvania Co. enl. 3/10/62 at Callands; Pvt.; Co. B. Admitted Chimborazo Hosp. #3 4/14/62. MWIA (thigh amputated) and POW at Gettysburg 7/3/63. Died 7/15/63.

BLAIR, THOMAS: Pvt.; Co. A. Detailed to bring in deserters 6/62.

BLAIR, WILLIAM T.: enl. 5/30/61 at Kentuck; Pvt.; Co. A. Prom. to 1st Cpl. prior to 4/1/64 and to Sgt. Maj./F & S prior to 2/27/65. Paroled at Appomattox C.H. on 4/9/65.

BLANKENSHIP, ARCHER F.: enl. 5/30/61 at Laurel Grove; Pvt.; Co. C. Present until discharged at Manassas on 9/1/61 due to hernia.

BLANKS, JOHN H.: enl. 6/20/61 at Clarksville; Pvt.; Co. I. Given medical discharge on 9/22/62, due to debility.

BLANKS, JOSEPH: enl. 3/10/62 at Republican Grove; Pvt.; Co. F. Present until wounded in 3/62. In hosp. 4/25/62 thru 7/1/63. Detailed as teamster at Kinston, N.C. 1/25/64. Present by 12/31/64. Deserted 2/2/65.

BLANKS, T. F.: enl. 6/20/61 at Clarksville. Pvt.; 1st Co. I. Present until admitted to Chimborazo Hosp. 6/2/62 due to shell wound (probably received at Seven Pines 5/31).

BLANKS, WILLIAM: enl. 11/4/63 near Petersburg; Pvt.; Co. F. Present until POW at Five Forks 4/1/65. Sent to City Point and then to Pt. Lookout 4/6/65. Released there 6/2/65.

BLAYLOCK, JOHN: enl. 4/18/64 at Richmond; Pvt.; Co. H. Conscript. Present until detached as shoemaker with regimental quartermaster prior to 8/31/64. Returned to duty prior to 12/31/64. Admitted Chimborazo Hosp. 1/14/65 with dysentery. Paroled at Huguenot Springs Hosp. 4/22/65.

BOGGS, ROBERT G.: enl. 3/1/62 in Norfolk Co.; Pvt.; 2nd Co. I. Detailed as Co. cook prior to 8/31/64. Deserted to Union forces on or about 2/17/65. Took oath and transportation was furnished to Norfolk.

BOHAMON, WILLIAM: enl. 5/30/61 at Laurel Grove. Pvt.; Co. C. Prom. to Color Cpl. prior to 9/62 and to Color Sgt. prior to 7/63. WIA (gunshot in thigh) at Gettysburg 7/3/63 and POW there 7/5/63. Sent to DeCamp G.H. on Davids Island and paroled there 8/24/63. Admitted to Chimborazo Hosp. 5/11/64 due to shell wound (probably received at Chester Station 5/10). 26 yrs. old in 1864. Trans. to Field Staff and prom. to Ensign on 8/16/64. POW and paroled at Appomattox CH on 4/9/65.

BOHANON, JOHN M.: enl. 5/30/61 at Kentuck; Pvt.; Co. A. Prom. to Color Sgt. prior to 10/61 and to Ensign for the regt. by 1/62. Admitted Chimborazo Hosp. 5/12/62 with fever. Deserted 9/15/62 at Leesburg.

BOLTON, HILRY: enl. 3/21/62 at Danville; Pvt.; Co. E. Present until admitted Chimborazo Hosp. 5/13/62 with debility. POW at Gettysburg 7/4/63 (CSR also states deserted at Gettysburg 7/4). Sent to Ft. Delaware 7/7-12/63 and died there 8/17/63, due to chronic diarrhea. Bur. Finn's Pt. Nat. Cem., N.J.

BOOKER, JAMES: Born 10/10/40, brother of John; enl. 5/24/61 at Whitmell; Cpl. Co. D. Present until admitted Richmond G.H. #18 3/2/62, with chronic diarrhea. Trans. to Danville Hosp. 5/11/62. Prom. to Sgt. by 4/1/64. WIA (flesh wound of right thigh) at Drewrys Bluff and admitted Chimborazo Hosp. 5/16/64. Died 1923.

BOOKER, JOHN: Born 10/10/40 (brother of James); enl. 5/24/61 at Whitmell; Pvt.; Co. D. Prom. to Sgt. prior to 4/1/64. WIA (chest) at Drewrys Bluff 5/16/64 and admitted to Chimborazo Hosp. Died 8/26/64.

BOOTHE, ALEX: enl. 10/14/64 at Danville; Pvt.; Co. C. Present until deserted 2/20/65 and "will be found near Danville, Va."

BOOTHE, BENJAMIN: enl. 5/30/61 at Laurel Grove; Pvt.; Co. C. Admitted Chimborazo Hosp. 2/28/62 and again 6/26/62 with debility. WIA ("struck in right side of forehead with grape shot") at Gettysburg 7/3/63. Returned to duty prior to 4/1/64. Deserted on 2/20/65 and "will be found near Danville, Va." Alive 6/16/84.

BOOTHE, WILLIAM T.: enl. 5/30/61 at Laurel Grove; Pvt.; in Co. C. Present until left at Winchester Hosp. 7/17/61. Returned to duty on or around 9/20/61. WIA (hand) at Seven Pines 5/31/62. Assigned detached service guarding commissary. POW at Amelia CH 4/2/65. Sent to City Point and then to Pt. Lookout 4/13/65. Res. of Pittsylvania Co., dk. complex., lt. brown hair, hazel eyes, 5'10". Alive at Malmaison 5/19/82.

BORDEN, G. F.: Co. B (no rank or enl. date given). Present for 6/62.

BOUSH, FRANKLIN: enl. 10/4/64 in Chesterfield Co.; musician in 2nd Co. I. Present thru last muster roll dated 2/25/65.

BOUSH, WILLIAM: enl. 2/13/62 in Norfolk Co.; Pvt.; 2nd Co. I. Assigned to duty in ambulance corps prior to 8/31/64. POW (date and place unknown) and confined in Libby Prison (apparently after occupation of Richmond). Paroled there 4/23/65.

BOWE, HENRY C.: enl. 6/2/61 at Cascade; Pvt.; Co. K. Present until POW at Five Forks 4/1/65. Sent to City Point and then to Pt. Lookout 4/6/65. Took oath and released there 6/16/65. Res. of Pittsylvania Co., fair complex., blk. hair, hazel eyes, 5'8".

BOWLIN, JOHN: enl. 6/20/61 at Clarksville; Pvt.; 1st Co. I. Present until detailed to Brigade slaughter pen 11/1/61. Returned to Co. and WIA (slightly) at Malvern Hill 7/1/62.

BOYD, JAMES O.: enl. 1/30/64 at Cascade; Pvt.; Co. K. Conscript. Present thru last recorded roll 2/25/65.

BOYD, JOHN B.: Appointed 2nd Lt. in Co. G 7/1/61. Present until failed to be reelected and dropped from roll 4/29/62.

BOYD, JOHN H.: enl. 6/2/61 at Cascade; Sgt.; Co. K. Present until sent to Richmond Hosp. 10/24/61. Died in Chimborazo Hosp. 11/13/61 of dyphtheria, at age 26.

BOYD, ROBERT: enl. 5/18/61 at Boydton; Sgt.; Co. G. "Hired a substitute who was to receive what was due him and want out of service" 7/16/62.

BOYD, THOMAS H.: Appointed 1st Lt.; Co. G 5/18/61. Present until resigned 12/11/62.

BOYD, W. B.: Lt.; Co. C. Admitted Chimborazo Hosp. 4/18/62.

BRADLEY, ROBERT: enl. 5/30/61 at Kentuck; Pvt.; Co. A. Present until WIA (slight in right foot) and POW at Gettysburg 7/4/63. Sent to Ft. McHenry 7/6/63 and then to Ft. Delaware 7/7-12/63 and then to Pt. Lookout 10/27/63. Exchanged 5/3/64 and admitted to Chimborazo Hosp. 5/8/64 with slight wound to right foot. Returned to duty by 10/26/64. Prom. to 1st Cpl. by 12/31/64. POW. Released 7/24/65. Res. of Pittsylvania Co., dk. complex., dk. brown hair, blue eyes, 5'8½".

BRADLEY, THOMAS D.: enl. 5/30/61 at Kentuck; 4th Cpl. in Co. A. Admitted Chimborazo Hosp. #2 5/13/62 with debility. Prom. to 4th Sgt. by 4/1/64 and to 2nd Sgt. by 12/31/64. POW at Petersburg 4/2/65. Sent to City Point and then to Pt. Lookout 4/4/65. Released there 6/24/65. Res. of Pittsylvania Co., fair complex., lt. brown hair, blue eyes, 5'11".

BRADLEY, WILLIAM T.: enl. 5/30/61 at Kentuck; Pvt.; Co. A. Present until given medical discharge 10/4/61, due to lung disease.

BRADNER, THOMAS H.: enl. 3/10/62 at Callands. Pvt.; Co. B. Present until admitted Richmond Gen. Hosp. #18 5/2/62, with measles. WIA at Seven Pines 5/31/62. Returned to duty, but WIA and POW at Gettysburg on 7/3/63. Apparently died while POW.

BRADNER, WILLIAM G.: Born Pittsylvania Co., farmer. Pvt.; Co. B. Admitted Richmond G. H. #4 11/2/62 and died there 11/18/62, due to bronchitis.

BRADSHAW, R. V.: enl. 10/14/64 at Halifax; Pvt.; Co. H. Detailed as clark at Gen. Stuart's Headquarters prior to 12/31/64 thru 2/26/65.

BRADY, WILLIAM: Born in Ireland; enl. 12/1 or 20/61, at Centreville; Pvt. and Musician; Co. E. Present until WIA at Seven Pines 5/31/62 and admitted Chimborazo Hosp. #4 6/4/62, with gunshot wound to penis. Admitted Richmond G.H. #21 9/6/62, with syphilis. Transferred to Camp Winder 9/27/62 and to Petersburg on 10/10/62. Admitted Camp Winder G.H. 10/17-11/1/62 with diarrhea. Admitted C.S.A. G.H. in Farmville 3/27-6/12/63, with rheumatism and deafness. POW at Gettysburg 7/4/63. Sent to Ft. McHenry 7/6/63 and to Ft. Delaware 7/7-12/63. Entered U.S. Service and trans. to 3rd Maryland Cavalry 9/22/63.

BRAME, DAVID: Pvt.; Co. G. AWOL 8/11/61.

BRAY, ELLIS H.: enl. 6/2/61 at Cascade; Pvt.; Co. K. Present until WIA (slightly) at Malvern Hill 7/1/62. WIA at Gettysburg 7/3/63. Admitted Chimborazo Hosp. #1 with wound 7/13/63, but returned to duty. Deserted 1/30/64 and entered Federal lines near Newbern, N.C. 2/17/64. Took oath of allegiance at Ft. Monroe 2/24/64 and sent to St. Louis, Mo. Res. of Henry Co., lt. complex. and hair, grey eyes, 5'8¾".

BRAY, JOHN: enl. 6/2/61 at Cascade; Pvt.; Co. K. Present until admitted Richmond G.H. #9 2/17/64 with left ankle injury. Assigned to extra duty in ambulance corps prior to 8/31/64. Paroled at Appomattox 4/9/65.

BRAY, MADISON H.: enl. 6/2/61 at Cascade; Pvt.; Co. K. Present until WIA (slightly) at Malvern Hill 7/1/62. POW at Gettysburg 7/3/63. Sent to Ft. McHenry 7/6/63 and to Ft. Delaware 7/7-12/63 and then to Pt. Lookout 10/27/63. Exchanged 2/10/65. Present at Camp Lee 2/17/65. Paroled at Appomattox 4/9/65.

BRIGHTWELL, WILLIAM C.: enl. 10/14/64 at Danville; Pvt.; Co. A. Admitted G.H. Farmville 3/11/65 with erisipilas and released 3/22/65. POW at Petersburg 4/2/65. Sent to City Point and then to Pt. Lookout 4/4/65. Released there 6/23/65, but admitted to Pt. Lookout G. H. 6/26 and died there 7/8/65, of scurvy and/or typhoid fever. Res. of Pittsylvania Co., fair complex., dk. hair, 5'7".

BROOKS, A. J.: Pvt.; Co. E. Deserted prior to 9/62.

BROWN, JOHN T.: enl. 6/8/61 at Danville; Pvt.; Co. E. Absent sick in Winchester of typhoid fever prior to 8/30/61, but returned to duty by 4/62. Prom. to Cpl. by 6/30/63. WIA (gunshot in arm and leg) POW at Gettysburg 7/3/63. Paroled at Baltimore at West's Building Hosp. 8/23/63. Admitted Danville G.H. with leg wound 5/22/64. Returned to duty and prom. to 4th Sgt. 8/31/64. POW at Five Forks 4/1/65. Sent to City Point to Pt. Lookout 4/5/65. Released there 6/4/65.

BROWN, JOHN W.: enl. 2/26/62, Norfolk Co. Pvt.; 2nd Co. I. Present until deserted to Federals 2/16/65. Oath taken at Bermuda Hundred and transportation furnished to Norfolk.

BROWN, T. J.: Sgt. (Co. and date of enl. unknown). Deserted and received by Provost Marshal Genl. (in Washington, D.C. 4/10/65. Took oath and transportation furnished to Philadelphia, Pa.

BROWN, WILLIAM: enl. 6/4/61 at Republican Grove; Pvt.; Co. F. Issued Surgeon's discharge on 8/31/61, due to general debility.

BROWN, WILLIAM C.: enl. 5/30/61 at Kentuck; Sgt.; Co. A. Elected 1st Lt. 10/1/61, but failed to be reelected and dropped from roll 4/29/62.

BROWN, WILLIAM J.: b. in Pittsylvania Co. enl. 6/8 or 14/61 at Danville; Pvt.; Co. E. Deserted at Richmond 7/6/61, but brought back by 8/30/61. Absent in hosp. from 4/62 until given medical discharge 9/30/62 due to chronic diarrhea, exhaustion, and bone deformity of elbow and top of thumb of left hand, varicose veins and general debility. Lt. complex., and hair, blue eyes, age 35, shoemaker.

BROWN, WILLIAM L.: enl. 3/7/62 at Danville; Pvt.; Co. E. Present until POW at Gettysburg 7/3/63. Sent to Ft. McHenry 7/6/63, to Ft. Delaware 7/12/63 and then to Pt. Lookout 10/15/63. Admitted to Hammond G.H. there 10/16/63 and died there 12/12/63 due to chronic diarrhea and scurvy. Bur. at Pt. Lookout, Md.

BRYANT, CHARLES W.: Born Pittsylvania Co., son of William Bryant; enl. 5/30/61; at Kentuck; Pvt.; Co. A. Admitted Chimborazo Hosp. #4 4/24/62. Present until KIA at Gettysburg 7/3/63. (with no wife or child).

BRYANT, FLEMING B. W.: enl. 5/30/61 at Laurel Grove; Pvt.; Co. C. Present until admitted Danville Hosp. 9/18/62 with debility. Returned to duty 12/12/62. WIA and POW at Gettysburg 7/5/63. Sick with chronic diarrhea. Paroled at DeCamp G.H., David's Island in N.Y. Harbor 9/8/63 and returned to duty. WIA (gunshot in shoulder) at Drewry's Bluff 5/16/64. Present for last muster roll dated 2/25/65.

BRYANT, JOHN: son of Jesse S. Bryant of Henry Co.; enl. 6/8/61 at Danville; Pvt.; Co. E. Present until KIA at Seven Pines 5/12(?)/62.

BUCHANNON, WILLIAM B.: Pvt.; Co. C. Postwar record only.

BUGG, JAMES R.: enl. 5/18/61 at Boydton; Pvt.; Co. G. Present until WIA (slightly) at Seven Pines 5/31/62. Detailed as enrolling officer for Mecklenburg Co. 8/6/62. Prior to 5th Sgt. 5/1/63 to 4th Sgt. by 12/31/64 and to 3rd Sgt. by 2/65. POW at Amelia CH 4/5/65. Sent to City Point and to Pt. Lookout 4/13/65. Released there 6/23/65. Res. of Mecklenburg Co., fair complex., lt. brown hair, blue eyes, 5'8", age 23.

BUGG, JOHN W.: enl. 3/13/62 at Boydton; Pvt.; Co. G. Detailed as guard for ordinance wagon 6/62. POW at Farmville (Saylers Creek?) 4/6/65. Took oath at Newport News 7/1/65. Res. of Mecklenburg Co., fair complex., lt. hair, blue eyes, 5'10".

BUGG, WILLIAM H.: Mother was Frances Bugg; Cpl.; Co. G. Admitted to Chimborazo Hosp. 12/1/61 and died there 12/16/61 of acute bronchitis. Bur. Oakwood Cem., Richmond.

BULLINGTON, JACKSON: Pvt.; Co. K. Died at home 5/62.

BULLINGTON, JOHN: Pvt.; Co. K. Died 8/25/61 of general debility.

BULLINGTON, JOHN R.: enl. 6/2/61 at Cascade; Pvt.; Co. K. Prom. to Color Cpl. 6/15/62. WIA at Malvern Hill 7/1/62, while carrying the colors. Admitted Richmond G.H. #21 7/2/62, wounded, but returned to duty 7/7/62. WIA at Gettysburg 7/3/63. Present until paroled at Appomattox 4/9/65.

BULLOCK, WILLIAM H.: enl. 3/12/62 in Norfolk Co.; Pvt.; 2nd Co. I. Present on only roll dated 8/31/64 and detailed to "daily duty as Co. cook." Deserted and received in Union hands 2/17/65. Received at Provost Marshal Genl. (office in Washington, D.C. 2/21/65. Oath taken there and transportation furnished to Norfolk.

BURKS, BENJAMIN: enl. 6/8/61 at Danville; Pvt.; Co. E. Deserted 7/18/61 and arrested 9/1/61. On detached service at Div. Head-qtrs. 6/30/63 and present 8/31/63. WIA 5/10/64 (at Chester Station?) and admitted to Chimborazo 5/11/64, due to being "stunned by explosion of shell." Present on last roll dated 12/31/64. Farmer, age 21.

BURKS, JAMES: enl. 6/8/61 of Danville; Pvt.; Co. E. Discharged at Richmond 7/2/61.

BURKS, JOSEPH: Age 17; enl. 7/1/61 at Richmond; Pvt.; Co. E. Deserted at Winchester 7/18/61 and arrested 9/1/61. Present until admitted to Richmond G.H. #18 5/31/62 and deserted there 6/26/62. Admitted Richmond G.H. #12 9/16/62, due to enlarged heart. Returned to duty 12/16/62. Admitted to Episcopal Church Hosp. in Williamsburg 3/3/64 and returned to duty 4/21/64. AWOL 12/31/64.

BURMAN, J. H.: Pvt.; (Co. and date of enl. unknown). POW at Gettysburg 7/4/63. Sent to Ft. Delaware 7/7-12/63.

BURNETT, ACHILLES H.: enl. 7/2/61, at Pittsylvania C.H.; Pvt.; Co. H. Prom. to 1st Sgt. by 4/1/64. Present until admitted to Chimborazo Hosp. on 3/5/65, with neuralgia.

BURNETT, EDWIN H.: enl. 5/18/61 at Boydton; Pvt.; Co. G. Present until POW at Williamsburg 5/5/62. Paroled 6/15/62 and name dropped from roll; however, present with company and detailed as cook by 5/1/63. WIA (gunshot in side) and POW at Gettysburg 7/3/63. Sent to Ft. McHenry and then to Ft. Delaware 7/7-/12/63 and then to Pt. Lookout on 10/27/63. Died there of diarrhea on 3/8/65. Buried at Pt. Lookout, Md.

BURNETT, JAMES D.: enl. 6/2/61 at Cascade; Pvt.; Co. K. Absent in Richmond Hosp. until given medical discharge 7/11/61, due to dysentery. Lt. complex., lt. hair, blue eyes; overseer in tobacco factory.

BURNETT, JOSEPH: enl. 2/19/62 at Richmond; Pvt.; Co. H. Present until detailed as nurse in Liberty Hosp. 9/62, thru 2/63. Returned to duty, but deserted from trenches near Bermuda Hundred 7/28/64.

BURNETT, JOSIAH: enl. 5/24/61 at Whitmell; Pvt.; Co. D. Present until admitted Chimborazo Hosp. 10/26/61 with typhoid fever, but returned to duty 12/16/61. Died 2/12/62, of meningitis.

BURNETT, SAMUEL H.: enl. 3/11/62 at Kentuck; Pvt.; Co. A. Present until admitted Chimborazo Hosp. 6/4/62, due to retention of urine. Admitted to Chimborazo Hosp. 6/12/63, with pneumonia, but returned to duty prior to 4/1/64. POW at Petersburg 5/10/64 (CSR may be in error as to Petersburg location, as the 38th was engaged in the Battle of Chester Station on this date). Sent to Ft. Monroe and then to Pt. Lookout 5/13/64 and then to Elmira, N.Y. on 8/17/64. Died there 12/21/64, of heart disease.

BURNETT, THOMAS S.: enl. 6/2/61 at Cascade; 2nd Lt.; Co. K. Present until under arrest by order of court martial until 11/10/61. Resigned office and remanded to ranks as Pvt. Deserted on 11/11/61.

BURNETT, WILLIAM C.: Born Pittsylvania Co.; occ. painter; enl. 5/24/61 at Whitmell; Pvt.; Co. D. Present until left sick at Old Camp on Broad Run. Admitted to Orange C.H. G.H. 11/8/61, with rheumatism. Died there 12/19/61. Dark complex., hazel eyes, black hair, 5'11", age 22.

BURRELL, SAMUEL: Pvt.; Co. A. Postwar record only.

BURTON, GILES A.: enl. 5/18/61 at Boydton; Pvt.; Co. G. Present until detailed as Co. cook 6/62. Absent on guard duty at South Quay 4/11/63. Present prior to 4/1/64. Paroled at Appomattox C.H. 4/9/65. Age 18, occ. laborer.

BURTON, HILLERY G.: enl. 8/23/62, at Boydton; Pvt.; Co. G. Present until assigned to guard duty at South Quay 4/11/63, but present prior to 4/1/64. WIA at Drewry's Bluff 5/16/64. Admitted Chimborazo Hosp. and furloughed 6/22/64. Retired from active duty 12/23/64, and given light duty by order of Medical Examining Board 12/27/64.

BURTON, HILLERY G., JR.: Born Mecklenburg Co.; enl. 5/18/61 at Boydton; mother M. J. Burton. Pvt.; Co. G. Present until admitted Chimborazo Hosp. 10/28/61 with rheumatism. Returned to duty 12/9/61. Issued Medical discharge 1/19/62, due to rheumatism. Ruddy complex., lt. hair, grey eyes, 5'11", age 22, occ. farmer. Wife: Virginia C. Burton (1838-1912). Bur. Liberty Baptist Ch. Cem., Rt. 677, Mecklenburg Co., stone marked Hillery G. Burton, so it may be grave of previously listed Hillery G. Burton.

BURTON, JAMES M.: enl. 10/14/64, at Danville; Pvt.; Co. C. Admitted Richmond G.H. #9 5/10/64 (possibly due to WIA at Chester Station). Present thru last roll dated 2/25/65.

BURTON, JAMES W.: enl. 3/10/62 at Cascade; Pvt.; Co. K. Present until admitted to Chimborazo Hosp. 4/14/62 and then trans. to Danville G.H. 5/6/62, with pneumonia. Returned to duty by 8/13/62. WIA (right arm) at Chester Station 5/10/64, and admitted to Chimborazo Hosp. 5/11/64. Trans. to Danville Hosp. 5/25/64 but returned to duty by 7/18/64. 26 years old in 1864. Probably paroled at Appomattox C.H. 4/9/65. Occ. farmer.

BURTON, JOHN: enl. 5/24/61 at Whitwell; Cpl.; Co. D. Present until MWIA at Seven Pines 5/31/62. Admitted Richmond G.H. and died there 6/16/62.

BURTON, JOHN M.: enl. 5/30/61 at Laurel Grove; Pvt.; Co. C. Present until admitted Chimborazo Hosp. 6/3/62 but returned to duty by 7/9/62. KIA at Bermuda Hundred 8/25/64.

BURTON, PAUL G.: enl. 5/18/61 at Boydton; Cpl.; Co. G. Died on furlough at home in Mecklenburg Co. of typhoid fever/pneumonia 1/17/62.

BURTON, ROBERT S.: enl. 6/2/61 at Cascade; Pvt.; Co. K. Present until admitted Chimborazo Hosp. 10/24/61 with remittant fever. Trans. to Petersburg Hosp. 11/11/61 and died there 12/14/61, of pneumonia.

BURTON, WILLIAM H.: Sgt.; Co. D. Sent to Gen. Hosp. 5/10/62.

BURTON, WILLIAM J.: enl. 5/24/61 at Whitmell. Pvt.; Co. D. Prom. to Sgt. and then elected 2nd Jr. Lt. 7/26/62. WIA at Sharpsburg 9/17/62 and sent to hosp. Present but under arrest 6/28/64 and present 12/31/64. POW at Dinwiddie C.H. 4/1/65. Sent to Old Capitol Prison in Washington, D.C. 4/5/65, then to Sandusky, Ohio, to Johnson's Island. Took oath and released there 6/18/65. Res. of Danville, fair complex., blk. hair, blue eyes, 6'1", age 30.

BURTON, WILLIAM T.: enl. 6/2/61 at Cascade; Pvt.; Co. K. Present until admitted to Chimborazo Hosp. 10/28/61 with remittent fever, but returned to duty 11/20/61. Detailed as cook 7/62. Present thru 2/25/65. Paroled at Appomattox C.H. 4/9/65.

BUTLER, THOMAS J.: enl. 5/30/61 at Kentuck; Pvt.; Co. A. Prom. to 1st Sgt. by 2/1/62. Elected 2nd Lt. 4/29/62. WIA (gunshot fractures of left leg which was amputated at knee and upper right leg) and POW at Gettysburg 7/3/63. Sent to Gen. Hosp. in Chester, PA., to McClellan Hosp. in Nicetown, Pa., to Baltimore Hosp. (age 28), to Ft. McHenry 4/23/64 and then to Pt. Lookout 9/28/64. Exchanged there 9/30/64. Admitted to Charlottesville Hosp. 10/13/64. Trans. to Stuart Hosp., Richmond 11/26/64 and then to Danville G.H. 12/1/64. Retired 2/2/65. Res. of Fairfax Co.

CABANISS, JAMES MATTHEW: Born 11/8/40. enl. 6/2/61 at Cascade; 4th Cpl.; Co. K. Present until sent home sick with fever 7/9/61, but returned to duty later. Prom. to 2nd Lt. 4/20/62 and to 1st Lt. 7/3/63. WIA at Gettysburg 7/3/63. Admitted Danville G.H. 7/20/63 with wounds, but returned to duty 10/8/63. Prom. to Capt. 12/17/64. Admitted Stuart Hosp. in Richmond 3/22/65, with acute bronchitis. Died 8/16/07.

CABANISS, JOHN GEORGE: Born 1/3/20 at Cascade. Married Mary Jane Astin 10/11/39. enl. 10/14/64, at Danville; Pvt.; Co. K. Absent on detached service with Brigade Quartermaster prior to 12/31/64. Admitted Chimborazo Hosp. 3/24/65 with debility. Paroled POW 4/25/65. Died 3/7/97 at Cascade.

CABANISS, WILLIAM GEORGE: Born 6/24/43. enl. 6/2/61 at Cascade; Lt.; Co. K. Present until WIA (fleshy part of arm) at Seven Pines 5/31/62. Admitted to Chimborazo Hosp. 6/3/62 and returned to duty 7/5/62 Prom. to Capt. 8/3/64. WIA (severely in jaw) at Bermuda Hundred 8/25/64, and admitted Richmond G. H. Furloughed 9/9/64 and retired by Medical Examining Board 12/17/64. Died 3/14/26 at Wren (Charlotte Co.)

CABELL, BENJAMIN E.: Co. E. Elected 2nd Lt. 1/1/62. Admitted Chimborazo Hosp. 3/10/62 and died there 3/17/62 with typhoid fever.

CABELL, JOHN ROY: Born Danville 3/24/23; graduate of VMI and a physician. Comm. Capt. of Co. B 6/4/61 at Callands. Present until on sick leave 12/20/61 but returned by 3/62. Absent sick 5/62, and in Danville Hosp. 6/62. Returned to duty 6/26/62. "Treatment" in Medical Directors office 12/8/62. Resigned on 12/10/62, debilitated by continual disease and to care for "five small motherless children." Died 8/26/97. Bur. Greenhill Cem., Danville.

CABELL, JOSEPH ROBERT: Born 5/28/40 at "Bridgewater" in Pittsylvania Co. enl. 4/23/61 at Danville; Pvt.; Co. A. 18th Va. Inf. Comm. Captain Co. E of 38th Inf. at Danville 5/29/61 and entered Confederate service 6/8/61. Present until admitted Danville G.H. 5/15/62, due to debility. Prom. to Major 5/12/62, to Lt. Col. 7/3/63 and to Col. 11/15/63. KIA at Chester Station near the Petersburg Turnpike 5/10/64. Bur. Grove St. Cem., Danville.

CALHOUN, WILLIAM A.: Res. of Pittsylvania Co.; enl. 10/14/64, at Danville; Pvt.; Co. E. Present until POW at Five Forks on 4/1/65. Sent to City Point and then to Pt. Lookout 4/5/65. Released there 6/24/65, but then admitted to Pt. Lookout G.H. 6/28/65. Died there 7/3/65, of chronic diarrhea. Dk. complex., dk. hair, grey eyes, 6'1".

CALLAHAM, WILLIAM R.: enl. 6/2/61 at Cascade; Pvt.; Co. K. Present until admitted to Chimborazo Hosp. 3/4/62 with pneumonia. Returned to duty by 5/1/62.

CALLAHAN, J. R.: enl. 3/8/62, at Clarksville; Pvt.; 1st Co. I. Present until admitted to Danville G.H. 5/27/62, with chronic diarrhea. Returned to duty by 10/22/62.

CALLEY, WILLIAM H.: enl. 3/8/62, at Kentuck; Pvt.; Co. A. Present until admitted Chimborazo Hosp. 3/30/62, with measles. Died there 4/10/62, due to measles and erysipelas. Bur. Oakwood Cem., Richmond.

CALLIS, HENRY: enl. 12/1/61 in Norfolk Co.; Pvt.; 2nd Co. I. Present from first muster roll in 7/64, thru last muster roll 2/25/65.

CAPPS, A. J.: enl. 3/10/62 in Norfolk Co.; Pvt.; 2nd Co. I. Present from first muster roll in 7/64, to POW at Petersburg 4/3/65. Sent to City Point and then to Pt. Lookout 4/13/65. Released there 6/24/65. Res. of Norfolk Co., fair complex., brown hair, blue eyes, 5'8¾".

CARR, JOHN ROBERT T.: Born 8/25/43 near Republican Grove, son of Paul and Margaret Carr; enl. 6/4/61, at Republican Grove; Pvt.; Co. F. Present until admitted Danville G.H. 1/21/62. Admitted Chimborazo Hosp. 12/6/62, with bronchitis. Admitted Farmville Hosp. 12/16/62, with debilitas. Prom. to 5th Sgt. 7/1/63. WIA (right arm) at Gettysburg on 7/3/63. Prom. to 3rd Sgt. by 11/1/64. Wife was Sarah Gutherie Carr. Died at South Boston 12/20/19.

CARR, PAUL W.: Born 3/26/19. Father of John Robert T. Carr; enl. 6/4/61, at Republican Grove; 2nd Lt.; Co. F. Admitted Chimborazo Hosp. 3/21/62, as convalescent and returned to duty 3/25/62. Failed to be reelected 4/29/62. Trans. to reserves as Capt. Died 6/22/03. Bur. in family cem. 1 mile off Rt. 765 south of Republican Grove.

CARR, SPENCER, M.: enl. 6/4/61 at Republican Grove; Pvt.; Co. F. Present until admitted Charlottesville Hosp. 1/8/63 with chronic rheumatism; returned to duty 3/4/63. Probably WIA (head and right thigh) at Drewry's Bluff 5/16/64. Admitted Chimborazo Hosp. 5/19/64, due to wounds. Trans. to Danville Hosp. 5/20/64. Returned to duty 6/15/64. Discharged 8/1/64.

CARRINGTON, EDGAR W.: enl. 7/2/61 at Pittsylvania C.H.; 1st Lt.; Co. H. Demoted to 2nd Lt. by 10/61. Elected Capt. 12/19/61. KIA at Seven Pines 5/31/62.

CARRINGTON, ISAAC HOWELL: Born 3/7/27 in Richmond; apptd. Maj. 6/12/61. Failed to be reelected and dropped from roll 5/12/62. Name appears on a list of prisoners dated 8/3/64, who were confined in E. D. M. Prison and volunteered in Winder Legion for defense of Richmond against 1864 Sheridan Raid and were pardoned by Pres. Married Mary Clayborn Coles.

CARTER, CHARLES SAMUEL: Born 1/24/44; enl. 3/7/62 at Kentuck; Pvt.; Co. A. Admitted Chimborazo Hosp. 11/5/62, with chronic diarrhea, but returned to duty 11/30/62. Detailed as Guard at Division Hqts. 4/1 to 11/24/64. Paroled at Appomattox C.H. 4/9/65. Married Judith Anne Travis 1/14/73. Alive in Salisbury, N.C. in 1912.

CARTER, CHRISTOPHER L.: enl. 10/14/64 at Danville; Pvt.; Co. D. Trans. to Co. D, 39th Va. Cav. Batt. 12/6/64, in exchange for G. W. King.

CARTER, EDWARD A.: b. Pittsylvania Co., enl. 5/30/61 at Kentuck; 2nd Cpl. in Co. A. Prom. to 3rd Sgt. prior to 7/5/63. Present until WIA (shot in left foot) and POW (captured in hosp.) at Gettysburg 7/5/63. Sent to DeCamp G.H., David's Island and released there 8/28/63. 20 yrs. old 1/16/64. Assigned detailed duty at Danville 4/1/64-2/25/65. Paroled at Appomattox CH "with horse and equipment" 4/9/65. Light complex., light hair, blue eyes, 5'7", farmer. Alive at Ingrams (Halifax Co.) 8/22/82.

CARTER, ELISHA K.: enl. 10/14/64, at Danville, Pvt.; Co. D. Present until POW at White Oak Road 4/1/65. Sent to City Point and then to Point Lookout 4/5/65. Released there 6/24/65. Res. of Pittsylvania Co., light complex. and hair, blue eyes, 6'0".

CARTER, GEORGE W.: enl. 5/18/61 at Boydton; Cpl. Co. G. Elected 2nd Lt. 4/29/62. Present until POW at Gettysburg 7/3/63. Sent to Fort McHenry 7/9/63; to Johnson's Island 7/18/63; to Pt. Lookout 2/14/64; and to Fort Delaware 6/25/64. Released there on 6/12/65. Res. of Mecklenburg Co., dk. complex., and hair, blue eyes, 5'10".

CARTER, HENRY C.: apptd. 2nd Lt., Co. B 5/23/61 at Callands. Failed to be reelected and dropped from roll 5/1/62.

CARTER, HENRY C.: enl. 10/14/64 at Danville; Pvt., Co. D. Present until paroled at Appomattox CH 4/9/65.

CARTER, JEDUTHAN, JR.: Born 1/22/21; apptd. Capt., Co. F 6/4/61, at Republican Grove. Detached to serve as recruiting officer beginning 2/16/62. Failed to be reelected and dropped from roll 4/29/62. Due to being unfit for military service because of health 10/9/62, he applied for appointment in Commissary Dept. Married Anne Hubbard; died 12/5/95. Bur. GreenHill Cem. (plot V37), Danville.

CARTER, JEDUTHAN: enl. 8/13/64 in Halifax Co.; Pvt.; Co. D. Present but assigned to light duty by division medical board prior to 8/30/64. Absent on detached duty with division commissary 10/28/64, through last roll dated 2/25/65. Paroled at Appomattox CH on 4/9/65.

CARTER, JESSE LAWSON: Born 3/27 or 28(?); enl. 3/5/62 at Kentuck; Pvt.; Co. A. Present until admitted to Danville Hosp. 8/2/62 with debilitas, but returned to duty by 2/13/63. WIA at Gettysburg 7/3/63. WIA (right leg) at Drewry's Bluff 5/16/64. Admitted to Chimborazo Hosp. 5/17/64 and returned to duty prior to 10/12/64. Died 11/16-17/75. bur. Carter family cem., Blairs.

CARTER, PHILIP VASS: enl. 10/14/64 at Danville; Pvt.; Co. A. Present until admitted Chimborazo Hosp. 11/14/64, for accidental wound to hand. Furloughed 1/7/65 and in Danville Hosp. on 4/5/65 with debilitas. Married Margaret Woody. Alive in 1912.

CARTER, ROBERT H.: enl. 3/12/62, at Clarksville, Pvt.; 1st Co. I. Trans. to Co. G 6/1/62. WIA (slightly) at Malvern Hill 7/1/62. Died (cause unknown) at Richmond 8/9/62. Probably buried Hollywood Cem., Richmond. Widow: Jane Carter.

CARTER, ROBERT W.: enl. 10/14/64 at Danville; Pvt.; Co. A. Present until POW at Dinwiddie C.H. 4/2/65. Sent to City Point and then to Pt. Lookout 4/4/65. Released there 6/10/65. Res. of Pittsylvania Co., dk. complex., dk. brown hair, gray eyes, 6'0".

CARTER, THOMAS M.: enl. 10/14/64 at Danville; Pvt.; Co. D. Trans. to Co. D of 39th Va. Battn. Cav. 11/64, in exchange for T. C. Allen.

CARTER, THOMAS W.: enl. 10/14/64 at Danville; Pvt.; Co. A. Present until POW at Dinwiddie C.H. 4/2/65. Sent to City Point and then to Pt. Lookout 4/4/65. Released there 6/10/65. Res. of Pittsylvania Co., dk. complex., dk. brown hair, hazel eyes, 5'11½".

CARTER, WILLIAM J.: enl. 5/18/61 at Boydton; 3rd Sgt.; Co. G. Elected 2nd Lt. 4/29/62. Prom. to 1st Lt. 11/15/63, age 23. Surrendered at Appomattox C.H. 4/9/65. bur. Boydton Presbyterian Church Cem.

CARTER, WILLIAM SPENCER: b. 5/31/41; enl. 6/8/61 at Danville; 2nd Sgt.; Co. E. Elected 2nd Lt. on 1/4/62. Prom. to 1st Lt. 5/12/62. WIA (slightly) at Malvern Hill 6/1/62. WIA at Gettysburg 7/3/63. Married Cornelia Guerrant 9/16/63. Absent sick 3/5-12/29/64. Died 6/14/96.

CASEY, JAMES: Pvt.; Co. H. Postwar record only.

CASEY, THOMAS W.: enl. 6/16/61 at Callands; Pvt.; Co. B. Present until admitted Chimborazo Hosp. on 3/30/62 (age 26) with chest disease. Admitted Richmond G.H. #13 on 12/30/64 and then trans. to No. 9 2/25/65, with wound.

CASSADA, HESAKIAH W.: enl. 2/4/64 at Kinston, NC; Pvt.; Co. C. Present until deserted 6/17/64. Captured and placed in guardhouse prior to 12/31/64. Escaped guardhouse by 1/6/65. Paroled POW 5/9/65.

CASSADA, JOHN J.: enl. 5/30/61 at Laurel Grove; Pvt.; Co. C. Present until detached as regt. teamster by 8/25/61. Returned and elected 2nd Lt. by 8/7/62. Admitted Danville Hosp. 7/20/63, with debilitas. Died in Chimborazo Hosp. 5/23/64 of g.s.w. (possibly sustained at Chester Station 5/10/64, or Drewry's Bluff 5/16/64.)

CASSADA, O. F.: enl. 3/4/63 at Petersburg; Pvt.; Co. C. Present until deserted 5/17/64. Paroled 4/25/65.

CHANDLER, L. B.: enl. 3/20/62 at Clarksville; Pvt.; 1st Co. I. Present until admitted to Chimborazo Hosp. 5/12/62, with debility. Returned to duty 5/18/62.

CHANDLER, WILLIAM C.: enl. 6/20/61 at Clarkville; Pvt.; 1st, Co. I. Present until detailed as teamster 5/20/62.

CHANDLER, WILLIAM J.: enl. 1/28/63 at Danville; Pvt.; Co. E. Present until deserted and confined by U.S. Provost Marshall at Bermuda Hundred 1/20/65. Sent to Washington, D.C. 1/24/65, where he took oath. Given trans. to Cincinnatti, Ohio 1/26/65.

CHANEY, BEVERLY WROE: Born 4/23/45. enl. 10/14/64 at Danville; Pvt.; Co. C. Present until last muster roll dated 2/23/65. Died 2/28/18. Bur. Laurel Grove.

CHANEY, CALVIN W.: enl. 10/4/63 at Danville; Pvt.; Co. C. Present until on detached duty with Provost Marshall prior to 8/30/64. Listed as having physical disability 9/17/64 (age 46).

CHANEY, CHARLES E.: Pvt.; Co. C. Hospitalized in Richmond prior to 5/62 and died there of typhoid fever.

CHANEY, DANIEL S.: enl. 5/30/61 at Laurel Grove; Pvt.; Co. C. Present until WIA (gunshot flesh wound in leg) at Seven Pines (according to CSR, but was probably Malvern Hill) 7/1/62 and admitted Chimborazo Hosp. 7/3/62. Prom. to 3rd Cpl. prior to 4/1/64, but back to Pvt. by 8/64.

CHANEY, E. B.: enl. 1/7/65, at Danville; Pvt.; Co. C. Absent on detached service at Danville prior to 2/25/65.

CHANEY, SAMUEL M.: enl. 6/24/61 at Richmond; Pvt.; Co. C. Present until sent to hosp. prior to 5/62 and then absent in hosp. thru last recorded roll 9/6/62.

CHAPLAIN, WILLIAM M.: elected 1st Lt.; 2nd Co. I on 3/9/62. Present until WIA (left foot) at Drewry's Bluff 5/16/64 and admitted Richmond G.H. 5/17/64. Retired on 12/1/64.

CHATTEN, M. COMAS: enl. 1/28/63, at Kinston, N.C.; Pvt.; Co. B. Present until sick at division hosp. prior to 10/31/64. Returned prior to 1/1/65.

CHATTEN, NATHANIEL C.: enl. 3/10/62, at Callands; Pvt.; Co. B. Present until admitted Chimborazo Hosp. 10/30/62 with debility. Admitted CSA Hosp. in Danville 4/23/63 with chronic rheumatism. WIA (nose) at Gettysburg 7/3/63. Present on 10/13/64. Alive 4/19/86.

CHATTEN, WILLIAM B.: enl. 5/30/61 at Kentuck; Pvt.; Co. A. Sent home unfit for duty prior to 10/31/61. Detailed as teamster 3/62. Hospitalized in Richmond 5-6/62. WIA (gunshot fractured left arm) at Gettysburg 7/3/63. POW at South Mountain, Md. 7/4/63. Sent to Ft. McHenry and then to Ft. Delaware between 7/7-12/6/63. Died there 8/24/63 of variola at age 23. Bur. Finn's Point Nat. Cem., NJ.

CHEATHAM, WILLIAM A.: enl. 3/6/62 in Appomattox Co.; Pvt.; 2nd Co. I. Present until POW at Fair Ground Hosp., Petersburg 4/3/65. Admitted Petersburg G.H. 4/9/65 with severe g.s.w. wound of right thigh. Died there 5/3/65. Bur. Fair Ground Cem.

CHICK, CHARLES B.: enl. 3/6/62 in Appomattox Co.; Pvt.; 2nd Co. I. Present until POW at Five Forks 4/1/65. Sent to City Point and then to Pt. Lookout 4/6/65. Released there 6/26/65. Res. of Appomattox Co.; lt. complex., brown hair, hazel eyes, 5'9½".

CHILDRESS, WILLIAM: enl. 3/6/62 in Appomattox Co.; Pvt.; 2nd Co. I. Present thru last muster roll 12/31/64.

CHILDRESS, WILLIAM T.: Trans. from Chamberlain's Battery prior to 12/31/64; Pvt., Co. C. Deserted 1/28/65 and took oath at Bermuda Hundred 1/30/65. Trans. furnished to Pittsburg.

CHISM (or CHISHOLM), JAMES H.: enl. 7/2/61 at Pittsylvania C.H.; Pvt.; Co. H. Absent on sick leave 8/19/61 and AWOL by 12/61. WIA and POW at Williamsburg 5/5/62. Died in Federal hands 6/2/62, age 26. Bur. Arlington Nat. Cem.

CHRISTIAN, WILLIAM E.: enl. 6/2/61 at Cascade; Pvt.; Co. K. Detailed as aide to Col. E. C. Edmonds since 9/4/61 and as post rider in 7/62. Detailed at Brigade Headqtrs. prior to 4/1/64. Present by 12/31/64. Admitted Chimborazo Hosp. 3/10/65 with catarrh fever.

CLAIBORNE, FELIX G.: Appointed 1st Lt.; Co. E 6/8/61, at Danville. Absent sick and resigned due to ill health prior to 8/30/61. Res. of Danville.

CLANTON, LEWIS: Pvt.; Co. K. Admitted Chimborazo Hosp. 4/14/62. Died there on 5/31/62 of typhoid fever.

CLARK, JAMES: enl. 3/12/62 at Clarksville; Pvt.; 1st Co. I. Admitted and discharged from Chimborazo Hosp. 6/3/62 for dysentery.

CLARK, THOMAS J.: enl. 3/5/62 at Republican Grove; Pvt.; in Co. F. Present until admitted to Chimborazo Hosp. 5/1/62, with diarrhea. Returned, but deserted from Guardhouse 3/27/63 (also listed as deserting 5/28/63). Under arrest by 8/31/64. Returned to be POW at Five Forks 4/1/65. Sent to City Point and then to Pt. Lookout 4/6/65. Released there 6/24/65. Res. of Halifax Co., fair complex., sandy hair, blue eyes, 6'2½".

CLARKE, EDWARD B.: Pvt.; Co. D. AWOL after being ordered to camp 7/20/62.

CLARKE, JOHN: enl. 5/4/64 in Rockingham; Pvt.; Co. H. Conscript. Present until POW at Drewry's Bluff 5/10/64.

CLAY, CHARLES M.: enl. 6/4/61 at Republican Grove; Pvt.; Co. F. Prom. to 2nd Cpl. by 7/22/62; to 3rd Sgt. by 7/1/63; and to 2nd Sgt. by 11/1/64. Absnt in division hosp. prior to 8/31/64. Present thru last muster roll dated 2/25/65.

CLAY, CHRISTOPHER J.: enl. 6/4/61 at Republican Grove; Pvt.; Co. F. Present until admitted to Manassas Hosp. 2/2/62. Died at Richmond G.H. of "sundries" (date unknown), but register received 6/27/63.

CLAY, GILES L.: enl. 3/19/62 at Republican Grove; Pvt.; Co. F. Present until sent to Richmond G.H. #21 4/13/62, with tuberculosis; trans. to Danville G.H. 6/4/62. Admitted Chimborazo Hosp. 6/23/62, with debility; trans. to Danville G.H. 6/29/62. Returned to duty 7/23/62. Deserted 3/16/64.

CLAY, JENNINGS: enl. 4/6/64, near Richmond; Pvt.; Co. F. Bounty due for enlisting voluntarily prior to 8/31/64. Present from enlistment thru last muster roll 2/25/65.

CLAY, THOMAS J.: enl. 3/14/62 at Republican Grove; Pvt.; Co. F. Present until admitted Chimborazo Hosp. 8/29/62 with debility. Detailed as division ordnance guard by 7/1/63. Under arrest by 4/1/64, but returned by 8/30/64. Under arrest at division guardhouse prior to 2/25/65. Paroled at Appomattox C.H. 4/9/65.

CLAYTON, JAMES C.: Born in North Carolina; enl. 2/19/62 at Danville; Pvt.; Co. C. Present until admitted to Chimborazo Hosp. 4/17/62; trans. to Danville G.H. 5/5/62, with pneumonia. Returned to duty 6/8/62, but back in Danville G.H. 9/7/62, with typhoid fever. Returned to duty by 2/13/63.

CLAYTON, WILLIAM R.: enl. 6/8/61 at Danville; Pvt.; Co. E. Present until admitted to Richmond G.H. #18 3/30/62, with typhoid fever. Returned to duty and on detached service 8-9/62. Returned by 6/30/63. Detailed as Co. cook 8/31/63.

CLEMENT, BEDFORD BOOKER: Born in 1836(?); enl. 3/17/62, at Republican Grove; Pvt.; Co. F. Present until admitted to Chimborazo Hosp. on 8/28/62, with intermittent fever. Returned to duty by 9/16/62. POW near Petersburg (Chester Station?) 5/10/64. Sent to Ft. Monroe and then to Pt. Lookout on 5/13/64 and then to Elmira on 8/17/64. Died there on 3/8/65 of diarrhea. Bur. Woodlawn Nat. Cem., Elmira, N.Y.

CLEMENT, BENJAMIN T.: Appointed 1st Lt.; Co. B 6/4/61, at Callands. Resigned 7/1/61, but reenlisted as Sgt. 8/30/61. Elected 2nd Lt. 5/1/62. Admitted to Danville G.H. 5/8/62, with inflammation of mouth. Returned to duty by 7/4/62. Prom. to 1st Lt. 12/22/62, age 24. Lived in Texas and Arkansas after War. Married and had one son. Probably alive in 1909.

CLEMENT, CHARLES HERBERT: Born 3/19/38; enl. 6/4/61, at Republican Grove, 3rd Cpl.; Co. F. Prom. to 1st Sgt. prior to 7/1/63. Admitted Chimborazo Hosp. 8/1-8/18/63, with wound to right leg. Appointed 2nd Lt. 8/27/64. POW at Dinwiddie C.H. 4/1/65. Sent to Old Capitol Prison 4/5/65; and then to Sandusky and Johnson's Island 4/9/65. Released there 6/18/65, after taking oath. Res. of Republican Grove; dk. complex. and hair, hazel eyes, 5'6''. Died 12/3/20. Bur. Highland Cem., Greenfield, Tenn.

CLEMENT, PARHAM BRANCH: Born 8/8/29; enl. 3/13/62, at Kentuck; Pvt.; Co. A. Present until admitted Chimborazo Hosp. 5/1/62 with remittent fever and furloughed from there 5/62 for 20 days. WIA at Gettysburg 7/3/63. Admitted Chimborazo Hosp. 7/13-7/17/63, with wound. WIA at Chester Station 5/10/64 and admitted to Chimborazo Hosp. 5/11/64, with compound fracture of left hand and amputated middle finger. Died 8/4/79. Bur. Stimson-Wiles Family Cem., west of Rt. 713 near Ringgold.

CLEMENTS, GREEN W.: Born in 1832(?) in Halifax Co.; enl. 4/13/62; Cpl.; Co. A. Absent sick in 5/62. Detailed to bring in deserters 6/62. Detailed as Brigade Provost Guard 8/62. KIA at Gettysburg 7/3/63.

COATES, JOHN C.: Born 2/13/42; enl. 6/4/61 at Republican Grove; Pvt.; Co. F. Prom. to 4th Sgt. prior to 7/1/63. Died 11/13/08. Bur. near Republican Grove off Rt. 647 behind Methodist Church approx. ½ mile in family cem.

COLE, BENJAMIN W.: Appointed 2nd Lt.; Co. A 5/30/61 at Kentuck. Present until resigned 10/13/61. Returned to duty as Pvt. prior to 1/1/65.

COLE, HARVEY J.: Appointed 1st Lt.; Co. C 5/30/61 at Laurel Grove. Failed to be reelected and dropped from roll 4/29/62. Returned home.

COLE, JAMES O. (or C.): enl. 3/4/62, at Kentuck; Pvt.; Co. A. Left sick in Richmond hosp. on or about 4/13/62, while regt. en route to Yorktown. Remained in hosp. thru 6/62. Died at Winchester 10/10/62. Bur. Stonewall Cem., Winchester. Widow: Lucy Ann Cole.

COLE, L. F.: enl. 10/14/64, at Danville; Pvt.; Co. A. Present thru last muster roll 2/25/65.

COLE, WILLIAM P.: enl. 10/14/64 at Danville; Pvt.; Co. A. Present until POW at Petersburg 4/2/65. Sent to City Point and then to Pt. Lookout 4/4/65. Released there 6/24/65. Res. of Pittsylvania Co., dk. complex., dk. brown hair, blue eyes, 5'9¾".

COLEMAN, JAMES MADISON: b. 1/37; Pvt.; enl. 3/12/62 at Boydton; Pvt.; Co. G. Present until discharged for disability (broken thigh and leg shortened 2") 6/8/62. Conscripted and assigned to Co. G 3/10/64. Light complex., dk. hair, 5'7", farmer.

COLEMAN, THOMAS BURWELL: Born 5/23/47. enl. 4/27/62 at Yorktown (according to CSR, but he may have enlisted as much as one year earlier); Pvt.; Co. G. Present until detached as Division Provost Guard 3/1/63. After 7/63, he was AWOL and arrested at his home in Mecklenburg Co. by 2nd Lt. Whitmell T. Adkins of Co. B prior to 9/16/63; however, he escaped from the county jail and returned to the Regt. ahead of Lt. Adkins. Admitted Richmond G.H. 3/26/64. Returned to Co. prior to 2/25/65. POW at Five Forks 4/1/65. Sent to City Point and then to Hart's Island, NY Harbor on 4/7/65. Released there 6/17/65, after taking oath. Res. of Mecklenburg Co., dk. complex. and hair, blue eyes, 5'10", occ. teamster. Married Annie V. Chapman of Bedford 12/1/67 and fathered 3 sons and 2 daughters in Roanoke. Died 7/14/14. Bur. Fairview Cem., Roanoke.

COLES, JOHN JR.: Born in 1836 in Pittsylvania Co.; son of John Sr. and Louisa Payne Coles. Appointed 1st Lt. of Co. H 7/2/61, at Pittsylvania C.H. Present until 12/20/61, when he was granted sick leave thru 2/62. Returned 3/62, but was not reelected 4/29/62. Later joined the cavalry. After the War, he worked as a farmer and served as a Justice of the Peace in the Bent Mtn. section of Roanoke Co.

COLLEY, WILLIAM: Pvt.; Co. A. Postwar record only.

COLLIE, DAVID N.: enl. 10/14/64 at Danville; Pvt.; Co. A. Present until admitted Chimborazo Hosp. 3/6/65, with bronchitis. Trans. to Danville G.H. 3/20/65, with chronic diarrhea. Returned to duty by 4/11/65, according to CSR.

COLLIE, JAMES HENRY: b. 4/13/45; enl. 9/2/63 at Danville; Pvt.; Co. D. Prom. to 2nd Cpl. by 12/31/64. Present until paroled at Appomattox C.H. 4/9/65. Bur. Chatham Cem.

COLLINS, AUGUSTINE H.: enl. 3/10/62, at Callands; Pvt.; Co. B. Present until admitted Chimborazo Hosp. 3/30/62, with typhoid fever. Died on 8/30/62, in Pittsylvania Co. Widow: Mary Collins.

COLLINS, CHRISTOPHER J.: enl. 6/4/61 at Republican Grove; Sgt.; Co. F. Present until discharged 8/3/62 at expiration of enlistment.

COLLINS, FRANKLIN: enl. 6/4/61, at Callands; Pvt.; Co. B. Present until admitted Chimborazo Hosp. 10/23/61, with kidney disease. Discharged there because of this 11/1/61.

COLLINS, IRA: enl. 3/10/62, at Callands; Pvt.; Co. B. Present until admitted Danville G.H. 6/29/62, with chronic diarrhea, but returned to duty by 9/16/62. WIA at Drewry's Bluff 5/16/64. Died in Chimborazo Hosp. 6/11/64 of pneumonia.

COLLINS, JOHN W.: enl. 5/24/61, at Whitmell; Pvt.; Co. D. Present, but sick due to injured hip and application for medical discharge refused. Admitted Chimborazo Hosp. 10/25/61, with rheumatism and furloughed until 1/24/62. Admitted Danville G.H. 5/8/62, with rheumatism. Deserted 7/24/62, but returned prior to 4/1/64. Paroled at Appomattox on 4/9/65. May be bur. Oakwood Cem., Richmond.

COLLINS, LILBURN: Pvt.; Co. B. Postwar record only.

COLLINS, TILMAN: Pvt.; Co. B. Sent to hosp. as nurse 3/25/62. Admitted to Chimborazo Hosp. 3/30/62 with bronchitis. Died there 4/23/62. (CSR also lists him dying on 4/25/62, due to catarrh).

CONNER, JACOB: Pvt.; 2nd Co. I. Paroled at Appomattox C.H. 4/9/65.

CONNER, JAMES O.: enl. 10/22/64 in Pittsylvania Co.; Pvt. Co. H. Present until deserted 1/12/65, and captured by Federals at Bermuda Hundred. Sent to Washington, D.C. 1/14/65. Took oath there and transportation furnished to Philadelphia, Pa.

CONSTABLE, CHARLES W.: enl. 3/1/62, in Norfolk Co.; Pvt.; 2nd Co. I. Present until admitted Chimborazo Hosp. 10/5/64, with chronic diarrhea. Furloughed 10/18/64. Returned to Chimborazo Hosp. 3/5/65, with chronic rheumatism. POW in hosp. in Richmond 4/3/65. Sent to Libby Prison and then to Newport News 4/23/65. Took oath there and released 6/14/65. Res. of Norfolk; fair complex., lt. hair, grey eyes, 5'4".

CONWAY, ALEXANDER F.: Born in Pittsylvania Co.; enl. 5/30/61 at Kentuck; Pvt.; Co. A. Present until WIA at Seven Pines on 5/31/62. KIA at Gettysburg 7/3/63.

COOK, JAMES R., JR.: enl. 2/18/62, at Clarksville; Pvt.; 1st Co. I. Present until detailed as nurse (probably especially for father, Pvt. James R. Cook, Sr.) at Orange Co. Hosp. 4/11/62. Died in Chimborazo Hosp. 6/8/62, of typhoid fever on the day following the death of his father there.

COOK, JAMES R., SR.: enl. 6/20/61, at Clarksville; Pvt.; 1st Co. I. Present until sick at camp near Centreville 12/26/61. Left at Orange Co. Hosp. 4/7/62. Admitted Chimborazo Hosp. 5/21/62, and died there 6/7/62, of typhoid fever and pneumonia. (See above record of son, Pvt. James R. Cook, Jr.)

COOK, WILLIAM H.: enl. 6/2/61, at Clarksville; Pvt.; 1st Co. I. WIA (slightly) at Malvern Hill 7/1/62.

COOPER, JAMES S.: enl. 2/20/62, in Norfolk Co.; Pvt.; 2nd Co. I. Present until deserted and captured by Federals 2/18/65, at Bermuda Hundred. Sent to Washington, D.C. where he took oath 2/21/65. Transportation furnished to Norfolk.

COSBY, JOHN S.: Appointed Chaplain of Regt. 7/10/61. Resigned 1/20/62.

COVINGTON, ANSALEM L.: enl. 3/13/62, at Republican Grove; Pvt.; Co. F. Present until deserted by 6/3/62, but returned by 4/1/64.

COX, BEDFORD B.: enl. 6/8/61 at Danville; Pvt.; Co. E. Present until admitted Richmond G.H. #24 9/18/62, with syphilis; returned to duty by 11/27/62. Prom. to 2nd Cpl. by 5/1/63, to 5th Sgt. by 7/1/64, to 4th Sgt. by 12/31/64; and to 3rd Sgt. by 2/25/65. WIA (right thigh) at Five Forks 4/1/65. POW at Fair Ground Hosp., Petersburg 4/14/65. Confined at Camp Hamilton 5/2/65. Released there 5/21/65.

COX, BENNETT: enl. 5/19/64, in Henry Co.; Pvt.; Co. K. Conscript. Present until admitted Chimborazo Hosp. 7/16/64 with scurvy, diarrhea and typhoid fever. Return to duty on or about 8/27/64. Paroled at Appomattox C.H. 4/9/65.

COX, EDWARD: enl. 5/1/64, at Boydton; Pvt.; Co. G. Absent and couldn't report until 8/28/64, due to disability. Admitted Petersburg Hosp. 3/29/65, and died there on the same day due to congestive fever.

COX, ELI: enl. 3/17/62, at Clarksville; Pvt.; 1st Co. I. Present until sent to Richmond G.H. #18 4/13/62, with chronic bronchitis. Trans. to Petersburg G.H. 5/16/62 but returned to duty by 5/7/62.

COX, ELIJAH H.: enl. 3/1/62, at Clarksville; Pvt.; 1st Co. I. Present until admitted Chimborazo Hosp. 5/12/62, with typhoid fever. Furloughed from there 6/12/62, for 30 days.

COX, GEORGE W.: Pvt.; Co. C. Sent to hosp. before or during 5/62 and remained there thru 7/62. Name appears on list of Claims of Deceased Soldiers filed 12/11/62, filed by his widow, Lucy A. Cox.

COX, JAMES: enl. 3/12/62, at Clarksville; Pvt.; 1st Co. I. Present until admitted Chimborazo Hosp. 4/24/62 and then trans. to Winder Hosp. 5/8/62.

COX, PETER B.: enl. 3/17/62, at Boydton; Pvt.; Co. G. Died in camp near Seven Pines on 6/22/62.

COX, POWHATAN: Pvt.; Co. K. Admitted Chimborazo Hosp. 3/31/62, with pneumonia, which caused his death 4/7/62.

COX, THOMAS A.: enl. 3/12/62, at Clarksville; Pvt.; 1st Co. I. Sent to Richmond Hosp. on 4/26/62.

COX, THOMAS PINCKNEY: Born 5/15/42. enl. 3/10/62 at Cascade; Pvt.; Co. K. Present until admitted Chimborazo Hosp. on 4/17/62. Trans. to Danville Hosp. 5/15/62 and deserted there 5/25/62. Returned and again admitted to Danville Hosp. 11/24/63 with wound. Trans. to Chimborazo Hosp. 1/7/64, with chronic rheumatism and gunshot wound of hand. Returned by 8/31/64 and detailed as camp cook. Retired to Invalid Corps 9/12/64. Died 2/2/28 at Cascade.

COX, WILLIAM: Pvt.; 1st Co. I. Present until received severe wound in shoulder and sent to hosp. 2/27/61; at home recuperating before or during 6/62.

COX, WILLIAM E.: Son of Alexander Cox; enl. 6/20/61 at Clarksville; Pvt.; 1st Co. I. Present until sent to hosp. from Manassas 2/10/62. Probably WIA (flesh wound in back) at Seven Pines 5/31/62. Admitted Chimborazo Hosp. 6/62. Died in Mecklenburg Co. 6/27/62, of typhoid fever.

COX, WILLIAM H.: enl. 11/10/63 in Henry Co.; Pvt., Co. H. Present until POW at Five Forks on 4/1/65. Sent to City Point and then to Hart's Island, NY Harbor. Took oath and released there 6/21/65. Res. of Henry Co., dk. complex. and hair, grey eyes, 5'10".

COX, WILLIAM S.: enl. 6/8/61, at Danville; Pvt.; Co. E. Left sick with typhoid fever in Winchester prior to 8/30/61, but returned by 4/30/62. Deserted and received by Provost Marshal Gen., Army of the Potomac on 3/30/65. Oath taken and trans. to Washington, D.C. 4/4/65.

CRADDOCK, DANIEL S.: enl. 3/10/62 at Callands; Pvt.; Co. B. Present until admitted Chimborazo Hosp. 8/28/62 with chronic diarrhea. Returned to duty by 10/18/62. WIA (compound fracture of right forearm) at Chester Station 5/10/64 and admitted Chimborazo Hosp. 5/11/64. Nailcutter. Alive in Burwellville 5/15/99.

CRADDOCK, WILLIAM B.: born 1827 in Pittsylvania Co. Married Mary Ann Hedrick in 1847. Enl. 6/4/61 at Callands; Pvt. in Co. B. Present until 2/4/62 when detailed to go after hay. Reenlisted or conscripted 2/28/64. WIA (forearm) Drewry's Bluff 5/16/64 and admitted Chimborazo #5. Furloughed for 60 days on 5/24/64 to recuperate from wound. 1/1/65 absent on furlough. POW at Five Forks 4/1/65. Sent to City Point and then to Hart's Island, NY on 4/7/65. Took oath and released there 6/20/65. Res. of Pittsylvania Co., dk. complex. and hair, grey eyes, 5'10½". Died in North Danville on 6/8/09 at 81 yrs. of age. Bur. Green Hill Cem., Danville.

CRANE, AARON W.: Born in 1830; enl. 5/24/61 at Whitmell; Pvt.; Co. D. Died of typhoid fever at Winchester 7/20/61.

CRANE, THOMAS E., JR.: Born Pittsylvania Co. 8/27; Pvt.; Co. E. WIA; died in Washington Co. in 1912. Postwar record only.

CRAWLEY, WILLIAM R.: enl. 3/8/62, at Danville; Pvt.; Co. E. Present until admitted Danville Hosp. 6/4/62, with rheumatism and returned 7/9/62. Detached as guard at Division Headqtrs. prior to 8/31/63. Admitted Danville Hosp. 4/19/64, with sprained knee. Paroled at Appomattox 4/9/65.

CREWS, ARMSTEAD C.: enl. 7/2/61, at Pittsylvania C.H.; Pvt., Co. H. WIA (2 broken ribs) at Seven Pines 5/31/62 and admitted Chimborazo Hosp. 6/1/62. Returned to duty 7/62. KIA at Gettysburg 7/3/63.

CREWS, JOSEPH B.: enl. 3/6/62, in Appomattox Co.; Pvt.; 2nd Co. I. Present until admitted to Chimborazo Hosp. 5/6/64, with rheumatism. Discharged, but readmitted there 8/15/64 and died there 8/19/64. Widow: Hester A. Crews.

CREWS, RAINEY W.: enl. 3/6/62, in Appomatox Co.; Pvt.; 2nd Co. I. Present until admitted to Chimborazo Hosp. 7/18/64, with fever; granted 30 day furlough 7/27/64, but CSR also states he was admitted to Farmville Hosp. 7/23/64, with chronic diarrhea for past 3 months; emaciation and debility. Furloughed for 40 days, but present by 12/31/64. Paroled at Appomattox 4/9/65.

CREWS, SAMUEL T.: enl. 3/15/62, at Laurel Grove; Pvt.; Co. C. Present until POW at Five Forks 4/1/65. Sent to City Point and then Pt. Lookout 4/6/65. Released there 6/24/65. Res. of Halifax Co., dark. complx. and hair, hazel eyes, 5'11".

CRIDLIN, RANSEL W.: Commissioned Chaplain for the Regt. 6/9/63. Present until surrender at Appomattox C.H. 4/9/65. Pastor of Stockton St. Baptist Ch. in Manchester (Richmond) 2/08.

CROWDER, JOHN W.: enl. 7/2/61, at Pittsylvania C.H.; Pvt.; Co. H. Present until detailed to drive wagons 4/62 and returned by 4/1/64. WIA (gunshot through left leg below knee) at Drewry's Bluff 5/16/64. Admitted Danville G.H. 6/9/64. Returned to duty by 8/31/64. Alive on 6/20/87.

CROWDER, SAMUEL W.: enl. 3/18/61 at Boydton; Pvt.; Co. G. Present until detailed as wagoner 1/62 and returned to Co. about 3/28/63. Deserted 4/10/63 and apparently arrested or returned. Deserted again 10/6/63, and later arrested. Broke arrest and deserted near Hanover Junction 5/7/64. Incarcerated in Division Guardhouse for desertion 2/65.

CULBREATH, (possibly CULBERT), JOHN: enl. 3/8/62, at Clarksville; Pvt.; 1st Co. I. Present until sent to Richmond Hosp. (Winder) 5/25/62 and apparently died there 6/1/62, of typhoid fever. Probably buried Hollywood Cemetery, Richmond.

CUMBY, EDWARD GREEN: enl. 5/18/61, at Boydton; Pvt.; Co. G. Present until listed as deserted on 7/22/62, but returned 5/1/63. Again listed as deserted 2/65, but returned in time to be POW at Amelia C.H. 4/5/65. Sent to City Point and then to Pt. Lookout 4/13/65. Released there 6/10/65. Res. of Mecklenburg Co., dk. complex., brown hair, grey eyes, 5'8¼".

CUNNINGHAM, JOHN: enl. 5/18/61, at Boydton; Pvt.; Co. G. Present until WIA seriously at Seven Pines 5/31/62 and admitted Richmond Hosp. Admitted Charlottesville Hosp. 12/2/62, with gonorrhea, but returned to duty by 3/26/63.

CUNNINGHAM, ROBERT: Pvt.; Co. G. CSR states: "surrendered by Lee as part of Army of No. Virginia 5/22/65, at Greensboro, N.C."

DABBS, JOSEPH D.: b. Pittsylvania Co.; merchant; age 27, a Mason; enl. 6/2/61 at Cascade. Cpl. in Co. K. Died at Camp Edwards near Bristow Sta. 9/11/61, of einteritis. Fair complex., dk. hair, blue eyes, 5'11". Bur. near Cascade.

DALGOOD, JOHN: Pvt.; Co. G. Postwar record only.

DALLAS, GEORGE T.: enl. 5/24/61, at Whitmell; Cpl.; Co. D. Present until KIA "on Chickahominy" at Seven Pines 5/31/62. Mother: Mrs. E. P. Dallas.

DALTON, DAVID W.: Pvt.; Co. H. WIA at Drewry's Bluff 5/16/64 and discharged. Postwar record only.

DALTON, JOHN R.: Born Pittsylvania Co.; enl. 6/2/61, at Cascade; Pvt.; Co. K. Present until medically discharged 2/12/62, due to gangrene. Dk. complex. and hair and eyes, 5'9", age 22, factory hand.

DALTON, RICHARD: enl. 7/2/61 at Pittsylvania C.H.; Pvt.; Co. H. Present until admitted Chimborazo Hosp. 3/7/62, with diarrhea; released 4/20/62. Detailed as nurse at Camp Winder Hosp. 5/16/62, and returned to duty 8/19/62. WIA (lost left leg) at Drewry's Bluff 5/16/64. Retired on 11/18/64. Res. of Chalk Level.

DALTON, THOMAS: Conscript enrolled 4/17/64 and assigned to 38th Va. Inf. 4/22/64.

DALTON, THOMAS R.: enl. 11/14/63 at Danville; Pvt. Co. H. Present until 6/2/64, when he "shot himself purposely...to obtain a furlough."

DANIEL, J. T.: enl. 3/6/62 at Clarksville; Pvt.; 1st Co. I. Present until sent to Richmond Hosp. 4/27/62.

DANIEL, LEWIS T.: enl. 3/1/62, at Clarksville; Pvt.; 1st Co. I. Present until he was sent to Danville Hosp. 4/62 to attend the sick. Returned in time to be WIA (hand) at Seven Pines 5/31/62.

DANIEL, LOT A.: enl. 6/20/61 at Clarksville; Pvt.; 1st Co. I. Present until admitted Chimborazo Hosp. 5/2/62, with debility and then sent to Camp Winder 5/6/62.

DANIEL, STEPHEN: enl. 6/2/61 at Clarksville; Pvt.; 1st Co. I. Present until detailed as teamster 6/20/62.

DAVICE, JOHN D.: enl. 5/30/61 at Kentuck; Pvt.; Co. A. Present until WIA (seriously) at Malvern Hill 7/1/62.

DAVICE, JOHN H.: enl. 5/30/61 at Kentuck; Pvt.; Co. A. Detailed as teamster in 1/62. Admitted Richmond G.H. #18 3/2/62 and died there 3/12/62, with typhoid fever.

DAVIS, AUGUSTINE H.: enl. 6/2/61 at Cascade; Cpl.; Co. K. Present until KIA at Gettysburg 7/3/63.

DAVIS, CREED O.: enl. 6/8/61 at Danville; Pvt.; Co. E. Detailed as orderly at Regt. Headqtrs. 8/31/63. Prom. 2nd Cpl. 7/1/64 and to Sgt. prior to 4/1/65. POW at Five Forks 4/1/65. Sent to City Point and then to Pt. Lookout 4/5/65. Released there 6/3/65.

DAVIS, ELZY: Born Norfolk Co.; enl. 6/26/61, in Norfolk Co.; Pvt.; 2nd Co. I. Present until deserted 8/4/64 and in Federal custody 8/6/64. Sent to Norfolk. Dk. complx., blk. hair and eyes, 5'7", age 34.

DAVIS, GEORGE W.: Son of Pvt. Israel Davis of Henry Co.; enl. 2/24/62, at Cascade; Pvt.; Co. K. Died at Richmond 6/18/62. Bur. Oakwood Cem., Richmond.

DAVIS, HENRY W.: enl. 6/4/61, at Republican Grove; Pvt.; Co. F. Detailed as nurse of Co. sick at Broad Run 10/61. Sent home with corpse of Pvt. John J. Stowe 11/61. Detailed as nurse at Orange C.H. 4/9/62. Admitted to Danville Hosp. 5/15/62, with inflammation of testicle, and returned to duty by 10/22/62. Probably WIA (gunshot in shoulder) at Chester Station 5/10/64, and admitted Chimborazo Hosp. 5/11/64. Returned to duty by 8/31/64. Paroled at Appomattox C.H. 4/9/65. Alive on 3/21/87.

DAVIS, H. M.: enl. 5/18/61, at Boydton; Pvt.; Co. G. Died at Manassas 8/31/61, of typhoid fever.

DAVIS, ISRAEL: Apparently father of Pvt. George W. Davis; Pvt.; Co. K. Absent in hosp. 5/62, and died there 6/25/62, of typhoid fever.

DAVIS, JAMES: enl. 2/25/62 at Danville; Pvt.; Co. E. Present until admitted Chimborazo Hosp. 7/28/62, with rheumatism. Trans. to Danville Hosp. 8/13/62. Returned prior to 8/31/64.

DAVIS, JAMES H.: Born in Halifax Co.; age 40; enl. 6/4/61 at Republican Grove; Pvt.; Co. F. Absent on furlough 8/31/61. Given medical discharge 11/9/61, due to lung disease. Light complex. and hair, blue eyes, 6'0", farmer.

DAVIS, JAMES T.: enl. 6/4/61 at Republican Grove; Pvt.; Co. F. WIA (slightly in hand) at Malvern Hill on 7/2(?),/62 and admitted Chimborazo Hosp. 7/3/62. Later deserted but returned by 11/12/64. Under arrest in Div. Guardhouse prior to 2/25/65.

DAVIS, JAMES W.: enl. 11/2/64 at Bermuda Hundred, Pvt.; Co. F. Present until admitted Chimborazo Hosp. 2/25/65 with skin inflammation and fever. Returned to duty by 3/6/65.

DAVIS, JOHN E.: enl. 6/2/61, at Cascade; Pvt.; Co. K. Present until WIA (slightly in hand) at Williamsburg 5/5/62. Present by 8/31/62. Deserted 3/63, but apparently returned voluntarily or was arrested. Listed as deserting again near Drewry's Bluff 5/18/64. Possibly buried Oakwood Cem., Richmond.

DAVIS, JOHN G.: enl. 2/9/63, at Mt. Jackson; Pvt.; Co. D. Present until paroled at Appomattox C.H. 4/9/65.

DAVIS, JOHN H.: b. 2/16/49; enl. 3/3/62, at Danville; Pvt.; Co. E. Present until admitted Chimborazo Hosp. 5/26/62, with diarrhea and trans. to Lynchburg Hosp. 6/3/62. WIA (gunshot in thigh) and POW at Gettysburg 7/3/63. Sent to DeCamp G.H. and paroled there 9/8/63. Returned to duty by 9/14/63. Died 2/10/23. Bur. Providence Baptist Ch. Cem., Providence, N.C.

DAVIS, JOHN T.: b. Pittsylvania Co.; Co. E. Postwar record only. Lived in Camp Lee Soldiers Home, Richmond. Died 9/7/03, at age 71. Bur. Hollywood Cem. (west section), Richmond.

DAVIS, JOHN W.: enl. 10/15/64 at Bermuda Hundred; Pvt.; Co. F. Present until incarcerated in Brigade Guardhouse as of 2/25/65. POW at Five Forks 4/1/65. Sent to City Point and then to Pt. Lookout 4/6/65. Released there 6/11/65. Res. of Pittsylvania Co., dk. complex., brown hair, grey eyes, 5'7-7/8".

DAVIS, LARKIN: enl. 3/4/62 at Danville; Pvt.; Co. E. Present until admitted Danville G.H. 5/9/62 with debilitas. KIA at Malvern Hill 7/1/62.

DAVIS, M. D.: enl. 3/10/62, at Cascade; Pvt.; Co. K. Present until admitted Danville CSA Hosp. 5/19/62 with catarrh. Returned to duty but listed as deserted at Drewry's Bluff 5/19/64.

DAVIS, THOMAS J.: enl. 6/2/61 at Cascade; Pvt.; Co. K. Present until WIA at Gettysburg 7/3/63; admitted Danville Hosp. 7/16/63. Returned to duty by 8/18/63. Paroled on 4/25/65.

DAVIS, WILLIAM L.: enl. 3/9/63, in Pittsylvania Co.; Pvt.; Co. H. Present until admitted Danville Hosp. 9/13/63, with debilitas. Deserted from hosp. 9/15/63, but returned 4/1/64. Bur. Oakwood Cem., Richmond.

DAVIS, WILLIAM G.: enl. 6/2/61 at Cascade; Pvt.; Co. K. Present until left in hosp. at Winchester prior to 10/31/61, with measles and fever; went home from there. Admitted to Danville Hosp. 5/5/62, with rheumatism and deserted from there 5/21/62. Returned by 5/28/62. (CSR also states: "died of disease in hosp. 6/62," in obvious conflict-possibly with Pvt. George W. Davis.) Admitted Danville Hosp. 12/16/62, with dyspepsia. Deserted 1/3 or 5/63, but returned prior to 4/1/64. CSR also states he deserted 5/16/64, near Drewry's Bluff, but was admitted CSA Gen. Hosp. Danville 5/23/64 with hand wound and then deserted 7/9/64. (Possibly he was WIA at Drewry's Bluff and later deserted in Danville.)

DAWSON, LEWIS H.: enl. 10/15/64, at Bermuda Hundred; Pvt.; Co. F. Present until admitted Chimborazo Hosp. 3/5/65, with inflammation of kidneys.

DAWSON, WILLIAM: enl. 6/4/61, at Republican Grove; Pvt.; Co. F. Present until deserted from Guardhouse 5/13/63. Returned to Co. by 8/7/64. Undergoing punishment in Salisbury, NC prior to 12/13/64.

DEER, EDWARD: enl. 3/15/62 in Norfolk Co.; Pvt.; 2nd Co. I. Present on daily duty as Co. cook as of 8/31/64. POW at Five Forks 4/2/65. Sent to City Point and then to Hart's Island, N.Y. Harbor 4/7/65. Released there 6/20/65. Res. of Norfolk Co., fair complex., lt. hair, blue eyes, 5'6".

DELANEY, LEWIS: enl. 6/20/61 at Danville; Pvt.; Co. E. AWOL 9/25/61, but returned in time to be WIA (gunshot in foot) probably at Williamsburg 5/5/62. Admitted Chimborazo Hosp. 5/11/62 with this wound. Gangrene set in and he died 5/21/62. Bur. Oakwood Cem., Richmond.

DENSMORE, M.: Pvt.; Co. B. Paid on 10/30/62.

DILLARD, GEORGE W.: enl. 1/1/62 at Manassas; Pvt.; Co. E. Present until admitted to Chimborazo Hosp. 3/13/62, with jaundice. Furloughed from hosp. for 30 days 4/1/62.

DILLARD, HENRY J.: enl. 8/14/62 at Danville; Pvt.; Co. E. Present until admitted Petersburg Hosp. 12/15/63, with intermittent fever. Admitted Petersburg Hosp. 1/28/64, with cholera. Admitted Williamsburg Episcopal Hosp. 2/22/64, with intermittent fever. Trans. to Petersburg Hosp. 5/7/64 with dyspepsia. Absent sick thru 2/25/65.

DILLARD, ROBERT M.: enl. 6/8/61 at Danville; Pvt.; Co. E. Present until absent sick by 2/28/62. Died in hosp. (probably near Manassas) by 9/62.

DILLION, WILLIAM D.: enl. 3/10/62 at Cascade; Pvt.; Co. K. Present until admitted Chimborazo Hosp. 4/14/62, with debilitas and trans. to Danville Hosp. on 5/6/62. Deserted on 8/23/62. Furloughed for 60 days 11/6/62. WIA at Drewry's Bluff 5/16/64. Admitted Danville Hosp. 9/13/64, with leg wound. Returned to duty 9/26/64.

DIX, JOHN R.: enl. 3/13/62 at Danville; Pvt.; Co. E. Pay deducted for being AWOL 4/16/63-8/12/63. Admitted Richmond G.H. #13 11/19/64, with syphilis, but returned to duty 11/26/64. Absent undergoing sentence of General Court Martial at Salisbury, N.C. prior to 12/31/64.

DIX, TANDA W.: b. Pittsylvania Co.; enl. 5/30/61, at Kentuck; Pvt.; in Co. A. Present until admitted Danville Hosp. 6/20/62, with diarrhea; returned 8/13/62. Admitted Chimborazo Hosp. 11/5/62, with acute diarrhea. KIA at Gettysburg 7/3/63.

DIX, WILLIAM: enl. 3/13/62 at Danville; Pvt.; Co. E. Pay deducted for being AWOL 4/10-8/12/63. Also absent undergoing sentence of General Court Martial at Salisbury, N.C. prior to 12/31/64. Returned in time to be POW at Burkeville 4/6/65. Sent to City Point and then to Newport News 4/16/65. Oath taken and released there 6/1/65. Res. of Pittsylvania Co., fair complex., lt. hair, grey eyes, 5'5".

DIXON, JOHN: enl. 10/4/64 at Danville; Pvt.; Co. D. Present until admitted Chimborazo Hosp. 12/23/64, with typhoid and pneumonia. Furloughed from hosp. 1/27/65, for 60 days.

DIXON, WILLIAM: enl. 6/2/61 at Cascade; Pvt. in Co. K. Admitted Danville Hosp. on 5/14/62 with hemorrhoids. Returned to duty on 7/23/62. KIA at Chester Station on 5/10/64.

DODD, BENJAMIN C.: enl. 6/4/61, at Callands; Pvt.; Co. B. Admitted Chimborazo Hosp. 3/30/62, with bronchitis and returned to duty 4/30/62. Admitted to Chimborazo Hosp. 6/26/62, with rheumatism and gastritis. Trans. to Danville G.H. 7/23/62 and died there 7/25/62, of typhoid fever.

DODD, JAMES W.: enl. 3/10/62, at Callands; Pvt.; Co. B. Admitted Richmond G.H. #18 5/2/62, with chronic rheumatism. Admitted Chimborazo Hosp. 7/3/62, with debility and returned to duty prior to 5/19/63. Admitted Chimborazo 5/23/64, with acute dysentery. Admitted Danville Hosp. on 5/29/64 with acute rheumatism and returned to duty by 6/21/64.

DODD, SAMUEL P.: enl. 6/4/61, at Callands; Pvt.; Co. B. Admitted Chimborazo Hosp. 3/7/62, with pneumonia and died there 3/17/62, of same, age 44. Widow: Malinda H. Dodd.

DODD, THOMAS W.: enl. 6/4/61, at Callands; Pvt.; Co. B. Admitted Danville Hosp. 6/4/62, with typhoid and returned 7/4/62. WIA (shot thru left forearm) at Drewry's Bluff 5/18/64, and admitted Chimborazo Hosp. Furloughed from hosp. for 60 days. POW at Five Forks 4/1/65. Sent to City Point and then to Hart's Island 4/7/65. Released there 6/20/65. Res. of Pittsylvania Co., lt. complex., dk. hair, grey eyes, 5'10½". Alive at Burwellville 5/15/99.

DODD, WILLIAM SAMUEL: b. at Chatham 8/16/40; son of Ralph and Nannie Johnston Dodd; enl. 8/14/62, at Danville; Pvt.; Co. B. WIA at Gettysburg 7/3/63 and admitted Danville Hosp. 7/12/63. Deserted from hosp. 9/5/63, but returned to hosp. 10/15/63. Returned to duty 10/22/63. WIA at Bermuda Hunded. Married Fannie Taylor Owen 11/10/70. Farmer and member of Halifax Co. Board of Supervisors. Died at Abell, Charlotte Co. in 1912.

DODSON, ALBERT J.: Pvt.; Co. C. WIA (gunshot in hand, slight) at Malvern Hill 7/1/62, and admitted Chimborazo Hosp., same date. Deserted 9/62.

DODSON, FELIX SHELBORNE: Born 12/15/23; enl. 10/14/64 at Danville; Pvt.; Co. A. POW at Dinwiddie C.H. 4/2/65. Sent to City Point and then to Pt. Lookout 4/4/65. Released there 6/11/65. Res. of Pittsylvania Co., iron grey hair, blue eyes, 6'¾". Died 9/12/76. Bur. Dodson. Clark Family Cem., west of Rt. 734 near Ringgold.

DODSON, HUGH A.: b. Pittsylvania Co.; enl. 5/30/61, at Laurel Grove; Sgt.; Co. C. Granted sick furlough for 20 days 9/20/61. Admitted Chimborazo Hosp. #5 3/30/62, with bronchitis. Granted furlough for 15 days 4/21/62, and returned by 5/10/62. KIA at Seven Pines 5/31/62.

DODSON, JAMES A.: enl. 5/30/61 at Laurel Grove; Pvt.; Co. C. Admitted Danville Hosp. 8/28/64, with abscess and furloughed from there for 60 days 12/1/64. Admitted Chimborazo Hosp. 2/25/65, with scrofula and furloughed from there 3/22/65. Bur. west of Rt. 912 near Laurel Grove.

DODSON, JOHN: Son of Elmira Dodson; enl. 5/30/61 at Laurel Grove; Pvt.; Co. C. KIA (shell fragment in head) at Seven Pines 5/31/62.

DODSON, JOHN A.: enl. 3/20/64, at Kentuck; Pvt.; Co. A. Present thru last muster roll dated 2/25/65.

DODSON, JOHN A.: b. in Pittsylvania Co. in 1839; enl. 6/27/61 at Richmond; Pvt.; Co. C. Issued medical discharge 3/28/62, due to consumption. Lt. complex., dk. hair, blue eyes, 6'0", age 22. Died in 1931. Bur. Chatham Cem.

DODSON, JOSEPH: enl. 6/2/61 at Cascade; Pvt.; in Co. K. Detailed as teamster 9/2/61. WIA at Malvern Hill 7/1/62. Discharged 9/62.

DODSON, JOSEPHUS B.: Pvt.; Co. C. In Richmond hosp. 5-6/62. WIA (leg amputated) and POW at Gettysburg 7/3/63. Died 7/6/63, due to primary shock of amputation.

DODSON, SILVANG: Pvt.; Co. C. Admitted Chimborazo Hosp. #2 4/14/62, with diarrhea. Died at home 4/28/62.

DODSON, TIMOTHY D.: enl. 5/30/61 at Laurel Grove; Pvt.; Co. C. Absent sick at home on 8/18/61 and in G. H. (location not stated) 2/27/62. Admitted Richmond G.H. #18 3/2/62, with chronic diarrhea. Returned to duty 3/26/62, but discharged due to disability 4/3/62.

DODSON, WILLIAM D.: enl. 3/12/62, at Laurel Grove; Pvt.; Co. C. Admitted Camp Winder Hosp. 4/4/63, with pneumonia. Admitted C.S.A. Hosp. Farmville 5/8/63, with rheumatism. POW at Bermuda Hundred 8/25/64. Sent to Ft. Monroe and then to Pt. Lookout 9/13/64. Died at USA Gen. Hosp. there 2/20/65, at age 39 of chronic diarrhea and scurvy.

DONNIVANT, HENRY: Pvt.; Co. G. WIA. Postwar record only.

DOOLEY, AUSTIN: enl. 3/18/62 at Danville; Pvt.; Co. E. Absent sick in hosp. 4-7/62.

DOOLEY, CARMILOUS W.: enl. 10/14/64, at Danville; Pvt. in Co. A. POW at Petersburg 4/2/65. Sent to City Point and then to Point Lookout 4/4/65. Released there 6/11/65. Res. of Pittsylvania Co. Lt. complex., dk. brown hair, brown eyes, 5'9-7/8".

DOOLEY, JESSE M.: enl. 5/30/61 at Laurel Grove; Pvt. in Co. C. WIA (gunshot in left shoulder, severe) at Seven Pines 5/31/62 and admitted Chimborazo Hosp. 6/1/62. Readmitted there 7/7/62 with gunshot wound of breast. Present by 4/1/64. Detailed as co. cook.

DOOLEY, SANDFORD D.: enl. 5/30/61 at Kentuck; Pvt. in Co. A. Died 8/12/61 of typhoid fever.

DOZIER, JAMES W.: enl. 3/15/62 in Norfolk Co.; Pvt. in 2nd Co. I. Assigned daily duty in ambulance corps prior to 8/31/64. Paroled at Appomattox CH on 4/9/65.

DRISKILL, CHARLES E.: enl. 10/31/61, in Appomattox Co.; Pvt in 2nd Co. I. WIA at Drewry's Bluff 5/16/64 and went home on furlough. Assigned to detached duty with Medical Dept. as cook at Division Hosp. prior to 12/31/64 and thru 2/25/65. Paroled at Appomattox CH(?) 4/9/65, listed on roll of enlisted men who were not present with their commands for parole, ... (but) ... paroled according to the terms of the surrender..."

DRISKILL, N. W.: enl. 3/6/62, in Appomattox Co., Pvt. in 2nd Co. I. Detailed as cook at Division Hosp. prior to 8/31/64.

DRISKILL, WILLIAM H.: enl. 4/15/64, in Henrico Co.; Pvt. in 2nd Co. I. Discharged due to being a deserter from the 11th Va. Regt. when he joined the Co. Returned to that regt. 7/6/64.

DUDLEY, CHISWELL: enl. 7/2/61, in Pittsylvania Co.; Pvt'; Co. H. Detailed as Co. cook 9/62. Prom. to 2nd Cpl. by 8/31/64 and to Sgt. by 2/26/65.

DUDLEY, G. T.: Pvt.; Co. H. WIA (slightly, spent ball struck leg) at White Pine (Seven Pines) near Richmond 5/31/62. Deserted 7/62.

DUFFIE, JAMES: Pvt.; Co. H. Postwar record only.

DUFFIE, WILLIAM T.: enl. 4/19/64, in Prince Edward Co.; Pvt.; Co. H. Deserted from Cold Harbor on or about 5/29/64, but apparently returned. Sent to hosp. prior to 12/31/64. Surrendered at Lynchburg in 4/65.

DUKE, JOHN M.: enl. 4/28/62, in Norfolk Co.; Pvt.; 2nd Co. I. Present thru last muster roll dated 12/31/64.

DUNN, JAMES: Pvt.; 1st Co. I. At home sick 10/61.

DUNN, JAMES M.: enl. 6/4/61, at Callands, age 20; Pvt.; Co. B. MWIA (gunshot in chest) at Malvern Hill 7/1/62. Died at Chimborazo Hosp. 7/8/62.

DUNN, SAMUEL B.: enl. 6/4/61, at Callands; Pvt.; Co. B. Prom. to 2nd Cpl. prior to 5/19/63. Apparently WIA (flesh wound in right thigh) at Drewry's Bluff 5/16/64 and admitted Chimborazo Hosp. on that date. Furloughed 6/16/64 for 40 days. Alive on 8/22/84.

DUNNWANT, HENRY: b. Mecklenburg Co. enl. 5/18/61, at Boydton; Pvt.; Co. G. Admitted Petersburg Hosp. 4/1/62, with bronchitis and returned to duty 4/24/62. WIA (gunshot in left hand) at Seven Pines 6/29/62, and admitted Chimborazo Hosp. 6/30/62. Detailed as nurse at Chimborazo #4 10/29/62. Given medical discharge there 2/4/63, due to epilepsy. Dk. complex. and hair, grey eyes, 5'7", age 22, farmer.

DURHAM, JAMES A.: b. 6/29/28; enl. 5/30/61, at Laurel Grove; Pvt.; Co. C. WIA (gunshot in left shoulder) 7/3/63 and POW at Gettysburg 7/4/63. Treated at U.S. XII Corps Hosp. and sent to Ft. McHenry, then to Ft. Delaware 7-12/63, and then to Pt. Lookout 10/27/63. Paroled there and sent to Aiken's Landing, Va. for exchange 9/18/64. Admitted Chimborazo Hosp. 9/22/64, for chronic diarrhea. Prom. to 4th Sgt. by 4/1/64 and to 3rd Sgt. by 8/31/64. Returned to duty by 2/25/65. Died 1/22/96. Bur. Green Hill Cem. (plot E37?) Danville.

DURHAM, JOHN H.: enl. 4/14/63, at Danville; Pvt.; Co. C. WIA (left hand) at Cold Harbor on or about 6/2/64 and admitted Chimborazo Hosp. 6/3/64. Returned to duty 8/2/64.

EANES, ROBERT: enl. 11/9/64, at Bermuda Hundred, Pvt.; Co. F. Deserted 1/10/65.

EANES, WILLIAM T.: enl. 5/24/61 at Whitmell; Pvt.; Co. D. Admitted Chimborazo Hosp. 5/11/62, with diarrhea and returned to duty 6/19/62. KIA at Gettysburg 7/3/63.

EARLES, HIRAM: enl. 6/2/61, at Cascade; Pvt.; Co. K. Admitted Chimborazo Hosp. on 5/28/62, with rheumatism and returned to duty 6/9/62. (CSR lists him as trans. to 57th Va. Inf. prior to 12/8/62, however there is no record of his having joined the 57th). CSR also lists him as died and dropped from roll in 9/62, which is apparently correct.

EARLES, ISAAC: enl. 6/2/61, at Cascade; Pvt.; Co. K. WIA at Seven Pines on 5/31/62. Died of those wounds and typhoid fever at Danville G.H. 7/2/62. Mother: Martha Earles.

EARLES, J.: Pvt.; Co. D. WIA (seriously) at Malvern Hill 7/1/62.

EARLES, JAMES G.: enl. 6/2/61, at Cascades; Pvt.; Co. K. Died at Richmond G.H. #12 on or about 3/4/62.

EARLES, RUFUS: enl. 6/20/61, at Clarksville; Pvt. in 1st Co. I. Admitted Danville Hosp. and sent to Chimborazo Hosp. No. 5 on 4/27/62 with dysentery.

EASLEY, HENRY W.: enl. 5/24/61, at Whitmell; Pvt.; Co. D. WIA (gunshot fracture of right thigh) and POW at Gettysburg on 7/3/63. Sent to West's Buildings Hosp. in Baltimore, then to Ft. McHenry 12/18/63, and then to Pt. Lookout on 1/24/64. Paroled and released there 2/14 or 15/65; and at Camp Lee by 2/17/65. POW at Fairground Post Hosp., Petersburg 4/3/65. Died there on 7/6/65, due to amputation of wounded right leg.

EASLEY, JAMES C.: enl. 5/24/61, at Whitmell; Pvt.; Co. D. WIA (fractured left arm) and POW at Gettysburg 7/3/63. Admitted Letterman G.H. at Gettysburg and then sent to West's Building Hosp. at Gettysburg 8/10/63 and to City Point for exchange on 11/12/63. Paroled and in Chimborazo Hosp. by 11/16/63, due to arm wound. Returned to Co., but then sick at Division Hosp. by 6/17/64. Returned and detailed as guard with Brigade Quartermaster prior to 12/31/64. Alive on 5/19/84.

EAST, JAMES D.: enl. 6/4/61, at Republic Grove; Pvt.; Co. F. Admitted Chimborazo Hosp. #3 on 10/22/61. Issued medical discharge 1/3/62, due to typhoid and pneumonia.

EATON, JOSEPH W.: enl. 7/2/61, at Pittsylvania C.H.; Sgt.; Co. H. Admitted Charlottesville Hosp. 3/10/62, with contusion. Furloughed 4/17/62, but returned to Co. by 7/14/62. Discharged 9/29/62, at Winchester for being over age, 35.

ECHART, JOB: enl. 4/28/64, at Pendleton Co., WVa.; Pvt.; Co. H. Conscript. POW at Five Forks 4/1/65. Sent to City Point and then to Hart's Island 4/7/65. Released there 6/21/65. Res. of Pendleton Co., W.Va.; dk. complx. and hair, black eyes, 5'6".

ECHOLS, JOSEPH W.: enl. 5/30/61, at Kentuck; Pvt.; Co. A. Medically discharged 9/25/61, due to consumption. Reenlisted 2/27/62, at Kentuck. Admitted Chimborazo Hosp. #5 on 5/3/62, with debility. Admitted Chimborazo Hosp. #4 6/4/62, with chronic diarrhea and returned to duty 7/62. Detailed as Co. cook. Paroled at Appomattox C.H. 4/9/65.

EDMONDS, EDWARD CLAXTON: b. 1/21/35, at Paris (Fauquier Co.); son of Dr. John Robert and Helen Carter Edmonds; graduated VMI 7/5/58; educator. Appointed Colonel of the 38th on 6/12/61, at Richmond. KIA leading the regiment in "Pickett's Charge" at Gettysburg on 7/3/63. Apparently buried in unmarked grave on the battlefield.

EDMONDS, JOSEPH W.: Born Pittsylvania Co.; enl. 6/4/61, at Republican Grove; Pvt.; Co. F. Sent to Lynchburg G.H. 10/25/61. Issued medical discharge 2/21/62, due to wound of left hand. Lt. complex. and hair, blue eyes, 5'11", age 24, farmer.

EDMONDS, WILLIAM BELL: b. 3/32 in Albemarle Co.; appointed Capt. 9/20/61. Present until dropped 5/27/63. Died 2/2/08. Bur. East Mount Cem., Greenville, Tenn.

EDMONDS, JAMES A.: enl. 10/14/64, at Danville; Pvt.; Co. D. POW at Five Forks 4/1/65. Sent to City Point and then to Pt. Lookout 4/6/65. Released there 6/26/65, but admitted to Pt. Lookout G. H. 7/28/65. Died there 7/15/65, due to chronic diarrhea. Res. of Pittsylvania Co., dk. complex. and hair, blue eyes, 5'8".

ELLIOTT, JOHN K.: enl. 6/8/61, at Danville; age 22; Pvt.; Co. E. MIA after Malvern Hill 7/1/62, but returned prior to 7/30/63. Paroled at Farmville between 4/11 and 21/65.

ELLIOTT, SAMUEL: enl. 10/14/64, at Danville; Pvt.; Co. D. Admitted to Chimborazo Hosp. 12/5/64, with chronic hepatitis. Trans. to Danville Hosp. 12/19/64 and deserted from there 1/6/65. Arrested in Barbour Co., WVa. 1/8/65 and returned to Danville Hosp. 1/14/65. Deserted from there 4/10/65. Florid complex., lt. hair, blue eyes, 5'7¼", age 59, farmer.

ELLIOTT, WILLIAM ANTHONY: Born 11/5/32; enl. 6/8/61, at Danville; Pvt.; Co. E. Admitted Danville Hosp. 5/6/62, with debilitas and returned to duty by 8/1/62. Admitted Danville Hosp. 8/30/62 and returned by 3/20/63. WIA (severely) at Gettysburg 7/3/63 and admitted Danville Hosp. for this wound 7/23/63. Returned to duty 1/5/64. Died 12/29/10. Bur. off Rt. 839 off Rt. 41 near Dry Fork.

ELLIS, F. M.: enl. 4/19/64, at Greenville; Pvt.; Co. H. Conscript. Admitted Chimborazo Hosp. 5/4/64, with carditis and bronchitis. Absent thru last roll dated 2/26/65.

EMERSON, JOHN D.: enl. 6/17/61, age 23; at Callands; Pvt.; Co. B. Sent to hosp. 2/27/62 and admitted Chimborazo Hosp. 3/4/62, with typhoid and pneumonia. Furloughed there 4/15/62 but returned by 7/62. Detailed as Co. cook.

EMMERSON, ELISHA W.: enl. 5/24/61, at Whitmell; Pvt.; Co. D. POW at Gettysburg 7/3/63. Sent to Ft. McHenry 7/6/63 and to Ft. Delaware 7/7-12/63. Took oath and released there 5/5/65. Res. of Pittsylvania Co., dk. complx. and hair, hazel eyes, 5'5".

EMMERSON, GEORGE C.: enl. 6/8/61 at Danville; Pvt.; Co. E. WIA (hand) at Williamsburg 5/5/62. CSR lists as deserting from camp near Richmond 5/63, but also indicates he was at Salisbury, N.C. undergoing sentence of General Court Martial. Age 34.

EPPERSON, PAUL: Born 7/16/30; enl. 3/14/62, at Replican Grove; Pvt.; Co. F. Admitted Chimborazo Hosp. 4/17/62. WIA (slightly) at Malvern Hill 7/1/62 and admitted Richmond Hosp. 7/3/62. Admitted Chimborazo Hosp. 3/10/65 with chronic diarrhea. Died 7/31/08. Bur. in family cem. on Rt. 647 near Republic Grove.

EPPERSON, SAMUEL: Son of Samuel Epperson; enl. 3/14/62, at Republican Grove; Pvt.; Co. F. Admitted Chimborazo Hosp. #5 5/1/62, with typhoid fever and died there 5/24/62.

ESTES, EDWARD H.: enl. 6/2/61, at Cascade; Pvt.; Co. K. Sent home on sick furlough 8/17/61. WIA at Seven Pines on 5/31/62 and admitted to hosp. Prom. to 3rd Sgt. and detailed as enrolling officer by 8/31/62. Elected 2nd Lt. by 12/18/64. Present thru last roll dated 12/31/64.

ESTES, JOSEPH H.: enl. 6/2/61, at Cascade; Pvt.; Co. K. Prom. to 5th Sgt. by 10/10/61, and to 1st Sgt. by 12/8/62. Elected 2nd Lt. by 1/13/62. WIA at Gettysburg 7/3/63 and admitted Danville Hosp. 7/20/63. Returned to duty by 9/18/63. Prom. to 1st Lt. on 12/17/64, and to Capt. in latter days of War.

EVANS, CHAMP T.: enl. 3/13/62, at Kentuck; Pvt.; Co. A. Admitted Farmville Hosp. 3/27/63, with dysentery, and deserted from there on 6/5/63. Returned to hosp. by 7/29/63, and to duty by 4/1/64.

EVANS, GEORGE W.: enl. 5/30/61, at Kentuck; Pvt.; Co. A. POW at Gettysburg 7/3/63. Sent to Ft. McHenry 7/6/63, to Ft. Delaware 7/7-12/63 and then to Pt. Lookout on 10/27/63. Died there on 11/19/63. Bur. at Pt. Lookout.

EVANS, GRIFFITH B.: enl. 5/31/61, at Kentuck; Pvt.; Co. A. Admitted hosp. 5/62.

EVANS, ISAAC S.: enl. 3/10/62, in Pittsylvania Co.; Pvt. (?) in Co. B. Died in Richmond hosp. 5/18/64, possibly from wounds sustained at Drewry's Bluff 5/16/64.

EVANS, JOHN W.: enl. 5/18/61, at Boydton; Pvt.; Co. G. Admitted Chimborazo Hosp. #4 10/28/61, with debility and dropsy. Issued medical discharge 11/9/61, for ascites.

EVANS, JOSIAH: Pvt.; Co. A. Died at Gordonsville Hosp. 3/20/62, of typhoid fever.

EVANS, ROBERT H.: enl. 5/30/61, at Kentuck; Pvt.; Co. A. WIA at Seven Pines 5/31/62. Returned to duty as Brigade Provost Guard by 8/62. WIA (gunshot in back and shoulder) 7/3 and POW 7/5/63, at Gettysburg. Paroled at West's Building Hosp., Baltimore 8/23/63. Arrived at City Point on 8/24/63 and returned to duty prior to 4/1/64. Detailed as ambulance driver by 10/12/64. Paroled at Appomattox C.H. 4/9/65. Alive at Chatham on 6/22/82.

EVANS, WILLIAM M.: enl. 3/13/62 at Kentuck; Pvt.; Co. A. Admitted Richmond Hosp. 5-8/62. WIA (gunshot in leg) 7/3 and POW 7/5/63, at Gettysburg. Paroled at West's Buildings Hosp., Baltimore 8/23/62. Arrived at City Point 8/24/63 and sent to Pettigrew G. H. #13, Raleigh, N.C. thru 11/26/64, due to stiffening right leg. Returned to duty by 12/6/64. Admitted Chimborazo Hosp. 1/6/65, but returned to duty by 3/28/65. Paroled at Appomattox C.H. 4/9/65. Alive at Chatham 6/22/82.

EVERETT, CHARLES: enl. 7/6/61, at Norfolk; Cpl.; 2nd Co. I. Admitted Chimborazo Hosp.

FACKLER, JEREMIAH W.: enl. 7/2/61, at Pittsylvania C.H.; Pvt.; Co. H. Asent on sick leave 8/19-12/61. Admitted Chimborazo Hosp. 6/23/62 and trans. to Danville Hosp. on 7/26/62. Still absent sick on last record 9/62.

FARGUS, JOSEPH T.: Born Henrico Co.; enl. 6/8/61, at Danville; Pvt.; Co. E. Discharged 12/1/61, due to old age, 57. Fair complex., sandy hair, blue eyes, 6'0", farmer.

FARGUSSON, JAMES M.: enl. 5/24/61, at Whitmell; Pvt.; Co. D. POW at Gettysburg 7/3/63. Sent to Ft. McHenry 7/6/63, then to Ft. Delaware 7/7-12/63, and to Pt. Lookout 10/27/63. Joined U.S. service there on 1/29/64, and released.

FARIS, WILLIAM S.: enl. 5/24/61, at Whitmell; Pvt.; Co. D. Absent on sick leave on 8/12/61. Discharged on Surgeon's Certificate of disability 1/27/62, by order of Brig. Gen. Wilcox.

FARMER, SAMUEL J(OHN?): enl. 5/2/64, at Pittsylvania CH; Pvt.; Co. H. Conscript. Admitted Chimborazo Hosp. #5 8/3/64, with chronic diarrhea. Admitted Chimborazo Hosp. #2 12/15/64 with hemorrhage of lungs. POW in Richmond hosp. 4/3/65. Paroled 4/24/65. Escaped hosp. 4/25/65.

FARRIS, JOHN: Pvt.; Co. D. Issued medical discharge 1/26/62, due to lung disease.

FARSON, STEPHEN: Born Pittsylvania Co.; enl. 5/30/61, at Laurel Grove; Sgt.; Co. C. Sent to Chimborazo Hosp. 10/24/61 and returned to duty 11/25/61, issued medical discharge on 12/17/61 due to general debility. Fair complex., grey eyes, red hair, 5'10", age 33, farmer.

FARTHING, JAMES: enl. 7/2/61, at Pittsylvania C.H.; Pvt.; Co. H. Sent to Manassas Hosp. 1/22/62, and Richmond Hosp. 6/15/62. WIA at Gettysburg 7/3/63 and admitted Danville Hosp. with wounds 7/16/63. Returned to duty 8/18/63.

FARTHING, JOHN C.: enl. 7/2/61 at Pittsylvania C.H.; Pvt.; Co. H. Admitted Orange C.H. Gen. Hosp. 12/6/61, for intermittent fever. WIA at Seven Pines 5/31/62, and admitted Chimborazo Hosp. on 6/1/62, with "slight contused wound of scalp." Sent to Wilmington, NC as nurse for yellow fever patients 10/5/62, and died there of disease 10/20/62. Widow: Nancy T. Farthing.

FERGUSON, HENRY: enl. 7/6/61 in Norfolk Co.; Musician in 2nd; Co. I. POW at Petersburg 4/2/65. Sent to City Point and then to Pt. Lookout 4/13/65. Released there 6/12/65. Res. of Richmond, lt. complex., black hair, dk. hazel eyes, 5'5".

FERGUSON, ISAAC H.: enl. 3/7/62, at Danville; Pvt.; Co. E. Absent sick in hosp. 4-7/62. Died in Petersburg Hosp. during 8 or 9/62. Bur. Oakwood Cem., Richmond.

FERGUSON, JOHN A.: Born Pittsylvania Co.; enl. 10/14/64, at Danville; Pvt.; Co. A. Admitted Chimborazo Hosp. 3/26/65, with wound in left hand. Paroled 4/25/65, at Headqtrs., 2nd Div., 6th Corps. Lived in Danville and Camp Lee Soldiers Home, Richmond. Died 6/21/12, at age 87. Bur. Hollywood Cem. (East sec.), Richmond.

FERGUSON, JOHN J.: enl. 6/8/61, age 36, at Danville; Pvt.; Co. E. Admitted Richmond Hosp. 11/23/61. Admitted Petersburg Hosp. 1/11/62 with pneumonia. Returned to duty 1/24/62. Died at Falling Creek 8/26/62. Widow: Julia H. Ferguson.

FERRELL, BENJAMIN F.: enl. 3/4/62, at Danville; Pvt.; Co. E. Admitted Chimborazo Hosp. 4/21/62, with diarrhea and then sent to Camp Winder 5/12/62. Absent thru 7/62. Died at Danville Hosp. 9/6/62, with epilepsy. Mother: Frances Ferrell.

FERRELL, EPAPRODITUS T.: enl. 5/30/61, at Laurel Grove; Pvt.; Co. C. Detailed as Commissary Sgt.; 7/15-8/6/61, and then acted as commissary officer for Regt. until 8/30/61. Admitted Chimborazo Hosp. 10/26/61, with debility. Detailed as Wardmaster at Chimborazo Hosp. 1/28/62-6/3/63 by Secretary of War (spl. order #22).

FERRELL, JAMES M.: enl. 5/30/61, at Kentuck; Pvt.; Co. A. Detailed as teamster 1/12/62 and as ambulance driver 2/62. Admitted Chimborazo Hosp. #3 4/14/62, wounded. Trans. to Lynchburg Hosp. 6/1/62. Admitted Chimborazo Hosp. 2/16/63 with diarrhea. Admitted Danville G.H. 3/14/63, with rheumatism, but returned to duty 4/10/63. 24 yrs. old in 1863. Probably WIA (right shoulder) at Drewry's Bluff 5/16/64. Admitted Howard's Grove Gen. Hosp.; Richmond 5/17/64. Returned to duty by 8/30/64.

FERRELL, JOSEPH B.: occ. harness maker; enl. 6/8/61; at Danville; Pvt.; Co. E. Assigned detached service at Bridade Headqtrs. 7-8/64 and returned prior to 12/31/64.

FERRELL, WILLIAM H.: enl. 8/30/62, at Kentuck or Danville; Pvt.; Co. A. Admitted Chimborazo Hosp. 11/5/62, with anemia and furloughed for 30 days 11/20/62. Admitted Danville Hosp. 1/2/63 with rheumatism, chronic diarrhea and dropsy. Returned to duty by 10/20/63.

FERRIS, JOHN: enl. 10/15/64, in Pittsylvania Co.; Pvt.; Co. H. Deserted and captured by Federals near Bermuda Hundred 1/10/65. Took oath in Washington, D.C. 1/15/65 and trans. furnished to Charleston, W.Va.

FIELD, JOHN S., JR.: Appointed 1st Lt.; 1st Co. I 7/1/61. Failed to be reelected 4/29/62. (Sgt. Joseph S. Yancey, elected 1st Lt.)

FINCH, GEORGE ALLEN: enl. 3/13/62, at Kentuck; Pvt.; Co. A. WIA (right eye shot out) at Malvern Hill 7/1/62. Admitted Danville Hosp. 3/23/63, with debilitas and returned by 7/1/63. AWOL as of 4/1-10/12/64, last roll.

FINCH, JOHN B.: enl. 8/10/63 at Camp Lee; Pvt.; Co. C. Detailed as teamster 11/1-12/9/63.

FINCH, MARCELLUS L.: enl. 3/13/62, at Kentuck; Pvt.; Co. A. Admitted Chimborazo 4/14/62 and returned by 6/2/62. Trans. to Co. C prior to 12/31/64. Admitted Chimborazo 3/5/65.

FINCH, NATHANIEL B.: enl. 5/30/61, at Laurel Grove; Pvt.; Co. C. WIA (slightly) at Chester Station 5/10/64. Paroled at Appomattox C.H. 4/9/65.

FINCH, WILLIAM R.: enl. 5/30/61 at Laurel Grove; Pvt.; Co. C. Died near Centreville 9/7/61 with typhoid fever. Lt. complex. and hair, 5'6".

FITCHETT, WILLIAM D.: enl. 2/25/62, in Norfolk Co.; Pvt.; 2nd Co. I. Deserted to the enemy at Bermuda Hundred 12/27/64. Took oath 12/29/64, and sent to Provost Marshall General in Washington, D.C. 1/3/65. Trans. furnished to Norfolk.

FITTS, TANDY W.: enl. 10/14/64, at Danville. Pvt.; Co. D. Present thru last roll dated 2/25/65. Paroled 4/25/65, at "Headquarters 2nd Div., 6th Corps."

FITZGERALD, THOMAS B.: enl. 5/30/61, at Kentuck; Pvt.; Co. A. Admitted Richmond Gen. Hosp. 10/24/61, and issued medical discharge 10/28/61.

FORBES, WILLIAM A.: enl. 10/14/64, at Danville; Pvt.; Co. C. WIA (slightly in left side) in trenches near Bermuda Hundred and sent to Chimborazo Hosp. #1 on 12/13/64. Trans. to Danville Hosp. 12/20/64, and returned to duty 3/7/65. Returned to Danville Hosp. 4/5/65.

FORTUNE, ROBERT C.: Son of Joel Fortune of Albemarle Co.; enl. 6/2/61, at Cascade; Pvt.; Co. K. Prom. to 3rd Cpl. by 9/17/61. KIA at Seven Pines 5/31/62.

FOSSETT, THOMAS: enl. 5/1/64, at Boydton; Pvt.; Co. G. Deserted 11/14/64.

FOSTER, ANDERSON: b. Bledsoe Co., Tenn.; enl. 10/6/63, age 25, at Richmond; Pvt.; Co. A. Dk. complex., hazel eyes, dk. hair, 5'10", farmer.

FOSTER, JOHN: enl. 5/4/64, at Rockingham. Conscript. Deserted from Hanover Junction 5/20/64.

FOSTER, WILLIAM: Pvt.; Co. A 10/6/63, Richmond; 24 at time of enlistment. Hazel eyes, lt. hair, lt. complex., 5'8", born Bledsoe Co., Tenn., a farmer.

FOUNTAIN, ROBERT B.: Pvt.; Co. D 10/14/64 Danville; present until POW White Oak Road 4/1/65; City Pt. to Pt. Lookout 4/5/65; died and bur. there 5/22/65, chronic diarrhea.

FOUST, BOLLING G.: Pvt.; Co. B 3/10/62 Callands; present until POW Gettysburg 7/3/63; Ft. McHenry 7/6/63 to Ft. Del. 7/7-12/63. Died of small pox and bur. Pt. Lookout 11/17/63.

FOUST, FOUNTAIN J.: Pvt.; Co. B 3/10/62 Callands; present until WIA, (g.s.w. leg) and POW Gettysburg 7/5/63; paroled West's Building Hosp., Balt. 8/23/63 delivered to City Pt. 8/24/63. Returned home on sick leave; admitted Chimborazo #5 3/5/65 wound left leg, frac. of tibia, POW in hosp., Richmond 4/3/65, turned over to Provost Marshal 4/14/65. Alive at Chatham 7/17/82.

FOWLER, JOSEPH L.: Co. B. Pvt.; Post war record only.

FOWLKES, GEORGE W.: Pvt.; Co. D (no date). Absent, sent to hosp. in Richmond 6/3/62; died Chimborazo #4, 6/13/62 diarrhea (acute) and catarrh.

FOX, MICHAEL: Pvt.; Co. H 10/14/64 Pittsylvania. Absent, detailed as teamster with Div. Supply Train prior to 12/3/64. Paroled Appomattox 4/9/65.

FRANCIS, WILLIAM: Pvt.; Co. F 12/4/63 near Nestor, N.C. Present until died 7/10/64 at Chester Hosp., cause not given. Born Halifax.

FROST, WILLIAM WASHINGTON: Born 8/2/40. Corpl.; 2nd. Co. I 2/25/62 Norfolk Co.; Present until deserted, captured and forwarded to Pro. Marshal office Suffolk, Va. 4/3/65. Died 5/13/98.

FULLER, BERRYMAN: Pvt.; Co. B 3/10/62 Callands; present until POW Gettysburg 7/3/63; Ft. McHenry 7/6/63 to Ft. Del. 7/7-12/63; died there 9/25/63 remittent fever. Bur. Finn's Point, N.J.

FULLER, DANIEL M.: Pvt.; Co. B 6/4/61 Callands; present until WIA Seven Pines 5/31/62; admitted Danville G.H. 6/4/62 wounded, died at home of same, 7/16/62 death reported on hosp. register 8/20/62.

FULLER, F. BRITTAIN: Pvt.; Co. B 6/4/61 Callands; present except AWOL. 1 month pay deducted accordingly dated 5/19/63; present until POW Gettysburg 7/4/63 while serving as nurse; Ft. McHenry 9/12/63 to Pt. Lookout 9/16/63; took oath and released to join U.S. services 1/29/64. Possibly bur. Finn's Pt. Nat'l. Cem., N.J.

FULLER, HENRY B.: Pvt.; Co. B 3/10/62 Callands; extra duty as teamster Iron Depot 3/62. Pvt. to 3 Sgt. 9/1/64; present until POW Gettysburg 7/3/63; Ft. McHenry 7/6/63 to Ft. Del. 7/7-12/63; to Pt. Lookout 10/27/63 to Hammond G.H. 11/6/63; paroled there and sent to Maj. J. E. Mulford for exchange 3/3-6/64. Returned to duty prior to 10/13/64; present until POW Five Forks 4/1/65; City Pt. to Hart's Island 4/7/65; released there 6/21/65; res. Pittsylvania; dk. complex., blk. hair, blk. eyes, 5'9".

FULLER, HENRY C.: Pvt.; Co. B 3/10/62; present until admitted Chimborazo 4/14/62; trans. to Danville Hosp. 4/30/62; acute diarrhea, returned to duty 6/18/62. Died Winder Hosp., Richmond 8/5/62. Bur. Hollywood Cem., Richmond. Father Absalom Fuller.

FULLER, JOSIAH E.: Sgt.; Co. B 6/4/61 Callands; Pvt. to 4 Sgt. 7/1/62; present from enlist. to WIA Seven Pines 5/31/62; returned to be POW Gettysburg 7/3/63; Ft. McHenry 7/6/63 to Ft. Del. 7/7-12/63; to Hammond G.H. at Pt. Lookout, Md. 11/21/63; died and bur. there 1/1/64 chronic diarrhea, age 25.

FULLER, RALEIGH W.: Pvt.; Co. B 6/17/61 Callands; present until discharged 9/4/62 on account of age; reenlisted [or conscripted] 10/6/64 Pittsylvania; Present until POW South Side RR 4/2/65; City Pt. to Hart's Island 4/7/65; released there 6/21/65; res. Pittsylvania Co., dk. complx., dk. hair, grey eyes, 6'1".

FULLER, WADDY THOMPSON: Pvt.; Co. B 3/10/62 Callands; present until admitted Danville G.H. 5/5/62 debilitas; returned to duty 8/20/62. Detailed as cook 9/62; paroled Appomattox 4/9/65.

FULTON, JAMES S.: Pvt.; Co. D 10/14/64 Danville. Present until paroled Appomattox 4/9/65.

FULTON, JOHN K.: Pvt.; Co. D 10/14/64 Danville; present until admitted Chimborazo #1 3/19/65; POW in Hospitals Richmond 4/3/65; sent to Pt. Lookout; admitted Pt. Lookout G.H. 5/6/65, chronic diarrhea. Discharged from service. Res. Pittsylvania Co., dark complex., dk. hair, grey eyes, 5'11".

FUNKHOUSER, JAMES D.: Pvt./musician; Co. F 6/4/61 Republican Grove; admitted Chimborazo Hosp. 8/28/62 bilous fever; 1st listed as Musician 7/1/63; present until paroled Appomattox 4/9/65.

FURLINES, GEORGE: Pvt.; 1st Co. I 2/20/62 Clarksville; present until left at Orange C.H. service 4/7/62 and admitted Charlottesville G.H. 4/16/62 measles; returned to duty 6/9/62 [also listed as rubeola].

FURLINES, J. R. (possibly Robert): Corpl.; 1st Co. I 6/20/61 Danville; [note: in remarks, states Pvt. to Sgt. 4/30/62, but, headings all 1st Furlines as Corpl.]; absent, admitted Danville G.H. 1/22/62; listed as sick since 2/28/62; returned, sent to Hosp. from Yorktown 4/26/62. Returned to duty, admitted Danville 6/2/62 shell wounds; returned to duty 6/9/62.

GAINES, GEORGE W.: Musician; 2nd Co. I 3/12/62 Richmond; absent, on detached service at Brigade Band, roll dated 12/31/64 through last roll dated 2/25/65.

GAINES, ROBERT R.: Pvt.; Co. E 6/8/61 Danville; WIA slightly 7/1/62 Malvern Hill; returned. Pres. until WIA (neck) 5/7/64; Chimborazo Hosp. 5/16/64; returned to duty 10/21/64, age 38; paroled Appomattox 4/9/65. Occupation machinist.

GAINES, THOMAS: Pvt.; Co. E 10/14/64 Danville. Present until surrendered and paroled at Appomattox 4/9/65.

GAMMON, ELISHA: Pvt.; Co. H 10/14/64 Pittsylvania; present through last roll dated 2/26/65.

GAMMON, GEORGE E.: Co. K. Pvt.; D. Post-war record only.

GAMMON, HARRIS E.: Pvt.; Co. K 6/2/61 Cascade; present until admitted Chimborazo 10/23/61 intermittent fever; returned 12/3/61; admitted Richmond G.H. #18 3/2/62 diarrhea; died there 5/29/62 phthisit pulmonalis.

GAMMON, H. J.: Pvt.; Co. H 10/14/64 Pittsylvania; present until POW Five Forks 4/1/65; Harts Island, no date; died there 6/8/65 chronic diarrhea.

GAMMON, JAMES A.: Pvt.; Co. K 6/2/61 Cascade; present until WIA, right arm and hand at Drewry's Bluff 5/16/64; admitted Chimborazo. Furloughed 60 days from 5/28/64; absent through 2/25/65 when admitted Chimborazo, v.s. right arm. Lived at Bachelors Hall, Pittsylvania Co. and Camp Lee Soldiers Home, Richmond. Died 1/1/13 at age 83. bur. Hollywood Cem., east sec., Richmond.

GAMMON, JOSEPH A.: Pvt.; Co. K 4/14/64 Cascade; died at Div. Hosp. 7/64 and dropped.

GAMMON, LEVI J.: 3 Sgt.; Co. K 6/2/61 Cascade; present until admitted Chimborazo #3 10/23/61 chronic rheumatism; Surgeon's Certificate of Discharge there 11/1/61 chronic rheumatism. Re-enlisted Co. I, 57th Va.

GARDNER, JOSEPH L.: 2 Lieut.; Co. A 5/30/61 Kentuck; 4th Sgt. to 1st Sgt. by 4/1/64, present from enlist. until WIA, (slightly) Malvern Hill 7/1/62; admitted Chimborazo 7/3/62 (gunshot flesh wound of back;) elected 2 Lieut. 10/4/64; surrendered by Lee at Appomattox 4/9/65.

GARDNER, WILLIAM B.: Pvt.; Co. A 5/30/61 Kentuck; absent, unable to report for duty, roll dated 8/31/61; admitted Chimborazo 4/14/62; medical discharge 4/14/62, consumption.

GARNER, JAMES W.: Pvt.; 2nd Co. I 2/25/62 Bedford; present on extra duty as a tailor, roll dated 12/31/64.

GARNER, JOHN L.: Pvt.; 1st Co. I 3/19/62 Clarksville; died at Orange Co. Hosp. 4/12/62.

GARNER, T. M. D.: Sgt.; 1st Co. I 6/20/61 Clarksville; pres. until sent to Orange Co. Hosp. 4/7/62; Corpl. to Sgt. 4/30/62.

GARNER, WILLIAM G.: Pvt.; Co. G 3/10/62 Boydton; pres. until sent to hosp. in Richmond on account of sickness, roll dated 7/16/62.

GARRETT, J. E.: Pvt.; 1st Co. I 3/11/62 Clarksville; present until sent to Chimborazo from Orange Co. Hosp. 4/7/62; admitted Chimborazo 4/11/62; returned to duty 6/2/62.

GARRETT, J. W.: Pvt.; 1st Co. I 3/18/62 Clarksville; pres. until admitted Chimborazo 5/10/62 remittent fever; returned to duty 6/6/62; sent to Richmond Hosp. 6/20/62.

GARROTT or GARRETT, WILLIAM T.: Pvt.; 2nd Co. I 7/6/61 Norfolk Co.; trans. to 38th from St. Bride's Heavy Artillery 5/4/64; present until admitted Chimborazo 8/4/64; died there of debility and chronic dysentery 10/9/64. bur. Oakwood Cem., Richmond.

GARTON, JAMES H.: Pvt.; Co. H 3/19/63 Orange C.H.; present until WIA severely leg and POW Gettysburg 7/3/63; to Balt. West Bldgs. Hosp.; paroled 9/27/63; to be transferred to City Pt.; admitted Richmond G.H. #9 9/29/63; nature of wound — "Ball enter below and in front of the tibia and passing through the leg." Operation 9/30/63, removed diseased portion; age 21 at time of operation; farmer, retired from active duty 1/27/65; on list of Invalid Corps, P.A.C.S.; detailed as a guard, Lynchburg 2/24/65.

GAULDEN, JABEZ S.: Pvt.; Co. B 6/4/61 Callands; Gen. Hosp. Richmond 3/2/62, diarrhea. Present until killed at Gettysburg 7/3/63. Widow Cynthia A. Gauldin.

GAULDIN, JOHN J.: Corpl.; Co. K 6/2/61 Cascade; present until absent in hosp. wounded as of 4/1/64; Danville Hosp. wound right hand 7/27/64; detailed by Med. Ex. Bd. for light duty with Brig. Quarter Master prior to 12/31/64; admitted Chimborazo #3 3/29/65 feb. intern; POW in Richmond hosps. 4/3/65; admitted Jackson Hosp., Rich. 4/8/65 then trans. from Libby Prison Richmond to Newport News 4/23/65; took oath 7/1/65; res. Pitts Co., fair complex., lt. hair, blue eyes, 5'8".

GAULDIN, WILLIAM: enl. 3/10/62 at Cascade; Pvt. Co. K. Admitted Chimborazo #2 3/30/62 with pleurisy and returned to duty 8/8/62. Admitted Farmville Hosp. 4/18/63 with rheumatism and returned duty 5/22/63. POW at Amelia C.H. 4/2/65. Sent to City Point and to Point Lookout 4/13/65. Released there 6/27/65. Res. of Pittsylvania Co. Dk. complex., dk. brown hair, blue eyes, 5'10".

GAULDING, JAMES H.: Pvt.; Co. D 5/24/61 Whitmell; present until WIA on Chickahominy 5/31/62; admitted Danville G.H. 6/15/62 wounded; reported deserted 7/7/62 but returned to duty 7/14/62; absent, detailed as Div. Prov. Guard 3/63-12/29/64 when returned to Co., deserted 2/23/65 to Pittsylvania Co.

GAULDING, JOHN D. H.: Pvt.; Co. D 3/30/64 Danville, Va.; conscript, present until deserted to Pittsylvania Co. 2/23/65.

GAULDING, JOHN F.: Pvt., Co. D 3/30/64 Danville; conscript, present until admitted Chimborazo #2 5/4/64 rubeola, transferred Danville Hosp. 5/7/64, debilitis deserted there 5/9/64; returned 12/19/64; present until POW White Oak Road 4/1/65; City Pt. to Pt. Lookout 4/4/65; rieleased there 6/27/65; res. Pitts Co., dk. complx., dk. bro. hair, blue eyes, 5'11".

GAULDING, SAMUEL H.: Pvt., Co. D, no date; admitted Richmond G.H. #18, Greaner's Hosp. 5/2/62 rubeola. Died there 5/13/62 rubeola and typhoid fever, both mentioned as cause.

GAULDING, WILLIAM D.: Pvt.; Co. H 7/2/61 Pitts. C.H.; present until sent to Richmond Hosp. sick, 6/62; remained absent sick through 9/62 when discharged 9/23/62, no cause given.

GIBBS, JOSEPH W.: Pvt.; Co. K 6/2/61 Cascade; 6/8/62 CSA Hosp. Danville, debility; present until killed Gettysburg 7/3/63. Dropped from roll.

GIBBS, ROBERT H.: Pvt.; Co. K 1/22/64 Cascade; conscript. Present until paroled, dated headquarters 2nd Div., 6th Corps., 4/25/65, list dated 5/4/65.

GIBSON, CURTIS: Pvt.; Co. D 6/15/61 Whitmell; died 8/27/61 typhoid fever; near Centerville.

GIBSON, HARRISON H.: Pvt.; Co. B 6/4/61 Callands; present, WIA slightly 7/1/62 Malvern Hill; present until POW Gettysburg 7/3/63; Ft. McHenry 7/6/63 to Ft. Del. 7/7-12/63; to Pt. Lookout 10/27/63; joined U.S. service and released 1/29/64.

GIBSON, HENRY CLAY: Pvt.; Co. B 6/4/61 Callands; present until sent to Richmond Hosp. 10/25/61; returned, medically discharged from camp near Centerville 11/19/61; consumption. Born Pitts. Co.; age 19, 5'11", dk. hair, dk. eyes, dk. complex., a farmer.

GIBSON, JOHN T.: 1st Lieut.; Co. C 5/30/61 Laurel Grove. Present, clerk for adjutant 9/62, elected 2 Lieut. from Pvt. 6/15/63; promoted 1st Lieut. 7/3/63; WIA left foot at Gettysburg; present until admitted Richmond G.H. #4 7/17/63 v.s. left foot; listed as deserted 10/19/63, but admitted Danville hosp. 10/8/63. Returned to duty 12/6/63 Gen. Hosp. Richmond; mercurial salivation, debility 11/4/64; POW near Richmond 4/3/65; Libby Prison 4/5/65 to Old Capitol Prison 4/11/65 to POW Depot Sandusky, Ohio 4/24/65 to Johnson's Island, no date. Released there 6/18/65; res. Danville, age 47; dk. complx., dk. hair, grey eyes, 6'0".

GIBSON, THOMAS P.: Sgt.; Co. B 6/4/61 Callands, present until died camp near Bull Run 1/6/62, typhoid fever.

GIBSON, WILLIAM J. W.: Pvt.; Co. B 6/19/61 Callands; present until admitted Chimborazo #3 10/23/61 chronic rheumatism, medically discharged for same 11/1/61.

GILBERT, CORNELIUS: Pvt.; Co. D 5/24/61 Whitmell; Pvt. to Color Corpl. by 7/62; WIA, mortally 7/1/62 Malvern Hill; carrying the colors. Died Chimborazo #2 7/3/62 g.s.w. of head. 5'7", dk. complex., grey eyes, dk. hair, farmer; born Pittsylvania Co. Father Preston Gilbert.

GILCHRIST, ALEXANDER: Pvt.; Co. G 5/18/61 Boydton; present until WIA slightly 5/31/62 Malvern Hill; admitted Gen. Hosp. #21, Richmond 6/4/62; returned 7/15/62; killed in battle near Sharpsburg 9/62.

GILES, GARRET: Pvt.; Co. H 7/2/61 Pittsylvania C.H.; listed as honorably discharged 8/17/61 and also on report of sick and wounded, having died of consumption same date 8/17/61.

GILES, GEORGE W.: Pvt.; Co. D 8/21/62 Danville; present until listed as sick in Danville Hosp. 8/62-12/31/64; absent, on detail at Danville hosp. by order of Med. Ex. Bd. by 2/25/65.

GILES, THOMAS H.: Pvt.; Co. B 6/6/61 Callands; present until sent to Richmond hosp. 10/25/61; admitted Chimborazo 10/23/61; medically discharged there 11/1/61 chronic rheumatism.

GILL, J. O.: Pvt.; Co. H, no date; paroled 4/9/65 Appomattox, no other information.

GILL, JOHN R.: Pvt.; Co. G 3/6/62 Boydton; present until sent to hosp., Richmond 5/1/62-5/7/63. Returned by 4/1/64; admitted Chimborazo #4 5/14/64, rheumatism chronic, returned to duty 7/11/64; present until paroled Appomattox 4/9/65.

GILL, THOMAS J.: 1 Sgt.; Co. G 5/18/61 Boydton; present until admitted Danville Hosp. 12/16/62 debilitas; supposed to report for duty 1/26/63 but muster roll doesn't have him reporting until 4/14/63; POW and WIA g.s. right leg, ankle Gettysburg 7/3/63, 7/19/63; treated at U.S. XII Corps. Hosp. from College Hosp. Gettysburg to Balt., Md. to Gen. Hosp., Chester, Pa. 7/31/63 to Hammond G.H. Pt. Lookout 10/4/63; paroled there and exchanged 3/6/64; returned home; retired by Med. Ex. Bd. 12/19/64.

GILLEY, D. J.: Pvt.; Co. K 5/19/64 Henry Co., Va.; conscript; present until entered Chimborazo #7 7/18/64; dysentery, died Chimborazo #4 7/30/64 typhoid fever. b. Oakwood Cem., Richmond.

GILLEY, HAYGOOD: Pvt.; Co. H 4/30/64 Henry Co., conscript. WIA Drewry's Bluff 5/16/64; entered Chimborazo #5 5/16/64; to Danville 10/22/64 v.s. right knee; there deserted 11/9/64; absent, returned to div. hosp. at Chester Station by 2/26/65; surrendered by Lee 4/65 Lynchburg. According to CSR.

GLASGOW, ASA H.: Pvt.; Co. A 10/14/64 Danville; present through last roll dated 2/25/65.

GLASS, JOHN B.: Pvt.; Co. C 10/14/64 Danville; present until deserted 1/12/65 to Danville.

GODFREY, JARVIS K.: Pvt.; 2nd Co. I 6/26/61 Norfolk Co.; present until deserted to Federals 2/20/65; oath taken Bermuda Hundred 2/21/65; trans. furnished to Norfolk, Va.

GODFREY, WILLIAM J.: Pvt.; 2nd Co. I 6/26/61 Norfolk; present until admitted Chimborazo #9 5/6/64 gonorrhoea; returned by 8/31/64; POW Farmville; 4/6/65; City Pt. to Newport News 4/14/65; oath taken there 6/25/65; res. Norfolk Co., dk. complex., dk. hair, blue eyes, 5'7". d. 1/89 Norfolk.

GOLD, CHARLES T.: Pvt.; 1st Co. I 6/20/61 Clarksville; present until admitted Charlottesville hosp. 1/7/62 pneumonia; returned to duty 2/11/62; listed as missing after battle Malvern Hill 7/1/62.

GOLD (or GOULD), JOHN B.: Born 2/9/35. Pvt.; 1st Co. I. Born 2/9/35 6/20/61 Clarksville, present. Died 1/25/21, bur. Buffalo Bapt. Ch. Cem., Mecklenburg Co.

GOLD, WILLIAM: Pvt.; 1st Co. I 6/20/61 Clarksville; present until admitted Chimborazo #2 3/30/62 catarrhal fever; returned to duty 7/29/62.

GOODE, WILLIAM W.: Pvt.; Co. D 5/24/61 Whitmell; Pvt. to Sgt. by 5/62; killed in action in Chickahominy 5/31/62, Seven Pines. Occupaton Smith

GOODMAN, JOHN H.: Pvt.; Co. D 3/1/62 Whitmell; present until entered Chimborazo #3 4/13/62; died there 5/24/62, cause not listed. Bur. Oakwood Cem., Richmond.

GOODMAN, SILAS: Pvt.; Co. K 3/6/62 Cascade; present until admitted Chimborazo #3 4/17/62; trans. to Danville hosp. 5/9/62; rubeola; returned to duty 8/15/62; present through 2/25/65, last roll dated.

GORDON, CHARLES G.: Pvt.; 1st Co. I 3/10/62 Clarksville; present until detailed to Orange Co. Hosp. to attend sick 4/7/62.

GORDON, JOHN C.: Asst. Surgeon; F & S. Appointed Asst. Sur. 6/12/61; present until resigned 11/6/61. Res. Albemarle.

GORMAN, W. B.: Co. A. Pvt.; Discharged. Post war record only.

GOSNEY, GEORGE H.: Pvt.; Co. E 6/8/61 Danville; absent, left at Winchester 7/61 as Co. marched for Manassas; to be discharged, disability by 11/61 but papers hand't been properly signed at time, no other information.

GOSNEY, JAMES L.: Pvt.; Co. A 5/30/61 Kentuck; present until WIA g.s.w. thigh and POW Gettysburg 7/3/63, paroled at DeCamp G. H., David's Island 8/24/63.

GOVER, JAMES M.: Pvt.; Co. E 10/14/64 Danville; present until POW Petersburg 4/2/65; City Pt. to Pt. Lookout 4/4/62; released there 6/27/65; res. Henry Co., dk. complex., dk. bro. hair, blue eyes, 6'0".

GRAHAM, JOHN B. (possibly BRAIDY): Pvt.; 2nd Co. I 3/13/62 Norfolk Co.; present until WIA 5/16/64 at Drewry's Bluff then admitted to Chimborazo #4 9/1/64 with g.s.w. of left shoulder; returned to duty 9/20/64; had been a guard in Richmond. Paroled at Libby Prison, Richmond 4/23/65. Probably died in 1888 in Norfolk.

GRAHAM, TILDSLEY: Pvt.; 2nd Co. I 7/6/61 Norfolk Co. Detailed as baker for brigade hosp. by 8/31/64; baker for Division hosp. by 2/25/65; POW Five Forks; 4/1/65; City Pt. to Hart's Island 4/7/65; released there 6/19/65; res. Norfolk Co.; dk. complex., dk. hair, blue eyes, 5'8".

GRANT, ISAAC S.: Pvt.; Co. B 3/10/62 Callands; present until admitted Farmville hosp. 1/15/63 rheumatism; returned to duty 5/15/63; POW Gettysburg 7/3/63; Ft. McHenry 7/6/63 to Ft. Delaware 7/7-12/63 to Pt. Lookout 10/27/63; admitted U.S.A. small pox hosp., Pt. Lookout 12/6/63; returned to Pt. Lookout 12/11/63; exchanged 4/27/64; admitted Chimborazo #3 5/19/64; died there 5/20/64 wound of right arm.

GRANT, WILLIAM C.: Pvt.; Co. K 6/2/61 Cascade; present until WIA Seven Pines 5/31/62; returned, but deserted near New Bern N.C. 1/30/64 to Federal hands; Ft. Monroe 2/17/64 where oath taken and released 2/24/64; sent to Jefferson Co., Ill., res. Pittsylvania Co., Va.; lt. complex., lt. hair, blue eyes, 5'7¼".

GRANT, WILLIAM H.: Corp.; Co B, no date. Absent, died in camp near Manassas, near Centerville also listed. 8/10/61 typhoid fever.

GRAVELY GEORGE W.: Pvt.; Co. E 10/14/64 Danville; present through last roll dated 2/25/65.

GRAVELY, ISAAC: Pvt.; Co. K 2/28/62 Cascade; present, until admitted Farmville 5/23/62 debility; returned 6/17/62; detailed guard for ordinance 9/62; listed as AWOL 4/1/64, last muster roll date.

GRAVES, MADISON: Pvt.; Co. G 5/18/61 Boydton, died near Centerville, Manassas 8/2/61 typhoid fever.

GRAVES, WILLIAM W.: Pvt.; Co. G 5/18/61 Boydton; present until WIA seriously 7/1/62 Malvern Hill; sent to Chimborazo then sent to Danville 7/3/62; g.s.w. in shoulder, moved to Farmville 7/6/63; returned to duty 7/21/62.

GRAY, G. J.: Pvt.; Co. K 5/19/64 Henry Co., conscript; present through last roll dated 2/25/65.

GRAY, JAMES D.: Pvt.; 2nd Co. I 6/25/63 Pitts. Co.; present until deserted and received by Provost Marshall Genl. Army of Potomac 3/30/65; took oath Wash. D.C. and trans. furnished to Washington Co. by 4/4/65.

GRAY, THOMAS W.: Pvt.; Co. K 6/2/61 Cascade; present until admitted Danville Hosp. 8/6/62; febris intermitteus; deserted from there 1/1/63; returned by time MWIA and POW Gettysburg 7/5/63, wounded in hosp. after battle, g.s.w., shot in back of right shoulder with ball piercing the right lung. Died of wounds at Camp Letterman hosp., Gettysburg 10/4/63. age 32 and unmarried. Bur. in Section 8, Grave #35 at hosp. cem.; disinterred to Richmond 6/13/72 in Box #98.

GRAY, WILLIAM R.: Pvt.; Co. K 6/2/61 Cascade; present until admitted Chimborazo #1 2/16/63 int. fever; returned to duty 7/24/63; present through last roll dated 2/25/65.

GREEN, JOHN A.: Pvt.; Co. E 3/11/62 Danville; present until admitted Chimborazo #3 4/18/63; died at his home in Pitts. Co. 6/11/63. Father Laban Green.

GREEN, JOHN B.: Pvt.; Co. A 10/14/64 Danville; present, extra duty repairing shoes for 38th Regt. prior to 2/25/65. Absent, admitted Farmville hosp. 3/11/65 Erysipelas of jaw; returned 3/22/65; present until POW. Five Forks 4/1/65; City Point to Pt. Lookout 4/6/65; released there 6/22/65; res. Pittsylvania Co.; fair complex., sandy hair, blue eyes, 5'4".

GREEN, THOMAS C.: Pvt.; Co. A 2/27/62 Kentuck; present until detached to hosp. at Huguenot Springs 7/27/62-10/1/62; returned by time POW Gettysburg 7/3/63; Ft. McHenry 7/6/63 to Ft. Del. 7/7-12/63; to Pt. Lookout 10/27/63; died and bur. there 8/11/64, no cause listed.

GREENWOOD, BENJAMIN P.: Pvt.; Co. C 5/30/61 Laurel Grove; Pvt. to 1 Sgt.; by 2/62; present until detailed as recruiting Sgt. in Pitts. Co. 2/16/62; admitted Chimborazo #2, 4/24/64 pneumonia; died there 4/27/62 of pneumonia. b. Oakwood Cem., Richmond.

GREENWOOD, ROBERT H.: Pvt.; Co. C 5/30/61 Laurel Grove; Pvt. to 4 Sgt. prior to 8/31/64; present until admitted Chimborazo 10/26/61 rheumatism; returned 4/15/62; present until POW Five Forks 4/1/65; City Pt. to Point Lookout 4/6/65; released there 6/27/65; res. Pitts Co.; lt. complex., brn. hair, hazel eyes, 5'9¼".

GREGORY, CHRISTOPHER C.: Pvt.; Co. B 7/10/61 Winchester; present until WIA seriously Malvern Hill, carrying the colors 7/1/62; present but detailed as Brigade blacksmith 5/62-1/1/65; paroled at Appomattox 4/9/65.

GREGORY, JAMES F.: Pvt.; Co. D 5/24/61 Whitmell. Admitted to Richmond hosp. on 7/13/63 and on sick furlough 7/20-8/29/63, may have been WIA at Gettysburg on 7/3/63. Present until WIA Drewy's Bluff 5/16/64; admitted Richmond hosp. Howard's Grove 5/17/64; v.s. left leg, severe; entered Danville hosp. 7/26/64; deserted there 8/26/64; returned by 12/31/64; POW White Oak Road 4/1/65; City Point to Pt. Lookout 4/5/65; there released 6/28/65; res. Pittsylvania Co.; lt. complex., lt. bro. hair, blue eyes, 5'9½".

GREGORY, JOHN B.: Pvt.; Co. B 7/10/61 Winchester; present until attached to Howard's Grove G.H. Richmond 6/14/62 as a nurse; returned to duty 3/8/63; killed at Gettysburg 7/3/63. Born Pittsylvania Co. Widow Martha J. Gregory, Swansonville, 3 children surviving.

GREGORY, JOHN L.: Pvt.; Co. B 8/4/62 Danville; present until WIA 7/1/62 Seven Pines; admitted Chimborazo 11/12/62 tonsillitis, transferred to Scottsdale 11/28/62; there through 6/3/63 as a patient; returned prior to WIA mortally Drewry's Bluff 5/16/64; died due to left leg amputated, Howard's Grove 5/29/64. bur. Oakwood Cem., Richmond.

GREGORY, JOHN R.: Pvt.; Co. D. 8/21/63 Danville; Present until admitted Chimborazo #2 5/4/64 rubeola; returned 6/16/64; there through last roll 2/25/65; paroled Appomattox 4/9/65.

GREGORY, NATHAN L.: Corpl.; Co. B 7/10/61 Winchester; present until died of wounds received at Seven Pines 7/1/62.

GREGORY, RICHARD P.: Pvt.; Co. B. 6/4/61 Callands; present until m. WIA Seven Pines 5/31/62; died 6/1/62. Bur. Hollywood Cem., Richmond.

GREGORY, ROBERT B.: Pvt.; Co. C 5/30/61 Laurel Grove; died in Pittsylvania Co. 8/6/61 typhoid fever; born Pitts Co.; age 26, 6'2", fair complex., hazel eyes, blk. hair, a farmer. Widow Susan A. Gregory.

GREGORY, T. R.: Pvt.; 1st Co. I. 3/19/62 Clarksville; present.

GRIFFIN, A. J.: Pvt.; 1st Co. I 3/6/62 Clarksville; absent, left at Orange Co. Hosp. 4/7/62; admitted Chimborazo #3 4/14/62; returned to duty 4/27/62.

GRIFFIN, CHARLES G.: Co. I; Pvt. Post war record only.

GRIFFIN, J. R.: Pvt.; 1st Co. I 6/20/62 Clarksville; absent in Chimborazo #4 10/28/61; returned 11/18/61; WIA slightly 7/1/62 Malvern Hill.

GRIFFIN, RALPH: Pvt.; 1st Co. I 3/1/62 Clarksville; present until sent to Chimborazo #2 6/2/62 dysentery; trans. to Huguenot Springs 6/23/62.

GRIFFIN, WILLIAM L.: Sgt.; 1st Co. I 6/20/61 Clarksville; present until entered Chimborazo 6/3/62 diarrhea; to Farmville H. 6/6/62 dysentery; returned to duty 7/22/62; probably elected 3rd Lt. Entered Charlottesville H. 7/31/62. Died there 8/8/62 typhoid fever.

GRIFFITH, ANDREW J.: Pvt.; Co. K/H 6/2/61 Cascade; trans. from Cascade Rifles Co. K to Co. H 38th Va. Regt. 7/6/61; present until POW Williamsburg 5/5/62; Ft. Monroe, no date. On a list of POWs on board steamer Coatzacoalcos; returned to duty by 9/62; deserted near New Bern, N.C. 2/2/64; received by Federals 2/17/64; Ft. Monroe, took oath 2/24/64 sent to Weakley, Tenn.; res. Pittsylvania C. [spelled Pennsylvania Co.]; sandy complex., brn. hair, blue eyes, 5'10".

GRIGGS, GEORGE K.: Born 9/12/39 near Dyers Store in Leatherwood community of Henry Co. Educated at VMI. Married Sarah E. Boyd on 4/5/61. Enl. 6/2/61 at Cascade; Capt. of Co. K. WIA (slight of forehead) 5/31/62 at Seven Pines. WIA (minie ball thru flesh of right thigh) at Gettysburg 7/3/63. Admitted Danville Hosp. with wound 7/20/63 and returned to duty 9/29/63. Prom. to Major effective 7/3/63 and to Lt. Col. effective 11/15/63. WIA (severely in left thigh) at Drewry's Bluff 5/16/64 and admitted Howard's Grove Hosp., Richmond. Prom. to Colonel in command of the 38th Regt. aff. 5/16/64. Transferred to Danville Hosp. 5/23/64 and furloughed 5/25/64. Returned to duty 7/29/64. Surrendered with army at Appomattox 4/9/65. Supt. of Danville and Western Railroad after war. Mason and member of Cabell-Graves Camp, Conf. Veterans. Died in Danville 9/18/14 and bur. in Green Hill Cem.

GROW, JOSEPH H.: Pvt.; 2nd Co. I 3/6/62 Appomattox Co., AWOL 8/22/64; but returned prior to 12/31/64; present through last muster roll 2/25/65.

GRUBBS, LEONARD B.: Pvt.; Co. B 6/12/61, Callands; present until WIA Seven Pines 5/31/62; died of wounds received Seven Pines 7/22/62. Bur. Hollywood Cemetery, Richmond.

GRUBBS, JOHN T.: Capt., Co. C 5/30/61 Laurel Grove, appted. 2nd Lieut. 6/8/61; promoted from 2 Lieut. to Capt. by election 4/29/62; present until arrested by Col. G. K. Griggs 3/13/65, for drunkenness and disobeying orders. Surrendered at Appomattox by Lee 4/9/65.

GRUBBS, WILLIAM J.: Corpl.; Co. C 10/10/63 Kinston, N.C.; Pvt. to Corpl. 7/1/64; present until WIA 5/10/64 near Richmond; admitted Chimborazo 5/11/64; v.s. right arm; returned to duty prior to 7/1/64; POW and WIA g.s.w. fractured humerous Farmville 4/3/65; to Newport News from City Pt. 4/5/65; took oath, Newport News 6/14/65; res. Leesburg, N.C.; dk. complex., dk. hair, blue eyes, 5'9", farmer, age 20. g.s.w. fractured humerous.

GUILL, WILLIAM: Pvt.; Co. G, no date. AWOL, but never been mustered into the service 10/61.

GUNN, JONES M.: Sgt.; Co. F 6/4/61 Republican Grove; present until admitted Charlottesville hosp. 1/22/62 nephritis, furloughed 8 days 1/31/62; Chimborazo #1 admitted 5/28/62 dysentery; returned to duty 6/9/62; on a register of claims of deceased soldiers, filed 4/4/64.

GUNNEL, JOHN T.: Pvt.; Co. A 5/30/61 Kentuck; present until discharged near Richmond 7/26/62 no reason given.

GUNNELL, HENRY: Pvt.; Co. A, no date; present until admitted Chimborazo #5 5/3/62 debility.

GUNNELL, JOSEPH L.: Pvt.; Co. A 5/30/61 Kentuck; present until WIA 5/31/61 Seven Pines in hosp.; killed 7/3/63 at Gettysburg. Born Pittsylvania Co.

GUNTER, CHARLES P.: Pvt.; 2nd Co. I 10/12/63 Henrico Co. Present until AWOL 12/7/64.

GUNTER, JOHN W.: Pvt.; 2nd Co. I 3/6/62 Appomattox Co.; AWOL 2/8/65; on roll of members of Army of N. Va. not with their commands for parole, but were taken up to be paroled by terms of Lee's surrender 4/9/65.

GUTHERY, JAMES T.: Pvt.; Co. F 6/4/61 Republican Grove Hosp., Chimborazo Hosp. 10/25/61, mumps. Present until WIA g.s.w., side and POW, Gettysburg 7/3/63; DeCamp G.H., Davids Island 9/8/63. Paroled there. Returned to duty by 4/1/64, WIA 5/10/64 at Chester Station. Admitted Chimborazo #2, 5/11/64 debility, returned to duty 8/29/64.

GUTHERY, THOMAS T.: Pvt.; Co. F 6/4/61 Republican Grove; present until admitted Chimborazo #4 10/25/61 calculus; returned to duty 12/4/61; medically discharged 12/13/61 bladder and kidney disorder; born Halifax Co., age 23, 5'9", dk. complex., grey eyes, dk. hair, a farmer.

GUTHRIE, PAUL W.: Pvt.; Co. F 3/14/62 Republican Grove; present until admitted Chimborazo #1 6/9/62 debility; trans. to Danville H. 7/2/62 chronic rheumatism; deserted 7/30/62; admitted Chimborazo #2 10/31/62 chronic rheumatism. Present 4-6/63. Probably KIA at Gettysburg in 7/3/63.

GUTHRIE, WILLIAM T.: Pvt.; Co. F 3/15/62 Republican Grove; present until WIA and sent to Hosp. 6/10/62 listed as convalescing in Farmville hosp., admitted 4/18/63; returned to duty 6/3/63; admitted Chimborazo #4 5/17/64 of g.s.w. to head; died there 6/25/64 v.s. face. bur. Oakwood Cem., Richmond.

HACKLER, PETER: Pvt.; Co. H, no date. Absent, deserted to the enemy. Received in Federal hands 12/17/64; took oath at Bermuda Hundred; to Wash. D.C. 12/27/64; transportation furnished to Cincinnati, Ohio.

HAILEY, JAMES T.: Corpl.; Co. K 3/1/62 Cascade; Pvt. to Corpl. prior to 12/31/64; present until admitted Chimborazo 5/16/64 wound in left hand; trans. to Danville H. 5/24/64; returned to duty 7/18/64; pres. through last roll dated 2/25/65. Paroled Appomattox 4/9/65.

HALEY, JOHN J.: Pvt.; Co. A 3/6/62 Kentuck; absent, admitted Chimborazo #4 4/24/62 measles and acute bronchitis, died there 5/9/62. Widow Mary F. Haley.

HALEY, THOMAS J.: Pvt.; Co. A, no date. Absent, left Richmond hosp. while on march to Yorktown 5/62; returned before killed Gettysburg 7/3/63. Born Caswell Co., N.C.

HALL, BEVERLY B.: Pvt.; Co. E 8/15/62 Danville; age 34, no date on roll. Present until absent wounded between 8 and 9/62. Returned prior to 6/30/63; Chimborazo #4 6/15/64 dysentery. Present through last roll 2/25/65.

HALL, H. W. G.: No rank listed; Co. B. Name appears on a Co. return for 9/62. No other information.

HALL, JAMES D.: Pvt.; Co. F 6/4/61 Republican Grove; pres. until WIA slightly 7/1/62 Malvern Hill; returned prior to 7/1/63; deserted 3/10/64; absent, in arrest as of 8/31/64; deserted and in Federal hands 2/17/65; oath taken at Bermuda Hundred; sent to Wash., D.C. 2/21/65; trans. furnished to Jefferson Co., Ill.

HALL, JAMES O.: Pvt.; Co. B 6/4/61 Callands; pres. until WIA Seven Pines 5/31/62; medical discharge, result of injury, right arm amputated 9/22/62.

HALL, JEREMIAH: Co. A; Pvt. Post-war record only.

HALL, JOHN O.: Pvt.; Co. E 2/24/62 Danville; absent sick 5-7/62; absent wounded for muster roll of 8-9/62; returned, killed at Gettysburg 7/3/63.

HALL, PEYTON T.: Pvt.; Co. C 5/30/61 Laurel Grove; present until admitted Chimborazo Hosp. #5 6/3/62; still absent as of last date 9/62.

HALL, WILLIAM C.: Pvt.; Co. E 2/24/62 Danville; absent sick 4/30/62; returned to be wounded 8-9/62; absent sick prior to 6/30/63; until died 8/9/64 of chronic diarrhea.

HALL, WILLIAM G.: Pvt.; Co. B 6/5/61 Callands; present until WIA Seven Pines 5/31/62; discharged from service, medically 11/29/62, result of wounds from Seven Pines, fracture of "humerous" of left arm; conscripted 10/15/64; present until POW Five Forks 4/3/65; City Pt. to Hart's Landing 4/7/63; released there 6/21/65; res. Pitts Co.; fair complex., lt. hair, blue eyes, 5'10". Born Pitts Co., age 19 as of 1st discharge 11/29/62. A farmer.

HALL, JACHARIAH: Pvt.; Co. A, no date; absent, sick in Richmond G.H. #21 3/30/62 bronchitis; sick through 8/62; died 3/19/63 of "fits" at Petersburg. Born Pittsylvania Co.

HALSTEAD, BENJAMIN F.: Lieut.; 2nd Co. I. Elected 2 Lieut. 3/9/62. Present until admitted Chimborazo 6/4/64 syphilis, furloughed 7/30/64. Returned, deserted to Federals. 3/30/64; sent to Wash., D.C. 4/4/65; oath taken.

HAMBRICK, JAMES B.: Pvt.; Co. E 6/8/61 Danville; present until discharged, medical, 12/1/61 paralysis. Born Halifax Co., age 24; 5'9", fair complex., grey eyes, brn. hair, farmer.

HAMPTON, JOHN A.: Pvt.; Co. A 10/14/64 Danville; present until discharged 1/14/65, amount of excessive corpulency.

HANBY, J. M.: No rank listed. Co. B, no date. No other information.

HANCOCK, COLEMAN: Pvt.; Co. H. Post-war record only.

HANCOCK, LAFAYETTE: Pvt.; Co. F 6/4/61 Republican Grove; present until WIA slightly 7/1/62 Malvern Hill. Sent to hosp. 7/2/62; returned prior to 7/1/63; POW Gettysburg 7/3/63; Ft. McHenry 7/6/63; to Ft. Del. 7/7-12/63; to Pt. Lookout 10/27/63; admitted to U.S.A. smallpox hosp. Pt. Lookout 11/28/63. Died at smallpox hosp. 1/8/64. Born Halifax Co.

HANCOCK, PRESLEY H.: Pvt.; Co. F 6/4/61 Republican Grove; pres. until WIA, slightly Malvern Hill 7/1/62; present until deserted 6/3/63. Returned prior to 4/1/64; present until POW Farmville 4/6/65; sent to Newport News from City Pt. 4/14/65; oath taken 6/25/65; res. Halifax Co., fair complex., lt. hair, blue eyes, 6'0''.

HANCOCK, RAWLEY W.: Pvt.; Co. H 7/2/61 Pitts C.H.; Chimborazo #2 5/11/62, Debility. Present until killed by a "bumshell" on Crewes Farm 6/29/62. Widow Susan J. Hancock.

HANCOCK, SAMUEL: Pvt.; Co. F 2/27/62 Republican Grove; pres. until POW Gettysburg 7/3/63; Ft. McHenry 7/6/63 to Ft. Del. 7/7-12/63 to Pt. Lookout 10/27/63. Paroled and exchanged from there 1/17/65; at Camp Lee, near Richmond 1/26/65. Also listed as died and bur. at Pt. Lookout.

HANKINS, HENRY C.: Pvt.; Co. B 6/9/63 Danville. Present until WIA, mortally Drewry's Bluff 5/16/64, v.s. right arm, upper ⅓. Admitted Chimborazo 5/17/64; died there 5/29/64; age 19 when died; occupation trader.

HANKINS, J. R.: Co. A; Pvt. Enl. 1864. Post-war record only.

HANKINS, REUBEN F.: Pvt.; Co. B 6/4/61 Callands; pres. until WIA Seven Pines 5/31/62; admitted to Danville hosp. 12/25/62 debilitas; there deserted 1/6/63; furloughed 6/18/63, had been in hosp. at Farmville for last 4 months, debility due to typhoid and diarrhea. Returned prior to WIA Drewry's Bluff 5/16/64. Retired and discharged on account of disability from wounds of right foot 12/23/64. Alive at Swansonville 4/19/97.

HANKINS, WILLIAM D.: Corpl.; Co. F 6/4/61 Republican Grove; Pvt. to 1 Corpl. by 7/1/63; pres. until admitted Charlottesville H. 2/26/62 rheumatism. Returned 4/16/62; POW Gettysburg 7/3/63; Ft. McHenry 7/5/63 to Ft. Del. 7/7-12/63 to Pt. Lookout 10/15/63; trans. to Hammond G.H. 12/11/63; died there 12/18/63 of chronic diarrhea.

HANKS, WILLIAM D.: Pvt.; Co. E 6/8/61 Danville, absent sick, had not rendered any service since mustered into service; but disability discharge not approved until 4/7/63 for diarrhea and phthisis pulmonary, age 25 as of 3/8/62. Occupation school teacher; born Pitts Co., 5'6'', fair complex., dk. eyes, fair hair.

HANNAH, JAMES C.: Pvt.; Co. K 9/2/62 Pittsylvania; C.S.A. Hosp. Farmville 3/14/65, diarrhea. Pres. until POW Farmville 4/6/65; City Pt. to Newport News 4/14/65; paroled there 7/1/65; res. Pitts. Co.; dk. complex., dk. hair, grey eyes, 5'10''.

HANNAH, JAMES P.: 2 Lieut.; Co. K 6/2/61 Cascade; present, resigned 9/18/61; took oath of Allegiance 6/2/65. Res. Davidson Co., N. Carolina.

HANNAH, JOHN W: Pvt.; Co. K 6/2/61 Cascade; present until detached 7/1/63 Brigade forage master; wagon master through 12/31/64; paroled Appomattox 4/9/63 "with private mule and equipments."

HARAWAY, WILLIAM L.: Pvt.; Co. A 10/14/64 Danville; present through last roll dated 2/25/65.

HARDY, JAMES B.: Pvt.; Co. B 8/6/64 Pittsylvania Co., conscript. Present until deserted 1/7/65.

HARDY, JAMES H.: Pvt.; Co. E 3/13/62 Danville; present until AWOL 8/1/62-5/1/63. Pay deducted accordingly; admitted Danville H. 5/23/64 wound in hand; returned to duty 7/26/64. Present through 2/25/65; admitted Danville hosp. 4/5/65 rheumatism chronic.

HARDY, JOHN W.: 2 Lieut.; Co. I. Appointed 6/26/61; failed to be elected, dropped 3/9/62.

HARDY, JOSEPH S.: Pvt.; Co. H 7/2/61 Pittsylvania C.H.; present until sent to hosp. Danville 1/15/62; returned by 5/62 when given extra duty ditching and trenching 6/8/62; deserted 7/26/62.

HARDY, OBADIAH: Pvt.; Co. H 7/2/61 Pittsylvania C.H.; WIA at Seven Pines 5/31/62. Present through last roll dated 2/26/65. Alive at Whittle 6/24/86.

HARDY, PRESLEY G.: Pvt.; Co. H 3/22/62 Orange C.H.; pres. until admitted Danville Hosp. 6/20/62 pneumonia; returned 8/28/62; MWIA at Gettysburg 7/3/63. Entered Staunton G. H. 7/14/63; died there of wounds 10/4/63. Father Banister Hardy. No wife or children. Bur. Thornrose Cem., Staunton.

HARDY, ROBERT THOMAS: Pvt.; Co. C 5/30/61 Laurel Grove; present until WIA slightly, g.s.w. of left hand, Seven Pines 5/31/62; returned 9/23/62; present until WIA (right foot) Gettysburg 7/3/63, POW 7/5/63 Chester, Pa. G.H. 7/31/63 to Hammond G.H., Pt. Lookout 10/4/63; amputated foot, followed by gangrene; exchanged from Hammond 3/17/64; retired 11/29/64; part of Invalid Corps Danville, assigned duty S.O. 293 to Comdt. 10/12/64. Alive at Sutherlin. (Halifax Co.) 4/19/86.

HARDY, SAMUEL H.: Pvt.; Co. E 6/8/61 Danville; pres. until admitted Chimborazo #4 5/16/64 g.s.w. left hand; apparently WIA at Drewry's Bluff; trans. Danville 5/23/64 contusion; returned to duty 7/26/64; paroled at Appomattox 4/9/65.

HARPER, GEORGE W.: Pvt.; Co. D 4/24/64 Danville; present until POW in Fairground Post Hosp., Petersburg 4/3/65; to Petersburg G.H. 4/13/65; furloughed 4/15/65 typhoid fever; to Pt. of Rocks Hosp. A of J. Pt. of Rocks, Va. 4/15/65; returned to duty 4/21/65.

HARRIS, E. K.: Pvt.; 1st Co. I 3/25/62 Clarksville; Pvt., elected Jr. 2 Lieut. 4/29/62; resigned 6/28/62.

HARRIS, GEORGE W.: Pvt.; Co. E 6/8/61 Danville; present until admitted hosp. 10/25/61 measles and sequelae; returned 12/13/61; entered Danville H. 8/9/62 debilitas; deserted 2/18/63; returned to be WIA severely, both legs and spine 7/3/63 Gettysburg. Absent sick through last muster roll dated 2/25/65; alive at Fall Creek on 3/19/83.

HARRIS, GEORGE W.: Pvt.; Co. K 3/1/62 Cascade; present until POW Winchester 12/22/62 to Ft. McHenry 1/22/63; paroled and returned prior to 4/1/64. Pres. through last roll dated 12/31/64.

HARRIS, JAMES G.: Pvt.; Co. K 3/6/62 Cascade; pres. until WIA right leg, Seven Pines 5/31/62; retired by Med. Ex. Bd. 4/23/64; part of Invalid Corps in Danville; alive at Cascade 9/18/82.

HARRIS, JOEL: Pvt.; Co. K 3/6/62 Cascade; absent sick 5/62-9/62; returned to be WIA, (no date or place listed) and retired by Med. Ex. Bd. 12/16/64; part of Invalid Corps. but possibly 4/2/64 bayoneted in arm by Pvt. John Q. Adams due to personal conflict. Alive at Cascade after war.

HARRIS, JOHN S.: Pvt.; Co. E 6/8/61 Danville; present, special duty as Co. Cook prior to 8/15/62; paroled Appomattox 4/9/65.

HARRIS, PETER M.: Pvt.; Co. K 8/14/62 Cascade; Jackson Hosp. 5/25/64 dia. act. Present through 2/25/65.

HARRIS, SAMUEL J.: Sgt.; Co. D 5/24/61 Whitmell; Sgt. to 2 Lieut. elected 3/14/63; absent, left at Winchester sick 7/18/61; returned prior to 3/14/63; POW Gettysburg 7/3/63 Ft. McHenry 7/6/63 to Ft. Del. to Johnson's Island 7/18/63; Pt. Lookout for exchange 3/14/63.

100

HARRIS, WILLIAM J.: Pvt.; Co. H 11/10/62 Henry; present through 2/26/65.

HARRIS, WILLIAM O.: Sgt.; Co. D 3/11/62 Whitmell; present, until WIA slightly Malvern Hill 7/1/62; WIA leg at Gettysburg 7/3/63 admitted to a Richmond Hosp. 7/13/63. Returned to duty prior to 4/1/64; POW White Oak Road 4/1/65; City Pt. to Pt. Lookout 4/5/65; released there 6/13/65; res. Pitts. Co.; dk. complex., dk. hair, dk. bro. eyes; 5'7¾". Alive 5/15/82.

HARRIS, WILLIAM P.: Pvt.; Co. E 6/8/61 Danville; present until absent sick 3/62 through until died 5/30/62 at his home in Pitts. Co. Father Robert Harris.

HART, W. J.: Co. A; Pvt. Post-war record only.

HARVEY, E. B.: Pvt.; Co. K 10/4/64 Danville; present through 2/25/65.

HARVEY, GEORGE A.: 3 Corpl.; Co. E 6/8/61 Danville; Corpl. to Pvt. by 5/62; present until detached as Brigade Teamster 7/62. Extra duty Picketts Div. as harness maker 12/64 until listed as present 2/25/65, admitted C.S.A. Hosp. Farmville 3/12/65 sprained ankle.

HARVEY, HENRY: Pvt.; 2nd Co. I 3/1/62 Norfolk Co.; present until deserted to Federals 12/30/64 Bermuda Hundred; to Wash., D.C. where took oath 1/6/65; transported to Norfolk.

HARVEY, JOHN: Pvt.; 2nd Co. I 7/6/61 Norfolk Co.; present until POW Five Forks 4/1/65; City Pt. to Harts Island 4/7/65; released there 6/20/65. Res. Norfolk Co.; lt. complex., lt. hair, blue eyes, 5'10".

HARVILLE, GEORGE A.: Born 1826. Pvt.; Co. K 6/2/61 Cascade; pres. until 10/24/61, when sent to Chimborazo Hosp. #4 with rheumatism and diarrhea; sick through 8/62; transferred to Danville Hosp.; returned by 5/26/62. Killed at Gettysburg 7/3/63; dropped from roll 8/19/64. Son of Joel C. and Betsy Callahan Harville. Married Mary A. Barker and had four sons.

HASTINGS, ROBERT H.: Pvt.; Co. D 3/11/62 Whitmell; pres. until WIA at Seven Pines 5/31/62; admitted Farmville H. 4/12/63 diarrhea. Returned to duty 5/20/63; WIA 5/10/64 near Chester Sta., Va. (Mini ball in arm fracturing humerus) left arm amputated upper 3d same day circular operation admitted in Rich. Hosp. 5/11/64; retired 9/12/64; part of Invaliad Corps; born Mecklenburg Co.; age 32 at retirement; 5'7½", dk. complex., grey eyes, dk. hair, farmer.

HATCHELL, JAMES L.: Pvt.; Co. G 5/18/61 Boydton; pres. until admitted Chimborazo #4 10/28/61 chronic rheumatism. Returned 12/9/61; admitted 3/7/62 Gen. Hosp. #18, Richmond, chronic rhematism. Absent sick through until discharged 9/62, over 35 years of age.

HATCHER, CHARLES R.: Pvt.; Co. K 6/2/61 Cascade; Pvt. to 2nd Corpl. by 6/62; pres. until admitted Richmond G.H. #18 6/17/62 rheumatism; trans. to Danville G. H. 6/24/62 pneumonia. Died at father's home 9/1/62 typhoid fever.

HATCHER, RICHARD J.: Sgt.; Co. K 6/2/61 Cascade; present, until wounded 9/17/62; admitted Richmond G.H. 10/4/62 flesh wound upper 3d left leg. Furloughed 30 days 10/19/62; absent 4/1/64. Detached service in Engineer Corps.

HATCHER, URIAH M.: Pvt.; Co. K 6/2/61 Cascade; pres. until WIA 5/31/62 Seven Pines; in Hosp., returned, WIA 7/1/62 Malvern Hill, slightly.

HAWKES, THOMAS S.: Pvt.; Co. A 3/13/62 Kentuck; present until WIA, probably at Drewry's Bluff; admitted Chimborazo #5 5/16/64. Furloughed for 60 days 6/21/64; left arm amputated while in Chimborazo #5, no date; retired 10/19/64; name on Register of Invalid Corps. P.A.C.S.

HAWKINS, W. H.: Conscript; no co. listed. Enrolled 4/23/64; assigned to 38th Regt. 4/25/64.

HAWTHORNE, BENJAMIN J.: Co. G; apptted. 2 Lieut. 12/11/61; promoted 1st Lieut. 4/29/62; promoted capt. 11/15/63; present until detailed in Conscript Bureau 7/3/63; wounded in left arm Gettysburg 7/3/63;enrolling officer 11/26/64; ordered to rejoin command 1/7/65.

HAY, WILLIAM P.: Pvt.; Co. A. 5/30/61 Kentuck; absent sick, died in Richmond 6/6/62. Widow Sarah Hay.

HAYES, RICHARD H.: Pvt.; Co. G 5/18/61 Boydton; present until detailed as ambulance driver 10/25/61-7/62; deserted 9/62. Returned to duty 3/26/63; discharged 4/4/63 being a mail contractor.

HAYMES, JOHN B.: Pvt.; Co. C 6/27/61 Richmond; present until sent to hosp. in Richmond sick 10/24/61, bronchitis. Discharged from service 1/9/62 disability. Re-enlisted 7/8/62 in 4th NC Cav. Bur. Sandy Creek Bapt. Ch. Cem., Pitts. Co.

HAYNES, R. A.: Pvt.; Co. C 10/14/64 Danville; pres. until deserted 1/19/65; signed oath of allegiance Campbell C.H. 5/29/65.

HAZLEWOOD, WALTER S.: Pvt.; Co. F 6/4/61 Republican Grove; present until detailed to Ordinance Dept. at Manassas Junction 2/25/62 and assigned there through 2/25/65.

HEATTS, LAWSON: Co. B. Pvt. Post-war record only.

HEDRICK, JACOB B.: Pvt.; Co. B 3/10/62 Callands; pres. until admitted Danville Hosp. 5/8/62 acute rheumatism; returned 10/10/62; absent, detailed as a shoemaker prior to 5/19/63; shoemaker through 1/1/65; POW Farmville 4/6/65; to Newport News, no date.

HENDERSON, HARTWELL: Pvt.; Co. C 5/30/61 Laurel Grove; pres. until admitted Petersburg hosp. 1/11/62 diarrhea; returned 1/24/62; admitted Danville 6/12/62 rheumatism; deserted 7/6/62; returned by time discharged 9/5/62, reason, over age.

HENDERSON, HARTWELL T.: Pvt.; Co. A 12/2/64 Kentuck; present, extra duty as orderly for Brig. Genl. Stewart; entered Chimborazo #5 3/5/65 debility.

HENDERSON, JOHN J.: Pvt.; Co. A 12/10/63 Kentuck; pres. until sent to hosp. 9/9/64; entered Chimborazo #5 10/4/64 rheumatism, furloughed 35 days 10/25/64. Returned by time detailed extra duty as Brig. teamster prior to 2/25/65; paroled Appomattox 4/9/65.

HENDRICK, JAMES: Pvt.; 1st Co. I 3/20/62 Clarksville; absent, sent to hosp. 4/20/62.

HENDRICK, JOSEPH B.: Pvt.; Co. G 5/18/61 Boydton; absent, died in hosp. in Richmond 5/5/62.

HENDRICK, MURRAY: Pvt.; Co. G 2/4/63 Mecklenburg; present until POW Amelia C.H. 4/5/65; City Pt. to Pt. Lookout 4/13/65; released there 6/13/65; res. Mecklenburg Co.; fair complex., dk. bro. hair, blue eyes, 5'11¾".

HENDRICK, WILLIAM L.: Sgt.; Co. G 5/18/61 Boydton; 8-9/62 Co. Cook. Pvt. to 4 Sgt. by 2/65; pres. until sent to Lynchburg Hosp. 1/27/63, sick. Returned prior to 4/1/64; present until POW Amelia C.H. 4/5/65; City Pt. to Pt. Lookout; 4/13/65; released there 6/13/65; res. Mecklenburg Co.; fair complex., bro. hair, blue eyes, 6'1-1/8"

HENDRICK, WILLIAM T.: Pvt.; Co. G 5/18/61 Boydton; present until discharged, disability 1/29/62; born Mecklenburg; age 32, 6'2", ruddy complex., blue eyes, dk. hair, a farmer. Reenlisted 8/23/62; WIA Gettysburg and POW 7/3/63; Ft. McHenry to U.S. Gen. Hosp., Chester, Pa., paroled there 9/23/63, exchanged. Returned but retired from service 1/29/64, discharged.

HENRY, JOHN: Pvt.; 1st Co. I 3/4/62 Clarksville; absent, sent to Orange Co. Hosp. 4/7/62; died Gen. Hosp. #20 4/15/62 typhoid fever.

HERALD, EDWARD: Co. A. 3rd Lt. Post-war record only.

HERBERT, JOSEPH T.: 1 Lieut.; Co. I; appted. 6/26/61. Dropped 3/9/62 failed to be reelected in reorganization.

HERNDON, DAVID B.: Born 3/29/42 at Callands. Pvt.; Co. B 6/4/61 Callands; present until entered Chimborazo #3 10/23/61; chronic rheumatism; discharged there 11/1/61. Member of Cabell-Graves Camp, UCV. Died 1912.

HERNDON, EDWIN T.: Born 1833. 1 Sgt.; Co. D 5/24/61 Whitmell; pres. until discharged surgeon; cert. 5/24/62; reenlisted conscripted 6/11/64 Danville; present detached as ambulance driver 8/20/64-12/31/64; listed as present 2/25/65.

HERNDON, JOHN A.: Born 5/30/38. Lt.; Co. D 5/24/61 Whitmell; appted. 2 Lieut. 4/16/62; promoted 1st Lieut. 7/1/62; promoted Capt. 7/17/62; present until WIA 5/31/62 Seven Pines, returned 6/62; present until POW Dinwiddie C.H. 4/1/65; to Old Capitol Prison 4/5/65 to Depot POW Sandusky, Ohio to Johnson's Island where took oath 6/18/65; res. Danville; age 27; florid complex., dk. hair, blue eyes, 5'11". Member of Cabell-Graves Camp, UCV, Lived in Lynchburg.

HERNDON, RALPH CLEMENTS: Born 9/4/36 at Whitmell. Capt.; Co. D 5/24/61 Whitmell; appted. Capt. 6/3/61; dropped, resigned 5/1/62. Failed to be reelected in Spring reorganization. School teacher, Comm. of Revenue for Pitts. Co., tobacconist, Ins. Agent. Mbr. of Cabell-Graves Camp, UCV. Died 2/18/98 at Danville. Bur. Green Hill Cem., Danville.

HICKS, JAMES: Pvt.; Co. G 4/18/64 Boydton; present until POW Amelia C.H. 4/5/65; City Pt. to Pt. Lookout 4/13/65; released there 6/13/65; res. Mecklenburg Co., dk. complex., dk. bro. hair, hazel eyes, 5'8¾".

HILL, JAMES O.: Pvt.; Co. H 3/9/63 Pittsylvania; pres. until detached at Div. Hosp. at Chester prior to 8/31/64. Present, detached as musician prior to 12/31/64. Present through 2/26/65. Surrendered at Appomx. C.H. 4/9/65.

HILL, JAMES S.: Born Pittsylvania Co. Pvt.; Co. C, on date. Present until admitted Chimborazo 4/14/62; returned to duty 4/29/62; died at home 5/17/62, no cause given.

HILL, JOHN ROBERT: Born 4/25/37. Pvt.; Co. A 5/30/61 Kentuck; Co. Cook 7-8/62. Present through detailed teamster 1/64; Episcopal Hosp., Williamsburg 4/27/64 pneumonia. Admitted Danville G.H. 5/23/64 chronic diarrhea; returned to duty 11/29/64. Teamster through 2/25/65; paroled Appomattox 4/9/65. Died 8/23/99 Pitts. Co.

HILL, JOSEPH W.: Pvt.; Co. A 5/30/61 Kentuck; present until admitted Farmville Hosp. 12/21/62, disease of scalp. Furloughed 30 days 5/30/63; absent 4/1/64-10/12/64; detailed Division Teamster; present prior to 12/31/64; on furlough of indulgence 2/25/65.

HILL, WILLIAM: Pvt.; Co. D 9/21/64 Halifax Co.; present until POW Five Forks 4/1/65; City Pt. to Hart's Island 4/7/65; released there 6/21/65; res. Halifax Co.; fair complex., red hair, blue eyes, 6'½".

HINES, G. D.: Pvt.; Co. D, no date. Paroled Appomattox 4/9/65.

HINES, HENRY DAVID: Pvt.; Co. H 10/14/64 Pittsylvania. Present until admitted Richmond G.H. #9 3/5/65, debility. POW Richmond Hosp. 4/3/65; Libby Prison to Newport News 4/23/65; took oath there 7/1/65; res. Pitts. Co.; dk. complex., dk. hair, blue eyes, 6'0". Died 1887.

HINES, JAMES L.: Pvt.; Co. D 10/14/64 Danville; pres. through 2/25/65.

HINES, THOMAS J.: Pvt.; Co. D 6/25/61 Richmond; pres. until WIA at Seven Pines 5/31/62; admitted Danville Hosp. 6/4/62 Returned to duty 7/9/62; discharged 9/5/62 expiration of service; reenlisted 10/14/64 Danville; present until paroled 4/9/65 Appomattox.

HITE, JAMES: Pvt.; 1st Co. I, no date. Absent, admitted Orange Court House Gen. Hosp. 12/6/61, pleuritis; discharged 1/12/62 consumption. Born Mecklenburg Co., age 26, 6'1", sallow complex., dk. eyes, dk. hair, carpenter.

HITE, THOMAS: Pvt.; Co. G 7/29/63 Mecklenburg; present through 2/65; paroled at Appomattox 4/9/65.

HODGES, DAVID F.: Pvt.; Co. K 6/2/61 Cascade; present, appointed wagon master 9/6/61-2/25/65. Paroled Appomattox 4/9/65.

HODGES, EDWARD P.: Pvt.; Co. B 6/4/61 Callands; Pvt. to 5 Sgt. by 4/1/64; to 2 Sgt. by 1/1/65; present until POW Gettysburg 7/3/63; Ft. McHenry 7/6/63 to Ft. Del. 7/7-12/63; to Pt. Lookout 10/27/63; exchanged 2/18/65; at Camp Lee 3/1/65; returned to duty, POW Five Forks 4/1/65; City Pt. to Harts Island 4/7/65; released there 6/21/65; res. Pitts Co.; lt. complex., dk. hair, blue eyes, 6'0".

HODGES, HARRISON L.: Pvt.; Co. A 10/14/64 Danville; present until POW Dinwiddie C.H. 4/2/65; City Pt. to Pt. Lookout 4/4/65; released there 6/13/65; res. Pitts Co.; lt. complex., brn. hair, blue eyes, 6'3". Blind in left eye.

HODGES, HIRAM H.: Pvt.; Co. K, no date. Mortally wounded Seven Pines 5/31/62; died in Danville G.H. 6/13/62.

HODGES, JOSEPH H.: Pvt.; Co. C 5/30/61 Laurel Grove; present until WIA, severely Gettysburg 7/3/63, g.s.w. forehead fracturing eye socket. Admitted 5/13/64 Chimborazo #4, g.s.w.; returned to duty 6/28/64. Paroled at Appomattox 4/9/65. Res. Ringold, Va.

HODNETT, DANIEL P.: Pvt.; Co. F 6/4/61, Republican Grove. Present until killed Malvern Hill 7/1/62.

HODNETTE, THOMAS: Pvt.; Co. F 10/18/64; Bermuda Hundred; present until POW Five Forks 4/1/65; City Pt. to Pt. Lookout 4/6/65; released there 6/13/65; res. Pitts. Co., dk. complex., brn. hair, grey eyes, 5'11½".

HOGAN, TIMOTHY: Pvt.; 2nd Co. I 3/6/62 Appomattox Co. Present until WIA at Drewry's Bluff 5/16/64 admitted Chimborazo #4 g.s.w. in foot; trans. to Farmville 6/3/64; diarrhea; returned to duty 6/26/64; present through 2/25/65.

HOLLAND, CONSTANTINE: Pvt.; Co. K 6/2/61 Cascade; present until WIA slightly Malvern Hill 7/1/62; present until admitted Chimborazo #9 4/12/64 ulcer of leg; trans. to Farmville Hosp. 5/4/64; rheumatism; furloughed there for 60 days 9/21/64 varicose veins, extensive, due to marching.

HOLLAND, JOHN: Pvt.; Co. K 3/10/62 Cascade; present until admitted Chimborazo 5/28/62; debility, absent through 7/62; returned prior to Gettysburg where KIA 7/3/63.

HOLLAND, JOHN: Pvt.; 2nd Co. I 3/10/62 Norfolk Co.; Pvt. to 3rd Corpl. by 12/31/64; present until POW Farmville 4/6/65; City Pt. to Newport News 4/14/65; took oath there 7/1/65; res. Norfolk Co.; dk. complex., dk. hair, blue eyes, 5'8".

HOLLAND, STEPHEN J.: Pvt.; Co. D 10/14/64 Danville; absent, admitted Chimborazo #1 1/7/65; furloughed 2/4/65, 40 days. Paroled 4/9/65, Appomattox.

HOLLEY, WILLIAM C.: Pvt.; Co. D 5/24/61 Whitmell; died 7/22 or 7/26/61 at Winchester. Born Pitts. Co.; age 20 as of death; 5'10", fair complex., lt. hair, blue eyes, farmer. Bur. Stonewall Cem., Winchester.

HOLLY, JOHN V.: Pvt.; Co. H 4/26/64 Dublin; Pvt. to Corpl. by 2/26/65; WIA at Chester Station 5/10/64; admitted Chimborazo 5/10/64; pres. through 2/26/65.

HOLMES, ROBERT: Pvt.; Co. G 5/18/61 Boydton; pres. until WIA, seriously Seven Pines 5/31/62 admitted Episcopal Church Hosp. Williamsburg 6/25/62 wounds; returned 9/15/62; pres. until POW near Petersburg 5/10/64; Ft. Monroe to Pt. Lookout 5/13/64; joined U.S. service, army, from there 5/31/64.

HOLT, JOHN B.: Pvt.; Co. D 6/15/61 Whitmell; pres. until detached to work on road 11/7/61. Returned by time killed in action 5/31/62 on Chickahominy, Seven Pines. Mother Rebecca Burnett.

HOOFMAN, MOSES: Pvt.; Co. H 7/2/61 Pittsylvania C.H.; pres. until slightly wounded on the hip with a spent ball 5/31/62 White Pines (Seven Pines) 3/28/64, branded on left hip with letter "D", head shaved and sentenced to work on breastworks for 12 months for desertion.

HOOVER, ISRAEL: Pvt.; Co. H. No other information.

HOPGOOD, ALBERT: Pvt.; 1st Co. I 6/20/61 Clarksville; pres. 6/62.

HOPPER, GEORGE W.: Pvt.; Co. K 2/24/62 Cascade; pres. until WIA Seven Pines 5/31/62; returned, killed at Gettysburg 7/3/63.

HOPPER, JOHN H.: Pvt.; Co. K 3/6/62 Cascade; present until missing, supposed killed Gettysburg 7/3/63 and dropped from roll 8/19/64.

HOPPER, JOHN T.: Pvt.; Co. K 3/1/62 Cascade; admitted Chimborazo #4 5/18/62, acute diarrhoea; trans. Danville Hosp. 5/19/62; absent through 8/31/62.

HOTELEN, HENRY: Sgt.; Co. G 5/18/61 Boydton; Sgt. reduced to Pvt. 4/1/62; present until WIA slightly 7/1/62 Seven Pines (according to CSR, but probably at Malvern Hill). Returned, but deserted 5/21/64 near Spotsylvania CH, POW near Hanover 5/22/64; Port Royal to Pt. Lookout 5/30/64; subject notes statement that he was in South when war broke out and was forced into Rebel army. Took first opportunity in giving self up; desires to take oath and return to native state of New Jersey; released Pt. Lookout 5/31/64; age 25.

HOUSE, GEORGE W. JR.: Pvt.; Co. G 5/18/61 Boydton; sent to hosp. in Richmond. Sick through 7/62; name on a Register of Claims of Deceased soldiers... filed 7/25/63 (no date of death). Died at Mecklenburg Co.

HOUSE, GEORGE W. SR.: Pvt.; Co. G 5/18/61 Boydton. Present, detailed as Ambulance Driver 1/62; deserted near Leesburg 9/62; returned, died at Mecklenburg 12/12/62 of small pox.

HOWERTON, JAMES H.: 1 Sgt. Co. E 6/8/61 Danville; present until put on detailed service 10/61 through 1/62; absent wounded 7/62 through 9/62.

HOWERTON, JOSEPH T.: Pvt.; Co. E 6/8/61 Danville; Pvt. to 2 Corpl. 1/1/62; 2 Corpl. to 5 Sgt. by 6/30/63; 5 Sgt. to 3 Sgt. by 8/31/64; 3 Sgt. to 2 Sgt. by 12/31/64; 2 Sgt. to 1 Sgt. by 2/25/65. Age 26. Present until admitted Danville G.H. 8/30/62 fever; deserted 10/29/62; returned prior to 6/30/63; pres. through 12/31/64; on furlough 2/25/65; Chimborazo Hosp. #5 3/10/65 Erysipelas Facial.

HOWERTON, WILLIAM H.: Pvt.; Co. E 3/13/62 Danville; Pvt. to 4 Sgt. by 6/30/63; 4 Sgt. to 2 Sgt. by 8/31/64; appointed 2 Lieut. 11/15/64. Present until admitted Chimborazo #4 7/1/62 gunshot wound, hand. WIA 7/1/62 Malvern Hill. Alive in Danville on 12/18/94.

HUBBARD, JOHN H. S.: Pvt.; Co. C 10/14/64 Danville; Present until POW Five Forks 4/1/65; City Pt. to Pt. Lookout 4/6/65; released there 6/13/65; res. Pitts Co.; dk. complex., brown hair, hazel eyes, 5'7½".

HUDGENS, WILLIAM H.: Pvt.; 2nd Co. I 7/6/61 Norfolk. Present through 12/31/61, last roll.

HUDSON, JOHN H.: Corpl.; Co. B, no date. Died in camp near Manassas 8/18/61 typhoid fever. Born Pittsylvania Co., age 20 as of death; 6'0", dk. complex., dk. hair, dk. eyes, farmer.

HUGHES, FRANCIS A.: Pvt.; Co. E 6/8/61 Danville. Present, listed as teamster 7/62; discharged by order of conscript act 9/15/62 at Camp near Leesburg.

HUGHES, WALTER B.: Pvt.; Co. E 6/18/61 Danville; pres. until medical discharge 2/28/62; age 26, 5'8", dk. complex., dk. hair, black eyes. Debility from typhoid and tuberculosis. Reenlisted 8/15/62; pres. until WIA 5/16/64; admitted Chimborazo #2 5/17/64 v.s. right thigh; furloughed 60 days 7/24/64, age 28; admitted Danville H. 9/18/64, v.s. right thigh. Deserted 11/12/64; returned, given detached duty with Brigade Qr. Master. Chimborazo, neuralgia #4 3/18/65.

HUGHEY, A. T.: Pvt.; Co. K 2/24/62 Cascade. Present in hosp. 5-6/62. Present through 2/25/65; paroled Appomattox 4/19/65.

HUGHEY, J. J.: Pvt.; Co. K 3/1/62 Cascade; admitted Chimborazo #4 6/4/62 typhoid fever; died there of same 6/11/62.

HUMPHREY, JOSEPH R.: (Also listed as James R.) Pvt.; Co. H 3/9/63 Orange C.H. Present until POW at Chester Gap 7/21/63 or Brandy Station 8/1/63; Old Capitol Prison to Pt. Lookout 8/8/63; died and bur. there 9/5/63, no cause given. CSR also states "Left sick at Front Royal in 8/63 and supposed to be in the hands of the enemy."

HUNDLEY, CHARLES W.: Pvt.; Co. D 6/15/61 Whitsnell; discharged 8/21/61 syphilis 4 years standing; conscripted and assigned Co. D 38th 7/31/62 Danville; present until WIA g.s. wound left temporal bone and POW Gettysburg 7/3/63; Ft. McHenry to Chester Gen. Hosp. 7/31/63; to Hammond H. Pt. Lookout 10/4/63; paroled there, sent to City Pt. 3/16/64 for exchange; returned to duty, no date; killed 6/17/64 Bermuda H.

HUNDLEY, JAMES M.: Corpl.; Co. K 6/2/61 Cascade; present until WIA Gettysburg 7/3/63 g.s.w. right foot, injuring bones. Gen'l. Hosp. #1 Richmond, given 30 day furlough 7/21/63; present by 1/64; Chimborazo #5 5/23/64; v.s. left leg, trans. Danville 5/26/64. Pres. but detailed to make Regimental Record by 8/31/64. Pvt. to Corpl. by 5/62, Corpl. to Pvt. by 4/1/64. Res. Sandy River.

HUNDLEY, JASON B.: Pvt.; Co. A 5/30/61 Kentuck; detailed as Commissary Sgt. 1/1/62-3/62. Chimborazo #5 5/3/62, catarrh. Present until POW Dinwiddie C.H. 4/2/65; City Pt. to Pt. Lookout 4/4/65; released there 6/13/65; res. Pitts. Co.; dk. complex., brn. hair, dk. hazel eyes, 5'11".

HUNDLEY, JOHN H.: Pvt.; Co. B 6/9/61 Winchester; pres. until died in Richmond hosp. 1/12/62.

HUNDLEY, JOHN M.: Pvt.; Co. D 7/31/62 Danville; conscript. Present, assigned teamster 10/62; paroled at Appomattox 4/9/65.

HUNDLEY, JOSEPH T.: Pvt.; Co. K, no date. Paroled Appomattox 4/9/65.

HUNT, BENJAMIN L.: Pvt.; Co. D 10/14/64 Danville. Present through 2/25/65.

HUNT, JOHN T.: Co. F. 2 Cpl. Post-war record only.

HUNT, JOHN W.: Pvt.; Co F 6/4/61. Republican Grove; pres. until deserted 3/16/64; returned 8/7/64 6 months pay deducted; deserted and received by Federals 2/17/65 Bermuda H. to Wash., D.C. where oath given 2/20/65 and furnished trans. to Jefferson Co., Ill.

HUNT, RYLAND LOGAN: Born 3/28/18. Pvt.; Co. F 6/4/61. Repl. Grove; present until sent to Manassas Junction to guard baggage 11/61-1/62; entered Chimborazo #4 5/18/62 Oedema; discharged 9/3/62 term of service having expired. Died 6/25/92 Pitts. Co.

HUTCHERSON, JAMES F.: Pvt.; Co. G 5/18/61 Boydton, Pvt. to Corpl. 4/1/62; pres. until WIA Malvern Hill 7/1/62; entered Charlottesville H. 1/6/62 with syphilis secondary; admitted Chimborazo #2 8/10/63 syphilis; returned to duty 10/28/63; POW in hosp. Richmond 4/3/65; escaped from hosp. 4/26/65.

HUTCHERSON, JOSEPH: Pvt.; Co. B 6/12/61 Callands; died in camp near Manassas 8/19/61 typhoid fever. Born Pittsylvania Co. Age 40, 6'2", fair complex., blue eyes, light hair, Farmer.

HUTCHERSON, NATHAN B.: Pvt.; Co. D 6/25/61 Richmond. Present until sent Gen. Hosp. Richmond with rheumatism 10/25/61; returned 2/10/62; sent Manassas G.H. 3/5/62 sick; discharged 6/12/62 at Richmond; reenlisted 8/5/63; POW Harpers Farm 4/6/65; City Pt. to Pt. Lookout 4/15/65; released there 6/14/65; res. Pitts Co.; fair complex., dark brown hair, grey eyes; 6'2¼".

HUTCHERSON, WILLIAM H.: Pvt.; Co. D 5/24/61 Whitmell; present until entered Orange Court House Genl. Hosp. 12/18/61, fever; returned to duty 3/4/62; Pvt. to Sgt. by 4/1/64; pres. until paroled Appomattox 4/9/65.

HUTCHESON, JOHN V.: Pvt.; Co. G 3/31/62 Boydton; absent, sick in hosp. 5/11/62-5/1/63.

HYLER, WILLIAM J.: Pvt.; Co. D 10/14/61 Danville,; pres. until deserted 1/28/65; POW in Richmond hosps. 4/3/65; Libby Prison to Newport News 4/23/65; paroled 5/2/65.

INGE, CASWELL F.: Pvt.; Co. F 6/4/61. Repl. Grove; Confed. Hosp. 12/3/62, Culpeper, Va., rheumatism. Present, detailed as Blacksmith prior to 7/1/63; deserted 2/26/64.

INMAN, HENRY W.: Pvt.; Co. D 5/24/61 Whitmell; left at Winchester, sick 7/18/61; discharged 9/4/61, no reason given.

INMAN, MEMORY A.: Pvt.; Co. D 5/24/61 Whitmell; absent sick from 6/21/61-10/61; medical discharge 11/11/61 general debility; reenlisted 8/28/62 Danville conscripted. Reassigned 38th Co. D; present until WIA Drewry's Bluff 5/16/64; admitted Howard's Grove 5/17/64. v.s. left breast; returned to duty 10/11/64; present through last roll 2/25/65. Alive 7/21/84.

INMAN, WILLIS A.: Pvt.; Co. D 5/24/61 Whitmell; died 7/27/61 or 8/5/61 at Winchester, no cause given. Buried Stonewall Cem., Winchester.

IRBY, EDMOND: Pvt.; Co. C (no date given); admitted Chimborazo #2 5/11/62 debility; returned to duty 7/20/62.

IRONMONGER, JAMES: Pvt.; 2nd Co. I 3/10/62 Norfolk Co.; admitted Chimborazo #4 5/13/64, rheumatism chronic. Returned 12/8/64; deserted to the Federals 2/17/65; Bermuda H. to Wash. D.C. 2/21/65. Oath taken and trans. furnished to Norfolk, Va.

IRONMONGER, WILLIAM C.: Pvt.; 2nd Co. I 3/15/62 Norfolk Co.; present until deserted to the Federals 2/20/65 Bermuda H.; to Wash. D.C.; oath taken there; trans. furnished to Norfolk, Va.

IRVIN, JOSEPH: Pvt.; Co. C, no date given. Mustered for 6/62.

JACKSON, ABEL: Pvt.; Co. A 5/30/61 Kentuck; present through 8/31/61; died in Lynchburg G.H. 12/20/62 variola; born Pittsylvania

JACKSON, CHESLEY: Pvt.; Co. B, no date given; died in Winchester 8/9/61 typhoid fever; buried Stonewall Cem., Winchester.

JACKSON, DAVID W.: Pvt.; Co. F 6/4/61 Repl. Grove; pres. until admitted Danville G.H. 1/7/62. Sent to Chimborazo #5 3/10/62 Parotills [?]; returned by 8/62 when detailed as Co. Cook; present until deserted to the Federals 2/23/65 near Bermuda H. to Wash. D.C. 2/24/65 where oath taken and trans. furnished to Utica, N.Y.

JACKSON, GREEN M.: Pvt.; Co. A 3/13/62 Kentuck; present through 2/25/65.

JACKSON, JAMES A.: 2 Lieut.; Co. B 6/4/61 Callands; appted. 2 Lieut. 6/8/61; present until sent on recruiting service 2/15/62-3/62; dropped 5/1/62, failed to be reelected.

JACKSON, JAMES H.: Pvt.; Co. C 5/30/61 Laurel Grove; present until admitted Richmond G.H. #18 3/2/62 chronic rheumatism; died there 3/11/62. b. Oakwood Cem., Richmond.

JACKSON, LEWIS H.: Pvt.; Co. A, no date given; absent in Hosp. Chimborazo #5 (8/20/62); transferred to Petersburg H. 11/14/62; returned prior to Gettysburg where WIA & POW 7/4/63; sent to Gen. Hosp. Chester, Pa. 7/17/63 where died 8/1/63 pyemia; Grave #100 Chester Cemetery.

JACOBS, AARON L.: Pvt.; Co. H, no date given; sent to Chimborazo 4/24/62; convalescent; returned for duty 7/30/62. Probably WIA at Chester Sta. 5/10/64.

JACOBS, C. A.: Pvt.; Co. H 2/17/62, Richmond; admitted Chimborazo #2 5/21/62 bronchitis; transferred to Farmville 6/6/62 there deserted 11/6/62; entered Howard's Grove G.H., Richmond 1/13/64; died there 1/27/64 variola. May be bur. Oakwood Cem., Richmond.

JACOBS, DAVID: Co. H. Pvt. Killed Chester Sta. 5/10/64. Post-war record only.

JACOBS, JOHN D.: Corpl.; Co. H 3/19/62 Lynchburg; pres. until deserted 7/62; returned by 4/1/64; pres. until POW Drewry's Bluff 5/10/64; Bermuda H. to Ft. Monroe 5/14/64 to Ft. Lookout 5/16/64; paroled there; exchanged from Aikens Landing 3/14/65.

JAMES, GEORGE T.: Pvt.; 2nd Co. I 7/6/61 Norfolk Co.; present until absent sick in Richmond Hosp. 6/20/64. Entered Chimborazo #5 7/16/64, haemoptysis; POW in Richmond Hosps. 4/3/65; Libby Prison to Newport News 4/23/65; oath taken there 7/1/65; res. Norfolk. Dark complex., dark hair, dark eyes, 5'6".

JAMES, JOHN E.: Sgt.; 2nd Co. I 7/6/61 Norfolk Co.; absent admitted 6/7/64 Chimborazo #3, syphilis; returned for duty 9/16/64; deserted to the Federals 2/20/65 near Bermuda H. Sent to Wash. D.C. 2/24/65; oath taken, trans. furnished to Norfolk.

JAMES, RICHARD: Pvt.; 1st Co. I 3/6/62 Clarksville; present admitted Chimborazo #2 4/14/62 rubeola.

JEFFERSON, HAILY R.: b. 5/24/42. Pvt.; Co. K 6/2/61 Cascade; present until WIA 8/25/64; admitted Chimborazo #3 8/26/64 v.s. left thigh mid 3rd, minnie ball; furloughed 45 days 9/13/64; admitted Chimborazo #4 12/10/64; g.s.w. left thigh; transf. to Danville H. 1/25/65; vulnus sclopeticum in leg; returned to duty 4/11/65. d. 4/1/26. bur. at site of Mt. Zion Methodist Ch. on Rt. 610 in Franklin Co. just west of Pittsylvania Co. line.

JEFFERSON, HENRY C.: Pvt.; Co. B 10/14/64 Pittsylvania; conscript; present until deserted 1/7/65.

JENNINGS, JOHN B.: Pvt.; Co. F 7/5/61 Hermitage Camp; Pvt. to 3 Corpl. by 7/1/63; 3 Corpl. to 5 Sgt. 11/1/64. Present, detailed Ambulance Driver 8/62; Chimborazo #2 5/11/62 diarrhea; returned 7/20/62; POW Gettysburg and WIA in left chest 7/5/63; paroled DeCamp Gen'l. Hosp., Davids Island 8/24/63; admitted Farmville H. 8/20/63 vul. selop., g.s.w. left breast; deserted 9/14/63 from there; returned to duty by 4/1/64; POW Five Forks 4/1/65; to Pt. Lookout 4/6/65; oath taken 6/28/65; res. Halifax Co.; lt. complex.; brown hair, hazel eyes, 5'7¼".

JENNINGS, JOHN W.: Pvt.; Co. A, no date given; admitted Chimborazo #2 5/12/62 fever; furloughed 5/13/62; died at home Pittsylvania Co. of fever 8/12/62. Widow: Winifred Jennings.

JENNINGS, LAFAYETTE: Enl.; Co. F 6/4/61 Republican Grove; elected from 1st Sgt. to Capt. 4/29/62; present until WIA Seven Pines 5/31/62; returned; present until WIA Gettysburg 7/3/63; grape shot wound face fracturing upper jaw; resigned 2/10/65; res. Republican Grove.

JENNINGS, WILLIAM W.: Born 7/32. Pvt.; Co. F 9/21/64 Bermuda H.; absent, assigned to light duty at Major Thompson's Quarters 10/64; deserted 2/2/65.

JENNINGS, WILLIAM H.: Pvt.; Co. A, no date given; sent to Richmond 6/62 sick.

JENNNINGS, WILLIAM T.: Pvt.; Co. K 6/2/61 Cascade; present until died 9/1/61 typhoid fever; born Pitts. Co.; age 32 at time of death; 5'9", dark complex., dark hair, blue eyes; trade mechanic.

JEWELL, SAMUEL: Pvt.; Co. H 5/4/64 Rockingham; conscript; deserted from Hanover Junction 5/20/64.

JEWELL, SOLOMON: Pvt.; Co. H 5/4/64 Rockingham; conscript; deserted from Hanover Junction 5/20/64.

JOHNS, JOHN H.: Pvt.; Co. H. Enlisted in 1864 and served 5 months. Post-war record only.

JOHNS, THOMAS J.: Pvt.; Co. C 5/30/61 Laurel Grove; present until WIA severely shoulder Seven Pines 5/31/62; absent through 2/25/65; returned to be POW Five Forks 4/1/65; City Pt. to Pt. Lookout 4/6/65; oath taken there 6/14/65; res. Pitts. Co.; fair complex., auburn hair, blue eyes, 5'7¾".

JOHNSON, RICHARD W.: Pvt.; Co. B 7/10/61 Winchester; present until WIA 5/31/62 Seven Pines; admitted Danville Hosp. 6/4/62 discharged from service 9/16/62, disability from wounds.

JOHNSON, THOMAS N.: Pvt.; 2nd Co. I 4/7/62 Lynchburg; deserted 4/27/64.

JONES, ALEXANDER M.: Pvt.; Co. K 3/10/62 Cascade; absent, sick Chimborazo #3 4/14/62; trans. to Danville H 6/4/62; returned to duty 7/30/62; transferred to 57th Va. Regt. by 8/31/62.

JONES, AMOS: Pvt. Co. H. Died at Manassas in 1861. Postwar record only.

JONES, ASA W.: Sgt.; Co. H 7/2/61 Pittsylvania C.H.; present until sent to Danville hosp. 1/2/62; returned to duty 6/15/62; pres. through 4/1/64. Killed at Chester Station 5/10/64.

JONES, CABOT: Pvt. Co. H. Postwar record only.

JONES, EDWARD: Pvt.; Co. H 10/14/64 Pittsylvania; absent 12/16/64 Danville Hosp.; chronic rheumatism; returned to duty 4/8/65.

JONES, EDWARD S.: Pvt.; Co. A, no date given. Admitted Chimborazo #1 5/28/62 diarrhea; died there 6/12/62 of diarrhoea. Probably bur. Oakwood Cem., Richmond. Widow: Frances Jones.

JONES, ELISHA: Pvt.; Co. H 7/2/61 Pittsylvania C.H.; present until died at Culpeper Hosp. 3/29/62.

JONES, GEORGE: Pvt. Co. H. Postwar record only.

JONES, GREEN WADE: b. 4/43. 6/4/61 Co. B Callands; pres. until WIA seriously 7/1/62 Malvern Hill; admitted Chimborazo #4 7/1/62 g.s.w. of forearm; reported for duty 10/11/63; detailed as regt. shoemaker by 10/13/64. Died 10/90, bur. off Rt. 57 west of Chatham near Ruby Fox's Store.

JONES, ICHABOD: Co. H. Pvt. Post-war record only.

JONES, J. ARMISTEAD: Pvt.; Co. K, no date given; Died at S. Carolina Hosp. Post Jefferson, Charlottesville, Va. 4/26/62, pneumonia.

JONES, JAMES T.: Pvt.; Co. H 3/62, Pittsylvania; present until POW Dinwiddie C.H. 4/3/65; City Pt. to Pt. Lookout 4/13/65; released 6/28/65; res. Pitts. Co.; light complex., brown hair, hazel eyes, 5'7¼". Occupation listed as both "laborer" and "mechanic".

JONES, JOEL T.: Lieut.; Co. F 6/4/61 Repl. Grove; elected 2nd Lieut. 4/29/62; promoted 1 Lieut. 3/14/64; present until extra duty as A.A.C.S. for Regt. 6/62-7/62; returned by time POW Gettysburg 7/3/63; Ft. McHenry 7/6/63 to Ft. Del., no date given; to Johnson's Island 7/18/63; paroled there, sent to Pt. Lookout 3/14/65 for exchange.

JONES, JOHN H.: Pvt.; Co. H 10/14/64; Pittsylvania. Listed as deserted 12/64; but on list of prisoners paroled at Appomattox 4/9/65.

JONES, JOHN W.: Pvt.; Co. H 5/4/64 Rockingham; conscript, absent, admitted Charlottesville hosp. 5/26/64; transferred to Staunton 5/28/64; had not returned to duty as of 2/26/65.

JONES, J. T.: Pvt.; 1st Co. I 6/20/61 Clarksville; absent and sent to Richmond 3/6/62; present, detailed as cook 6/62.

JONES, L. C.: Pvt.; 1st Co. I 3/5/62 Clarksville; admitted Chimborazo #2 5/12/62 catarrh.

JONES, PETER: Pvt.; 1st Co. I 3/12/62 Clarksville; absent, sent to Chimborazo 4/24/62 measles.

JONES, PLEASANT: Pvt.; Co. G 3/2/64 Mecklenburg; present, reported back to Regt. under guard 8/28/64; admitted Chimborazo #4 12/26/64 chronic rheumatism, absent sick through 2/65.

JONES, SAMUEL J.: Pvt.; Co. F 6/4/61 Repl. Grove; Pvt. to 4 Corpl. by 7/1/63; to 1 Corpl. 11/1/64. Pres. until admitted Danville H. 8/6/62 debilitas; there deserted 1/1/63; returned by 7/1/63; WIA Drewry's Bluff 5/16/64 sent to hosp Chimborazo on same date, v.s. left leg; furloughed 60 days; paroled at Farmville, no date given.

JONES, THOMAS J.: Pvt.; Co. H 7/2/61 Pittsylvania C.H.; present until sent to Orange Court House Gen. Hosp. 12/18/61 paraplegia; disability discharge about 3/28/62.

JONES, T. JEFF.: Pvt.; 1st Co. I 6/20/62 Clarksville. Present, no other information.

JONES, YANCEY B.: Pvt.; Co. H 7/2/61 Pittsylvania C.H.; present until admitted Chimborazo #3 10/23/62; g.s.w. in arm; deserted there 10/26/62; arrested and returned 10/28/62; detached as nurse in Chimborazo #4 11/6/62; returned to duty 2/5/63; deserted to the enemy 2/1/64 near Newbern, N.C.; sent to Ft. Monroe 2/17/64 took oath there; sent to Baltimore, Md.; res. Orange Co., N.C.; sallow complex.; brown hair, blue eyes, 6'0". Died 11/5/1908 in Ky.

JORDAN, MILES H.: Pvt.; 2nd Co. I 7/6/61 Norfolk Co.; POW 8/25/64 near Howletts House Bermuda H. to Ft. Monroe 8/26/64 to Pt. Lookout 8/28/64; released there 6/13/65.

JOYCE, RICHARD J.: Sgt.; Co. A 5/30/61 Kentuck; 2nd Sgt. elected to 2 Lieut. 10/13/61; promoted 1 Lieut. 12/29/61; promoted Capt. 7/3/63; present until WIA Seven Pines 5/31/62; absent through 7/62; returned 8/62; captured 8/25/64 near Bermuda Hundred and soon died as POW.

KASEY, JAMES: Pvt.; Co. H 4/26/64 Dublin; conscript; present through last roll 4/26/64.

KEATTS, LAWSON S.: Pvt.; Co. B 8/14/62 Danville. Gen. Hosp. Camp Winder 12/19/62, no cause given. Present until admitted Danville H. 3/14/63 debilitas; returned 5/19/63; present through 1/1/65.

KELLY, JOHN: Pvt.; Co. G, no date given. Substitute for R. Boyd; deserted 6/4/62, same day Boyd brought him to Regt.

KELLY, MICHAEL: Pvt.; Co. D 7/29/62 substitute for John P. Millner. Deserted about 8/1/62.

KELTER, JAMES: Pvt.; 1st Co. I 3/5/62, Clarksville; present until reported missing after Battle Malvern Hill 7/1/62.

KENDRICK, JAMES: Pvt., Co. H. Killed at Gettysburg, Post War record only.

KENDRICK, THOMAS: Pvt.; Co. B 6/4/61 Callands; present until Chimborazo #1 2/20/63 fracture of leg; returned 3/28/63; absent, confined at Castle Thunder for desertion by 4/1/64; deserted 6/10/64; on a list of prisoners, confined in E. D. M. Prison; who volunteered in Winder Legion to defend Richmond against Sheridan's '64 raid. Pardoned by Pres. dated 8/3/64.

KENDRICK, WILLIAM O.: Pvt.; Co. C 5/30/61 Laurel Grove; pres. until sent to hosp., admitted Danville H. 6/29/62 chronic diarrhea. Died at his father's home 9/14/62. Father: Barksdale Kendrick.

KENNEDY, THOMAS: Co. K; Pvt. Enl. 4/62, substitute. Deserted. Post-war record only.

KIDD, GEORGE WASHINGTON: Born 12/45. Pvt.; Co. H 5/4/64 Petersburg, conscript. Pres. until deserted to the Federals 2/17/65; near Bermuda Hundred, sent to Wash. D.C. 2/21/65 there oath taken and trans. furnished to Wash. D.C. Died 9/4/09 at Beach, Chesterfield Co. Bur. 2nd Branch Bapt. Ch. Cem., Winterpock.

KINDRICK, HARDEN: Pvt.; Co. B 7/28/64 Pittsylvania; conscript. Present until deserted 1/7/65.

KINDRICK, LINWOOD: Pvt.; Co. H 2/8/63 at Guinea Station. KIA Gettysburg, 7/3/63.

KING, GEORGE W.: Pvt.; Co. D 6/1/63 Danville; transferred to 38th Co. D from 39th Va. Battn. Cav. in exchange for C.L. Carter 12/6/64; present until paroled at Greensboro, N.C. 5/1/65, in terms of agreement between Sherman and Joe E. Johnston 4/26/65.

KING, JOHN R.: Pvt.; Co. K 3/5/62 Cascade; absent, admitted Charlottesville G.H. 3/31/62; medical discharge there 8/29/62 chronic rheumatism.

KING, JOSHUA W.: Corpl.; Co. D 10/11/64; pres. until POW White Oak Road 4/1/65; City Pt. to Pt. Lookout 4/5/65; released there 6/28/65. Admitted Pt. Lookout Genl. Hosp. 6/29/65, chronic diarrhea; released 7/3/65. Res. Pitts. Co.; light complex., brown hair, hazel eyes, 5'8".

KIRBY, RICHARD M.: Pvt.; Co. C, no date given. Absent, sent to Richmond hosp. 5-9/62.

KISSINGER, JAMES: Co. H. Pvt. Enl. 5/64. Post-war record only.

KISSINGER, THOMAS H.: Pvt.; Co. H 2/9/64 Fredericksburg, conscript. Deserted in trenches near Bermuda H. 7/28/64; captured by Feds 12/29/64; sent from Bermuda H. to Wash. D.c. 1/4/65; there took oath; trans. furnished to Phila., Pa.

KITTER, JAMES: Co. I. Post-war record only.

KNIGHT, HENRY C.: Pvt.; Co. E 6/8/61 Danville; Pvt. to 1 Sgt. 1/1/62; elected to 2nd Lieut. 4/29/62; resigned 9/1/64; present until resignation.

KUHN, THOMAS C.: Pvt.; 2nd Co. I 8/29/61 Norfolk Co.; present as of 8/31/64, only muster roll date.

LAMBERT, JOHN N.: Pvt.; 2nd Co. I 2/15/62 Norfolk Co.; Present until admitted Chimborazo #2 5/6/64 continued fever; returned 6/13/64; deserted to the Federals 12/20/64; 1/30/64 captured near Bermuda H.; took oath there; sent to Wash. D.C. 2/4/65; trans. furnished to Norfolk, Va.

LAMBERT, THOMAS J.: Pvt.; 2nd Co. I 3/1/62 Norfolk Co.; Pres. until deserted to enemy 12/20/64; received by Federals 1/10/65 Bermuda H. to Wash. D.C. 1/14/65; there oath taken and trans. provided to Norfolk.

LAMBKIN, JAMES: Pvt.; Co. K 3/1/62 Cascade; present until WIA 5/31/62 Seven Pines; returned by 9/62 when given extra duty in Ambulance Corps in Confed. Hosp. Culpeper 11/3/62, pneumonia. Name on list of soldiers killed in battle or died of wounds or disease, no date or place given.

LAMONT, HENRY: Pvt.; 2nd Co. I 3/15/62 Norfolk Co.; pres. until Chimborazo 5/25/64. Bilious fever; returned 6/2/64; POW 8/25/64.

LAND, HENRY: Pvt.; 2nd Co. I 3/20/62 Norfolk Co.; Pres. til POW Amelia C.H. 4/3/65; City Pt. to Pt. Lookout 6/13/65; there released 6/14/65; res. Richmond; light complex., brown hair, hazel eyes, 5'5¼".

LAND, HENRY M.: Pvt.; Co. K 3/10/62 Cascade; Pres. til sick in hosp. 5-6/62; returned by 12/18/62; Chimborazo #4 12/5/62, neuralgia; present through 2/25/65; admitted Richmond G.H. #9 3/5/65. Paroled at Lynchburg 4/15/65.

LAND, JOHN L.: Pvt.; Co. K, no date given; admitted Chimborazo #2 3/20/62; died there 4/10/62 pneumonia.

LAND, THOMAS J.: Pvt.; Co. K 3/10/62 Cascade; absent on register of Farmville hosp. dated 4/19/62, listed as having died.

LANDRUM, JAMES A.: Pvt.; Co. E 6/8/61 Danville; present until admitted Chimborazo #3 10/21/61; discharged there 11/1/61 variocelli.

LANE, HILARY: Pvt.; Co. H 7/6/61 Richmond; Pres. til sent to Richmond hosp. 2/27/62; died there 3/17/62.

LANIER, ADOLPHUS M.: 1 Lieut.; Co. D 5/24/61 Whitmell; Corpl. to Sgt., no date given; apptd. through election to 1 Lieut. 7/26/62; POW & WIA Gettysburg 7/3/63, g.s.w. both legs, in body and head; hosp. Gettysburg to Gen. Hosp. Chester, Pa. 7/31/63 to Sandusky, Ohio 8/31/63 to Johnson's Island; to Pt. Lookout 3/21/65; to Ft. Del. 4/28/65; there released 6/12/65; res. Pitts. Co.; ruddy complex., dark hair, grey eyes, 5'9". Alive on 5/19/84.

106

LANIER, JAMES A.: Pvt.; Co. A 10/14/64 Danville; Pres. til POW. Dinwiddie C.H. 4/2/65; City Pt. to Pt. Lookout 4/4/65; there released 6/14/65; res. Pitts Co.; lt. complex., blk. hair; brown eyes, 5'6½".

LANIER, WILLIAM S.: Cpl.; Co. D 5/24/61 Whitmell; Corpl. to 5 Sgt. by 12/31/64. Present through 2/25/65.

LATHAM, JAMES W.: Pvt.; Co. F 6/4/61 Repl. Grove; pres. til detailed wagoner for Regt. 11/61-1/62; admitted Richmond Gen. H. #18 3/2/62 diarrhoea. Returned 4/12/62; Chimborazo #5 admitted 7/8/62; admitted Charlottesville 11/6/62 toncilitis; returned prior to 7/1/63; absent in arrest 4/1/64, no reason given. Returned to be WIA 8/25/64 admitted Chimborazo #4 8/25/64 g.s.w. left knee joint; absent wounded through 2/25/65.

LAW, GEORGE D.: Pvt.; Co. D 3/1/62 Whitmell; died 6/12/62 at camp near Richmond. Father: Burwell Law.

LAW, GEORGE W. C.: Pvt.; Co. K 6/2/61 Cascade; pres. til WIA 5/31/62 Seven Pines, returned by time "supposed killed" at Gettysburg; dropped from roll 8/19/64.

LAW, JAMES T.: Pvt.; Co. D 10/14/64 Danville; pres. til admitted Chimborazo Hosp. #1 11/6/64 rheumatism; to Danville 11/25/64 chronic rhematism to Raleigh, N.C., Pettigrew G.H. 11/26/64 same; returned duty 12/22/64; POW White Oak Rd. 4/1/65; City Pt. to Pt. Lookout 4/5/65; released there 6/5/65.

LAWSON, JOHN O. (possibly James): Pvt.; Co. H 3/9/63 Green Co.; absent, "deserted from battlefield of Gettysburg" according to CSR. Post-war records but most probably KIA at Gettysburg 7/3/63.

LEATH, JOSIAH W.: Sgt.; 2nd Co. I 7/6/61 Norfolk Co.; WIA 5/16/64 Drewry's Bluff; admitted Chimborazo #3 5/20/62; g.s.w. through right leg; furloughed 6/10/64 for 40 days; returned prior to 12/31/64; POW Five Forks 4/1/65; City Pt. to Hart's Island 4/7/65; released there 6/20/65; res. Norfolk; light complex., light hair, blue eyes, 5'9".

LEE, HENDERSON LEWIS: Born 10/23/26. Appted. 2 Lieut. 5/15/61; promoted 1st Lieut. 12/11/61; promoted Capt. 4/29/62; promoted Major 11/15/63; present until WIA Gettysburg 7/3/63; in hosp. from wounds, g.s.w. top of upper arm, requiring surgical removal of part of bone, from report of Medical Director's office Richmond, dated 10/14/64; retired 12/2/64 result of wounds; res. Non intervention, Va., Lunenburg Co. Died 3/5/94 at Lee Hall in Nottoway Co.

LEE, THOMAS J.: Pvt.; 2nd Co. I 6/26/61 Norfolk Co.; pres. til WIA on skirmish 8/25/64, Chester Station; admitted Chimborazo #3 8/27/64 v.s. right thigh amputated; admitted Charlottesville 2/17/65 same; transferred 3/1/65 Chimborazo #3; application for retirement approved 3/13/65. Res. Norfolk Co.; died 1903.

LEFTWICH, ANDREW J.: Pvt.; Co. D 5/24/61 Whitmell; WIA, seriously 7/1/62 Malvern Hill; died of wounds received there 7/11/62 at Pitts. Co.

LEGIN, ALEXANDER: Pvt.; 1st Co. I, no date given; died of typhoid fever 10/14/61.

LEMONS, JACKSON: Pvt.; Co. K 2/4/62 Cascade; pres. til WIA Second Manassas 8/30/62; lower third left leg amputated; retired from active service 4/23/64 on a list of Invalid Corps, P.A.C.S.; dropped from rolls 8/19/64.

LENCAVE, JOHN S.: Pvt.; Co. I 6/20/61; died 9/2/61; father: John Lencave.

LESSEE, THOMAS: Co. A. Pvt. Post-war record only.

LEWIS, BENJAMIN H.: Pvt.; Co. C 5/30/61 Laurel Grove; present until on furlough 2-3/62; absent in hosp. 5-6/62; returned to be WIA, slightly, Malvern Hill 7/1/62; contusion of the scalp, admitted Chimborazo #2 7/4/62.

LEWIS, CHARLES JAMES: Born 1848. Pvt.; Co. C 11/9/64 Danville; admitted Chimborazo #4 12/16/64, typhoid fever; furloughed 60 days 2/8/65. Died 1924 in Danville.

LEWIS, DANIEL L.: Pvt.; Co. A 8/10/63 Kentuck; pres. til admitted Chimborazo 8/7/64 chronic diarrhea; furloughed from there 40 days 8/16/64; returned by 12/31/64; admitted Rich. G.H. #9, double scrotal hernia.

LEWIS, ELI J.: Pvt.; Co. C 3/7/62 Laurel Grove, pres. til WIA, right hand, 7/1/62 Malvern Hill; admitted Chimborazo #2; g.s., flesh wound of wrist 7/4/62; retired active service on account of wounds 9/19/64 Part of Invalid Corps. Alive at Pickaway on 7/19/80.

LEWIS, FLEMING J.: Pvt.; Co. A 5/30/61 Kentuck; died at house near camp on Broad Run 8/14/61 of typhoid fever. Father: Royall Lewis.

LEWIS, JOHN: Pvt.; Co. C, no date given; WIA 5/31/62 Seven Pines; admitted Chimborazo #4 6/1/62 contused wound of left arm; transferred to Danville 6/9/62; returned to duty 7/30/62.

LEWIS, JOHN J.: Pvt.; Co. C 3/19/62 Laurel Grove; died Chimborazo #4 4/24/62 pneumonia, bur. Oakwood Cem. Father: Abner C. Lewis.

LEWIS, RICHARD BULLOCK: Born 1843. Sgt.; 1st Co. I, no date given. Transferred to 14th Va. Regt. 1/19/62. Died 1924. Bur. Mecklenburg Co., grave moved due to Buggs Island Lake.

LEWIS, THOMAS J.: Co. C. Pvt. Died in Chimborazo. Post-war record only.

LEWIS, VINCENT W.: Born Va. Pvt.; Co. A 5/30/61 Kentuck; absent on furlough 8/31/61; absent sick at Richmond 2/27/62; returned to be killed on battlefield 5/31/62 Seven Pines, according to Confederate records; Union POW records shows subject a POW after battle; Ft. Monroe to Ft. Del. 6/5/62; exchanged Aiken's Landing 8/5/62. Age 20, 5'3", dark hair, grey eyes, sallow complex. Father: Royal K. Lewis.

LEWIS, WILLIAM H.: born Pitts Co.Pvt.; Co. C 5/30/61 Laurel Grove; pres. til admitted Chimborazo #4 10/26/61 measles; returned to duty 4/15/62; back at Chimborazo #4 4/20/62 colic; returned to duty 4/29/62; Danville 6/20/62; rubeola; returned 7/18/62; admitted Danville H. 4/25/63; erysipelas; medical discharge for same 7/13/63. Age 43, 5'4", dark complex., blue eyes, grey hair, farmer.

LEWIS, WILLIAM L.: Born 1837. Corpl.; Co. B 6/16/61 Callands; Pvt. to 4 Corpl. 12/1/64. Age 20, roll not dated. Pres. til entered Chimborazo #3 3/14/62 neuralgic; returned 4/13/62; readmitted Chimborazo #3 5/10/62 typhoid; returned to be WIA Williamsburg 5/62; returned to be POW Five Forks 4/1/65 City Pt. to Harts Island 4/7/65; released there 6/20/65; res. Pitts Co.; dark complex., dark hair, hazel eyes, 5'9½". Died 1907, buried Chatham, Va. Cem.

LEWIS, WILLIAM T.: Pvt.; Co. C 11/9/64 Danville; present through 2/25/65; paroled Appomattox 4/9/65.

LIGHT, CHARLES M.: Pvt.; Co. F 6/20/61 Hermitage Camp; pres. til POW Gettysburg 7/3/63; WIA, shot in shoulder, there also; from Gettysburg Hosp. to DeCamp Genl. Hosp., Davids Island, N.Y. 7/17/63; died there 7/30/63; Bur. Cypress Hill Cemetery, Long Island, Grave #710.

LINDSEY, JOHN S.: Born: Pittsylvania Co. Sgt.; Co. A 5/30/61 Kentuck; pres. til admitted Danville H. 6/18/62 Febris Int.; returned 7/13/62; detail Provost Guard 8/62; KIA Gettysburg 7/3/63. Father: James H. Lindsey.

LITTRELL, WILLIAM C.: Born Northumberland Co. Musician/Pvt.; 2nd Co. I 5/5/63 Albemarle Co.; detached service Brigade Band from, prior to 12/31/64-2/25/65; paroled Appomattox 4/19/65. Lived in Fredericksburg and Camp Lee Soldiers Home, Richmond. Died 12/24/23 at age 79. Buried Hollywood Cem., east section, Richmond.

LOCKETT, JOHN K.: Born Mecklenburg Co., age 23. Sgt.; 1st Co. I 6/20/61 Clarksville; daily duty in Commissary Dept. 10/61; absent sick 2/2/62-7/17/62, last dated roll. Probably elected 2nd Lt. Father: H. A. Lockett. Blue eyes, dark hair, light complexion, 5'8".

LOGAN, JOHN K.: Sgt.; Co. A 5/30/61 Kentuck; absent on furlough, which expired but unable to report 8/31/61; pvt. to 4 Corpl. 10/1/61; 4 Corpl. to 5 Sgt. 10/19/61; to 4th Sgt. by 1/1/65; present by 10/61; on recruiting service 2/62. Present until 5/12/62 Chimborazo #2 catarrh; returned 6/19/62. Pres. through 2/25/65. Lived in Danville and Camp Lee Soldiers Home, Richmond. Died 2/13/22 at age 86. Bur. Hollywood Cem., east section, Richmond.

LOVE, WILLIAM: Co. I. Pvt. Post-war record only.

LOVELACE, CHARLES M.: Pvt.; Co. C 5/30/61 Laurel Grove; present til admitted Chimborazo #4 6/26/62 "fever interm. great". Returned to duty 8/3/62; cook for Co. 9/62.

LOVELACE, JAMES N.: Pvt.; Co. D 5/24/61 Whitmell; furlough at home near Danville 9/26/61 reported as convalescent 10/15/61. Present until left camp without leave 7/5/62.

LOVELACE, JOHN F.: Pvt.; Co. A, no date given; admitted Chimborazo #4 4/24/62; measles and pneumonia; died there 5/6/62 pneumonia; widow: Amanda Lovelace.

LOVELACE, JOHN H.: Pvt.; Co. C 6/10/61 Richmond; discharged at Richmond 7/1/61, disability.

LOVELACE, NATHANIEL: Corpl.; Co. C 5/30/61 Laurel Grove; Pres. til admitted Chimborazo #4 10/25/61, rheumatism; returned 4/15/62; corpl. to Pvt. by 5/62; discharged 9/5/62, reason, overage.

LOVELACE, THOMAS W.: Born Pitts. Co. Pvt.; Co. E 6/8/61 Danville; pres. til hosp.; Petersburg 1/11/62 with pneumonia. Returned to duty 1/24/62, Charlottesville 3/31/62 with pleurisy; returned to duty 5/1/62; AWOL 8-9/62; died at home, Danville 12/1/62 of typhoid fever. Widow: Narcissa A. Lovelace.

LOVELACE, WILLIAM O.: Pvt.; Co. A 3/11/62 Kentuck; pres. til 3/30/62; admitted Richmond Gen. Hosp. #21, rheumatism; transf. to Lynchburg 5/5/62; absent through 8/62; died at G.H., Liberty, Va. 9/19/62 of pericarditis. Father: John Lovelace.

LOVELACE, WILLIAM A.: Born 2/12/33. Pvt.; Co. C 5/30/61 Laurel Grove; pres. til admitted Chimborazo #5 5/10/62 diarrhea; absent through 9/62; pres. by 12/31/64; pres. through 2/25/65. Died 2/14/18. Buried Stokesland Cem., W. Main St. & Clearview Dr., Danville.

LOYD, JAMES W. B.: Pvt.; 6/14/61 Callands; present until detached to Gainesville to guard hay 12/61-2/62; admitted G.H. #18, Richmond 5/2/62 debilitus; transf. to Lynchburg H. 5/5/62; Charlottesville H. 12/7/62 chronic dysentery; furloughed 12/18/62; Charlottesville admitted 2/1/63 pneumonia conv.; returned to duty 3/28/63; muster roll dated 5/19/63; listed as deserted.

LUKE, SHIELDS S.: enl. 4/23/61 in Co. I "Chatham Grays" of 53rd Regt. at Chatham. Transferred to Co. H of the 38th on 7/8/61 and appointed Sgt. Maj. on 7/9/61. Promoted to 2nd Lt. on 4/29/62. Elected Capt. 5/5/62, according to CSR which may be in error. KIA at Seven Pines 5/31/62. CSR also indicates he served in Co. D of 38th at some time.

LUMPKINS, GEORGE W.: Pvt.; Co. A 10/14/64 Danville; Pres. til killed in Trenches Bermuda H. 11/1/64 by Federal sharpshooters.

LUMPKINS, T. J.: Pvt.; Co. A 10/14/64 Danville; pres. til POW Petersburg 4/2/65; City Pt. to Pt. Lookout 4/4/65; released there 6/14/65; res. Pitts Co.; light complex., auburn hair, blue eyes, 5'6¼".

LYNCH, GEORGE C.: Pvt.; Co. B 6/11/61 Callands; pres. til WIA, severely in right foot at Seven Pines 5/31/62; wounded furlough through 1/1/65. Alive 2 miles west of Dry Fork on 6/19/82.

MACKASEY, ROBERT F.: Sgt.; Co. G 3/24/62 Boydton; pres. til 11/12/62; admitted Winder Hosp.; returned to duty 3/26/63; pres. til admitted Chimborazo #3 2/25/65; returned to duty 3/6/65; POW Farmville 4/6/65; oath taken at Newport News 7/1/65; res. Mecklenburg; fair complex., lt. hair, blue eyes, 5'11".

MACKASEY, THOMAS S.: Pvt.; Co. G 1/26/63 Richmond; Pres. til POW Amelia CH 4/5/65; City Pt. to Pt. Lookout 4/13/65; released there 6/15/65; res. Mecklenburg; fair complex., lt. hair; blue eyes, 5'8¼".

MAHON, GEORGE W.: Pvt.; Co. K 6/2/61 Cascade; present til MWIA 5/31/62 Seven Pines, exact date of death not shown.

MAHON, PLEASANT: Pvt.; Co. K 6/2/61 Cascade; pres. til sick in hosp. 5/62; returned prior to 8/31/62; present, extra duty as Brig. Butcher by 12/31/64; pres. through 2/25/65; paroled Appomattox 4/9/65.

MAHON, PLYANT: Pvt.; Co. K 6/2/61 Cascade; pres. til sent to Chimborazo #4 10/24/61, typhoid fever; returned 11/24/61; present til POW Gettysburg, 7/3/63; took oath at Ft. Del. and released there 6/20/65; res. Henry Co.; dark complex., dark hair, dark eyes, 5'8".

MALLETT, BEVERLY: Pvt.; Co. G 5/18/61 Boydton. Pres. til admitted Petersburg H. 4/27/62, chronic rheumatism; furloughed 6/6/62, 20 days; absent sick at home 6/1/63; admitted Petersburg hosp. 12/5/63 acute diarrhoea, trans. to Episcopal Ch. Hosp., Williamsburg 2/22/64, chronic diarrhoea, transf. to Petersburg 5/7/64 to hosp. at Kittiel Springs, N.C. 6/18/64; returned to duty by 12/31/64.

MALLETT, HORACE L.: enl. 3/13/62 at Boydton. Pvt. in Co. G. Sick in hosp. 4/62 thru 7/62, but present by 5/1/63. Absent in hosp. sick 12/15/64 thru 2/65. Admitted Chimborazo #3 2/25/65 with rheumatism. Paroled at Appomattox CH 4/9/65.

MALLETT, SILAS C.: Pvt.; Co. G 3/12/62 Boydton; pres. til 4/13/62 Chimborazo (chronic diarrhea) through 10/22/62; bronchitis; returned to duty 11/30/64; pres. til POW Five Forks 4/1/65; City Pt. to Hart's Island 4/7/65; released there 6/21/65; res. Mecklenburg; fair complex., lt. hair, hazel eyes, 5'9".

MANN, JOHN T.: Pvt.; Co. K/H 6/2/61 Cascade; transferred to Co. H 38th Va. 7/6/61. Present, extra duty Building Bake Ovens for Brigade 2/62; deserted 9/62; present by Gettysburg when POW 7/3/63 Ft. McHenry 7/6/63 to Ft. Del., no date; there released 6/20/65; res. Pitts Co.; dk. complex., dk. hair; blue eyes, 5'5½".

MANN, WILLIAM H.: Pvt.; Co. E 6/8/61, Danville; pres. til admitted Danville G.H. 8/27/62 erysipelas; returned to duty 10/10/62; but CSR also states deserted 8/31/62 to 2/1/64. Pay deducted accordingly but pardoned by pres.; present through 2/25/65, P.O.W. Five Forks 4/1/65. Took oath 6/15/65. Res. Richmond. Dark complex., brown hair, blue eyes, 5'6¾".

MARSHAL, REUBEN J.: Pvt.; Co. K 6/2/61 Cascade; present until 10/24/61 sent to Rich. Hosp.; WIA 5/31/62, Seven Pines; returned by 8/31/62; extra duty as Co. Cook prior to 8/31/64. Present through 2/25/65.

108

MARSHALL, CLEMENT C.: Sgt.; Co. K 6/2/61 Cascade, 4 Sgt. to Pvt. by 8/31/64; pres. til admitted Chimborazo #4 6/26/62 dysentery, acute; trans. to Danville 7/20/62, debilitas; returned to duty 11/25/62; WIA Gettysburg 7/3/63. Pres. til admitted Danville H. 7/30/63. Returned to duties 8/25/63; pres. til admitted Danville 2/2/65 acute rheumatism; returned to duty 3/9/65. Alive 11/2/21, age 82 in Kentucky.

MARSHALL, DAVID P.: Pvt.; Co. E 2/25/62 Danville; pres. til admitted G.H. #18, Rich. 5/2/62 chronic bronchitis; transferred to Lynchburg H. 5/5/62; absent sick through 6/62; absent, detached provost guard roll, dated 6/30/63; returned by roll dated 8/31/63; pres. until admitted Farmville 6/12/63, v.s. left shoulder, age 17; returned, admitted Danville 6/15/64 v.s. left shoulder; returned to duty 8/2/64; pres. til 2/25/65. Occupation: farmer.

MARSHALL, GEORGE M.: Pvt.; Co. A 5/30/61 Kentuck. Pres. til Chimborazo #5 4/17/62 bronchitis; returned, by 4/1/64; pres. til died of wounds at Rich. Hospital #9 5/13/64; b. Oakwood Cem.

MARSHALL, HUMPHREY: Born 5/13/43 in Pittsylvania Co. Pvt.; Co. K 6/2/61 Cascade; pres. til sent to hosp. Chimborazo #4 10/24/61 typhoid. Returned 12/4/61; 9/62 detached ambulance corps; returned by 4/11/64 Chimborazo #5, no date given; right leg, flesh wound; furloughed 6/3/64; admitted Chimborazo #4 11/16/64 syphilis; returned to duty 12/13/64; present til POW Amelia C.H. 4/3/65 City Pt. to Pt. Lookout 4/13/65; released there 6/15/65. Res. Pitts. Co.; light complex., brown hair, hazel eyes, 5'11¾". Post-war occupation Lumberman. Died 2/1/19, buried Mt. Pleasant, N.C.

MARSHALL, JAMES M.: Sgt.; Co. A 5/30/61 Kentuck; 1st Corpl. to 2 Sgt. by 4/1/64 to 1st Sgt. by 2/25/65; present til POW WIA Gettysburg 7/3/63; Ft. McHenry 7/6/63 to Ft. Del. 7/12/63; paroled there 7/30/63; admitted Rich-Howard's Grove Hosp. 5/17/64 v.s. left knee; returned to duty 8/5/64. Present through 2/25/65. Res. Pittsylvania Co., dark complexion, black hair, dark hazel eyes, 5'10¼".

MARSHALL, THOMAS L.: Pvt.; Co. K 2/25/62 Cascade; was sick in Chimborazo 5/14/62 typhoid til detached to Danville hosp. as ward master 6/10/62, unfit for field duty through 2/25/65.

MARSHALL, WILLIAM B.: Pvt.; Co. A 5/30/61 Kentuck; pres. til died Lynchburg G.H. 4/2/62 typhoid fever.

MARSHALL, WILLIAM M.: Pvt.; Co. E 2/22/62; pres. til deserted 7/3/62.

MARTIN, GARLAND A.: Pvt.; Co. G 9/6/64 Albemarie; listed as deserted 2/65.

MARTIN, GEORGE ALEXANDER: Born 9/3/33 in Norfolk Co. Lawyer. Appointed Capt. 6/26/61, Norfolk Co., Co. B, "St. Bride's Artillery, 20th Bn. Va. Heavy Artillery. Transferred to 38th Regt. as (2nd) Co. I on 5/3/64. Admitted Howard's Grove Hosp., Richmond 5/17/64-8/31/64 with debility. Admitted Richmond Gen. Hosp. #4 9/19/64 with fever. Prom. to Lt. Col. of 38th Regt. on 3/28/65 to be eff. from 12/2/64. In Lynchburg hosp. on 4/9/65. Joined President Davis at Charlotte, NC and accompanied him to Washington, Ga. Surrendered and paroled at Augusta, Ga. Lawyer in New York and Norfolk after war ended Va. State Senator and Delegate.

MARTIN, GEORGE W.: Pvt.; Co. K 5/19/64 Henry Co., conscript; present through 2/25/65; paroled Greensboro 5/8/65.

MARTIN, JAMES M. D.: Pvt.; Co. F 6/4/61; Repl. Grove; present til died. at Camp Manassas 3/2/62, cholera morbus.

MARTIN, MALLORY: Pvt.; Co. H 3/9/63, Orange, POW Gettysburg 7/3/63; CSR also states given detached service by order of Med. Ex. Bd. prior to 12/31/64 at Petersburg.

MARTIN, PLEASANT J.: Born Halifax Co., age 19. Pvt.; Co. F 3/8/62 Republican Grove; pres. until admitted Chimborazo #3 4/17/62. Trans. to Lynchburg 5/16/62; admitted Farmville 9/5/62 diarrhea; medical discharge from there 10/13/62, hypertrophy of heart. 5'7", sallow complex., grey eyes, light hair, farmer.

MARTIN, ROBERT W.: Born Va. Pvt.; Co. F 6/20/61 Hermitage Camp; pres. til admitted Chimborazo #4 10/25/61, typhoid fever and dysentery; returned to duty 12/11/61; present, extra duty as provost guard; court martial Gen. Order #136, 12/27/62); present as of 7/1/63; POW Gettysburg 7/3/63; received Ft. Del. 7/12/63; there released 6/20/65; res. Halifax Co.; dark complex., dark hair, dark eyes, 5'6".

MASON, FLOYD L.: Sgt.; 1st Co. I, no date given; absent at home on sick furlough 8/16/61-10/61. Discharged Surgeons Cert., disability 11/13/61, paralysis.

MATHERLY, BENJAMIN: Born Henry Co. Pvt.; Co. K 3/3/62 Cascade; pres. til entered Danville Hosp. 5/14/62 debilitas; deserted from there 5/19/62; returned to duty 7/4/62; died Spotsylvania 12/27/62, pneumonia. Mother: Elizabeth Matherly.

MATHERLEY, JACKSON: Pvt.; Co. K 6/2/61 Cascade; pres. til entered Chimborazo #1 5/28/62; debility; returned 6/9/62; killed in action 7/1/62, Malvern Hill.

MATHERLY, MADISON: Pvt.; Co. K 3/3/62 Cascade; WIA at Gettysburg; present til 7/16/63 when entered Danville H. for wound; deserted from there 9/9/63; returned Danville hosp. 9/29/63; returned to duty 10/6/63; pres. til admitted Richmond G.H. #9; POW in Richmond Hosp. 4/3/65; admitted Jackson Hosp. 4/8/65; turned over to Pro. Mar. 4/14/65; transferred from Libby Prison to Newport News 4/23/65. Took oath there 6/16/65; res. Danville; light complex., light hair, blue eyes, 6'0".

MATTHEWS, ALEXANDER: Pvt.; 1st Co. I 3/14/62 Clarksville; pres. til admitted Chimborazo #3 4/17/62; returned by time WIA slightly 7/1/62 Malvern Hill.

MATTHEWS, J. KEMP: Pvt.; 1st Co. I 6/20/61; Clarksville; sick at camp near Centerville 12/26/61; returned prior to 7/17/62; admitted Richmond GH #18 4/13/62 chronic bronchitis; returned 4/22/62; res. Mecklenburg.

MATTHEWS, JOHN A.: Pvt.; Co. G 9/6/64 Albemarle, deserted 2/65.

MATTHEWS, JOHN H.: Pvt.; Co. G 5/18/61 Boydton; absent at home 2/5/62, sick; returned prior to time when killed at Malvern Hill 7/1/62. Occupation: teamster, age 21, dark eyes, dark hair, light complex., 5'9".

MAY, JAMES H.: Pvt.; Co. D 5/24/61 Whitmell; pres. til sick with yellow jaundice 9/6/61. Sent to hosp. sick 7/15/62. Died 7/22/62 at Richmond. Father: George May.

MAYHAM, JOHN W.: Pvt.; Co. B 8/1/62, Danville; pres. til POW Gettysburg 7/3/63; Ft. McHenry 7/6/63; to Ft. Del. 7/12/63; died there 10/2/63. Widow: Matilda A. Mahan (sic). Bur. Finn's Point, N.J.

MAYHAN, ALEXANDER: Born Pitts Co. Pvt.; Co. B 6/4/61 Callands; pres. til died Manassas 9/10/61; of conjestive fever; age 25; 6'0", florid complex., blue eyes; dark hair, farmer. Widow: Levinia Mayhan.

MAYS, CHARLES W.: Pvt.; Co. C 10/14/64 Danville; pres. til deserted 1/20/65; went to Danville.

McALPINE, JAMES N.: Surgeon; F & S; apptd. commissioned 6/3/61; absent sick 1/25/62; returned prior to 5/13/62. Present 9/23/64 near Bermuda Hundred.

McCARTHY, DANIEL: Pvt.; Co. D 3/5/62 Whitmell; AWOL since 1/31/64, roll dated 4/1/64.

McCARTHY, JAMES M.: Pvt.; Co. E 3/13/62 Danville; present til WIA, slightly, Williamsburg 5/5/62; wounded in ankle; slight, Malvern Hill 7/1/62, entered Chimborazo #1 7/3/62 wound of hand; transf. to Danville 7/6/62 pneumonia; returned duty 10/29/62; pres. til rebel deserter received at Provost marshal Genl., Wash., D.C. 4/4/65. Took oath there.

McCLANEN, THOMAS A.: 2 Lieut.; 2nd Co. I 10/15/61 Norfolk Co.; 1st Sgt. Elected to 2 Lieut 11/3/64; pres. til admitted Danville H. 6/29/62 febris vites; returned 7/16/62; pres. til 15 day furlough 1/18/65; deserted to enemy 2/18/65 and desires to take oath and reside in Princess Anne Co.

McCORMIC, COSMAS B.: Pvt.; Co. E 10/21/62 Danville; pres. til POW Five Forks 4/1/65; City Pt. to Pt. Lookout 4/6/65; released there 6/15/65; res. Pitts. Co.; light complex., black hair, dark hazel eyes, 5'8".

McCORMICK, JOHN (possibly James): Pvt.; Co. H 3/3/63 Campbell; pres. til MWIA Gettysburg, fractured hip. POW, died in U.S. Corps. Hosp. 7/23/63 and bur. in yard B, row 2 of hosp. cem., on the hill between Schwartz's & Buchanan's, disinterred to Richmond 6/13/72 in Box #211.

McCORMICK, JOHN B.: Born 7/3/41. Pvt., Co. C 5/30/61 Laurel Grove; Pvt. to 4 Corpl. prior to 4/1/64; 4 Corpl. to 2 Corpl. 8/64; pres. til 4/24/62 Chimborazo #2; debility; returned duty 5/3/62, admitted Danville H. 5/16/62, debilitas; returned 7/23/62; pres. til WIA and POW, Gettysburg 7/5/63, concussion of shell explosion taking place near his head; also suffering chronic diarrhoea. Sent to DeCamp Hosp., Davids Island where paroled 8/24/63; admitted Farmville H. 8/30/63; v.s.; sent to Danville H. 9/5/63, admitted 9/9/63; debilitas; deserted 9/25/63; returned by time WIA 5/16/64 near Richmond; admitted Chimborazo #4; g.s.w. left hip, flesh wound; admitted Danville H. 5/23/64 vulnus sclopeticum. Furloughed 7/9/64; deserter, received by Federals 3/3/65; taken to Fed. Provost Mar. Headquarters Bermuda H. 3/4/65; to Wash., D.C. 5/8/65; oath taken and trans. furnished to Boston, Mass. Died 1/11/1917.

McCORMICK, ROLLIN S.: Pvt.; Co. C 5/30/61 Laurel Grove; pres. til sent to hosp. 3/4/62; died at Lynchburg G.H. 3/16/62, pneumonia.

McCORMICK, WILLIAM LOGAN: Born Halifax Co. 8/22/37. Pvt., Co. C 5/30/61 Laurel Grove; pres. til sent to Richmond Hosp. 12/31/61; disability, discharged 4/2/62; reenlisted 8/6/62 Danville; pres. til WIA, shot in leg; and POW Gettysburg 7/5/63; from hosps. in and around Gettysburg to DeCamp Hosp. at Davids Island, no date given. Paroled there 8/24/63 and rec'd. at City Pt. for exchange on 8/28/63. Entered Danville hosp. 2/16/64 vulnus sclopeticum, absent sick through last dated roll 2/25/65; 5'7", fair complex., light hair, blue eyes, farmer. Died 3/1/1910.

McCUNE, HENSON T.: Pvt.; Co. D 5/24/61, Whitmell. Pres. til admitted Chimborazo 10/25/61 rheumatism; returned 1/10/62; admitted Chimborazo #4 3/2/62; gastritia; trans. to Farmville 5/7/62, rheumatism; furloughed 20 days 5/19/62; discharged 9/5/62 expiration of service, being conscript.

McDANIEL, ALBON JR.: Pvt., Co. H 7/26/61 Bull Run; Pvt. to 1 Sgt. 6/13/62; sent to Danville Hosp. 1/22/62; sent to Orange Co. Hosp. 3/28/62 sick; absent sick at home 6/62; returned 7/62; discharged, Leesburg 9/5/62, being over 35 years old.

McDONALD, GEORGE C.: Pvt.; Co. K 6/2/61 Cascade; Pres. til sick in hosp. 5/62-7/62; listed as deserted 9/62; WIA Gettysburg 4/1/64, home on furlough; absent in arrest, provost guard prior to 8/31/64; present, 6 months pay deducted by order of Gen. Court Marshal, prior to 12/1/64; present through 2/25/65; POW Five Forks 4/1/65; City Pt. to Pt. Lookout 4/6/65; released there 6/15/65; res. Pitts Co.; lt. complex., brown hair, brown eyes, 5'11".

McDOWELL, DAVID T.: Born 1847. Pvt., Co. K, no date given. Died at hosp. 5/62.

McDOWELL, JOSEPH M.: Pvt.; Co. K 3/10/62 Cascade; pres. til admitted Danville 6/4/62 debilitas; returned to duty 10/22/62; present, extra duty in ambulance corps prior to 8/31/64; pres. til POW Farmville 4/6/65; Newport News, no date given; oath taken there 7/1/65; res. Pitts Co.; dark complex., dark hair, dark eyes, 5'8".

McDOWELL, PETER W.: Color Sgt. 5/30/61 Laurel Grove; Pvt. to Color Sgt. by 5/62; killed Seven Pines 5/31/62, musket ball passing through the body.

McDOWELL, ROBERT A.: Born 1829. Pvt.; Co. A 3/12/62 Kentuck. Pres. til WIA 7/1/62 Malvern Hill; entered Chimborazo #9 7/4/62 diarrhea; admitted Danville H. 8/18/62 vulnus selopeticum and debilitas, returned to duty 11/25/62; pres. through 2/25/65.

McDOWELL, ROBERT B.: Pvt. Co. K 6/2/61 Cascade; pres. til WIA Seven Pines 5/31/62; returned by time MWIA & POW Gettysburg, 7/3/63; g.s.w. in shoulder; died in Gettysburg hosps. 7/22/63.

McGRAW, WILLIAM: Pvt.; 2nd Co. I 3/6/62 Appomattox Co.; died of disease at hosp. 7/29/64. May be bur. Oakwood Cem.

McGREGOR, THOMPSON L.: Sgt.; Co. F 6/20/61 Hermitage Camp; medical discharge 11/16/61 general debility.

McGREGOR, WILLIAM H.: Pvt.; Co. F 3/17/62, Repl. Grove; Genl. Hosp. #18 Richmond 4/13/62, chronic diarrhea. Pres. until admitted Chimborazo #2 2/20/63 dropsy.

McHANEY, WILLIAM R.: Pvt.; Co. F 6/4/61, Repl. Grove; pres. til admitted Chimborazo #4 10/25/61 fever; returned 11/22/61; Chimborazo #1 5/28/62 diarrhea; admitted Danville H. 6/4/62 chronic dysentery, returned 7/16/62; Camp Winder, admitted 4/4/63; deserted 4/23/63; returned by 7/1/63; pres. through 11/16/64; deserted to Federals 2/15/65; Bermuda H. to Wash. D.C. 2/21/65. Took oath there; trans. furnished to Jefferson Co., Ill.

McMILLAN, SAMUEL H.: Co. K. Pvt.; wded. at Five Forks. Post-war record only. Died 1/25/26, age 93, at Axton. Bur. family cem. near Boxwood.

McNEALY, ELIJAH: Pvt.; Co. B 3/10/62 Callands; deserted 9/62; voluntarily returned 2/29/64; Deserted 1/7/65.

McNEALY, WYATT K.: Pvt.; Co. D 6/15/61 Whitmell; pres. til admitted Chimborazo #4 10/25/61 dyspepsia; returned prior to 3/62; sent to hosp. 3/5/62; died of disease in Richmond 3/21/62.

McNUNER, CHARLES: Pvt.; Co. D, no date given. Deserted on or about 6/62.

McQUENNEY, JOHN: Pvt.; Co. F, no date given; absent 8/62, nature of absence not shown.

MEACHAM, WILLIAM B.: Born Mecklenburg Co. Pvt.; Co. G 5/18/61. Boydton; pres. til sent to hosp. 12/61; absent and detached as Ward Master Bird Island Hosp., Richmond 2/62-5/62; present, detailed as Sgt. Major on 6/62; ward master Gen. Hosp. #25 9/15/62; detailed ward master Chimborazo H. 4/15/63, through roll dated 5/1/64; apptd. hosp. steward 4/27/64-12/3/64; clerk through 1/25/65 at Chimborazo #1, note, subject is listed as being discharged 11/15/61; but no record of different reenlistment dates. Age 19 as of 11/15/61; 5'11"; light complex., black hair; dark eyes; a clerk; probably died 1912.

MEADE, HARRISON W.: Pvt.; Co. D 5/24/61, Whitmell; pro. to Cpl. by 7/3/63; pres. til WIA Gettysburg 7/3/63 g.s.w., right arm amputated, leg also. POW Gettysburg; hosps. in Gettysburg to DeCamp hosp., no date given; paroled there 8/24/63; absent from co.; disabled, on furlough for the war, result of wounds from Gettysburg.

MEADE, ROBERT W.: Pvt.; Co. D 5/24/61 Whitmell; detailed as teamster 8/13/61; sent to hosp. sick 3/5/62; entered Chimborazo #2 3/14/62. Died there 3/20/62; sudden death from disease of the heart. bur. Oakwood Cem.

MEADE, WILEY W.: Pvt.; Co. B 6/4/61 Callands; present; extra duty Wagoner 11/61-3/62; pres. til deserted prior to 5/19/63; captured, confined in Castle Thunder prior to 4/1/64; deserted 6/10/64; pardoned by pres. for volunteering to defend Richmond, Winder Legion, against Sheridan's raid of 1864 8/3/64; paroled after Johnston's surrendering Greensboro, N.C. 5/18/65.

MEADOWS, FRANCIS D.: Pvt.; Co. D 3/13/62 Whitmell; present til admitted Chimborazo #5 4/15/62, pneumonia; transf. to Lynchburg 5/9/62; returned prior to 4/1/64. Admitted Chimborazo #3 5/16/64 debilitas.

MEADOWS, JAMES R.: Pvt.; Co. B 6/4/61 Callands; Pres. til sent to hospl. 2/27/62. Returned prior to 5/19/63; WIA & POW Gettysburg, fractured clavicle; paroled at Baltimore, MD 8/23/63; delivered City Point 8/24/63 for exchange; retired from active duty due to wounds received at Gettysburg 8/4/64. Name on Registry of Invalid Corps.

MEADOWS, WORLEY W.: Co. B. Pvt. Post-war record only.

MEAKES, GEORGE W.: Co. K. Pvt. Enl. 4-62. Post-war record only.

MEAKES, HENRY D.: Born: Henry. no rank listed; Co. K 3/10/62. Pres. til admitted Chimborazo #3 4/17/62; returned 5/3/62 but in Camp Winder Hosp. 5/26/62; diarrhoea; returned to duty 6/8/62; medically discharged 7/24/62, disease of the eyes which has resulted in partial blindness. Age 27, 5'10", dark complexion, dark hair, occupation farmer.

MEAKES, POWHATAN J.: Pvt.; Co. K 3/10/62 Cascade; pres. til admitted Chimborazo #2 3/31/62 debility; returned 4/14/62; admitted Danville H. 5/15/62; returned 6/8/62; admitted Danville, no date given, vulnus selopetium; died there 2/23/62.

MEAKES, W. D.: Pvt.; Co. K, no date given; 5-7/62 sick in hosp.; 9/62 absent at home.

MEAKS, GEORGE W.: Pvt.; Co. K 3/10/62 Cascade; pres. til admitted Chimborazo #5 4/14/62; trans. to Danville 5/22/62; debilitas; returned 9/23/62; arrested as of 4/11/64, undergoing sentence of Genl. Court martial; present, discharged from military prison at Salisbury, NC by Sec. of War. 12/16/64; Chimborazo #5 3/22/65 erysipelas facial; captured in Richmond hosp. 4/3/65. Turned over to Provost Marshal 4/14/65; transferred from Libby Prison to Newport News 4/23/65 took oath there 7/1/65; res. Danville, Va. Dark complex., dark hair, dark eyes, 5'6".

MEAKS, T. W.: Pvt.; Co. K, no date given. Admitted Chimborazo #2 3/30/62 catarrh; returned 4/14/62; died at Rich. hospital 5/1/62, cause not given; bur. Oakwood Cem., Richmond.

MEEKS, JOHN THOMAS: Born 9/17/38 in Henry Co. Pvt.; Co. C 5/30/61 Laurel Grove; Chimborazo #3 3/14/62 with pleuritis. Pres. til 5/20/62; admitted Danville hosp. with debilitas; returned 10/22/62 [?] WIA seriously in face and eye 7/1/62 Malvern Hill; returned prior to WIA g.s.w. left thigh, POW Gettysburg 7/5/63; Gettysburg 7/3/63, treated in U.S. XII Corps hosp. from Gettysburg hosp. to DeCamp Hosp., no date given. Paroled there 9/16/63. Shot in shoulder at Drewrys Bluff; shot in right side while on picket duty at Hanover Junction; Danville Hosp. 5/24/64, head wound Chimborazo #2 9/29/64, remittent febris. Returned prior to 2/25/65; paroled 4/25/65. Farmer. Alive in Henry Co. in 1889. Wife: Caroline Matilda Hopper. Son of John & Catherine Daniels Meeks.

MELSON, CHARLES H.: Sgt.; 2nd Co. I 7/6/61 Norfolk Co.; present thru 8/31/64 and possibly transferred to Navy.

MIDKIFF, LINTON L.: Pvt.; Co. B 6/4/61 Callands; pres. til died 4/22/62 Richmond.

MIDKIFF, WILLIAM R.: Pvt.; Co. B 6/4/61 Callands; present til POW near Howletts House 8/25/64; Bermuda H. to Ft. Monroe 8/26/64; to Pt. Lookout 8/28/64; exchanged from there 10/30/64; Ocmulgee Hosp. 11/15/64, diarrhoea; returned to be POW Five Forks 4/1/65; City Pt. to Hart's Island 4/7/65; released there 6/21/65; res. Pitts Co. Fair complex., black hair, grey eyes, 5'7".

MILAM, JAMES M.: Pvt.; Co. E 6/18/61 Danville; pres. til WIA Seven Pines 5/31/62; admitted Chimborazo #2 6/2/62, g.s. flesh wound of hand. Furloughed 30 days 6/15/62. CSA Hosp., Danville 3/14/63 glut. Returned 8/31/63; absent confined for desertion in Div. Provost Guard House from 12/31/64-2/25/65. Age 23, occupation Farmer.

MILES, RICHARD G.: Pvt.; Co. G 5/18/61 Boydton; present til detailed as hearse driver at Moores' Hosp. Manassas 12/31/61-2/62; detailed as cook for Co. C 6-7/62; detailed as ambulance driver for regt. 8-9/62. Pres. til entered Chimborazo 5/24/64, v.s. left hand, transferred to Petersburg; returned about 8/5/64; paroled prisoner, took amnesty oath 5/9/65; res. Mecklenburg.

MILLAIN, JAMES M.: Co. E. Pvt., wded. during war. Post-war record only.

MILLER, JOSEPH T.: 6/8/61 Danville; Pvt. to 2 Corpl. 12/1/61; 2 Corpl. to Sgt., no date given. Elected 3 Lieut. 5/10/62; elected 2 Lieut. 7/25/62; pres. until severely wounded Gettysburg, 7/3/63 right leg amputated below knee by Surgeon McAlpine of 38th; POW there 7/5/63, held at Gettysburg Hosp. until sent to Letterman Gen'l. Hosp. 8/10/63; then to Ft. McHenry 10/22/63; to Pt. Lookout 1/23/64; paroled, exchanged 3/3/64; retired due to wounds 8/3/64. Res. Farmville; on Register of Invalid Corps.

MILLER, WILLIAM: Pvt.; Co. H 4/28/64 Pendleton; conscript; absent sick, sent to Chimborazo #4 5/13/64; gunshot wound, left hand.

MILLNER, JAMES W: Sgt.; Co. K 6/2/61 Cascade; Sgt. elected to 3 Lieut. 9/17/61; promoted 2 Lieut. 11/14/61. Resigned to join cavalry 1/13/63 but pres. til WIA slightly at Malvern Hill 7/1/62; WIA g.s.w., right side of neck, Five Forks 4/1/65. POW Fairgrounds Hosp. 4/3/65; to Ft. Monroe. USA Genl. Hosp. 5/14/65. Discharged from there upon taking oath on 7/22/65, age 23.

MILLNER, JOHN P.: Pvt.; Co. K/D 6/2/61 Cascade; pres. til admitted Chimborazo #1 5/28/62; dysentery, returned 6/10/62; admitted Danville G.H. 6/3/62 chronic diarrhoea; returned to duty 8/20/62; pres. til transferred from Co. K to Co. D 38th Va. 7/28/62 and discharged 7/29/62 for having found substitute Michael Kelly.

MILLNER, JOSEPH T.: Pvt.; Co. K 6/2/61 Cascade; absent, home sick furlough 8/21/61-10/61; entered Chimborazo #1 3/10/62 chronic bronchitis; left without permission; at Danville H 1/10/63 debilitas; returned 3/17/63.

MILLNER, WILLIAM H.: 2 Lieut.; Co. K 6/2/61 Cascade; Pvt. to 2 Jr. Lieut. 11/14/61; dropped 4/1/62 failed to be reelected at Spring Reorganization.

MILLS, CALEB W.: Pvt.; Co. D 5/24/61 Whitmell; pres. til admitted Chimborazo #1 3/21/62 diarrhea; returned 4/17/62; pres. til sick at Div. Hosp. 7/28/64; Co. cook prior to 12/31/64; deserted 2/19/65 to Pitts. Co.

MILLS, CHARLES F.: Pvt.; 1st Co. I 3/14/62 Clarksville; sent to Richmond hosp. 4/20/62.

MILLS, GEORGE C.: Pvt.; Co. H 10/14/64 Pitts Co.; pres. til deserted, supposed to have gone home by 2/26/65.

MILLS, JOHN H., JR.: Pvt.; Co. D 5/24/61 Whitmell; Chimborazo #5 4/18/62, debility. Pres. til WIA Malvern Hill 7/1/62, sent to Danville G.H., wound of right arm. Returned to duties 1/5/63, admitted 2/14/64 old wound; returned 4/25/64; admitted Chimborazo 5/4/64-11/1/64; captured Hosp. in Richmond 4/3/65; escaped from Hosp. 5/4/65. Farmer, age 21.

MILLS, JOHN H., SR.: Pvt.; Co. D 5/24/61 Whitmell; pres. til Surgeon's Cert. of Disability 3/1/62; conscripted 5/2/64 Danville; pres. til deserted 2/19/65 to Pitts. Co.

MILUM, W. E.: Pvt.; Co. C 1/7/65 Danville; pres. through 2/25/65.

MINOR, WILLIAM B.: Pvt., 2nd Co. I 7/6/61 Norfolk Co.; pres. til WIA, (middle finger of left hand); Chimborazo #2 from 5/17/64 until returned to duty 8/29/64; deserted to Federals 12/27/64; Bermuda H. Prov. Mar. to Prov. Mar. Gen'l., Wash, D.C. 1/3/65. Took oath there and trans. furnished to Norfolk Co. Age 18, tinner.

MITCHELL, DAVID W.: Pvt.; Co. H 7/2/61 Pitts Co.; pres. til absent, Gen'l. Hosp. 10/25/61; returned prior to time sent to Richmond H. 5/1/62-7/62; CSA Hosp. Danville 8/20/62 rheumatism. Absent, sick in hosp. in Richmond prior to 4/1/64-12/21/64, Danville 7/28/64 abscess of right foot. Deserted 9/26/64, returned to Chimborazo #2 9/28/64; discharged 11/27/64, inflammation right foot. Age 29, farmer.

MITCHELL, GEORGE WILLIAM: Born 7/1/32. Pvt.; Co. G 5/18/61 Boydton; pres. til WIA slightly, Seven Pines 5/31/62; admitted Richmond G.H. #21 6/4/62 vulnus selopeticum; returned 7/15/62; pres. til POW Five Forks 4/1/65, City Point to Hart's Island 4/7/65; released there 6/20/65; res. Mecklenburg Co., fair complexion, dark hair, hazel eyes, 5'6". Died 6/18/14.

MITCHELL, HENRY C.: Pvt.; Co. D 5/24/61 Whitmell; pres. til sent to Gen'l. Hosp. 4/20/62 Chimborazo #1 6/9/62-7/62 with typhoid fever; returned, pres. til 5/16/64, admitted Chimborazo #4 debility; returned 8/27/64; admitted Chimborazo #2; 8/28/64 neuralgia; furloughed 35 days 10/15/64; absent on sick furlough through 2/25/65.

MITCHELL, JAMES: Born in Pitts Co. Pvt.; Co. H 7/26/61 Bull Run; present til discharged, medical; 9/23/61 consumption. Age 32 at discharge, 5'11", light complex., dark grey eyes, dark hair, farmer.

MITCHELL, JAMES R.: Pvt.; Co. B 6/4/61 Callands; pres. til sent to hosp. 2/27/62; died 3/5/62 Richmond. Buried Oakwood Cem. Richmond 3/6/62.

MITCHELL, JOHN A.: Pvt.; Co. H 10/14/64; Halifax; pres. til POW Five Forks 4/1/65; City Point to Hart's Island 4/7/65; released there 6/21/65.

MITCHELL, KELLY: Co. C. Pvt. Deserted 8/1/62. Post-war record only.

MITCHELL, WILLIAM D.: Pvt.; Co. H 10/14/64 Pittsylvania; pres. til admitted Danville 2/3/65 pneumonia; returned 2/25/65 listed as being in jail in Danville for desertion; POW Richmond hosp. 4/3/65. Escaped hosp. 4/18/65. Res. Pittsylvania Co., tanner.

MITCHELL, WILLIAM R.: Pvt.; Co. E 6/8/61 Danville; pres. til deserted 7/6/61 at Richmond. Joined 11th N.C. Regt.; arrested and brought back by 8/30/61; Chimborazo #1 5/28/62, rheumatism; CSA Hosp., Farmville 4/19/63, injury to back, returned to duty 4/24/63. Present through 2/25/65. Age 29, no date on roll.

MOON, HENRY M.: Pvt.; 1st Co. I 2/20/62 Clarksville; absent, sent to Orange C.H. Hosp. 4/10/62.

MOON, JAMES B.: Corp.; Co. F 12/4/63 Kinston, N.C.; Pres. til WIA Drewry's Bluff 5/16/64; admitted Chimborazo #4 g.s.w., hand 5/17/64. Returned by 8/31/64; Pvt. to 4th Corpl. 11/1/64; pres. til POW Five Forks 4/1/65 City Point to Point Lookout 4/6/65. Released there 6/5/65.

MOON, JOHN B.: Pvt.; 1st Co. I 3/1/62 Clarksville.

MOORE, HARPER C.: Born Mecklenburg Co. Pvt.; Co. G 5/18/61 Boydton; pres. til sick at camp near Broad Run in 10/61, admitted Orange C.H. Hosp. 11/8/61 debility; transferred to Chimborazo #5 3/18/62 scrofula. Medical discharge, Surgeons Cert. of disability 5/13/62, no reason given. Age 19 at discharge, 5'6", dark complex., black eyes and dark hair, farmer.

MOORE, HENRY H.: Born 3/28/40. 1st Sgt.; Co. G 5/18/61 Boydton; Pvt. to 2nd Sgt. prior to 5/1/63; 2 Sgt. to 1 Sgt. by 2-65; pres. til WIA seriously 7/1/62 Malvern Hill. Returned by 5/1/63; pres. til POW Amelia C.H. 4/5/65; City Point to Point Lookout 6/13/65; there released 6/24/65; res. Mecklenburg Co. Wife: Susan Chandler. Light complexion, brown hair, gray eyes, 5'10". Died 3/11/29. Buried Bluestone Baptist Church Cem. at Int. Rts. 49 & 15 in Mecklenburg Co.

MOORE, JAMES A.: Pvt.; Co. G 2/28/62 Boydton; absent, sent to hosp. in Richmond prior to 4/30/62. Reported to duty 3/26/63; sent to Episcopal Ch. Hosp. Williamsburg 4/8/63 diarrhoea; returned to duty 6/4/63; absent, home on furlough for 30 days as of 4/1/64; returned by time WIA 5/16/64 at Drewry's Bluff; Chimborazo #1 5/17/64, v.s. right leg amputated below knee; discharged 10/12/64.

MOORE, JAMES R.: Pvt.; Co. E 10/14/64 Danville. Present through 2/25/65.

MOORE, WARNER F.: Pvt.; Co. G 5/18/61 Boydton; absent, sent to hosp. at Manassas 11/61; as of last dated muster roll 5/1/63.

MOREFIELD, JAMES R.: Pvt.; Co. C 10/14/64 Danville; pres. through 2/25/65.

MOREFIELD, JOHN H.: Pvt.; Co. C 5/30/61 Laurel Grove; present, detailed as Teamster 11/28/61; present until absent with leave, roll dated 2/25/65.

MORGAN, GEORGE T.: Pvt.; Co G 5/18/61 Boydton; pres. til wounded slightly Malvern Hill 7/1/62; deserted 4/10/63; absent in arrest, as of 4/1/64; in military prison Salisbury, N.C. from roll dated 8/31/64-2/65; returned to be POW Five Forks 4/1/65; City Point to Hart's Island 4/7/65; released there 6/20/65; res. Mecklenburg Co.; dark complex., light hair, hazel eyes, 5'10".

MORGAN, JOHN J.: Pvt.; Co. G 5/18/61 Boydton; pres. til WIA Malvern Hill 7/1/62; deserted 4/10/63; absent in arrest by 4/1/64; volunteered Winder Legion, pardoned by Pres. 8/3/64; present as of 8/31/64; listed as deserter for month 2/65; POW Five Forks 4/1/65; City Point to Hart's Island 4/7/65; released there 6/20/65; res. Mecklenburg Co.; dark complex., light hair, hazel eyes, 5'10".

MORGAN, LAFAYETTE: Pvt.; Co. E 6/8/61 Danville; pres. til admitted Danville H. 6/20/62 pneumonia; returned 7/19/62; pres. but confined in Prov. Guardhouse for desertion prior to 8/31/64. Admitted Gen. Hosp. #9, Richmond 3/6/65 to Chimborazo #1 3/7/65.

MORGAN, WILLIAM G.: Pvt.; Co. G 5/18/61 Boydton; died Manassas 8/26/61, pneumonia.

MORRIS, ANDREW J.: Born 10/25/28. Pvt.; Co. E 6/8/61 Danville; Pres. til absent, sick at hosp. 5/62-7/62; absent, admitted Winder Hosp. 11/19/62-2/63 with rheumatism. Returned to duty prior to 4/1/64; present, confined in Div. Provost Guardhouse for desertion by 8/31/64; Gen. Hosp. #9 3/14/65; to Chimborazo #3 3/15/65, nyctalopia; on list of Confederate POW's, paroled at Farmville between 4/11/65 and 4/21/65. Died 10/24/19. Buried Stokesland Cem. at W. Main St. and Clearview Dr., Danville.

MORRIS, JOHN H.: Pvt.; 1st Co. I 3/5/62 Clarksville. Absent, admitted Chimborazo #1 4/24/62 parotidis, left without permission.

MORRIS, N. W.: Pvt.; 2nd Co. I 7/6/61 Albemarle Co.; deserted to enemy 12/20/64. Received by Federals 1/10/65; taken to Provost Mar., oath taken at Bermuda H. 1/15/65; to Wash. D.C.; trans. to Norfolk.

MORRIS, WILLIAM: Pvt. 2nd Co. I 3/15/62 Norfolk; present til deserted to the Federals. Received by them 2/16/65; Bermuda Hundred to Wash. D.C.; oath taken there; trans. furnished to Norfolk, Va.

MORRISON, GEORGE W.: Pvt.; Co. K 6/2/61 Cascade; Pvt. to 1 Corpl. 9/17/61; 1 Corpl. to Sgt. Major by 12/8/62; WIA arm Seven Pines 5/31/62; admitted Chimborazo #5 6/3/62 remit. fever; returned 6/9/62 admitted Danville H. 7/11/62; chronic diarrhea; deserted from there 8/23/62.

MORRISON, JOHN A.: Pvt.; Co. H 7/2/61 Pitts. Co.; pres. til on detached service packing hay for Brigade 2/7/62; returned to be WIA 1/13/62 White Pine, slightly wounded on shoulder and arm with spent ball and piece of "bumshell"; discharged 9/5/62, reason over 35.

MORRISON, JOHN R.: Corpl.; Co. K 3/10/62 Cascade; Pvt. to 1 Corpl. by 8/31/64; pres. til admitted Danville 5/27/62 debilitas; returned to duty 9/7/62; admitted Danville H. 5/26/64 wound in hand; returned 7/22/64; present through 2/25/65.

MORRISETT, WILLIAM B.: Pvt.; Co. E 3/15/62 Danville; Gen. Hosp. Farmville 5/7/62 debility; furlough 25 days 5/20/62; returned to duty 6/28/62; deserted 5/9/63. Returned order Presidential amnesty 8/14/63. Pay deducted accordingly; pres. til admitted Chimborazo 3/5/65, debility. Admitted Farmville 4/2/65 phythisis. Transferred to Lynchburg 4/2/65.

MORTON, HENRY S.: Pvt.; 1st Co. I 3/5/62 Clarksville. Elected from Pvt. to 2 Lieut. 4/29/62 at Lebanon Church; pres. until absent at Brigade hosp. 6/23/62.

MOTLEY, DANIEL J.: Pvt.; Co. B 3/10/62 or 4/62 Pittsylvania; pres. til POW Five Forks 4/1/65; City Point to Hart's Island 4/7/65; released there 6/21/65; res. Pitts Co.; fair complex., auburn hair, grey eyes, 5'6".

MOTLEY, J. W.: No rank listed; Co. H, no date given. Deserted 9/62.

MOTLEY, NATHANIEL C.: Pvt.; Co. D 10/14/64 Danville; pres. through 2/25/65.

MOTLEY, RICHARD WASHINGTON: Born 6/30/34. Pvt.; Co. H 7/2/61 Pitts. Co.; pres. til deserted from camp near Centerville 9/28/61; returned by time sent to Richmond Hosp. 6/10/62-7/62. Returned prior to 4/1/64; absent, detached with Division Pioneer Corps by 8/31/64; returned by 12/31/64; pres. til 2/65; at Div. Hosp. sick; Chimborazo #5 3/5/65. Died 11/23/15. Buried Mill Creek Ch. Cem., Rt. 685, Pitt. Co.

MOTLEY, ROBERT J. O.: Pvt.; Co. E 6/18/61 Danville; Pvt. to 3 Sgt. 12/1/61; 3 Sgt. to 2 Sgt. 1/1/62; WIA Seven Pines; died in hosp. in Field 5/31/62. Father: William Motley.

MOTLEY, WASHINGTON: Co. H. Pvt. Post-war record only.

MOTLEY, WILLIAM D.: Pvt.; Co. A 1/15/62 Kentuck; sent to hosp. 10/9/64; pres. through 2/25/65.

MOTT, LEWIS T.: Pvt.; 2nd Co. I 3/15/62 Norfolk Co.; pres. til deserted to Federals 2/16/65; received at Bermuda Hundred 2/17/65; to Wash. D.C. oath taken and trans. furnished to Norfolk.

MUCK, DANIEL H.: Pvt.; Co. K 2/28/62 Cascade; pres. til admitted Chimborazo #3 5/1/62 hepatitis; to Danville H. 5/14/62 debilitas; returned to duty 8/15/62; pres. til 3/23/64 admitted Danville H. vulnus selopeticus of foot 5/22/64; returned prior to 8/31/64; pres. through 2/25/65; POW Five Forks 4/1/65 City Point to Point Lookout 4/6/65; released there 6/15/65; res. Henry Co.; florid complex., light hair, blue eyes, 5'7¼".

MUCK, SAMUEL H.: Pvt.; Co. K 2/28/62 Cascade; pres. til 7/8/62 Chimborazo #5 pneumonia; to Danville Hosp. with debility where deserted 7/28/62; returned to duty 8/5/62; pres. til admitted hosp. Danville 5/23/64 wound, foot and hand. Returned by 8/31/64; POW White Oak Road 4/1/65, City Point to Point Lookout and released there 6/15/65. Res. Henry Co., florid complexion, brown hair, grey eyes, 5'5½".

MULLINS, JOSHUA: Pvt.; Co. H 7/2/61 Pitts. C.H. Pres. til died at Culpeper C.H. "Horsepittle" 4/62.

MURPHY, CORNELIUS W.: Pvt.; Co. F 6/4/61 Republican Grove; present til discharged at Camp Falling Creek 7/29/62 expiration of service.

MURPHY, JOHN R.: Pvt.; Co. K 11/9/63 Cascade; pres. til sent to hosp. 12/64. Returned by 2/25/65. Admitted Chimborazo #5 3/5/65 with cystitis. POW in Richmond hosps. 4/3/65. Listed as admitted to Jackson Hosp., Richmond 4/8/65; paroled 4/29/65, Richmond. Deserted 5/11/65 according to CSR.

MURRELL, JAMES W.: Pvt.; Co. A 5/30/61 Kentuck; absent at home unfit for duty by 8/31/61; sent to hosp. 4-6/62; returned prior to POW Gettysburg 7/5/63 where serving as nurse. Baltimore, Md. to Point Lookout 8/21/63; transferred to Hammond Genl. Hosp. 11/63; admitted small pox hosp., Point Lookout 12/14/63; returned to camp 1/15/64; detailed as Camp Police; paroled Pt. Lookout and transferred to City Point 3/16/64 for exchange on 3/20/64.

MURREY, R. A.: Pvt.; 1st Co. I 6/20/61 Clarksville; absent 2/62, detailed as nurse 2/27/62; admitted to Chimborazo #4 3/19/62 with injury to foot; furloughed 5/9/62; returned 5/29/62.

MURRY, WILLIAM W.: Pvt.; Co. C 10/14/64 Danville; pres. til POW Farmville 4/6/65; oath taken at Newport News 7/1/65; res. Halifax Co., dark complexion, dark hair, grey eyes, 5'6".

MUSSEN, JAMES: Co. A. Pvt. Post-war record only.

MYERS, C.A.: Co. B. Pvt. Post-war record only.

MYERS, ROBERT: Pvt.; Co. A 5/30/61 Kentuck; pres. til sent to Richmond hosp. 7/62-8/62; returned prior to 4/1/64; pres. til POW Dinwiddie C.H. 4/1/65; City Point to Point Lookout 4/4/65; released there 6/15/65; Pitts Co.; light complex., sandy hair, blue eyes, 5'9".

MYERS, STEPHEN R.: Pvt.; Co. D 5/24/61 Whitmell; pres. til sent to Genl. Hosp. 5/27/62, sick; returned by 9/62 when made guard of ordinance train; pres. til POW Harper's Farm (Sayler's Creek) 4/6/65; City Point to Point Lookout 4/15/65; oath and released there 6/15/65. Res. Pitts Co.; light complex., auburn hair, grey eyes, 5'10½".

MYERS, WILSON P.: Pvt.; Co. A 5/30/61 Kentuck; pres. til Chimborazo #4 5/18/62 rheumatism; to Danville 6/15/62 debilitas; returned 7/15/62; pres. til POW, Farmville 4/6/65; City Point to Newport News 4/14/65.

NANCE, JOHN A.: Pvt.; Co. D 4/6/64 Henry Co.; conscript; absent, in custody of Div. Provost Guard 11-12/64-2/25/65; paroled, Headqrs. 2nd Div., 6th Corps 4/25/65; list dated 5/8/65.

NEAL, DAVID R.: Pvt.; Co. F 10/8/64 Bermuda Hundred; pres. til POW. Five Forks 4/1/65; also WIA in Petersburg area to Lincoln USA Gen'l. Hosp., Wash. D.C. 4/8/65, g.s.w. left thigh, flesh lower third, ball passing through anterior portion, slight; oath taken there 6/12/65; res. Pitts. Co.; light complex., brown hair, blue eyes, 6'0".

NEAL, PASCHAL: Born Pittsvylania. Pvt.; Co. A 10/14/64 Danville; absent, admitted Chimborazo #4 12/26/64 debility; discharged 1/11/65; complete nervous prostrating debility and age 37. 5'5", fair complexion, grey eyes, dark hair, farmer.

NEAL, W. W.: Pvt.; Co. G 10/24/64 Mecklenburg; Present, had deserted 11/14/64 but returned 12/20/64; listed as deserter 2/65.

NEATHERY, HENRY H.: Born Mecklenburg Co. Pvt.; 1st Co. I 6/20/61 Clarksville; discharged, surgeon's order 12/20/61, rheumatism. Age 27, 5'11", light complex., light eyes, dark hair, farmer.

NEDDOM, WILSON: Pvt.; 2nd Co. I; 2/20/61 Norfolk Co. Deserted to the Federals 12/20/64; Prov. Mar. Bermuda Hundred to Wash. D.C.; oath taken there 1/13/65; sent to Norfolk, 1/14/65.

NELSON, WILLIAM G.: Pvt., 1st Co. I 2/28/62; Pvt. to Corpl. by 5/1/62.

NETHERY, ALEXANDER: Pvt.; Co. G 5/18/61 Boydon; pres. til WIA exhibiting "gallant conduct", Malvern Hill 7/1/62; returned prior to 5/1/63; listed as missing since expedition to Newburn, N.C. 2/1/64.

NETHERY, GEORGE H.: Pvt.; 1st Co. I 6/20/62 Clarksville; absent, sent to Richmond hosp. 4/26/62; missing after battle Malvern Hill 7/1/62.

NEW, JOHN D.: Pvt.; Co. F 12/4/63 near Kinston, N.C.; deserted 1/31/64.

NEWCOMB, HENRY W.: Pvt.; Co. C 5/30/61 Laurel Grove; absent, sent to Chimborazo #5 2/25/62 debilitas; there through 7/62; deserted 9/62.

NEWCOMB, JAMES A.: Pvt.; Co. G 9/15/63 Petersburg; present extra duty as drummer for the 38th Va. Regt.; on roll dated 8/31/64; pres. til paroled Appomattox 4/9/65.

NEWCOMB, WILLIAM T.: Pvt.; Co. G 8/24/62 Boydton; pres., made cook for Co. G, pres. through 2/25/65; paroled Appomattox 4/9/65.

NEWTON, E. H.: Pvt.; 1st Co. I 2/21/62 Clarksville; absent, sent to hosp. from Lebanon Church 4/20/62; entered Chimborazo #4 6/26/62 acute diarrhea. Had been in service earlier 6/24/61, Clarksville; but had surgeon's cert. of discharge 7/1/61.

NEWTON, GEORGE W.: Pvt.; Co. D 5/24/61 Whitmell; pres. til admitted Chimborazo #4 6/4/62, acute diarrhea; returned by 8/31/61; AWOL since 1/31/64.

NEWTON, HENDERSON: Pvt.; 1st Co. I 3/4/62 Clarksville; pres. til admitted Chimborazo #3 4/24/62; died in Lynchburg G.H. 5/12/62 eryspelas. Bur. Lynchburg Cem.

NEWTON, HENRY J.: Pvt.; 1st Co. I 3/12/62 Clarksville; absent, sent to Chimborazo #1 from Lebanon Church; admitted there 4/24/62, pneumonia; left without permission.

NEWTON, JAMES S.: Pvt.; 1st Co. I 2/26/62 Clarksville; absent, sent to hosp. 4/26/62.

NEWTON, JAMES S.: Pvt.; 1st Co. I 3/8/62 Clarksville; joined by enlistment from Grover Battalion, never reported to Co. Possibly same as preceding individual.

NEWTON, JOHN: Pvt.; 1st Co. I 6/20/62 Clarksville. No further information.

NEWTON, P. J.: Pvt.; 1st Co. I 6/20/62 Clarksville; pres. til sent to hosp. 2/27/62 according to CSR.

NEWTON, R. H.: Corpl.; Co. I, no date given; discharged 8/8/61, chronic rheumatism.

NEWTON, WILLIAM T.: Pvt.; 1st Co. I 6/20/62 Clarksville; pres. til sick in Mecklenburg Co. 12/16/61-1/62; returned by 4/30/62; admitted Chimborazo #2 6/2/62 Int. Fever; returned 6/16/62; entered Richmond Gen'l. Hosp. #24 7/5/62, wounded.

NICHOLSON, JOSEPH: Pvt.; Co. H 4/29/64 Madison; conscript; absent, deserted from Hanover Junction 5/20/64; returned by time POW Five Forks 4/2/65; City Point to Point Lookout 4/6/65; released there 6/15/65; res. Madison Co.; dark complex., black hair, brown eyes, 6'1".

NICHOLSON, J. P.: Pvt. Co. H 4/29/64 Madison; conscript; deserted from Hanover Junction 5/20/64. Alive in 1926.

NOBLIN, JOHN H.: Born Mecklenburg Co. Pvt.; 1st Co. I 6/20/61 Clarksville; Chimborazo #4 7/2/62 bronchitis. Returned to duty 7/4/62. Age 36, grey eyes, light hair, dark complexion, 5'5", farmer.

NOEL, JESSE R.: enl. 10/14/64 at Danville; Pvt. Co. K. Admitted Richmond Gen. Hosp. #9 3/5/65. Paroled 4/25/65 on list dated 5/5/65.

NOELL, CHARLES P.: Sgt.; Co. K 6/2/61 Cascade, 2 Corpl. to Sgt. by 5/62; back to 4 Corpl. by 8/31/62; absent in hosp. 5-8/62.

NORMAN, COURTNEY W.: Pvt.; Co. K, no date given; admitted Orange C.H. hosp. 3/28/62; died in Charity hosp., Gordonsville 4/5/62, pneumonia.

NORMAN, GEORGE S.: Born 5/22/45. Pvt.; Co. C or D (?) 7/22/63 Laurel Grove; Pvt. to 5th Sgt. prior to 12/31/64; pres. through 2/25/65. Paroled Appomattox 4/9/65. Died 8/4/11. Buried Cem. Chatham, Va.

NORMAN, HENRY J.: Born Henry Co. Pvt.; Co. K 3/10/62 Cascade; pres. til admitted Chimborazo #2 3/30/62 catarrhal fever; to Danville H. admitted 5/3/62 debilitas; deserted 8/9/62; admitted Winder hosp. 9/26/62; returned to duty 11/14/62; pres. til admitted Danville H. 7/26/64; fistula. Returned 11/22/64; medical discharge 2/27/65 phythisis and fistula; disability permanent. Age 28, dark complexion, blue eyes, dark hair, 6'0", farmer.

NORMAN, JAMES M.: 2 Lieut.; Co. C 5/30/61 Laurel Grove; 2 Lieut. to 2 Sgt. 4/29/62. Declined in election and returned home, dropped 2 Sgt. to Pvt., no date given. Pres. til returned home after election; returned to duty prior to 4/1/64; pres. til POW in hosps. in Richmond 4/3/65; Libby Prison to Newport News. 4/23/65, same date paroled in Richmond.

NORMAN, JOHN: Pvt.; Co. C 3/30/61 Laurel Grove. Pres. til WIA Seven Pines 5/31/62. Sent to Richmond Hosp., sick through 6/62; returned, detailed Ambulance Corps 9/62.

NORMAN, WILLIAM: Pvt.; Co. C 5/30/61 Laurel Grove; Pvt. Elected to 1 Lieut. 4/29/62; killed in action Seven Pines 5/31/62, musket ball passing through the head.

NORTON, HUGH: Pvt.; Co. D 5/24/61 Whitmell; pres. detached service, teamster 8/13/61; AWOL from wagon camp 7/5/62; returned, but AWOL since 1/31/64.

NORWOOD, BEN: Pvt.; 1st Co. I 3/24/62 Clarksville; pres. til admitted Chimborazo #3 4/24/62; died there 6/3/62 typhoid fever.

NOWLIN, WILLIAM S.: Asst. Surgeon; F & S, commissioned 3/6/63; pres. til POW Gettysburg 7/5/63 while attending wounded; Baltimore, Md. to Ft. Monroe 8/3/63 to Ft. Norfolk, no date given, to Ft. McHenry 8/10/63; paroled at Ft. McHenry and sent to City Point for exchange 11/21/63; 8/14/64 Gen'l. Hosp. #4 diarrhea chr. Paroled at Appomattox 4/9/65.

NUCHOLS, JAMES A.: Pvt.; Co. B 6/14/61 Callands; age 19, roll not dated. Pres. til admitted Chimborazo #4; 10/25/61 typhoid fever and rheumatism; returned 1/17/62; present until POW and WIA Gettysburg 7/4/63; amputated lower third right arm which led to death at Letterman Gen. Hosp. 9/2/63. 22 years old in 1863 and single. Bur. in Section 8, grave #21 of Hosp. Cem., dinsterred to Richmond in Box #95 on 6/13/72.

NUCKOLDS, DAVID R.: Pvt.; Co. B 3/10/62 Callands; pres. til admitted Chimborazo #2 6/25/62, debility; transferred to Danville 6/29/62 chronic rheumatism; returned to duty 7/30/62; present, extra duty as cook 9/62; 20 years old in 1863 and married. Pres. til WIA dissection of left hand and POW Gettysburg 7/4/63. Died Letterman Gen. Hosp., Gettysburg 9/17/63. Bur. Section 8, grave #13 of hosp. cem. Disinterred to Richmond in Box #113 on 6/13/72.

OAK, A.: Pvt.; Co. B, no date; entered Farmville Hosp. 3/17/65 coxalgia; returned 3/22/65; admitted Chimborazo #5 anchylosis, right knee, joint. Captured in hosp. Richmond 4/3/65; escaped from hosp. 5/6/65; died 4/1919 in Pitts. Co. at 99 years old.

OAKES, CHRISTOPHER P.: Pvt. Co. D, no date given, Danville; pres. til killed near Chester Station 5/10/64.

OAKES, EDWARD B.: Pvt.; Co. D 5/24/61 Whitmell; pres. til WIA on Chickahominy 5/31/62; absent sick as a result through 7/62; returned prior to 4/1/64; killed near Drewry's Bluff 5/16/64. Father: John B. Oakes.

OAKES, JAMES ALLEN: Pvt.; Co. B 3/10/62 Callands; pres. til WIA & POW Gettysburg, g.s., upper one third of leg amputated, died as a result 7/15/63. Widow: Margaret C. Oakes.

OAKES, JAMES LAFAYETTE: Pvt., age 23 in 1860. Co. B 8/14/62 Danville; pres. til entered Chimborazo #1 2/17/63 cont. fever; to Danville H. 4/20/63 debilitas; returned 5/12/63, probably WIA Gettysburg on 7/3/63, left shoulder. Pres. til WIA, right leg, severely; Chester Station 5/10/64; entered Chimborazo #2 5/11/64. Furloughed 40 days 6/10/64; admitted Danville Hosp. 10/18/64 v.s. right leg. Transferred to Pettigrew Gen. Hosp. #13, Raleigh, N.C. 11/26/64, transferred 3/8/65; res. Pitts. Co. Age 28, farmer. Died in 1920 at age 83.

OAKES, JOHN K.: Born 6/38. Corpl.; Co. B 6/4/61 Callands; Pvt. to 3 Corpl. 7/1/62; pres. til admitted Danville 4/2/63, debility; chronic diarrhea; returned to duty 6/12/63. Pres. through 10/13/64. Wife Susan A. Oakes. Died in 1934. bur. North of Danville "beyond Rt. 818 off Rt. 41" on left .2 mi. behind barn.

OAKES, THOMAS C.: age 25 in 1860. Sgt.; Co. B 6/4/61 Callands. Pvt. to 3 Sgt. 7/1/62; pres. til admitted Danville 6/29/62 chronic diarrhoea; returned 8/20/62; pres. til POW and WIA, mortally, Gettysburg, fractured thigh, died 8/2/63 at U.S. II Corps Hosp. and buried in Yard B, Row 2 of the hosp. cem. on the hill between Schwartz and Bushman's. Disinterred to Richmond on 6/13/72 in Box #213.

OAKS, ELIAS J.: Pvt.; Co. C 3/12/62 Laurel Grove; was sent to Richmond hosp., date not known. Died of typhoid fever at hosp. 5/15/62. Widow: Elizabeth J. Oakes.

OAKS, ROBERT J.: Pvt.; Co. E 6/8/61 Danville; sick at camp near Lewis House; pres. til 2/28/62. Died of typhoid fever 7/11/63 at Williamsport, Md. Born: Pittsylvania, Va.

OLIVER, ISAAC T.: Pvt.; Co. C 5/30/61 Laurel Grove. Pres. til admitted Richmond GH #18. 3/2/62 chronic bronchitis; discharged from service from there 4/5/62 for disability; born Halifax, age 40, 5'9", dark complex., dark hair, dark eyes, farmer.

OLIVER, JOHN J.: Pvt.; Co. F 3/1/62 Republican Grove; admitted Chimborazo #3 5/3/62 dysentery. Transf. Lynchburg 5/9/62. KIA at Gettysburg 7/3/63.

ORRENDER, MATHEW T.: Pvt.; Co. E 3/10/62 Danville; pres. til 5/6/62; admitted Danville H., acute rheumatism; returned 3/23/63; Chimborazo #5 by 5/24/64 when transferred to Danville, wound forearm. Pres. til POW Dinwiddie C.H. 4/2/65; City Point to Point Lookout 4/4/65; released 6/15/65; res. Pitts Co.; dark complex., brown hair, blue eyes, 5'6¾".

OVERBY, ANDREW J.: Pvt.; Co. K 6/2/61 Cascade; died at Camp Edmonds 8/20/61 conjestive fever.

OVERBY, SILAS: Pvt.; Co. F 3/14/62 Republican Grove; pres. til admitted Chimborazo #4 debility 6/23/62 to Danville 6/29/62; died at home 8/16/62; typhoid fever.

OWEN, BEVERLY B.: Pvt.; Co. A 8/30/62 Kentuck. Pres. til KIA Gettysburg 7/3/63.

OWEN, BEVERLY B.: Pvt.; Co. C 5/30/61 Laurel Grove, discharged Manassas 7/27/61 by order of Gen. J. E. Johnston, for disability.

OWEN, C. M.: Pvt.; 1st Co. I 3/12/62 Clarksville; died of fever at Orange C.H. Hosp. 4/10/62.

OWEN, DAVID L.: Pvt.; Co. B 6/4/61 Callands; pres. til AWOL in Pitts. Co. 11/61; can't afford the funds to return; returned by 2/62 when detailed as teamster; pres. til WIA and POW Gettysburg, captured 7/5/63 in hosps. g.s.w. shoulder, amputation at joint; paroled at Wheat's Building Hosp., Baltimore, Md. 8/23/63. Sent to City Point for exchange 8/24/63; returned to Va. but on indefinite furlough due to injury as of 1/1/65.

OWEN, EDWARD: Pvt.; Co. F 6/4/61 Republican Grove; pres. til admitted Chimborazo #4 10/25/61, fever; returned 11/22/61; died in camp near Richmond of disease 7/2/62.

OWEN, GEORGE RUFUS: Pvt.; Co. C 5/30/61 Laurel Grove; pres. til WIA Seven Pines 5/31/62, admitted Danville H. 6/4/62 with wounds; returned to duty 8/20/62; WIA & POW Gettysburg 7/3/63; g.s.w. thigh to Chester G. Hosp. where paroled and exchanged 9/23/63 at Camp Lee 9/29/63; returned prior to time when POW 5/10/64 Petersburg and Richmond Turnpike; Bermuda Hundred to Camp Hamilton, Va.; to Ft. Monroe 5/14/64 to Point Lookout 5/16/64; exchanged from Aiken's Landing 3/15/65. Alive at Pickaway on 10/21/95.

OWEN, JAMES H.: Pvt.; Co. K 6/2/61 Cascade; present, detailed teamster 7/62; CSA Hosp. Danville 12/15/63, chr. diarrhea, medical board detailed subject for teamster prior to 12/31/64; pres. til POW White Oak Rd. 4/1/65; City Point to Point Lookout 4/5/65; released there 6/15/65. Res. Pitts Co.; dark complex., brown hair, blue eyes, 5'8¾".

OWEN, JAMES J.: Pvt.; Co. E 2/28/62 Danville; Pvt. to 3 Corpl. prior to 8/31/64; CSA Hosp., Danville 6/1/64, hand wound; prom. to 4 Corpl. prior to 8/31/64. Pres. til POW Five Forks, 4/1/65; City Point to Point Lookout 4/5/65; there released 6/5/65; res. Pitts Co. Fair complex., light hair, gray eyes, 5'5".

OWEN, JOHN A.: Pvt.; Co. K 6/2/61 Cascade; present. No further record.

OWEN, JOHN WILLIAM: Pvt. Co. H. "Served 4 years." Postwar record only.

OWEN, JOSEPH T.: Pvt.; Co. K 6/2/61 Cascade; present teamster 9/3/61, cook 7/62, C.S.A. Hosp., Danville 8/20/62, debilitas; ret. 9/16/62. Pres. til POW Farmville 4/6/65; Newport News, oath taken there 7/1/65; res. Pitts Co.; dark complex., light hair, blue eyes, 6'0".

OWEN, THOMAS W.: Pvt.; Co. A 5/30/61 Kentuck; WIA Drewry's Bluff; admitted Howard's Grove G.H. v.s. left knee 5/17/64; returned by 10/12/64; pres. through 2/25/65.

OWEN, WADE: Co. H. Pvt. Post-war record only.

OWEN, WILLIAM: Pvt.; Co. F 6/4/61 Republican Grove; pres. til admitted Chimborazo #4 10/25/61 wound in foot; returned 11/22/61; present, detailed as teamster 6/62; pres. until paroled. Parole dated headqrs., 2nd Div. 6th Corps. 4/25/65.

OWEN, WILLIAM R.: Pvt.; Co. A 8/30/62 Kentuck. Present until admitted Chimborazo #3 6/1/64 debilitas; returned 6/13/64; pres. through 2/25/65.

OWEN, WILLIAM T.: Pvt.; Co. A 5/30/61 Kentuck; absent, sent to Gen. hosp. in Richmond 10/23/61. Discharged from service 5/2/62 at Richmond, paralysis; born Pitts. Co., age 21; 5'11"; fair complexion, blue eyes, red hair, farmer.

OWEN, WILLIAM T.: Pvt.; Co. G 3/10/62 Boydton; absent in hosp. sick 5/62-7/62; returned prior to 5/1/63; pres. til POW & WIA Gettysburg, shot in left leg, flesh wound, 7/3/63 captured. Ft. Del. 7/63 to Chester G.H., Pa. 7/31/63 to Point Lookout, Hammond hosp. 10/4/63; paroled there, and transferred for exchange 3/6/64. Returned prior to 5/10/64 when WIA at Chester Station. Entered Chimborazo #1 5/27/64, vulnus cont.; returned 10/6/64; admitted Chimborazo #3 3/5/65 feb. interm; POW Rich. Hosp. 4/3/65; escaped from hosp. 4/26/65; but CSR also states paroled Appomattox 4/9/65.

OWEN, WILSON: Pvt.; Co. H 7/2/61 Pitts. C.H.; pres. til sent sick to Richmond hosp. 12/23/61, til returned to duty 7/17/62; pres. til KIA Gettysburg 7/3/63.

OWEN, W. J.: Pvt.; 1st Co. I 6/20/61 Clarksville; pres. til admitted Chimborazo #4 10/28/61 rheumatism. Transferred to Petersburg 11/25/61; returned prior to 7/17/62.

PALMER, GEORGE H.: Pvt.; Co. D, no date given; pres. til admitted Chimborazo #1 3/30/62. Self-inflicted incised wound of right hand; returned 6/1/62; pres. til WIA slightly Malvern Hill 7/1/62; sent to hosp. Died in Richmond hosp. 8/10/62.

PALMER, WILLIAM R.: Born 11/14/18. Pvt.; Co. G 5/18/61 Boydton; in Ambulance Corps 8-9/62; pres. til deserted 4/10/63; returned by 4/1/64; Chimborazo #4 5/14/64, chronic rheumatism. Discharged from service 7/10/64, over age. Died 10/30/03 Danville.

PAMPLIN, JAMES R.: Pvt.; 2nd Co. I 3/15/62 Appomattox Co.; present as of only muster roll, dated 8/31/64.

PARISH, JOHN W.: Corpl.; Co. B 6/4/61 Callands; Corpl., reduced to Pvt. by 7/62; pres. until WIA seriously Malvern Hill 7/1/62; admitted Danville hosp. 7/7/62 vulnus selopeticum; returned 7/27/62.

PARKER, CHURCHWELL: Pvt.; Co. F 6/4/61 Republican Grove; present until killed in action, Malvern Hill carrying the colors 7/1/62.

PARKER, JOHN W.: Pvt.; Co. G, no date listed; pres. til entered Chimborazo #3 3/5/65, rheumatism. POW in Richmond Hosp. 4/3/65; Libby Prison to Newport News 4/23/65; took oath there 7/1/65; res. Mecklenburg Co.; fair complex., light hair, dark eyes, 5'8".

PARROTT, LEWIS: Pvt., 1st Co. I 6/20/61 Clarksville; absent, sent to hosp. 10/24/61, typhoid fever; returned 11/12/61; sent to hosp. 2/27/62; at hosp. 3/62 through last dated muster roll 7/17/62.

PARSONS, ALLEN: Pvt.; Co. B, no date given. Sent to hosp. 6/25/62.

PARSONS, SPENCER: Pvt.; Co. B 4/12/62 Richmond; pres. til attached to Camp Winder hosp. 7/24/64 as nurse. There through 1/1/63. Returned to duty by 5/19/63; pres. til absent div. hospital by 1/1/65; admitted Chimborazo #3 2/25/65 rheumatism.

PARSONS, W. H.: Pvt.; Co. H, no date given. Deserted to Federals 12/29/64; from Bermuda Hundred where took oath, to Wash. D.C. 1/4/65. Transportation furnished to Phila. Pa.

PATTERSON, JOHN R.: Pvt.; Co. A 5/30/61 Kentuck; pres. til admitted 3/2/62. G.H. #18, Richmond, debility. Died there 3/24/62.

PATTERSON, WILLIAM H.: Born in Pitts. Co. Pvt.; Co. A, no date given. Pres. til left at hosp. at Richmond on march to Yorktown 5/62. Admitted Danville hosp. 11/13/62 contusion and debilitas; returned to duty 1/17/63. Died in Gordonsville, Charity hosp. 2/3/63 pneumonia.

PAYNE, CRISPIN: Pvt.; Co. K 6/2/61 Cascade; absent sick from prior to 8/31/61, CSA Hosp., Charlottesville 4/23/62 pneumonia; trans. to Lynchburg #2 hosp. Died there 5/17/62 of typhoid pneumonia. Bur. Lynchburg Cem.

PAYNE, JOHN R.: Pvt.; Co. C 5/30/61 Laurel Grove, Chimborazo #1 4/12/62 convalescent, left without permission. Present, extra duty, ambulance corps 9/62; pres. til WIA at Drewry's Bluff 5/16/64; admitted Chimborazo #5 5/16/64 v.s. left elbow; died there 7/9/64. Brother of Joseph T. and Leroy Payne.

PAYNE, JOSEPH T.: Pvt.; Co. C 5/30/61 Laurel Grove. In hosp. sick in late June or early July, 1862. Apparently detached with 53rd Regt. sometime in 1862. WIA and POW at Gettysburg on 7/3/63. Died at U.S. II Corps. Hosp. on 7/22/63. Bur. in Yard B, Row 2 of hosp. cem. on the hill between Schwartz's and Bushman's; disinterred to Richmond on 6/13/72 with 110 others in 10 large boxes marked "S". Brother of John R. and Leroy Payne.

PAYNE, LEROY: Pvt.; Co. D 5/24/61 Whitmell; present ambulance corps, litter bearer 9/62; present until entered Chimborazo #5 5/16/64 v.s. right shoulder; furloughed 60 days 5/22/64; returned to be POW near Howlett's House 8/25/64; Bermuda Hundred to Ft. Monroe 8/26/64 to Point Lookout 8/28/64; paroled there and exchanged from Aiken's Landing 3/14/65. Brother of John R. and Joseph T. Payne.

PAYTHIESS, GEORGE W.: Co. I. Pvt. Post-war record only.

PEAK, HENRY B.: Pvt.; Co. F 3/14/62 Repub. Grove; absent, sick in hosp. 4/62. Returned to be WIA 6/20/62; admitted Chimborazo #4 debility 6/23/62; entered Danville 6/29/62 chronic diarrhea; returned 8/28/62; entered Petersburg hosp. 3/21/63, cause not given. Entered Farmville 4/24/63 debility from fever. Furloughed 30 days from 4/24/63.

PEAKE, JOHN J.: Pvt.; Co. F 3/13/62 Republican Grove; absent, in hosp. in Richmond 4/14/62; returned to be WIA and sent to hosp. 7/10/62; returned to duty by 9/15/64; pres. until POW Farmville 4/6/65; to Newport News, where took oath 7/1/65; res. Halifax; dark complex., dark hair, grey eyes, 5'10".

PEAKE, LUKE R.: Pvt.; Co. F 6/4/61 Republican Grove; Chimborazo #3 4/14/62, no cause and furlough, 20 days. Pres. til slightly WIA Malvern Hill 7/1/62; detailed with ambulance corps 8/62. Present til POW 8/23/64.

PEAKE, MARK L.: Pvt.; Co. F 6/4/61 Republican Grove; present, detailed ambulance corps 8/62; detailed litter bearer prior to 7/1/63; deserted 3/16/64; returned to company 8/18/64, 6 months pay deducated by gen. court martial. Pres. through 2/25/65.

PEAKE, THOMAS L.: Pvt.; Co. F 3/13/62 Republican Grove; pres. til under arrest by 4/1/64; sent to Castle Thunder to do gov't. work by sentence of court mar. prior to 8/31/64; present prior to 12/31/64; pres. til POW Farmville 4/6/65; City Point to Newport News 4/14/65. Oath taken there 6/14/65; res. Halifax Co.; dark complex., dark hair, blue eyes, 5'5".

PEATROSS, JOHN D. L.: Pvt.; Co. D 10/14/64 Danville, Va.; present through 2/25/65.

PEED, CHARLES W.: Pvt.; 2nd Co. I 3/10/62 Norfolk Co.; present til POW 10/2/64. Confined at Bermuda Hundred, to go to Wash. D.C.

PENICK, CHARLES CLIFTON: born 12/9/43 in Charlotte Co. Enlisted 5/24/61 at Whitmell. Q.M. Sgt.; Co. D/F & S; appted. from Pvt. to QM Sgt. 6/30/61. Pres. til paroled Appomattox 4/9/65 with "horse & equipments". Son of Edwin A. Penick. Missionary to Blacks in West Africa 1878 (?) to 10/83. Bishop of Protestant Episcopal Church Richmond at Shenandoah Flats in 2/08.

PENICK, EDWARD (EDWIN?) A.: born in Prince Edward Co. 2/24/20. Farmer. Pvt.; Co. D 4/62. Pres. til admitted Richmond G.H. #18 5/2/62 measles; transferred to Danville H 5/6/62; died near Winchester 10/2/62, probably from wounds sustained in the Maryland campaign. Father of C. C. Penick. Widow: Mary M. Penick. Buried Stonewall Cem., Winchester.

PENICK, NATHAN: 2 Lieut.; Co. F 6/4/61; Republican Grove; appted. 2 Lieut. 6/4/61; resigned 7/61.

PERKINS, J.: Pvt.; no company listed. Took oath of allegiance at Hart's Island 6/20/65. Res. Prince George; light complex., light hair, blue eyes, 5'3".

PERKINS, JAMES R.: 2 Lieut; Co. H 7/2/61 Pitts Co. C.H.. Elected 4/29/62 to 3 Lieut.; promoted 5/31/62 2 Lieut.; pres. til admitted Orange C.H. Hosp. 11/8/61 rheumatism. Returned to duty 11/23/61; admitted Chimborazo #5 11/29/61, chronic rheumatism; returned to duty 12/16/61. Present til WIA White Pine near Richmond 5/31/62, slight wound on leg, with a piece of spent bomb; returned, present til detached to command Co. G 38th Va. prior to 8/31/64; returned by 12/31/64.

PERKINS, THOMAS M.: Pvt.; Co. F 6/20/61 Hermitage Camp; pres. til sent to Gen'l. Hosp. at Manassas Junction 2/62; died Gen'l. Hosp. Warrenton, Va., 2/27/62 pneumonia.

PERKINS, WILLIAM M.: Pvt.; Co. E 6/8/61, Danville; absent, on sick furlough prior to 8/30/61; left camp sick 9/61; discharged 9/7/61 with surgeon's certificate of disability.

PERKINS, WILLIAM P.: Pvt.; Co. D 10/14/64 Danville; absent under civil process as of 12/31/64; present by 2/25/65; paroled 4/25/65 Headqrs. 2nd Div., 6th Corps.

PERSON, ALLEN: enl. 1861 in 1st Co. I. Postwar record only.

PETTY, DAVIS A.: Born in Pittsylvania Co. Pvt.; Co. K 6/2/61; absent sick in hospital 5/62 Cascade; present detailed teamster 9/62; died Lynchburg G.H. 1/6/63 typhoid pneumonia.

PHELPS, ROBERT S.: Pvt.; 2nd Co. I 3/6/62 Appomattox Co.; absent, admitted Chimborazo #4 6/25/64 typhoid fever; died 7/3/64.

PHILLIPS, ALUSTON D.: Pvt.; 2 Co. I 4/7/64 Henrico Co.; pres. til WIA at Chester Station 5/10/64. Admitted Chimborazo #4 5/11/64 g.s.w. to face; admitted Chimborazo #4 again 10/8/64, old g.s.w., face; v.s. left eye; retired 11/14/64 disability permanent; on list of Invalid Corps, Military Station, Richmond. Occupation harness maker.

PHILLIPS, HOWELL: Pvt.; 1st Co. I 6/20/61 Clarksville; pres. til listed as missing, sick since 12/26/61.

PHILLIPS, JAMES D.: Pvt.; 1st Co. I 3/12/62 Clarksville; pres. til admitted Chimborazo #1 4/24/62 Haemoptysia.

PHILLIPS, R. W.: Pvt.; Co. I 6/20/61 Clarksville; discharged surgeon's cert. 8/26/61 chronic rheumatism.

PIERCE, ALBERT W.: 1 Lieut.; Co. F 6/4/61 Repl. Grove; appted. 5/13/61; dropped 4/29/62; failed to be reelected spring reorganization.

PIERCE, EDGAR T.: Cpl.; Co. F 6/4/61 Republican Grove; 4 Corpl. to 2 Sgt. prior to 7/1/63; appted. 1 Sgt. 11/1/64; pres. til POW Five Forks 4/1/65; City Point to Point Lookout 4/6/65; released there 6/16/65. Res. Pitts Co.; light complex., auburn hair, dark blue eyes, 5'8½".

PIGG, HEZEKIAH FORD: Born 12/18/25 in Pittsylvania Co. Corpl.; Co. H 7/2/61 Pitts. Co.; honorably discharged. Surgeon's cert. 8/23/61 rheumatism or possibly 9/5/62, overage. Died 9/08 in Pittsylvania Co. Buried in Pigg family cem. in Pittsylvania Co. North of Int. Rts. 703 & 834.

PIGG, THOMAS C.: Pvt.; Co D 5/24/61 Whitmell; admitted gen. hosp., Richmond 5/2/62, debility; pres. til WIA 5/31/62 on Chickahominy R.; admitted Danville H. prior to 6/10/62 vulnus selopeticum; returned duty 10/22/62; pres. til admitted Chimborazo #1 2/18/63 Whitlow; returned to duty 3/19/63.

PINCKMAN, THOMAS: Pvt.; 1st Co. I 6/20/61 Clarksville. No further record.

PINSON, ALLEN: Born Mecklenburg Co. Pvt.; 1st Co. I 6/20/61 Clarksville; absent, sick since 12/26/61-7/17/62. Age 22, 5'10", dark complexion, grey eyes, dark hair, farmer.

PIPER, JACOB: Pvt.; Co. H 5/4/64 Rockingham; conscript; deserted from Hanover Junction on or about 5/20/64.

PITT, JULIAN V.: Musician, drummer; Co. G. Resided in Catawba Co., N.C. and enlisted in Co. F, 32nd N.C. Regt. at Portsmouth, Va. Age 14 on 4/1/62. Present or accounted for until transferred to Co. G, 38th Va. on 8/10/64. Present thru 2/25/65. Paroled at Appomattox 4/9/65.

POINDEXTER, JAMES EDWARD: Born Chatham 11/17/38. U.Va. graduate. Appted. 2 Lieut. Co. H 6/7/61 Pittsylvania C.H.; promoted to 1 Lieut. 12/13/61 or 4/29/62; promoted Capt. 5/31/62; pres. til WIA White Pine [Seven Pines] 5/31/62, thigh broken; returned during 6/62; absent 7-9/62 due to wounds from White Pine. Returned to duty 6/6/62; POW Gettysburg 7/3/63; Ft. McHenry 7/6/63 to Ft. Del. 7/7/63 to POW Depot, Johnson Island, Sandusky, Ohio 7/20/63 to Point Lookout for exchange 3/14/65. Married Katharine Gordon Wallace in 1883. Episcopal Minister in Md., Va. and N.C. Died 5/31/12.

POINDEXTER, WILLIAM R.: Born 8/6/44. Sgt.; Co. H 3/22/62, Orange; CSA Hosp. Danville 9/7/62 rheumatism; ret. to duty 9/10/62. Sent to Genl. Hosp. #8 Richmond 9/15/62, effects of typhoid fever, transferred to Camp Winder 9/24/62. Furloughed 20 days 10/27/62. Returned, WIA Gettysburg 7/3/63. Present until admitted G.H. #9, Richmond 3/5/65.

POLK, LEWIS: Pvt.; Co. F 5/27/62 near Richmond; WIA Battle Seven Pines sent to hosp. 5/31/62 in Richmond.Last roll dated 2/25/65.

POSEY, BENJAMIN: Pvt.; Co. A 3/30/61 Kentuck; Chimborazo #4 12/3/61 bronchitis and dysuria; pres. til 6/23/62 admitted Danville H. nephrites; returned to duty 10/2/62. CSA Hosp. Danville 10/3/64, febris int. quo through 2/25/65. Alive on 3/28/87.

117

POSEY, GEORGE W.: Corpl.; Co. A 5/30/61 Kentuck; pres. til POW Dinwiddie C.H. 4/2/65; City Point to Point Lookout 4/4/65; released there 6/16/65; res. Pitts. Co.; dark complex., black hair, blue eyes; 5'6".

POULTON, JOHN F.: Chaplain, F & S; appted. 5/20/62; dropped 6/8/63. Failed to be reelected at reorganization, ceased to be officer due to continued long absence.

POWELL, ELLIS: Pvt.; Co. H 7/2/61 Pitts. C.H.; Chimborazo #1 4/24/62 convalescent; pres. til discharged 9/5/62, over 35.

POWELL, JAMES A.: Pvt.; Co. E 3/21/62 Danville; pres. til 5/23/62 Farmville H. Diarrhea, returned 6/30/62; admitted Danville H 8/28/62 debilitas; furloughed 11/11/62; CSA Hosp., Danville 4/19/63, aphonia; returned prior to 6/30/63; pres. til WIA Drewry's Bluff 5/16/64; admitted Chimborazo #2 5/17/64; v.s. left hand, loss of 2 fingers, age 20 as of 5/17/64; farmer; admitted Danville 5/26/64, wound of hand; returned to duty 11/8/64; present through 2/25/65.

POWELL, JOHN C.: Pvt.; Co. D 5/24/61 Whitmell; pres. til discharged 9/15/61, no reason given.

POWELL, JOSEPH W.: Born 7/7/43. Pvt., Co. D 3/11/62 Whitmell; pres. til admitted Danville H. 5/8/62, debilitas; returned 6/1/62; pres. til admitted 8/22/62; Chimborazo #5; furloughed 9/13/64 for 30 days, returned and admitted Danville H. 4/3/65 vulnus incisum; furloughed 4/8/65 30 days. Died 7/29/19.

POWELL, ROBERT H.: Pvt.; Co. D 5/24/61 Whitmell; pres. til WIA on Chickahominy 5/31/62; admitted Danville H. 6/4/62 vulnus selopeticum; returned to duty 7/23/62; admitted Danville H. 8/28/62, chronic diarrhoea; present until WIA Drewry's Bluff 5/16/64; admitted Chimborazo 5/17/64; v.s.; furloughed for 60 days 8/12/64.

POWELL, THOMAS J.: Pvt.; Co. H 7/2/61 Pitts. C.H. b. 1843. Present until admitted Chimborazo #1 5/28/62 rheumatism; supposed to return to duty 6/21/62 but didn't report according to Co. roll until 7/17/62; detailed as cook for Co. 9/62; pres. til deserted near Newbern 2/2/64. Post war record lists as "killed at Seven Pines".

POWER, JOHN J.: Pvt.; Co. B 11/13/64 Pittsylvania, conscript. pres. til admitted Chimborazo 3/5/65 debility.

POYTHRESS, GEORGE W.: Pvt.; 1st Co. I 6/20/61 Clarksville; absent sick 2/10/62, furloughed through 7/17/62.

PREWETT, DAVID D.: Pvt.; Co. D 5/24/61 Whitmell; pres. til admitted Danville H. 5/8/62 debilitas; sent to Genl. Hosp. 11/24/62; returned prior to 4/1/64; pres. til absent sick at Div. Hosp. 8/10/64; returned prior to 12/31/64; pres. through 2/25/65; POW High Bridge 4/6/65; City Point to Point Lookout 4/15/65; released there 6/16/65; res. Pitts. Co.; dark complex., black hair, hazel eyes, 5'7". Lived in Pitts. Co. and Camp Lee Soldiers Home, Richmond. Died 7/25/16 at age 77. Buried Hollywood Cem., east section, Richmond.

PREWETT, EPHRAIM: Pvt.; Co. D 5/24/61 Whitmell; pres. til entered Danville H 5/8/62 pneumonia; sent to Genl. Hosp. 11/24/62; returned, prior to 4/1/64; WIA 5/10/64 near Chester; admitted Chimborazo #2 5/11/64; v.s. right leg and knee; age 23 as of 5/11/64, farmer. Returned to duty prior to 12/31/64. Pres. til deserted 2/19/65 to Pitts. Co.

PREWETT, RALPH B.: Pvt.; Co. D 5/2/64 Danville; conscript; pres. through 2/25/65; POW White Oak Road 4/1/65; City Point to Point Lookout 4/5/65; there released 6/16/65; res. Pitts. Co.; light complex., brown hair, dark hazel eyes, 5'3".

PREWETT, WILLIAM C.: Pvt.; Co. D 5/24/61 Whitmell; pres. but sick as of 8/30/61; died 9/4/61 of colic.

PREWETT, WILLIAM E.: Pvt.; Co. D, conscript, joined Co. on the march 9/20/62; admitted Rich. G.H. #4 11/2/62, sequele of rubeola; returned to duty 1/23/63. Occupation tobacconist.

PREWITT, ABEL: Pvt.; Co. D 8/14/62 Danville. WIA at Gettysburg 7/3/63. Present through 2/25/65.

PREWITT, ALEXANDER: Pvt.; Co. C 5/30/61 Laurel Grove; pres. til WIA, seriously Malvern Hill 7/1/62; admitted Chimborazo #2 7/4/62; g.s.w., arm and erysipelas; died there of same 7/9/62. Widow: Jenette Prewitt.

PRICE, DAVID: Co. A. Pvt. Post-war record only.

PRICE, DORSEY M.: Pvt.; Co. D, no date given. Pres. til admitted Richmond G.H. #18 5/2/62 measles in Wayside Hosp., Richmond 10/11/62 rheumatism; absent sick through roll dated 9/62.

PRICE, JACKSON M.: Corpl.; Co. F 6/20/61 Hermitage Camp; Pvt. to 3 Corpl. 11/1/64; pres. til admitted Chimborazo #4 6/10/62; returned, sent to hosp. at Winchester 6/18/63; present prior to 4/1/64; pres. through 2/25/65; pres. til POW Five Forks 4/1/65; City Point to Point Lookout 4/6/65; released 6/16/65; res. Halifax Co.; light complex., light hair, dark blue eyes, 5'8¼".

PRICE, NAPOLEON D.: 1 Lieut.; Co. D 5/24/61 Whitmell; appted. 1 Lieut. 6/3/61. Pres. til WIA Malvern Hill 7/1/62. Died of g.s.w. abdomen at Chimborazo #4 7/3/62. Mother: Nancy R. May.

PRICE, NATHANIEL: Born 5/12/31 in Pittsylvania Co. Pvt.; Co. H 7/2/61 Pitts. C.H.; pres. til sent to Richmond Hosp. as a nurse 4/62; also sick there until 9/23/62 when discharged, no reason given. Reenlisted 10/14/64 Pittsylvania; pres. through 2/25/65; pres. til POW South Side R.R. 4/2/65, City Point to Hart's Island 4/7/65; released 6/6/65. Res. Pitts Co., dark complex., dark hair, grey eyes, 5'7". Died 5/12/84 in Pittsylvania Co.

PRICE, WILLIAM T.: Born Campbell Co. Pvt.; Co. B 10/10/64 Pittsylvania; pres. til admitted Chimborazo #5 1/24/65. Chron. rheumatism. Lived in Brookneal and Camp Lee Soldiers Home, Richmond. Died 1/27/18 at age 97. Buried Hollywood Cem., East section, Richmond.

PRITCHARD, WILLIAM B.: Commissioned 1st Lieut. Co. B 7/7/61 at Richmond; promoted Capt. 12/10/62; pres. til WIA Seven Pines 5/31/62. Returned by 7/62; WIA (finger amputated and thigh wound). Battle of Chester Station 5/10/64; absent, detached service as Brig. Recorder 10/14/64. Surrendered Appomattox 4/9/65; given amnesty oath as of 5/13/65. Married Margaret Strother Johnston, 4th child of Gen. A. S. Johnston, in 1876. Lived in Los Angeles and San Francisco after war.

PRITCHETT, CHARLES WESLEY: Born 11/26. Pvt.; Co. D 9/29/64 Danville; pres. til POW White Oak Road 4/1/65; City Point to Point Lookout 4/5/65; released there 6/16/65; res. Pitts. Co.; dark complex., brown hair, hazel eyes, 5'6", farmer. Married Lydia A. Robertson. Died 10/30/06. Buried in family cem. near Whitmell.

PRITCHETT, CLAUDIUS A.: Pvt.; Co. K 6/2/61 Cascade; at home sick 10/61 furlough; pres. til transferred to Cavalry 6/6/62.

PRITCHETT, CULBRETH J.: 1 Sgt.; Co. D 5/24/61 Whitmell; elected from 1 Sgt. to 2 Lieut. 7/26/62; while absent sick. Admitted Danville H, no date given; serofula; returned to duty 8/26/62; sent to hosp. 9/20/62; resigned commission 9/30/62 disabled; born Pitts Co.; age 21; 5'7", sallow complex., grey eyes, dark hair, a farmer. Father: William E. Pritchett.

PRITCHETT, JAMES H.: Sgt.; Co. D 5/24/61 Whitmell; Sgt. demoted to Pvt. 5/2/62; WIA on Chickahominy R. 5/31/62; admitted Chimborazo #2 3/14/62 chronic bronchitis; returned 5/2/62; WIA on Chickahominy R. 5/31/62; admitted Chimborazo #2 6/2/62 bayonet wound of hand; furloughed there 20 days 6/5/62; returned prior to time POW White Oak Rd. 4/1/65 City Point to Point Lookout 4/5/65; released there 6/16/65; res. Pitts. Co.; fair complex., brown hair, grey eyes, 5'9½".

PRUETT, ABRAM: Pvt. Co. D. Postwar record only. WIA (head of penis) at Gettysburg 7/3/63. Alive on 3/16/86.

PRUETT, JOHN: Pvt. Co. H. WIA at Gettysburg, post-war record only.

PUGH, ABRAHAM: Pvt.; 2nd Co. I 3/1/62 Norfolk Co.; present til detached service at Division Pioneer Corps prior to 2/25/65. Paroled Appomattox 4/9/65.

PURYEAR, J. A.: Pvt.; 1st Co. I 6/20/61 Clarksville; sent to hosp. at Orange C.H. 4/7/62.

PURYEAR, JOHN R.: Pvt.; 1st Co. I 3/19/62 Clarksville; absent, sent to hosp. at Orange C.H. 4/7/62; admitted Chimborazo #2 4/14/62 rubeola; furloughed 20 days 5/1/62.

PURYEAR, RICHARD: Pvt.; 1st Co. I 6/20/61, Clarksville; pres. til detailed wagoner 1/29/62; admitted Chimborazo #1 5/12/62 contused wound of foot received 5/5/62 at Williamsburg; returned to duty 6/1/62.

PURYEAR, WILLIAM M.: Pvt.; 1st Co. I 3/12/62 Clarksville; absent, sent to hosp. at Orange C.H. 4/7/62; admitted Petersburg H. 5/1/62 sorditus; returned to duty 5/7/62; admitted Chimborazo #5 5/17/62, pneumonia. Died there of same 5/21/62.

QUINN, THOMAS R.: Pvt.; Co. D 5/24/61 Whitmell; Chimborazo #1 3/30/62 bronchitis; returned to duty 4/17/62. Pres. until deserted 7/5/62; arrested and in Castle Thunder, Richmond under sentence of death by court martial, this list dated 4/1/64. Sentence not carried out and is returned to Co. D (possibly due to plea for clemency by his capt. and other members of Co. D) deserted, 2nd offense, from trenches to Federals near Bermuda H. 7/7/64; received Ft. Monroe 7/11/64; released 7/16/64; took oath Ft. Monroe 7/17/64; sent to Wash. D.C.; res. Pitts. Co.; dark complex., light hair, blue eyes, 5'5".

QUINN, WILLIAM: Pvt.; Co. D 5/24/61 Whitmell; pres. til admitted Chimborazo #4 10/25/61 hyposadias; discharged surgeon's cert. 11/8/61.

RAGSDALE, JAMES W.: Pvt.; Co. E 3/2/62 Danville; absent sick 4-5/62-7/62; died at Genl. Hosp. #12, Richmond, 9/2/61. Bur. Hollywood Cem., Richmond.

RAINEY, MALACHI: Pvt.; 2nd Co. I 3/11/62 Norfolk Co.; absent POW 8/25/64 near Howlett's House near Petersburg. Bermuda Hundred to Fort Monroe 8/26/64 to Point Lookout 8/28/64; released there 5/14/65; res. Norfolk, occupation grocer.

RAINEY, MATHEW J.: Pvt.; Co. G 5/18/61 Boydton; present, extra duty as Postmaster for 38th Va. 10/61; pres. til WIA slightly at Seven Pines 5/31/62; sick in hosp. Reported for duty 4/14/63; died Chimborazo #1 hosp. 8/10/64, typhoid fever. Bur. Oakwood Cem., Richmond.

RAINEY, PETER: Pvt.; Co. G 5/18/61 Boydton. Discharged Surgeon's cert. 8/28/61, rheumatism.

RAINEY, PHILIP: Pvt.; Co. G 3/13/62 Boydton; present, detailed with Capt. William B. Edmonds Commissary prior to 7/16/62; acting as Commissary Sgt. for Brigade; discharged 1/3/63, no reason given.

RAMSEY, WARREN: Pvt.; 1st Co. I 6/20/61 Clarksville; absent, sick 12/26/61; returned prior to 4/62; admitted Chimborazo #1 7/2/62 wound of hand.

RAY, GEORGE F.: Pvt.; Co. A 5/30/61 Kentuck; CSA Hosp., Danville 5/15/62, diarrhea. Returned to duty 5/25/62; sent to Richmond hosp. sick 6/62. Present through 2/25/65.

READ, JAMES W.: Pvt.; Co. D 3/11/62 Whitmell; pres. til sent to hosp. 4/27/62-6/62. Returned prior to POW and WIA Gettysburg 7/3/63; g.s.w. left arm below shoulder; treated at U.S. 1st Div., I Corps Hosp. Died 7/25/63 in hosp. around Gettysburg.

REDMAN, JOHN G.: Pvt.; 1st Co. I 6/20/61 Clarksville; pres. til POW Fair Oaks 5/31/62; Ft. Monroe to Ft. Delaware 6/5/62; to Aiken's Landing to be exchanged 8/5/62; age 18, 5'9", sandy hair, blue eyes, fair complex., born in Va.

REED, DAVID: Pvt.; 2nd Co. I 2/10/62 Norfolk Co.; pres. til WIA skirmish 8/25/64 in hosp. Richmond; deserted to enemy 12/27/64 captured 12/28/64 Bermuda Hundred. Oath taken there; to Wash. D.C. 1/3/65. Trans. furnished to Norfolk.

REED, JOHN: Pvt.; 2nd Co. I 2/10/62 Norfolk; pres. til POW, a deserter, Dept. Head Qrs. 10/2/64; turned over to Provost Marshal Genl. to go to Norfolk, Va.

REESE, JOHN W.: Born Lunenburg, Va. Pvt.; Co. G 5/18/61 Boydton; Gen. Hosp. Orange C.H. 3/9/62 rheumatism, absent, admitted Petersburg H. 3/31/62; discharged 8/4/62; acute rheumatism. Age 48, 5'6", dark complex., blue eyes, light hair, farmer.

REESE, JOSEPH M.: Pvt.; Co. G 5/18/61 Boydton. Pres. til admitted Chimborazo #5 6/1/62, returned 6/8/62; slight wound of arm. WIA Malvern Hill 7/1/62; absent 7/62; returned prior to 5/1/63; deserted 5/16/64 near Drewry's Bluff.

REYNOLDS, COLEMAN: Born in Pittsylvania. Pvt.; Co. B 6/4/61 Callands, age 31, roll not dated. Pres. til Chimborazo #4 5/8/62, transferred Danville 5/27/62; chronic diarrhea; returned duty 7/4/62; WIA at Gettysburg on 7/3/63. Died in Pittsylvania Co. of wound 7/30/63.

REYNOLDS, JOHN H.: Pvt.; Co. B 10/14/64 Pittsylvania; conscript; present through 1/1/65.

REYNOLDS, JOHN WARD: Born 9/24/31. Pvt.; Co. B 6/4/61 Callands; pres. til sent to hosp. 4/25/62 and admitted Chimborazo #2 on 5/13/62, catarrah. Returned to duty by 5/17/62; deserted prior to 5/19/63; also listed as having deserted 6/10/64; captured and confined in Castle Thunder, Richmond. Paroled by Pres. for volunteering in Winder Legion to defend Richmond from Sheridan's '64 raid 8/3/64. Died 5/3/10. CSR also states he died 12/30/64 in Richmond of typhoid fever. Buried Reynolds family cemetery, Chatham, Va.

REYNOLDS, JOSEPH D.: Pvt.; Co. B 6/4/61 Pittsylvania; left camp near Broad Run and went home sick on 8/26/61. Pres. til AWOL 3 months prior to 4/30/63; returned, POW Gettysburg 7/3/63; Ft. McHenry 7/6/63 to Ft. Del. 7/12/63 to Point Lookout 10/26/63; exchanged 10/30/63; returned before WIA 5/11/64; Chimborazo #2 5/11/64 v.s. right arm. Trans. to Danville Hosp. 5/23/64. Returned prior to 4/65; POW Farmville 4/6/65; City Point to Newport News 4/14/65; took oath there 7/1/65; res. Pittsylvania; fair complex., light hair, blue eyes, 5'11", farmer.

REYNOLDS, JOSEPH D.: Pvt.; Co. B 9/14/64 Pittsylvania; conscript; pres. til POW Five Forks 4/1/65; City Point to Hart's Island 4/7/65; released there 6/20/65; residence Pitts Co.; fair complex., light hair, grey eyes, 6'2".

REYNOLDS, JOSEPH J. D.: Pvt.; Co. B 12/10/64 Pittsylvania; present through 1/1/65. Possibly died 6/15/61 and bur. Greenlawn Cem., Newport News.

REYNOLDS, WYATT: Pvt.; Co. B, no date given; only information is that he was in hospital, but no date on Co. return.

RICE, HENRY C. (or CHARLES HENRY): Born 1845. Pvt.; Co. C 10/6/63 Danville; pres. til paroled with Army of N. Va. 4/25/65. Died 5/24/19.

RICE, JAMES J.: born in N.C. Pvt.; Co. H 3/3/63 Campbell; pres. til POW Gettysburg and WIA, g.s. right side of thorax and abdomen from Gettysburg to USA Genl. Hosp., Baltimore, Md. Died there 1/13/64; 39 years old in 1863. Bur. London Park Cem., Baltimore, Md. Also listed in CSR as J. R. Rice.

RICE, JAMES P.: Born Pitts. Co. Sgt.; Co. E 6/8/61 Danville; Pvt. to 2 Sgt. prior to 6/30/62; pres. til killed at Gettysburg 7/3/63. Son of Joseph L. Rice.

RICE, WILLIAM C.: Pvt.; Co. C, no date listed. Present until Chimborazo #5 5/1/62; cont. fever; died there 6/2/62, cont. fever.

RICHARDS, DAVID B.: Born Pittsylvania. Pvt.; Co. H 7/2/61 Pittsylvania; pres. til admitted Chimborazo 10/27/61; measles and sequelas, pneumonia; died there 11/12/61. Bur. Oakwood Cem., Richmond. 5'10".

RICHARDS, JESSE H.: Pvt.; Co. A 5/30/61 Kentuck; present, detailed teamster 8/10/61; wded. Seven Pines 5/31/62, pres. til WIA slightly Malvern Hill 7/1/62; returned, pres. til Genl. Hosp. #9 Richmond 4/24/64, no date of returning to duty. Last muster roll 2/25/65.

RICHARDS, JESSE N.: Born Pitts Co. Pvt.; Co. H 7/2/61 Pittsylvania C.H.; pres. til Danville H. 1/16/62. Died 1/18/62 pneumonia at Moore hosp.; Manassas Junction. Age 17, 5'8", sallow complex., black eyes, dark hair, no occupation, a minor before war.

RICHARDS, WILLIAM W.: Pvt.; Co. A 7/20/63 Danville; conscript, pres. til POW Dinwiddie C.H. 4/2/65, City Point to Point Lookout 4/6/65; released 6/30/65; res. Pitts. Co.; light complex., brown hair, dark gray eyes, 5'11¾".

RICHARDSON, ALFRED or ALBERT: Pvt.; Co. C 5/30/61 Laurel Grove; present til discharged, surgeon's cert. 10/8/61 rheumatism. Lived in Camp Lee Soldiers Home, Richmond. Died 8/10/01 at age 66. Buried Hollywood Cem., west section, Richmond.

RICHARDSON, GEORGE THOMAS: Born 9/15/24 at Pitts. Co. Pvt.; Co. E 6/8/61 Danville; pres. til Chimborazo #4 10/25/61, returned 1/28/62, fever and lumbago; admitted Chimborazo #3 4/14/62; trans. to Lynchburg 6/1/62; returned by time WIA 8/27/61 through thigh, compound fracture of femur of right leg; admitted Richmond Genl. Hosp. #8 1/5/63, discharged surgeon's cert., compound fracture femur 1/28/63. Age 40 at time of discharge, 5'10", light complex., blue eyes, gray hair, farmer. Died at home at Ringgold 12/17/94 and bur. nearby.

RICHARDSON, HENRY: Pvt.; Co. A, no date listed; pres. til Chimborazo #2 4/24/62 rubeola complicated with bronchitis. Died there 5/9/62 typhoid fever.

RICHARDSON, JOHN S.: Pvt.; Co. C 5/30/61 Laurel Grove; pres. til Richmond Genl. Hosp. #18 3/2/62 typhoid fever. Returned 4/2/62; pres., WIA slightly Gettysburg 7/3/63; WIA severely 5/16/64 at Drewry's Bluff; g.s.w. in right hand and shoulder blade, Chimborazo #4 5/16/64, transf. 5/24/64 to Danville 5/27/64, furloughed 6/21/64; retired and put in Invalid Corps 12/12/64. Alive in Peytonsburg on 11/20/99.

RICHARDSON, ROBERT: Corpl.; Co. C 5/30/61 Laurel Grove; Corpl. to Pvt. by 8/31/62; absent, left in Richmond sick 7/9/61. Still absent 8/30/61, returned prior to 8/62; killed at Manassas 8/31/62.

RICHARDSON, ROBERT H.: Pvt.; 1st Co. I 6/20/61 Clarksville; absent, sent to hosp. 2/27/62; returned prior to 4/18/62.

RICHRDSON, SAMUEL: Pvt.; Co. A 1/23/62 Danville. Present as of only roll dated 2/25/65.

RICHARDSON, SAMUEL S.: Pvt.; Co. A 5/30/61 Kentuck; pres. til admitted Danville #1 12/21/61; to Richmond 4/22/62 debility.

RICHARDSON, THOMAS T.: Pvt.; Co. A 10/14/64 Danville, pres. through 2/25/65.

RICHARDSON, WILLIAM D. H.: Pvt.; Co. A 5/30/61 Kentuck; Chimborazo #4 5/1/62, cont. fever. Pres. til WIA at Drewry's Bluff 5/16/64 and admitted Howard's Grove Hosp. 5/17/64, v.s. right hip; on wounded furlough 5/29/64 through last roll 2/25/65; alive at Laurel Grove on 3/20/82.

RICKETTS, JAMES: Corpl.; Co. H 7/2/61 Pitts C.H.; pres. til admitted Chimborazo #3 10/22/61; chronic rheumatism; discharged 11/22/61.

RICKETTS, JOHN W.: Pvt.; Co. A 5/30/61 Kentuck. Pres. til admitted Camp Winder Genl. Hosp. 5/9/62 pneumonia. Returned 5/23/62; pres. til WIA, slightly Malvern Hill 7/1/62.

RICKETTS, REUBEN B.: Pvt.; Co. E 3/11/62 Danville; pres. til Rich. Genl. Hosp. #18 5/2/62. Transferred 5/5/62 chronic rheumatism; Danville H. 6/16/62; returned 7/18/62 debilitas; pres. til detached to Brigade Head Qrs. prior to 8/31/64; returned prior to 2/25/65. Died 7/9/91 at age 61. Buried in Danville, Va. off Piney Forest Rd. about ¼ mile south of Franklin Turnpike.

RIDDLE, BENJAMIN: Pvt.; Co. H 2/2/64, conscript; pres. til WIA 5/16/64 Drewry's Bluff; died of wounds received v.s. right foot, in Howard's Grove Hosp., Rich. 7/26/64. Widow: Mary A. Riddle.

RIDDLE, JOHN A.: Sgt.; Co. B 6/4/61 Callands; Pvt. to 4 Sgt. 12/1/64. Present on Division Provost Guard prior to 4/1/64, age 33, roll not dated. Present until POW. Five Forks 4/1/65; City Point to Hart's Island 4/7/65; released there 6/20/65; res. Pitts Co.; light complex., light hair, blue eyes, 5'7".

RIGGINS, ROBERT D.: Pvt.; Co. G 5/18/61 Boydton; pres. til AWOL 3/26/63 to 4/10/63; present, returned through 2/25/65; paroled, headquarters 6th Army Corps, no date given but list dated 5/13/65.

RIGNEY, CHARLES W.: Pvt.; Co. B 10/3/63 Petersburg; Drewry's Bluff 5/16/64, Chimborazo #3 WIA (left shoulder); returned 7/10/64. Present 7/10/64 through to last roll dated 1/1/65. Alive at Whittles on 9/16/95.

RIVES, ABRAM: Pvt.; Co. C 5/30/61 Laurel Grove; pres. til Danville Hosp. 12/16/62. Returned 2/19/63, nephralgia, Farmville Hosp. 8/29/63. Returned 9/12/63, calculus, Chimborazo #2. 6/14/64 dysentary; pres. until POW Five Forks 4/1/65; City Point to Point Lookout 4/6/65; released there 6/17/65; Halifax Co., light complex., iron grey hair, grey eyes, 5'5".

RIVES, DANIEL D.: Pvt.; Co. C, no date given. Admitted Danville Hosp. 6/20/62 icterus. Deserted 7/17/62.

RIVES, EPHRAIM: Pvt.; Co. C 3/19/62 Laurel Grove; pres. til WIA Gettysburg, severely in left side of neck causing partial paralysis of left arm and shoulder. POW 7/3/63, to Baltimore, Md. Hosp., no date listed, West's Building Hosp. 8/14/63. Paroled there, sent to City Point for exchange 8/24/63; present in Co. by 8/30/64; pres. through 2/25/65. Paroled Appomattox 4/9/65. Alive on 10/20/84.

ROACH, ELIJAH T.: Born Charlotte Co. Pvt.; Co. F 6/4/61 Republican Grove; pres. til transferred to Co. K 18th Regt. Va. Vols. 12/61. Age 25, 6'0", dark complex., dark eyes, dark hair, farmer.

ROARK, BOOKER: Pvt.; Co. F 6/4/61 Republican Grove; pres. til Chimborazo #4 6/23/62 Intermittent fever; trans. Farmville 7/1/62, int. fever; returned to duty 7/26/62. Pres. til WIA severely ball fracturing third rib, exit upper edge of shoulder blade, Gettysburg 7/3/63. Farmville Hosp. 8/20/64-1/17/65 when furloughed 60 days.

ROARK, WILLIAM P.: Corpl.; Co. F 6/4/61 Republican Grove; appted. from Pvt. to 2 Corpl. 11/1/64; present until POW Five Forks 4/1/65; City Point to Point Lookout 4/6/65; released there 6/17/65; res. Halifax Co.; light complex., light red hair, grey eyes, 5'8¾".

ROBERTS, SAMUEL P.: Pvt.; Co. G 5/18/61 Boydton; pres. til sent to hosp. at Manassas 1/2/62. There through 5/1/63; name on a list of deceased, but no date; died Genl. Hosp. #12, Richmond.

ROBERTS, ZACHARIAH H.: Pvt.; Co. A 5/30/61 Kentuck; pres. til Chimborazo #1 7/28/62 diarrhoea; transferred to Danville 9/24/62; returned to duty 9/28/62. Name appears on register of Medical Directors Office, Richmond, Va. on 3/1/64 as diseased by old age, 57 and defective vision, but CSR provides no record of discharge.

ROBERTSON, CHRISPIN D.: Pvt.; Co. D 9/29/64, Danville; pres. through 2/25/65.

ROBERTSON, DANIEL C.: Pvt.; Co. K 6/2/61 Cascade; present til admitted Orange C.H. Hosp. 11/8/61 debilitas; returned 12/6/61. Killed at Gettysburg 7/3/63.

ROBERTSON, EDWARD S.: Born 1827 Pitts. Co. Pvt.; Co. H 7/2/61 Pitts. C.H.; Pvt. to 2 Sgt. by 12/61; elected 2 Lieut. 12/19/61. Pres. til Rich. Gen. Hosp. #21 4/29/62 rheumatism. Returned 8/7/62; present til dropped, failed to be reelected on 4/29/62. Died 1886. Bur. Davis Cem. near Chatham.

ROBERTSON, GEORGE J.: Pvt.; Co. D 10/14/64 Danville; pres. til WIA skirmish near Chester Station 11/17/64. g.s.w. left thigh, admitted Chimborazo #4 11/18/64; trans. 2/18/65; in hosp. Richmond 4/3/65; sent to Jackson Hosp. 4/15/65; trans. to 3rd Div. 5/1/65; paroled Richmond 5/15/65. Alive Mt. Cross on 5/15/82.

ROBERTSON, HENRY H.: Pvt.; Co. K 6/2/61 Cascade; left at Camp Edmonds to nurse sick 9/2/61; returned prior to 8/31/61; pres. til WIA Gettysburg 7/3/63; admitted Charlottesville 7/12/63, vulnus selopeticum; trans. to Camp Winder Hosp. where died 8/5/63.

ROBERTSON, JAMES: Pvt., Co. E 6/8/61 Danville; pres. til listed as absent sick at hosp. 5/62-7/62; died Liberty, Va. Hosp. 10/13/62.

ROBERTSON, JOHN E.: Pvt.; Co. K 6/2/61 Cascade; pres. WIA slightly 7/1/62 Malvern Hill; discharged due to over age 8/16/62; born in Pitts Co.; 37 years old, 5'11", fair complex., blue eyes, light hair, farmer.

ROBERTSON, JOHN S.: Pvt.; Co. D 4/24/61 Tuskegee, Ala. Pres. til WIA, g.s.w., arm and arm amputated. POW Gettysburg, 7/4/63; from Gettysburg hosp. to DeCamp Hosp. David's Island, no date given. Paroled there 9/8/63. Returned by 9/14/63, but disabled, so retired 5/10/64; part of Invalid Corps.

ROBERTSON, NATHANIEL T.: Born Pittsylvania Co. Pvt.; Co. D 5/24/61 Whitmell. Furloughed 2/15/62-3/17/62 and permitted to go to Whitmell to recover health. Age 17, 5'9", fair complex., gray eyes, dark hair, farmer.

ROBERTSON, SAMUEL S.: Pvt.; Co. D 5/24/61 Whitmell; discharged, surgeons cert. 8/12/61 consumption.

ROBERTSON, WILLIAM E. F.: Corpl.; Co. B 6/4/61 Callands; pres. til sent to hosp. 1/19/62 at Danville; WIA slightly 7/1/62 Malvern Hill; returned, pres. by 5/19/63; pres. til WIA Drewry's Bluff, entered Chimborazo #5 5/16/64, v.s. abdomen; to Danville, no date given; returned 6/21/64; but still absent on rolls through 1/1/65. Alive 11/23/85.

ROBERTSON, WILLIAM T.: Pvt.; Co. K 6/2/61 Cascade; Gen. Hosp. #18 Richmond 3/2/62, debility. Returned to duty 4/12/62. Pres. til detailed for Division Pioneer prior to 8/31/64. Paroled Headqrs. 2d Div., 6th Corps 4/25/65.

ROBEY, AUSTIN B.: Pvt.; Co. F 6/4/61 Republican Grove; pres. til slightly WIA at Malvern Hill 7/1/62. Returned prior to 7/1/63; admitted 6/3/64 Farmville; acute rheumatism; deserted 8/31/64.

ROBEY, GEORGE WILLIAM: Pvt.; Co. F 9/21/64 Bermuda Hundred, absent sent to Div. hosp. 10/15/64; admitted Chimborazo #2 12/23/64 chronic hepatitis, furloughed 40 days 1/28/65.

ROBINSON, JOHN H.: Corpl.; Co. E 6/8/61, Pvt. to 4 Corpl. demoted to Pvt. 1/1/62; performed extra duty near Winchester 9/9 thru 10/30/62, near Culpeper and F'burg 11/1-10, also 1-3/63. Pres. til confined for desertion in Division Provost Guardhouse. Returned prior to 12/31/64. Pres. through 2/25/65; paroled Lynchburg 4/14/65.

ROBINSON, JAMES K. P.: Pvt.; Co. K 4/29/64 Dublin; conscript; admitted Chimborazo #5 6/20/64 rubeola; furloughed 7/19/64, 40 days. Paroled, dated Headqrs. 2d Div., 6th Corps 4/25/65.

RODGERS, RODRICK E.: Pvt.; 2nd Corpl. I 3/1/62 Norfolk Co.; pres. til POW Dept. Head Qrts., Bermuda Hundred (deserted?) 10/2/64; to go to Norfolk, Va.

ROFFE, CHARLES SAMUEL: Pvt.; Co. G 5/18/61 Boydton; pres. til killed Malvern Hill 7/1/62; age 20.

ROFFE or ROLFE, EDWARD E.: b. 1824. Pvt.; Co. G 3/12/62 Boydton; pres. til sent to hosp. in Richmond 5/1/62; admitted Chimborazo 10/23/63 ascites; doing guard duty Chimborazo Hosp. by 4/1/64; trans. 5/4/64; furloughed 50 days from Farmville Hosp. 6/1/64, chronic hepatitis and sponites of 5 months. Continued standing with obstinate constipation; absent sick through 2/65. Died 1921. Bur. Mt. Horeb Bapt. Ch. Cem., Mecklenburg Co.

ROFFE or ROLFE, LEWIS J.: Born Mecklenburg Co. Pvt.; Co. G 5/18/61 Boydton; pres. til Danville H. 7/2/62-10/22/62 v.s.; POW Gettysburg 7/5/63 and WIA, (grapeshot in right knee at Gettysburg, g.s. thigh); paroled from DeCamp Gen. Hosp., David's Island 8/24/63. Admitted Chimborazo #3 3/10/64 g.s.w. knee; age 29 as of 4/10/64, farmer. Farmville Hosp. 5/4/64. Retired 1/27/65 on list of Invalid Corps; detailed light duty in Chimborazo H 2/3/65. 5'10", light complex., blue eyes, dark hair.

ROSS, JOHN E.: Corpl.; 2nd Co. I 2/26/61 Norfolk Co.; Color Bearer, Pvt. to 4 Corpl. 8/10/64; 4 Corpl. to 2 Corpl. by 12/31/64; present til POW Farmville 4/6/65; City Point to Newport News 4/14/65; took oath there 7/1/65; res. Norfolk; fair complex., light hair, blue eyes, 5'5".

ROSSER, JOHN W.: Co. F. Pvt. Furnished substitute. Post-war record only.

ROPER, JOHN W.: Pvt.; Co. F 6/8/61 Hermitage Camp. Present til discharged by reason of substitute 5/27/62.

ROWLAND (or ROLAND), JOHN D.: Pvt.; Co. H 7/2/61 Pitts. C.H.; Pvt. to Sgt. by 2/62; Chimborazo #4 4/19/62 remitt. fever, returned to duty 5/29/62. Pres. til killed at Seven Pines 5/31/62.

ROYALL, JOHN C.: Sgt.; Co. D 10/14/64 Danville; appted. 3 Sgt. 10/27/64; pres. til entered Chimborazo #4 1/18/65; chronic rheumatism. Returned 2/21/65; paroled 4/25/65.

ROYALL, RICHARD J.: Pvt.; Co. D 10/14/64 Danville; pres. til POW White Oak Road 4/1/65; City Point to Point Lookout 4/5/65; released there 6/17/65; res. Pitts Co.; light complexion, brown hair, grey eyes, 5'10".

ROYSTER, GRANVILLE: Corpl.; Co. F 6/4/61 Republican Grove; pres. til WIA Seven Pines 5/31/62; absent at hosp. through last roll 7/1/63.

RUSSELL, HOUSON G.: Sgt.; Co. C 5/30/61 Laurel Grove; Corpl. to Pvt. by 5/62; Pvt. to Sgt. by 6/62; pres. til admitted Danville H. 11/3/62; debilitas; deserted 11/14/62.

SADLER, ROBERT H.: Sgt.; 2nd Co. I 7/6/61 Norfolk; transferred to the 15th Cavalry 8/10/64.

SAUNDERS, JAMES B.: Pvt.; Co. F 3/5/62 Republican Grove. Absent sick in 6/62. On provost guard 8/62. Admitted Windor Hosp. 10/28/62 and transf. to Lynchburg 11/6/62. WIA Gettysburg 7/3/63. Adm. Gen. Hosp. No. 9 Richmond 7/13/63; present through 2/25/65.

SAUNDERS, WILLIAM: Pvt.; Co. F 6/20/61 Hermitage Camp; pres. til admitted 10/25/61, with rheumatism to Chimborazo #4. Returned to duty 11/22/61. Adm. Orange C.H. hosp. 12/6/61 fever; returned to duty 1/24/62; admitted Chimborazo #1 5/28/62 with dysentery, returned 6/10/62. Present until died 5/16/64; Drewry's Bluff.

SAWYER, CALEB T.: Pvt.; 2nd Co. I 2/20/62 Norfolk Co.; present until deserted to the Federals 12/29/64; received by Federals at Bermuda Hundred 1/30/65; took oath there and sent to Wash. D.C. 2/4/65; trans. furnished to Norfolk.

SAWYER, MADISON M.: Sgt.; 2nd Co. I 6/26/61 Norfolk Co.; appted. 5 Sgt. 8/10/62; 5 Sgt. to 3 Sgt. prior to 12/31/64; 1st roll dated 12/31/64, lists as absent on furlough; deserted 2/20/65 to enemy; Bermuda Hundred to Wash. D.C. 2/24/65; trans. furnished to Norfolk.

SCEARCE, DAVID W.: Pvt.; Co. K 6/2/61 Cascade; adm. Gen. Hosp. #18 on 3/30/62, debility. Returned 4/12/62. Pres. til absent sick in Chimborazo #4 5/18/62 with acute dysentery, trans. 5/26/62. Returned prior to 9/62 when listed as deserted and dropped from rolls. Also listed as deserting 3/63 and 2/63.

SCEARCE, RICHARD: Pvt.; Co. K 6/2/61 Cascade; admitted Gen. Hosp. #1 12/21/61. Pres. through 2/25/65. Sick in hosp. 5 and 6/62 when absent on 15 day furlough.

SCHOEFIELD, JAMES T.: 2 Lieut.; Co. C, elected 2 Lieut. 10/4/64; absent 2/25/65. On list of Army of N. Va. surrendered by Lee at Appomattox 4/9/65.

SCORCE, ED H.: Pvt.; Co. K, no date given. Paroled at Appomattox 4/9/65.

SCOTT, CHARLES: 2 Lieut.; Co. H 7/2/61 Pittsylvania C.H.; 4 Corpl. to Sgt. prior to 2/62; Sgt. to Lieut. elected 4/29/62; pres. til killed Seven Pines near Richmond 5/31/62.

SCOTT, WILLIAM L.: Pvt.; Co. H 3/22/62 Orange; pres. til sent to Richmond H. 4/25/62 for duty; returned some time prior to 4/1/64; pres., detailed as Co. cook 8/31/64-12/31/64; pres. through 2/25/65.

SCRUGGS, JOHN WILBURN: Born 7/12/42 in Pittsylvania Co., son of Rhoda Scruggs. Enl. 7/2/61 at Pittsylvania CH., Pvt. Co. H. Present until admitted C.S.A. Gen. Hosp. Danville 8/21/62 with debilitas, but returned to duty on 9/10/62. Admitted Camp Winder Gen. Hosp. on 9/11/62 with neuralgia but returned to duty 9/13/62. Prom. to Cpl. by 2/26/65. Present until admitted Chimborazo #5 on 3/5/65 with neuralgia. POW in Richmond Hosp. on 4/3/65. (CSR also states POW near Farmville 4/6/65) Libby Prison to Newport News on 4/23/65. Took oath and released at Newport News 7/1/65. Dark complex. and hair, black eyes, 5'6". Farmer near Whittles. Married Nannie Jane Hamlett on 4/26/66 and had 12 children. Died 9/1/11. Buried fam. cem. Pittsylvania Co. 300 yds. E. of Rt. 29 near Whittles and ½ mi. N. of Rt. 649.

SCRUGGS, POWHATAN B.: Born in 1840 (?) in Pittsylvania Co., son of Rhoda Scruggs. Farmer. Enl. 7/2/61 at Pittsylvania C.H., Pvt. in Co. H. Given medical discharge 7/12/61. Reenlisted 3/22/62 at Orange C.H. Admitted Camp Winder G.H. 5/25/62 with diseased nervous system and returned to duty 6/18/62. Admitted Danville G.H. 9/7/62 with diarrhea and returned to duty 9/10/62. Prom. to Sgt. prior to 7/63. Present until KIA at Gettysburg 7/3/63. Brown hair and eyes, fair complex., 5'10", age 21.

SEGAR, ARTHUR SIMPKINS: Born in Accomac Co. 10/9/44. 2 Lieut.; Co. H 5/14/61 Hampton, Va.; promoted from 2 Lieut. to 1st Lieut. 5/3/62. Slightly wounded at Gettysburg 7/3/63. Pres. til WIA in both legs at Drewry's Bluff 5/16/64 and sent to hosp.; admitted Danville H. 6/4/64 vulnus selopeticum, furloughed 6/19/64; returned prior to 8/31/64; paroled at Headqrs., Dept. of Va., Richmond 4/17/65. 5'10", fair complex., dark eyes, black hair. Teacher in Northampton Co. and Hampton 1865-1874 and state legislator 1869-70 from Norfolk; lawyer 1874 in Newport News til after 1890 including 8 years as Commonwealths Attorney in Elizabeth City Co. Married Mary Sue Winder 6/19/76. Died 11/28/1901. Bur. St. John's Cem., Hampton.

SEGAR, JOHN ADAMS: Sgt.; Co. H 3/10/62 Craney Island, Norfolk; pres. til admitted Chimborazo #1 5/4/64 rheumatism; returned 6/20/64; admitted Petersburg Gen. Hosp. 4/1/65; POW there 4/3/65; Fairground Post Hosp.; paroled 5/5/65. Died 1918.

SEYMORE, HENRY: Pvt.; Co. H 10/14/64 Halifax; pres. til POW Five Forks 4/1/65; City Point to Hart's Island 4/7/65; released there 6/20/65; res. Halifax Co.; dark complex., dark hair, black eyes, 5'6½".

SHACKLEFORD, _____: Pvt.; Co. E, no date given; absent with leave for period 8-9/62.

SHACKLEFORD, ARMISTEAD A.: Pvt. Co. E 6/8/61 Danville; pres. til accidently killed when fell off wagon 8/19/62; at Louisa CH., Va.

SHACKLEFORD, ARMISTEAD F.: Pvt.; Co. E 6/8/61 Danville; pres. til admitted Chimborazo #4 7/9/62 g.s.w. left arm; returned to duty 9/1/62; pres. til absent, detached duty as a nurse in Danville Hosp. prior to 6/30/63; on detached duty Danville Provost Guard by 12/31/64; absent sick as of 2/25/65; paroled at Appomattox 4/9/65.

SHACKLEFORD, FRANCIS S.: Pvt.; Co. E 3/12/62 Danville; pres. til killed in action 7/3/63 Gettysburg; born Pittsylvania. Wife: Elizabeth Shackleford.

SHACKLEFORD, JAMES T.: 1 Sgt.; Co. E 6/8/61 Danville. Corpl. to 5 Sgt. 12/1/61; to 4 Sgt. 1/1/62; to 1st Sgt. prior to 6/30/63; absent, left at Winchester with typhoid fever prior to 8/30/61; returned by 4/62; pres. til WIA Gettysburg 7/3/63; admitted Danville 10/19/63, severe; transferred 1/6/64. Returned to be hospitalized Chimborazo #2 9/17/64 int. fever. Returned 12/15/64, admitted Danville H. 3/18/65 erysipelas, in leg; deserted 4/6/65. Retired and in Invalid Corp. by 12/23/64, but also listed as deserted 4/6/65.

SHACKLEFORD, JOHN M.: Pvt.; Co. E 3/20/61 Danville; pres. til admitted Chimborazo #4 4/24/62 measles; furloughed 8/1/62; died at home 8/7/62 in North Carolina.

SHACKLEFORD, RUFUS J.: Pvt.; Co. E 3/3/62 Danville; pres. til admitted Richmond Gen. Hosp. #18, measles; died there 5/5/62; bur. Oakwood Cem., Richmond.

SHACKLEFORD, WILLIAM A.: Pvt.; Co. E 3/20/62 Danville; pres. til admitted Camp Winder Hosp. where died 4/22/62, no cause listed.

SHAW, OTIS A.: Pvt.; Co. A, no date. On a list of POW's. Paroled at Staunton, Va. 5/1/65.

SHELL, R.: Pvt.; Co. D, no date given; on record of POW's, "Amnesty Oath at Richmond, Va. 5/30/65"; residence Petersburg.

SHELTON, ADOLPHUS: Pvt.; Co. H 10/22/64, Danville.

SHELTON, A. F.: Pvt.; Co. E, no date given; absent with leave 8-9/62.

SHELTON, EDWARD T.: Pvt.; Co. H 12/17/63 Richmond; post war record states "served 4 years."

SHELTON, GEORGE J.: Born 4/3/41. Pvt.; Co. B 6/12/61 Callands. Pres. til 11/61, sent in charge of dead brother home; returned prior to 2/62; pres. til POW Five Forks 4/1/65; City Point to Hart's Island 4/7/65; released 6/20/65; res. Pittsylvania Co.; dark complex., dark hair, gray eyes; 5'5½". Died 1/6/1916. Buried in Shelton Family Cem. Chalk Level Road, w. of Chatham, Pitts. Co.

SHELTON, JAMES A.: Pvt.; Co. F 6/4/61 Republican Grove; pres. til admitted 11/8/61 Orange C.H. Gen. Hosp., rheumatism; returned to duty 12/1/61; pres. til admitted Farmville 6/6/62 hosp. with diarrhea. Returned to duty 7/16/62; pres. til admitted Chimborazo #2 5/11/64 wounded by shell 5/10/64 at Chester Station; transferred to Lynchburg H. 5/21/64. Age 28, farmer as of hosp. reporter. Returned prior to 12/31/64; pres. til POW Farmville 4/6/65; City Point to Newport News 4/14/65.

SHELTON, JAMES E.: Pvt.; Co. B 6/12/61 Callands; pres. til admitted into hosp. at Manassas where died 11/15/61 of typhoid fever.

SHELTON, JOHN: Pvt.; Co. H 10/22/64 Pittsylvania; pres. til POW Farmville 4/6/65; took oath at Newport News 6/25/65; res. Halifax Co.; fair complex., light hair, blue eyes, 5'9".

SHELTON, JOSEPH: Pvt.; Co. F 3/8/62 Republican Grove; pres. til admitted Chimborazo #2 6/2/62, shell wound of hand; transferred to Lynchburg 6/5/62.

SHELTON, P. K.: Pvt.; Co. B 8/14/63 Danville.

SHELTON, RALPH S.: Pvt.; Co. B 6/4/61 Callands; pres. til admitted Orange C.H. Gen. Hosp. 12/4/61, debilitas; returned to duty 1/13/62; pres. til admitted Chimborazo #2 6/17/64 diarrhea; returned 7/5/64; present, detailed Div. Pioneer Corps prior to 4/1/64. Listed as having retired and on Invalid Corps list 8/20/64. Admitted Farmville 3/13/65, rheumatism.

SHELTON, ROBERT M.: Pvt.; Co. E 3/12/62 Danville; pres. til WIA, admitted Chimborazo #5 5/16/64; v.s. left hip; returned to duty 8/12/64, age 21. Pres. til POW Five Forks 4/1/65; City Point and Point Lookout 4/5/65; released there 6/20/65. Res. Pittsylvania Co., light complex., light hair, blue eyes, 5'6". Farmer.

SHELTON, TAVENOR S.: Pvt.; Co. K 6/2/61 Cascade; pres. til admitted Charlottesville H. 2/25/62 catarrh; furloughed 4/25/65 for 8 days; returned, present til deserted 6/16/64; but paroled with rest of Army of N. Va. 4/25/65; list dated 5/4/65.

SHELTON, WILLIAM: Pvt.; Co. F 6/4/61 Republican Grove; pres. til entered Orange C.H. Gen. Hosp. 11/8/61; fever, returned 12/1/61; admitted Richmond Gen. Hosp. #18 3/2/62; rheumatism; returned 7/1/62; sent to hosp. in Winchester 9/21/62; listed as absent, sent to hosp. on last roll dated 4/1/64.

SHELTON, WILLIAM J.: Pvt.; Co. E 3/14/62 Danville; pres. til admitted Richmond Gen. Hosp. #9 10/11/62, spinal affliction; furloughed for 20 days 10/29/62. Returned, pres. til 3/14/63, admitted Danville H. with bronchitis; deserted 3/26/63.

SHELTON, WILLIAM L.: Pvt.; Co. H 11/14/63 Danville; conscript; absent sick through 12/31/64. Present by 2/25/65; pres. til POW South Side R.R. 4/6/65; City Point to Newport News 4/16/65; admitted Newport News Prison Hosp. 5/7/65; died there of chronic diarrhoea 5/24/65. Buried Greenlawn Cem., Newport News.

SHELTON, WILLIAM T.: Pvt.; Co. C 5/30/61 Laurel Grove; pres. til admitted Chimborazo #1 4/30/62 typhoid fever; left without permission; admitted Camp Winder 7/18/62, diarrhea. Returned to duty 7/28/62, admitted Danville H. 1/1/63 diarrhea; returned to duty 1/17/63.

SHELTON, W. T.: Pvt.; Co. B 8/14/62 Danville.

SHEPHERD, WILLIAM A.: Pvt.; Co. E 6/8/61 Danville; pres. til admitted Richmond Gen. Hosp. #21 4/14/62, diarrhoea. Returned prior to 2/20/63 when admitted Richmond Gen. Hosp. #21 for vulnus selopeticum; transferred to Danville H. 4/2/63 burn. Returned 6/5/63; present until detailed in Danville arsenal as of 4/1/64; detailed in Brigade Qr. Master Dept. as of 12/31/64, still absent at Brig. Qr. M. Dept. as of 2/25/65; detailed Q.M. Dept. for medical reasons, burn of leg and epilepisia; paroled Appomattox 4/9/65.

SHUMATE, JAMES L.: Pvt.; Co. K 6/2/61 Cascade; Pvt. to 5 Sgt. prior to 12/8/62; 5 Sgt. to Pvt. prior to 8/31/64; present, extra duty in Ambulance Corps as of 8/31/64. Present through 2/25/65.

SHUMATE, JOHN S.: Pvt.; Co. K 6/2/61 Cascade; pres. til admitted Chimborazo #4 10/28/61; with typhoid fever; returned to duty 11/12/61; present, extra duty as pioneer 7/62; extra duty as cook 9/62. Pres. til POW Five Forks 4/1/65; City Point to Point Lookout 4/6/65; released there 6/19/65; res. Pitts Co.; dark complex., dark brown hair, grey eyes, 5'11".

SHUMATE, M. N.: Pvt.; Co. K 2/20/62 Cascade; absent sick 5/62-6/2/62 in Danville Hosp. for debility. Died in Richmond 8/5/62.

SHUMATE, SAMUEL H.: Born Pitts Co. in 1843. Pvt.; Co. K 6/2/61 Cascade; pres. til discharged 10/4/61 at Camp Centerville, disability due to wound from an engine in Richmond; reenlisted 2/20/62 Cascade; pres. til WIA 5/31/62 at Seven Pines. Returned by 8/62; Age 19 as of 1st unofficial medical discharge 10/4/61; 5'11"; fair complex., blue eyes, light hair, a factory hand. Died 1930. Bur. on Rt. 861 near Cascade next to J. B. Jarrett's home.

SHURMADINE, WILLIAM: Born Norfolk. Pvt.; 2nd Co. I 3/11/62 Norfolk Co.; pres. til admitted Jackson Hosp., Richmond 5/25/64 acute diarrhea; trans. to Chimborazo #1 6/3/64; returned prior to desertion on 8/6/64; POW 8/9/64 at Bermuda Hundred Dept. Hd. Qrs.; returned to Norfolk; age 39 as of 8/9/64; 5'5", blue eyes, light hair, fair complex.

SIMMONS, HENRY W.: Pvt.; Co. C 6/27/61 Richmond. Pres. til admitted Orange C.H. Gen. Hosp. 11/8/61; debilitas, died there of same 12/16/61; age 38, 5'8", light complex., blue eyes, black hair, farmer.

SIMMONS, WILLIAM B.: Pvt.; Co. C 5/30/61 Laurel Grove; pres. til admitted Chimborazo #4 10/25/61 rheumatism and carditis. Discharged 11/8/61; reenlisted 3/18/62; detailed Camp Winder Hosp. 5/24/62 as nurse through 11/1/63; detailed as an orderly at Danville Hosp. by 3/64. Returned to Co. by 12/31/64. Present through 2/25/65. Pres. til POW Petersburg 4/2/65. City Point to Point Lookout 4/4/65. Released there 6/20/65; res. Pittsylvania Co., dark complex., brown hair, gray eyes, 5'7¼".

SIMPSON, ARCHER M.: Born Pitts. Co. Pvt.; Co. C, no date given; present til admitted Danville Hosp. 9/8/62 febris. Deserted 1/6/63; returned prior to 7/3/63 Gettysburg where WIA mortally, g.s. abdomen and leg. Died 7/6/63.

SIMPSON, WILLIAM B.: Capt.; Co. C 5/30/61 Laurel Grove; apptd. Capt. 5/11/61; pres. til detached as recruiting officer 2/15/62. Dropped 4/29/62 declined reelection and returned home.

SINGLETON, ABRAM: Pvt.; Co. F 6/4/61 Republican Grove; pres., detailed as cook for Co. 8/62; detailed as shoemaker for Brigade by 8/31/64-2/25/65.

SINGLETON, CHARLES R.: Pvt.; Co. G 5/18/61 Boydton; sick hosp. by 7/16/62-9/62.

SINGLETON, JAMES: Pvt.; Co. G 5/18/61 Boydton; pres. til WIA at Seven Pines 5/31/62; shell wound of leg, Chimborazo #2, admitted 6/2/62; returned by time WIA 7/1/62 Malvern Hill; g.s.w. in shoulder. Returned prior to 5/1/63; POW and WIA at Gettysburg 7/3/63.

SINGLETON, JOSEPH: Pvt.; Co. F 6/4/61 Republican Grove; Prom. to Color Cpl. Pres. til deserted 3/16/64; returned to Co. 8/7/64; assigned to light duty Div. Hosp. prior to 12/31/64. Paroled Appomattox 4/9/65. Bur. north of Volens, Halifax Co. near Rt. 501 and 645.

SINGLETON, WILLIAM T.: Pvt.; Co. F 6/4/61 Republican Grove; present, detailed as Wagoner 6/6/62; deserted 6/3/63; returned by 4/1/64; paroled Appomattox 4/9/65.

SIZEMORE, ELI D.: Pvt.; 1st Col. 3/14/62 Clarksville.

SIZEMORE, THOMAS L.: Born 1846. Pvt.; 1st Co. I 6/20/61 Clarksville; present until extra duty at Manassas Junction guarding baggage belonging to 38th Va. Died 1928. Buried State Line Assembly cem. end of Rt. 721 near Clarksville. Wife: Martha Y.

SLATE, ISAAC J.: Pvt.; Co. E 6/8/61, Danville; present til WIA 7/1/62 Malvern Hill; died at home Pittsylvania Co. 7/19/62 of wounds.

SLAUGHTER, GEORGE W.: Pvt.; Co. K 6/2/61 Cascade; pres. til admitted Chimborazo #1 5/28/62 rheumatism; returned 6/9/62; killed in action 7/1/62 Malvern Hill.

SLAUGHTER, PETER D.: Pvt.; Co. K 6/2/61 Cascade; pres. til WIA slightly Malvern Hill 7/1/62; returned prior to 8/62. Present til WIA, no date given; admitted Chimborazo #4 6/5/64; g.s.w. arm; furloughed 40 days 7/23/64; returned prior to 12/31/64. deserted to Federals 2/19/65 near Bermuda Hundred Head Qrs.; took oath there. To Wash. D.C. 2/24/65; trans. furnished to Columbus, Ohio. Lived in Pitts Co. and Camp Lee Soldiers Home, Richmond. Died 7/10/13 at age 75. Buried Hollywood Cem., east section, Richmond.

SLAYTON, DANIEL T.: Born 9/13/45. Pvt.; Co. E 3/19/62 Danville; Pvt. to 1 Corpl. 7/1/64; 1 Corpl. to 4 Sgt. prior to 2/25/65. Present, daily duty with surgeon 4-5/62. Present until paroled at Appomattox 4/9/65. Died 12/5/24. Buried off Rt. 360 in Halifax Co. about ¾ miles from Pittsyvania Co. line.

SLAYTON, WILLIAM B.: Born 2/24. Pvt. Co. D 10/14/64 Danville; pres. til admitted Chimborazo #3 2/25/65 Feb. intern. Died ca 1907-08. Occupation tanner and farmer.

SLEDGE, FRANCIS L.: Pvt.; Co. E 3/12/62 Danville; pres. til admitted Chimborazo #3 4/17/62. Trans. to Danville 5/2/62 rubeola. Returned to duty 6/11/62; pres. til possibly WIA and POW 7/3/63; Gettysburg; Ft. McHenry 7/5/63 to Ft. Del. 7/30/63. Paroled there 7/30/63. Pres. til POW Five Forks 4/1/65; City Point to Point Lookout 4/5/65; released there 6/3/65.

SMITH, ALBERT GALLATIN: Born 1/4/34. 1 Lieut./Adjutant; F & S; commissioned 9/20/61, adjutant by 7/62; pres. til WIA slightly 7/1/62 Malvern Hill, wded. in hip and arm; returned and tendered resignation 2/20/65. POW paroled 4/23/65 at Winchester. Died 5/4/92. Founded Bethel Academy near Warrenton after war. Buried Alton Cem., Warrenton.

SMITH, E. J.: Pvt.; Co. K, no date given; died at hosp. 5/62.

SMITH, E. M.: Pvt.; Co. I, no date given; absent, deserted to the Federals 2/16/65; oaths taken at Bermuda Hundred 2/18/65; to Wash. D.C.; trans. furnished to Norfolk.

SMITH, GEORGE W.: Pvt.; Co. G 8/26/62 Richmond. Absent, admitted to Chimborazo #3 11/23/62 debilitas, absent at hosp. through 2/65.

SMITH, HUGH L. W.: Pvt.; Co. K 6/2/61 Cascade; pres. til sent to Chimborazo #4 10/24/61. Discharged med. cert. 11/9/61 hypertrophy of heart.

SMITH, JAMES: Pvt.; Co. C 3/18/62 Laurel Grove. Absent, sent to Camp Winder Hosp. 5/62; died there 5/16/62 typhoid fever. Bur. at Hollywood Cem., Richmond.

SMITH, JAMES L.: Pvt.; Co. F 3/1/64 near Camp Richmond. Pres. til WIA at Chester Sta. 5/10/64, admitted Chimborazo #2 5/11/64 v.s. left hand, lost hand. Age 18, farmer. Returned to duty prior to 12/31/64.

SMITH, JAMES W.: Pvt.; Co. A 5/30/62 Kentuck; pres. til admitted 6/29/62 Danville Hosp., typhoid fever; deserted from there 10/29/62; returned prior to Gettysburg where he was POW 7/4/63 and WIA, flesh w. right thigh, upper third; Chester Hosp., Pa. 7/31/63 to Hammond Hosp., Pt. Lookout 10/4/63; paroled there 3/6/64. Returned to duty by 8/64; pres. til POW Petersburg 4/2/65; City Point to Point Lookout 4/4/65; released there 6/30/65; Res. Pitts. Co.; dark complex, brown hair, grey eyes, 5'11½". Alive 7/21/84.

SMITH, J. E. W.: 2nd Co. I 2/20/62 Norfolk Co.; pres. through 12/31/64.

SMITH, JOSEPH S.: Born Pitts. Co. Pvt.; Co. D 5/24/61 Whitmell; died 7/25/61 at Newtown, Va. Age 26, 5'9", fair complex., gray eyes, dark hair, farmer.

SMITH, JOSIAH: Pvt.; Co. D 5/24/61 Whitmell; discharged 7/3/61 at Richmond by order of Genl. Lee.

SMITH, MARCELLUS W.: Pvt.; Co. F 6/4/61 Republican Grove; pres. til sent as nurse for sick of Co. at Broad Run 10/61; returned, WIA and sent to hosp. 6/1/62; returned and put on extra duty as Provost Guard 8/62; present til WIA, mortally at Chester Sta. 5/10/64. Died 5/12/64.

SMITH, S. R.: Pvt. Co. H. Post war record only.

SMITH, W. H.: Co. K; Pvt., no date given; POW paroled 4/23/65 Winchester, Va. Age 19 when took oath, 5'8", fair complex., light hair, hazel eyes.

SMITH, WILLIAM H.: Born 1842. Pvt.; 1st Co. I 6/20/61 Clarksville; pres. til sent to Richmond Hosp. 10/24/61 typhoid fever at Chimborazo #4; returned 11/20/61; pres. til WIA 7/1/62 Malvern Hill; admitted Chimborazo #1, wound of foot; died there 7/12/62. Bur. Oakwood Cem., Richmond.

SMITH, WILLIAM S.: Cpl.; 2nd Co. I 6/26/61 Norfolk Co.; 1st Corpl. to 4 Sgt. prior to 12/31/64. Pres. til POW Five Forks 4/1/65; City Point to Hart's Island 4/7/65. Released, took oath there 6/20/65. Res. Princess Anne Co.; fair complex., dark hair, blue eyes, 5'6".

SNEED, HENRY H.: Cpl.; Co. G 5/18/61, 2 Corpl. to 4th Sgt. prior to 2/62; 4th Sgt. to 3rd Sgt. 5/1/63; present til detailed in Commissary Dept., Pickett's Div. 12/25/62 by order of Pickett. Returned to Co. prior to 12/31/64; pres. through 2/65.

SNEED, JOHN J.: Pvt. Co. G 3/1/62 Boydton; pres. til WIA 7/1/62 Malvern Hill. Returned by 7/16/62. Pres. til POW Five Forks 4/1/65; City Point to Hart's Island 4/7/65; released there 6/20/65. Res. Halifax Co., fair complex., light hair, hazel eyes, 5'7½".

SNEED, ROBERT L.: Pvt.; Co. C 5/30/61 Laurel Grove; pres. til admitted Chimborazo #4 10/25/61 fever; returned to duty 11/1/61; admitted Richmond Gen. Hosp. #18 3/2/62 chronic rheumatism; returned to duty 4/7/62; admitted Chimborazo 5/12/62, diarrhoea; returned. KIA Gettysburg 7/3/63.

SNOW, ABNER: Corpl.; Co. H 7/2/61 Pitts. C.H. Died 8/21/61 typhoid fever.

SNOW, MARTIN VAN BUREN: Pvt.; Co. H 7/2/61 Pitts. C.H.; pres. til admitted Chimborazo #4 10/27/61 jaundice, hernia and varicola; discharged medical certificate hernia and varicula 11/9/61; reenlisted 2/17/62, Richmond; pres. til WIA (shoulder) Seven Pines 5/31/62.

SNOW, WILLIAM D.: Pvt.; Co. H 7/2/61 Pitts. Co. C.H. Present til sent to hosp. 12/10/61; died in Richmond 1/12/62, no cause listed. Bur. Oakwood Cem., Richmond.

SOLOMON, ANDERSON: Pvt.; 1st Co. I 6/20/61 Clarksville.

SOYARS, WILLIAM A.: Pvt.; Co. D 3/15/62 Whitmell; pres. til WIA, left leg and knee; Seven Pines 5/31/62; admitted Chimborazo #2 6/2/62; shell wound, leg, furloughed 30 days. Remained absent due to wounds from Seven Pines through last muster roll dated 2/25/65. Also has two POW listings of a W. O. Sayers 38th Va. Co. F. POW Winchester 8/17/64; Old Capital Prison 8/22/64 to Elmira 8/29/64; released 7/7/65. Alive at Whitmell 6/19/82.

SOYERS, ROBERT O.: Pvt.; Co. K 3/1/62 Cascade; pres. til absent sick in hosp. 6-7/62; detailed Co. cook 9/62; absent, in Danville Hosp. 3/63 debilitas; detailed to Danville hosp. to work there 3/13/63; unfit for field duty. Age 35 as of 3/15/63. Hosp. duty through 2/25/65.

SPARKS, PINKNEY A.: Pvt.; Co. D 3/1/62 Whitmell; admitted hosp. 4/16/62; died Richmond Hosp. 5/10/62 of disease.

SPARROW, ABNER W.: Pvt.; Co. C 10/14/64 Danville. Pres. til left camp 9/17/61 to escort remains of his brother home, to return 9/24/61 but is home sick in Pittsylvania until discharged, med. cert., disability 4/5/62 by order of Genl. Toombs.

SPARROW, ASA E.: Born Pittsylvania Co. Pvt.; Co. C 5/30/61 Laurel Grove; pres. til died of typhoid fever 9/16/61 at Broad Run.

SPENCE, ABNER: Pvt.; 2nd Co. I 3/15/62 Norfolk; deserted 8/1/64; POW by Federals Petersburg 8/3/64; Bermuda Hundred to City Point to Point Lookout 8/5/64; to Elmira 8/12/64; released there 6/21/65; on a roll of POW's. Remarks: conscripts 4/62, assigned Battery O of Heavy Artillery at Richmond, no chance to escape, was transferred to 38th Va. in 5/64, managed to escape 8/1/64; came over lines in Chesterfield same day; was told would be able to take oath, said he had seen Pres.'s Amnesty Proclamation and claims benefit of it. He claims to be a union man. Res. Norfolk; dark complex., dark hair, blue eyes, 5'7".

STALLINGS, ARCHIBALD A.: Pvt.; Co. K 6/2/61 Cascade; pres. til admitted Orange Court House G. H. 11/8/61; debilitas; returned to duty 1/3/62; pres. til WIA 5/31/62 Seven Pines; 21 in 1863. Returned prior to Gettysburg where POW 7/3/63 and WIA, flesh right thigh and shoulder; at Letterman Genl. Hosp., Gettysburg 7/16/63; to West's Bldgs. Hosp., Baltimore 11/12/63; to City Point for exchange, no date given. To Chimborazo #2 11/18/64 v.s. right thigh; retired 5/17/64, part of Invalid Corps. Farmer.

STAPLES, CLARENCE L.: Corpl.; Co. E 4/22/64 Staunton; appted. 3 Corpl. 7/1/64; pres. til POW Five Forks 4/1/65 City Point to Point Lookout 4/5/65; released there 6/20/65. Res. Albemarle Co. Light complex., brown hair, hazel eyes, 5'8½".

STAPLES, JOHN: Pvt.; Co. E 11/11/64 Henrico Cty. Pres. through 2/25/65.

STEPHENS, BENJAMIN F.: Pvt.; Co. K 6/2/61 Cascade; pres. til POW 5/31/62 (Fair Oaks), Seven Pines. POW on Steamer Coatzacoaloos; to Aiken's Landing for exchange 8/5/63. WIA at Drewry's Bluff 5/16/64; died in Chimborazo #4 6/1/64. Result of amputation of left leg. Age 25 as of 1862 when POW; 6'2", light brown hair, blue eyes, light complex.

STEVENS, JAMES W.: Pvt.; Co. F 6/20/61 Hermitage Camp. Pres. til admitted Chimborazo #4 10/25/61 fever and hemorrhoids. Returned 1/10/62; pres. til admitted Chimborazo #4 6/23/62. Fever interim, returned prior to 7/1/63. WIA fractured thigh Gettysburg 7/3/63 and POW. Died 7/29/63 U.S. II Corps hosp. Bur. in Yard B, Row 2 of hosp. cem. on hill between Schwartz's and Bushman's. Disinterred to Richmond on 6/13/72 in Box #200.

STOKES, ALLEN W.: Pvt.; Co. B 6/4/61 Callands; age 22, roll not dated. Pres. til sent to hosp. Richmond 10/25/61; returned prior to 2/62. Pres. til POW Gettysburg 7/3/63; Ft. McHenry 7/6/63 to Ft. Del. 7/12/63. Died there 9/17/63 of typhoid fever. Bur. Finn's Point National Cem., N.J.

STOKES, BARTLETT: Pvt.; Co. K 6/2/61 Cascade; pres. til POW Seven Pines, (Fair Oaks). 5/31/62 held on steamer Coatzocoalcos to Ft. Del. 6/21/62; to Aiken's Landing for exchange 8/5/63. Absent from Co., in arrest as of 4/1/64. Sentenced to death and confined in Castle Thunder, volunteered in Winder Legion for defense of Richmond. Pardoned by Pres. 8/3/64, but failed to return to his Co.

STOKES, COLLINS: Pvt.; Co. K 6/2/61 Cascade; pres. til POW and WIA, (g.s. breast), Gettysburg 7/3/63; to West's Buildings Hosp., Baltimore, Md. 8/23/63; to City Point for exchange 8/24/63; returned to duty prior to 4/1/64; POW Petersburg 5/10/64; Ft. Monroe to Point Lookout 5/13/64; joined U.S. Army 5/31/64.

STOKES, JOHN: Pvt.; Co. B 6/4/61 Callands; pres. til 10/25/61 Chimborazo #4 went as nurse, also had fever; returned 12/5/61; pres. til WIA Seven Pines 5/31/62. Died of wounds received 7/10/62.

STOKES, MADISON: Pvt.; Co. K, no date given. Pres. til admitted Chimborazo #1 5/28/62 diarrhoea. Died there 6/16/62 of typhoid fever; bur. Oakwood Cem., Richmond.

STOKES, WILLIAM C.: Pvt.; Co. D 5/24/61 Whitmell; pres. til WIA 5/31/62 Seven Pines; pres. detailed as Co. cook 9/62; pres. til missing in skirmish 2/18/65; had deserted to Federals 2/18/65; Bermuda Hundred to Wash. D.C. 2/21/65 there oath taken; trans. furnished to Phil., Pa.

STONE, JOHN McHANEY: Born 6/4/44. Pvt.; Co. F 6/4/61 Republican Grove; pres. til sent to hosp. 6/22/62 accidental wound; returned; detailed litter bearer prior to 7/1/63; present til detailed teamster for Brigade prior to 12/31/64. Still absent as of 2/25/65; assigned light work with Brigade, paroled 4/9/65 at Appomattox. Died 8/12/26 in Halifax Co.

STONE, JOHN J.: Pvt.; Co. F 6/4/61 Republican Grove; pres. til sick at Broad Run 10/61; died 11/15/61 at Broad Run.

STRAIGER, JAMES W.: Born Norfolk. Pvt.; Co. I, no date given. Rebel deserter 8/9/64 Bermuda Hundred; sent to Norfolk, age 23, 5'8", blue eyes, light hair, light complex.

STRICKLAND, EDWIN C.: Pvt.; Co. C 5/30/61 Laurel Grove; pres. til sent to hosp. 3/28/62; died at Chimborazo #5; 4/11/62 of pneumonia.

STRICKLAND, JAMES L.: Pvt.; Co. C 3/19/62 Laurel Grove. Pres. til admitted Chimborazo #4 6/23/62 acute diarrhea; there through 7/62. Returned prior to 8/64; pres. through 2/25/65.

STRINGER, THOMAS J.: Pvt.; 2nd Co. I 3/20/62 Norfolk Co.; pres. til 5/14/64 Chimborazo #4 fever int. Returned to duty 6/2/64; pres. til deserted 8/6/64.

SUMMERHILL, JAMES: Pvt.; 1st Co. I 6/20/61 Clarksville.

SUTHERLIN, GEORGE H.: Born 11/28/20. 2 Lieut.; Co. E 6/8/61 Danville; appted. 2 Lieut. 5/28/61; absent sick 10/61 until died in Richmond while returning to regt. after sick furlough 12/13/61. Buried Leemont Cem., Danville.

SWANSON, SAMUEL A.: Pvt.; Co. D 6/15/61 Whitmell. Elected from Pvt. to 2 Lieut. 5/1/62; killed in action on Chickahominy R. Seven Pines 5/31/62.

SYDNOR, GILES: Pvt.; Co. H 10/14/64 Halifax. Present through 2/26/65. Paroled, no date.

SYKES, JESSE F.: Pvt.; 2nd Co. I 3/20/62 Norfolk Co. Paroled Appomattox 4/9/65.

SYKES, WILLIAM W.: Pvt.; 2nd Co. I 6/26/61 Norfolk Co.; pres. til Chimborazo #1 6/15/64. Diarrhea, returned 7/11/64; pres. til POW Fairground Post hosp. Petersburg 4/3/65; transferred to Pt. of Rocks Hosp., with high fever 4/15/65. Died there 4/22/65.

TALBOTT, JOHNSON: Pvt.; Co. F 6/20/61 Hermitage Camp; pres. til discharged 4/7/62 surgeon's cert.

TALLEY, H. M.: Cpl.; 1st Co. I 6/20/61 Clarksville; 3 Corpl. to Sgt. 4/30/62. Pres. til sick 2/27/61. Returned by 7/17/62.

TANKERSLEY, ALEXANDER: Pvt.; Co. C 3/14/62 Laurel Grove; according to CSR deserted 2/62; returned after 9/62 and prior to 2/20/65; deserted again 2/20/65 to Danville.

TARPLEY, GEORGE W. L.: Pvt.; Co. D 5/24/61 Whitmell; died 7/17/61 at Winchester.

TARPLEY, LUKE P. H.: Color Cpl.; Co. D 5/24/61 Whitmell; Corpl. to Col. Sgt. by 7/62; pres. til KIA at Malvern Hill 7/1/62, carrying the colors.

TATE, RICHARD A.: Pvt.; Co. C 5/30/61 Laurel Grove; pres. til WIA Seven Pines 5/31/62 in arm; returned prior to 8/64. Admitted Danville 8/23/64, paralysis from wound from Seven Pines. Returned 9/7/64. Admitted Chimborazo #3 3/13/65 paralysis, no date given for leaving hospital.

TATUM, JAMES H.: Pvt.; Co. B 6/23/61 Richmond; age 21, roll not dated. Pres. til admitted Chimborazo #5 4/18/62 fever remit. to #4 Chimborazo 6/26/62 dysuria.

TATUM, JOHN T.: Pvt.; Co. B 6/4/61 Callands. Pres. til 7/2/62 Danville H., debilitas. Furloughed 12/7/62; returned but deserted on 5/19/63. Returned and deserted again 8/63. Voluntarily returned 3/29/64; pres. til WIA (gun shot wound, leg, flesh), Chester Station 5/10/64, admitted Chimborazo #4 5/11/64. Furloughed 7/2/64. Given light duty when returned, prior to 2/65. Alive 6/21/86.

TERRELL, THOMAS: Pvt.; 1st Co. I, no date given. Died at Manassas 1/15/62, no cause listed.

TERRY, EDWARD W.: Born Pitts. Co. Pvt.; Co. C 3/62. Sent to hosp. 5/62. Returned prior to missing 7/1/62 Malvern Hill; returned Co. Cook 7-9/62; entered Farmville Hosp. 11/12/62 rheumatism; discharged, med. cert. 12/5/62, deformed left foot. Never should have been in service. Age 39, 5'8", pale complex., blue eyes, dark hair, farmer.

TERRY, JOHN H.: Born Pitts Co. Pvt.; Co. C 6/27/61 Richmond; pres. til admitted Howard's Grove, variola 12/22/62. Died there of variola 1/2/63.

TERRY, JOSEPH M.: Capt.; Co. H 7/2/61 Pitts. C.H.; appted. Capt. 7/7/61; resigned 12/13/61. Married Katherine Thompson Coles.

THOMAS, ABRAHAM J.: Pvt.; Co. D 5/24/61 Whitmell. Pres. til admitted Orange C.H. hosp. 11/8/61, rheumatism. Admitted Gen. Hosp. #18, Richmond 3/2/62 diarrhoea. Returned 4/7/62; admitted Danville Hosp. 7/2/62 debilitas; returned 8/13/62. WIA and POW at Gettysburg 7/3/63. Died at U.S. II Corps Hosp. at Balt., Md. 7/9/63 or 7/14/63 of wounds received at Gettysburg. Bur. in Yard D of hosp. cem. in Jacob Schwartz's cornfield on Rock Creek. Disinterred to Richmond on 6/13/72 with 110 others in 10 large boxes labelled 'S'. Father was Abraham Thomas.

THOMAS, A. J.: No rank listed; Co. F, no date listed. died in Federal hands, Gettysburg 7/9/63.

THOMAS, CAMPBELL H.: Pvt.; Co. D 5/24/61 Whitmell; pres. til WIA Seven Pines 5/31/62; in Danville Hosp., no date given, Returned duty 8/13/62. Pres. til WIA Chester Station 5/10/64. Minnie ball in thigh, fracturing bone middle third; admitted Richmond Gen. Hosp. #9 5/11/64; died 5/15/64 v.s. Bur. Oakwood Cem., Richmond.

THOMAS, CREED T.: Pvt.; Co. E 10/14/64 Danville; pres. through 2/25/65.

THOMAS, HOWELL: Born Mecklenburg. Pvt.; 1st Co. I 6/20/61 Clarksville; discharged from Culpeper C.H. 1/20/62, rheumatism. Age 28, 6'0", light complex., gray eyes, light hair, farmer.

THOMAS, JOHN H.: Pvt.; 1st Co. I 6/20/62 Clarksville; absent, sent to Richmond Hosp. 1/26/62; admitted Chimborazo #5 3/7/62 bronchitis, furloughed 20 days 3/27/62.

THOMAS, ROBERT W.: Pvt.; Co. G 8/22/62 Boydton; absent, admitted Chimborazo #1 12/6/62 typhoid fever; died there 12/24/62, pneumonia. Bur. Oakwood Cem., Richmond.

THOMAS, STOKELY: Pvt.; 1st Co. I, no date given. At home sick 10/61.

THOMAS, WILLIAM P.: Born Pittsylvania. Pvt.; Co. E 3/13/62 Danville; pres. til AWOL 5/9/63 to 8/17/63. Pay deducted accordingly; pres. til killed 5/10/64 Chester Station.

THOMPSON, GEORGE H.: No rank listed; Co. B, no date given. Died Richmond 7/15/61.

THOMPSON, J. A.: Pvt.; 1st Co. I 2/19/62, Clarksville. Pres. til admitted 4/11/62 Chimborazo #3. Returned 6/21/62.

THOMPSON, JOHN: Pvt.; Co. B, no date given. Died 8/9/61 of typhoid fever.

THOMPSON, JOSEPH S.: Pvt.; Co. F 6/4/61 Republican Grove; pres. til detailed wagoner for Regt. 4/8/62; present by 4/1/64; absent, teamster prior to 8/31/64; present by 12/31/64; absent, wagoner prior to 2/25/65: paroled at Appomattox 4/9/65.

THOMPSON, J. S.: Pvt.; Co. H. Enl. 1861 and "served 3 yrs. 6 mos." Post war record only.

THOMPSON, SAMUEL J.: Born Pitts Co. Pvt.; Co. C 5/30/61 Laurel Grove. Pres. til admitted Chimborazo #4 10/25/61 debility; returned 11/27/61; admitted Danville Hosp., no date, but list dated 5/6/62 chronic rheumatism. Returned 6/18/62. Discharged 8/28/62, overage and having served his term. Age 35, 5'8", fair complex., blue eyes, dark hair, farmer.

THOMPSON, SAMUEL J.: Pvt.; Co. D 10/14/64 Danville. Pres. til POW Five Forks 4/1/65; City Point to Point Lookout 4/6/65. took oath there 6/20/65. Res. Pitts. Co.; fair complex., auburn hair, blue eyes, 5'7¼".

THORNTON, FELIX F.: Cpl.; Co. F 1/5/62 near Kinston, N.C. Color Corpl. to 4 Sgt. 11/1/64; pres. til POW Five Forks 4/1/65 City Point to Point Lookout 4/6/65; released there 6/20/65. Res. Halifax Co.; fair complexion, light brown hair, hazel eyes, 5'7¾".

THORNTON, JAMES R.: Pvt.; Co. K 6/2/61 Cascade; pres. til WIA Seven Pines 5/31/62; absent through 7/62. Pres. til admitted Danville Hosp. 3/13/63, rheumatism, furloughed from there 11/27/63; absent sick as of 4/1/64; retired by Medical Examining Board and dropped from roll 8/19/64.

THORNTON, JOHN L.: Pvt.; Co. F 6/20/61 Hermitage Camp; Pvt. to 2 Lieut. Elected 9/18/61; absent sick 10-11/61; absent sick 3/62, debility. Dropped 4/29/62, failed to be reelected in spring reorganization; also had chronic diarrhoea, unable to fulfill duties.

THORNTON, MOSES T.: Pvt.; Co. K 6/2/61 Cascade; pres. til POW Gettysburg 7/3/63; Ft. McHenry to Ft. Delaware, no date given to Point Lookout 10/27/63; exchanged there 2/18/65; at Camp Lee 3/1/65.

THORNTON, ROBERT F.: Pvt.; Co. F 6/4/61 Republican Grove; Pvt. to 2 Lieut. Elected 4/29/62; pres., extra duty dispatch bearer for Regt.; absent due to wounds received 5/31/62, Seven Pines. Returned by 7/62, WIA (left eye) Gettysburg 7/3/63; resigned 3/14/64. Died 4/10.

TILMAN, COLLINS: Co. B. Post-war record only.

TINSLEY, ALFRED H.: Pvt.; Co. D 10/14/64, Danville.

TINSLEY, GEORGE W.: Pvt.; 2nd Co. I 3/4/64 Henrico Co.; admitted Chimborazo #5 6/20/64 wound to thorax involving left lung. Died of wounds received in skirmish 8/15/64.

TINSLEY, JESSE NOELL: Born 6/10/29. Pvt.; Co. D 10/14/64 Danville, Va. Absent, admitted Chimborazo #4 12/5/64 debility. Returned 12/19/64. Admitted Danville Hosp. 3/2/65 hemmorrhoids. Returned 4/11/65. Died 7/25/05 Pitts. Co.

TOLER, JOHN D.: Pvt.; Co. H 3/17/64 Orange; pres. til sent to Richmond Hosp. 6/62 and again 7/62; returned, WIA Drewry's Bluff 5/16/64 left leg. Admitted C.S.A. hosp., Richmond 5/19/64 wounded; furloughed 6/7/64; absent through 2/25/65; paroled Appomattox 4/9/65. Alive near Sandy Level on 5/15/99.

TOMPKINS, GEORGE G.: Born Pitts. Co. Pvt.; Co. H 10/14/64 Pitts. Co.; admitted Chimborazo #4 11/28/64 phthisia pulmonalis. Discharged from service, med. cert. for phthisia pulmonalis 12/20/64. Age 35, 5'10", fair complex., dark eyes, dark hair, farmer.

TOONE, ED H.: 1st Co. I; appted. 2 Lieut. 7/8/61; failed to be elected 2 Lieut.; was elected 2 Jr. Lieut. 4/9/62; absent 11/61 "attending a young lady medically." Returned by 1/62; absent 2-3/62, furlough.

TOWLER, JOSEPH L.: Pvt.; Co. B 7/10/61 Winchester, age 26, roll not dated. Present until admitted Richmond Gen. Hosp. #9 4/2/64. No later dates available.

TOWNES, DANIEL C.: Born Pittsylvania Co. Capt.; Co. A 5/30/61 Kentuck; appted. Capt. 8/20/60. Present until killed in action at Gettysburg 7/3/63.

TOWNES, STEPHEN HALCOURT: Corpl., Co. A 3/13/62 Kentuck; corpl. to Pvt. by 6/62. Present, extra duty as commissary sgt. 5/62; present til detached as hospital steward 7/23/62; appted. by Sec. of War. Howards Grove; appointed acting hosp. steward 6/20/63 by Genl. Winder; relieved from duty by special order #13 Med. Div. 1/19/64; assigned small pox hosp., Richmond 1/22/64; reported for duty at Howards Grove 5/8/64 as hosp. steward. Farmer and lawyer in Pitts. Co. Died in 1913.

TOWNES, WILLIAM, JR.: Capt.; Co. G; appted. Capt. 5/18/61. Dropped 4/29/62. Failed to be reelected spring reorganization. Pres. til admitted Seminary Hosp., Williamsburg, diptheria 4/18/62, sent to Genl. Hosp. 4/23/62.

TOWNSHEND, THOMAS J.: Pvt.; Co. A 5/30/61 Kentuck; absent, went home from Richmond hosp. and reported unfit for duty prior to 8/31/61; discharged, surg. cert. 8/12/61.

TOWSEN, JOSEPH: Co. C. Pvt. Post-war record only.

TRENT, WILLIAM J.: Pvt.; Co. K 3/5/62 Cascade; absent, sick in hosp. 4/30/62 to 6/30/62; attached Danville Gen. Hosp. 5/18/62 as a nurse. Admitted as patient Danville Hosp. 10/16/62 hernia; sent to Genl. Hosp. 10/6/63; transfer to Petersburg Hosp. 10/6/63; returned to duty as a nurse at Camp Winder 10/9/64; absent, regt. hosp. steward at Chester Station prior to 2/25/65.

TREVILIAN, JOHN G.: Born Goochland Co. 4/1/40. Surgeon, F & S; Appted. Asst. Surgeon 10/15/61. Paroled Appomattox 4/9/65. Died Richmond 11/24/13. Bur. Hollywood Cem., Richmond.

TRIBBLE, GEORGE T.: Born Halifax Co. Pvt.; Co. F 6/20/61 Republican Grove or Hermitage Camp; pres. til sent to Genl. Hosp. at Manassas Junction 11/13/61; admitted Genl. Hosp. #18, Richmond 3/1/62, diarrhea; returned 4/12/62; discharged, medical certificate 10/20/62, paralysis. Age 23, 5'10", dark complex., gray eyes, dark hair, farmer.

TRIPPLE, CHARLES: Pvt.; 2nd Co. I 3/14/62 Norfolk Co.; absent in Chimborazo #2 5/6/64, carditis; transf. to Danville 5/10/64; acute rheumatism; admitted Danville Gen. Hosp. 3/1/65, acute rheumatism. POW, paroled at Burkeville Junction, Va. 4/20/65.

TROTTER, PETER D.: Cpl.; Co. K 6/2/61 Cascade; appted. from 3 Corpl. to 1 Sgt. 9/17/61; discharged for disability at Richmond Hosp. 11/8/61.

TRUE, LEVI: Pvt.; Co. E 3/5/62 Danville. Pres. til admitted Gen. Hosp. #21, Richmond 11/1/62, rheumatism, age 18. To Gen. Hosp. Howard's Grove 12/15/62, variola; returned to duty 3/31/63; AWOL 4/8/63 to 8/18/63; pay deducted. Pres. til admitted Chimborazo #2 1/16/65, incontinence of urine; trans. to Chimborazo #1 3/5/65; furloughed from there 3/19/65.

TRUE, LEWIS J.: Pvt.; Co. E 6/8/61 Danville; admitted to Chimborazo #3 Richmond 4/14/62. Pres. til AWOL 4/9/63 to 5/18/63, pay deducted; pres. til admitted Chimborazo #2 5/11/64 wound from explosion of shell 5/10/64 at Chester Station. Returned to duty 6/2/64, age 25, a farmer; readmitted Chimborazo #4 6/15/64 diarrhea, returned 7/10/64.

TUCKER, GEORGE T.: Pvt.; Co. G 5/18/61 Boydton; sick in camp near Broad Run 10/61, 30 day furlough at home, 2/62 WIA (slightly) 5/31/62 Seven Pines. Killed at Crews Farm, Malvern Hill 7/1/62.

TUCKER, GEORGE W.: Pvt.; Co. F 6/4/61 Republican Grove; discharged from service 7/5/61.

TUCKER, JAMES P.: Pvt.; Co. F, no date given; absent, was transferred to Co. F; 38th Va. 1/23/65. He never reported.

TUCKER, JAMES W.: Pvt.; Co. F 6/4/61 Republican Grove; detached as Co. cook 8/62; present through 2/25/65. Paroled Campbell CH on 5/29/65.

TUCKER, JOEL P.: Pvt.; Co. F 3/13/62 Repubublican Grove; pres. til WIA, (shot in chin); sent to hosp. from Yorktown 4/20/26. Died in Richmond Hosp., no date given; burial on or about 6/10/62.

TUCKER, RALEIGH W.: Pvt.; Co. F 6/4/61 Republican Grove; pres. til admitted Chimborazo #1 4/24/62 rheumatism, left without permission; admitted Winder Hosp. 10/15/62, no reason given. Deserted from guard house 5/13/63; returned to duty by 4/1/64; present through 2/25/65.
present through 2/25/65.

TUCKER, RICHARD: Pvt.; Co. C 5/30/61 Laurel Grove. Present from 1st recorded roll 12/31/64 through last 2/25/65.

TUCKER, SAMUEL: Pvt.; 2nd Co. I 7/6/61 Norfolk Co.; deserted 8/6/64; captured by Federals 8/9/64, confined at Bermuda Hundred; sent to Norfolk, Va.. Age 26, 5'7", gray eyes, light hair, light complex.

TUCKER, WESLEY H.: Pvt.; Co. F 6/4/61 Republican Grove. Discharged from service 7/5/61.

TUCKER, WILLIAM H.: Pvt.; 2nd Co. I 7/6/61 Norfolk Co.; present until deserted into Federal hands 2/17/65; Headquarters Bermuda Hundred 2/18/65 to Wash. D.C. 2/21/65; oath taken there. Transportation furnished to Norfolk.

TURNER, JOHN W.: Sgt.; Co. A 5/30/61 Kentuck; present Pvt., to Sgt., no date given. Died at Richmond of wound 6/20/62 or 6/2/62 of wounds received at Seven Pines on 5/31/62. Bur. family cemetery on Route 726 on "left side of road inside wire fence" between Kentuck & Ringgold. Son of Joseph H. and Sarah E. Turner. 25 years of age.

TURNER, JOSEPH H.: Pvt.; Co. C 5/30/61; Laurel Grove; pres. til POW Gettysburg 7/3/63; Ft. McHenry 7/5/63 to Ft. Del. 7/12/63; to Point Lookout 10/27/63; exchanged there 2/18/65. Pres. at Camp Lee 3/1/65.

TURNER, THOMAS J.: Born 6/10/10. Co. A 5/30/61 Kentuck; appted. 1st St. 10/19/61; elected 2 Lieut. 2/1/62. Admitted Chimborazo #1, Richmond 5/4/62, rubeola; ret. to duty 5/10/62; promoted 1st Lt. 7/3/62; promoted to Capt. 8/25/64. Pres. til WIA 5/31/62 Seven Pines. Absent through 6/62; returned 7/62; POW with Army of N. Va., surrendered by Lee 4/9/65 Appomattox. Died 4/27/66 "of disease contracted in Army". Bur. Townes-Turner family cemetery on Rt. 726 on "left side of road inside wire fence" between Kentuck & Ringgold.

TURNER, WILLIAM W.: 1 Sgt.; Co. C 5/30/61 Laurel Grove; 5/23/62 admitted Gen. Hosp., Farmville, dysentery; Pvt. to 1 Sgt. prior to 4/1/64. Pres. slightly wounded Gettysburg 7/3/63; severely wounded leg and foot at Chester Station 5/10/64, admitted Chimborazo #2 5/11/62, bronchitis and diarrhoea 5/23/62 transferred to Lynchburg, Va., age 33, farmer, as of 5/11/64. Omitted Danville Gen. Hosp. prior to 8/17/64, returned 11/22/64, vs. right foot; admitted Chimborazo #3 v.s. right foot 12/1/64; admitted Chimborazo #3 2/10/65; admitted Danville Gen. Hosp. 2/25/65 v.s. right foot. Alive near Malmaison 6/22/82.

TURNER, WILLIS W.: Pvt.; Co. K 3/5/62 Cascade; absent sick in hosp. 5/62-12/8/62. Court martialed by Gen. Order No. 6 Army of Northern Virginia 1/20/63. Returned prior to POW Gettysburg 7/3/63; Ft. Del. 7/12/63 to Point Lookout 10/27/63; joined U.S. Army service 1/29/64.

TYREE, DAVID A.: Pvt.; Co. E 12/1/64 Danville; pres. til POW White Oak Road 4/1/65 City Point to Point Lookout 4/5/65; released there 6/3/65.

TYREE, THOMAS MARTIN: Appted. 2 Lieut. Co. E 5/28/61 at Danville promoted 1 Lieut. 10/29/61. Present til severely WIA at Crews Farm at Malvern Hill 7/1/62; admitted Richmond Gen. Hosp. #7 7/2/62 wound of right arm and left leg. Furloughed 7/4/62; returned. Promoted to Capt. 7/12/62; pres. til admitted Gen. Hosp. Howard's Grove, Richmond, 5/20/64; hemorrhage of lungs; trans. to Danville 6/20/64 hoemoptysis; returned 8/8/64. Pres. til POW Dinwiddie C.H. 4/1/65; Old Capitol Prison 4/5/65; to Sandusky, Ohio POW Depot 4/11/65 to Johnson's Island. Released and oath taken 6/20/65; res. Danville; age 24, blue eyes, dark hair, fair complex., 5'10". Died 6/27/02 age 66 years. Bur. Leemont Cem., Danville.

UHLES, DAVID: Born Halifax Co. Pvt., Co. B 6/4/61 Callands; Pvt. to 4 Corpl. 7/1/62; present WIA, slightly at Crew Farm, Malvern Hill 7/1/62. Present til WIA and POW, captured 7/3/63; (shot in leg and thigh); from Gettysburg hosp. to DeCamp Genl. Hosp. David's Island, New York Harbor 7/17/63; exchanged there 9/16/63. Returned to company prior to 4/1/64; discharged 8/5/64 for being over 45 years old and having served out term of enlistment. Lived in Camp Lee Soldiers Home, Richmond. Died 10/10/04 at age 85. Buried Hollywood Cem., west section, Richmond.

UMPLING, J. R.: Co. H. Died 10/63 while POW at Point Lookout, Md. No other record.

UPTON, THOMAS W.: enl. 6/4/61 at Republican Grove; Pvt. Co. F. Admitted Chimborazo #3 4/14/62 and 4/22/62. Detailed with Brigade Surgeon prior to 7/1/63. Absent on furlough after 8/31/64. Died at home in Campbell Co. 9/14/64.

VANDERBERG, JAMES: Pvt.; 2nd Co. I 3/20/62 Norfolk Co. Deserter received by Federals, 2/17/65; Bermuda Hundred to Wash. D.C. 2/21/65; oath taken there and trans. furnished to Norfolk.

VAUGHAN, ENOCH: Pvt.; 1st Co. I 2/21/62 Clarksville. Died 4/8/62 at Orange C.H. Hosp. of typhoid fever. Conflicting records indicate died at Gen. Hosp., Farmville.

VAUGHAN, JAMES T.: Pvt.; 1st Co. I 3/1/62 Clarksville. Sent to Orange C.H. Hosp. prior to 7/17/62.

VAUGHAN, JOSEPH: Pvt.; Co. F 3/14/62. Republican Grove; admitted Chimborazo Hosp. #1 5/28/62, released 6/1/62. Pres. til deserted 3/28/63.

VAUGHAN, PETER G.: Pvt.; 1st Co. I 6/20/62 Clarksville; pres. til admitted Chimborazo #4 6/23/62 nephritis.

VAUGHAN, R. W.: Pvt.; 1st Co. I 6/20/62 Clarksville. Present through 7/17/62, last roll.

VERNON, JAMES D.: Pvt.; Co. C 3/18/62 Laurel Grove; pres. til listed as missing, Malvern Hill 7/1/62. Returned by time admitted Danville Gen. Hosp., debilitas; returned to duty 8/11/62; died at Chester Station 5/10/64, cause not listed. Born Pittsylvania Co.

VERNON, JAMES H.: Pvt.; Co. C 4/22/62 Fort Dillard, N.C.; Pvt. to 3 Corpl., 7/1/64. Pres. til POW Gettysburg 7/3/63; Ft. McHenry 7/6/63; to Ft. Delaware, no date given; to Point Lookout 10/27/63; to Hammond's Hosp., Point Lookout, Md. 10/28/63, chronic rheumatism. Paroled Pt. Lookout and exchanged from City Point 3/16/64. Last muster roll dated 2/25/65 lists him as AWOL in Danville.

VERNON, WILLIAM H.: Pvt.; Co. A 3/13/62 Kentuck; pres. til sent to Richmond hosp. Chimborazo #5, int. fever 6/3/62; trans. to Lynchburg Gen. Hosp. 6/10/62 and died 6/23/62 there, rheumatism. Buried by Diuguid Funeral Home 6/30/62 in Lynchburg.

VERNON, WILLIAM T.: Sgt.; Co. C 5/30/61 Laurel Grove; pres. til WIA Seven Pines 5/31/62; admitted Chimborazo #4 6/26/62 fever interim. Returned prior to 7/3/63; WIA slightly Gettysburg; returned prior to 4/1/64; WIA 6/17/64; admitted Chimborazo #5 6/19/64; furloughed 40 days 7/2/64; pres. by 8/64; pres. through 2/25/65. Alive at Cascade 3/15/97.

VOSS, BEDFORD B.: Pvt.; Co. E 6/14/61 Danville; Pres. til absent; admitted to Chimborazo #4 10/26/61, rheumatism. Discharged, surgeons cert. 12/26/61 rheumatism. Discharged from service 12/30/61.

VOSS, WILLIAM H.: Born Pitts. Co. Pvt.; Co. E 2/24/62 Danville; pres. til admitted Danville Hosp., prior to 5/6/62; debilitas; returned to duty 6/27/62. Killed at Gettysburg 7/3/63.

WADDILL, CHARLES M.: Pvt.; Co. A/F & S 5/30/61 Kentuck; Pvt. to 3 Corpl. 10/1/61; 3 Corpl. Detailed as Ord. Sgt. 9/11/62. Pres. til absent wounded 7/62; returned prior to 2/27/65. Paroled Appomattox 4/9/65.

WADE, JOHN T.: Pvt.; Co. F 3/17/62 Republican Grove. Pres., detailed as teamster for Regt. 8/62; returned to Co. prior to 8/63. Present through 2/25/65.

WALDRON, JOHN D.: Pvt.; Co. B 6/4/61 Callands. Pres. til absent, detached to Manassas Junction guarding heavy baggage of 38th Regt. 10/61-2/62. Admitted Danville Hosp. 6/20/62, chr. rheumatism; deserted 7/1/62; returned 7/10/62; discharged 9/14/62 on account of age.

WALKEL, JOHN B.: Pvt., Co. I, no date given; POW Gettysburg 7/3/63. Died in hosp. in or about Gettysburg 8/13/63.

WALKER, CHAPLES WEST, DR.: Asst. Surgeon; Co. G 5/18/61 Boydton. Absent, hosp. Steward at Camp near Broad Run 10/61-2/62. Promoted Ass't. Surgeon 3/62. Appointed a surgeon A.S.A. 4/29/62 at Orange CH.

WALKER, JAMES H.: Enl. 1861. Pvt. 1st Co. I. "Served 9 years." Post war record only.

WALKER, JOHN H.: Pvt.; Co. B, no date given. Pittsylvania. Pres. through last dated roll 1/1/65.

WALKER, JOHN H.: Pvt.; Co. D 5/24/61 Whitmell. Present Co. Cook 9/62; admitted Chimborazo #3 4/17/62-5/3/63. Pres. til WIA, (g.s. right buttock) and POW 7/3/63 Gettysburg; Ft. McHenry to Ft. Del. 7/12/63; paroled there 7/30/63; admitted Farmville 8/29/63, g.s.w. right buttock, from Gettysburg; 30 day furlough 9/8/63. Returned prior to 4/1/64; WIA near Drewry's Bluff 5/16/64; admitted 5/17/64 Howard's Grove Hosp. v.s. right leg, severe, furloughed 60 days 5/25/64.

WALKER, JOHN M.: Pvt.; Co. H 10/9/64 Camp Lee. Pres. through 2/26/65.

WALKER, JOHN W.: Pvt.; Co. H 7/2/61 Pitts. Co. H. Admitted Chimborazo #1 12/11-12/26/61; granted 30 day furlough on 2/12/62. Deserted to 7/62. Returned prior to time discharged 10/4/62, no reason given.

WALKER, MOSES: Pvt.; Co. B 6/4/61 Callands; present til died pneumonia 9/10/61.

WALKER, WILLIAM G.: Pvt.; Co. B 10/14/64 Pittsylvania; pres. through last recorded date 1/1/65.

WALLER, ALBERT R.: Corpl.; Co. F 6/4/61 Republican Grove; pres. til WIA, (slightly) Malvern Hill 7/1/62; sent to hosp. 7/2/62 in Richmond. Discharged 9/3/62.

WALLER, JAMES A.: Pvt.; Co. F 3/5/62 Republican Grove; elected from Pvt. to 1 Lieut. 4/29/62; reduced to ranks 3/7/64. Pres. til absent sick 4-7/62, admitted Chimborazo #4 5/23/62, catarrh. Returned by 8/62; pres. til AWOL 5/20/63. Returned prior to 4/1/64.

WALLER, JOHN W.: Pvt.; Co. H 7/26/61 Bull Run; pres. til sent to Richmond Hosp. 3/28/62; admitted Farmville hosp. 5/23/62 rheumatism. Returned 6/21/62; WIA, (slightly by shell) 6/29/62; discharged at Leesburg 9/5/62 reason being over 35. Alive 5/20/96.

WALLER, WOODLEY: Born Halifax Co. Pvt.; Co. F 6/4/61 Republican Grove; pres. til admitted Orange C.H. Genl. Hosp.; 12/6/61 catarrh fever; returned 1/24/62; admitted Farmville 3/27/63 dysenteria; returned 4/27/63; POW at Gettysburg 7/3/63; sent to Ft. McHenry and Ft. Delaware 7/7-7/12/63; to Point Lookout 10/26/63. Pres. til died at Point Lookout 9/3/64.

WALNE, JOHN: Pvt.; Co. A 5/30/61 Kentuck; pres. til admitted Chimborazo #4 6/26/62 acute diarrhea; deserted 9/5/62, Leesburg. Returned prior to 3/2/64. Pres. through 2/25/65; paroled Appomattox 4/9/65. "Walno" on Appox. parole list.

WALTERS, CHARLES W.: 2 Lieut.; Co. C. Elected 4/29/62 to 2 Jr. Lieut.; promoted to 2 Lieut. 5/31/62; present until killed 7/3/63. at Gettysburg.

WALTERS, JAMES B.: Sgt.; Co. C 5/30/61 Laurel Grove; present on a register of claims of deceased soldiers, filed 5/29/62, no date, cause of, or place of death listed.

WALTERS, JOSEPH: Sgt.; Co. C, no date given. Died 9/30/61 typhoid fever, near Centerville.

WALTON, WILLIAM J.: Born 2/23/40. Pvt.; Co. D 5/24/61 Whitmell; pres. til admitted Chimborazo #4 10/25/61 rheumatism; there through 6/62; sent to Danville Hosp. 7/23/62, chronic diarrhea. Deserted 2/18/63; admitted Danville hosp. prior to 11/19/63, debilitas, according to muster rolls, absent sick from 10/23/64-12/31/64; detailed at Danville hosp. by Medical Examining Board by 2/25/65. Died 12/27/30. Bur. Walton Cem. on Rt. 750 13 miles north of Danville.

WARD, JOHN M.: Sgt.; Co. F 6/8/61 Hermitage Camp; admitted Chimborazo #4 5/8/62 with debility. Transf. to Lynchburg 5/9/62. Present until discharged by reason of providing a substitute 7/3/62.

WARD, JOHN W.: Pvt.; Co. G 3/29/62 Boydton; absent, sent to Richmond Hosp. prior to 4/30/62. Returned, sent to hosp. in Richmond 4/10/63; WIA, (shot in left thigh) at Gettysburg 7/3/63; admitted Chimborazo #1 10/23/63 g.s.w., of leg. Furloughed 30 days 1/14/63; admitted Chimborazo #4 2/19/64, ulcer on left thigh; to Farmville prior to 6/10/64; admitted Chimborazo #1 11/23/64; v.s. and c.d. Returned to duty 3/17/65.

WARF, THOMAS A.: Pvt.; Co. E 3/15/62 Danville. Pres. til detached duty with Div. Provost Guard. Prior to 8/31/64; guard duty through 2/25/65.

WARF, WILLIAM G.: Pvt.; Co. A 5/30/61 Kentuck; pres. til POW Gettysburg 7/4/63; Ft. Delaware 7/12/63; released there 5/4/65; res. Pittsylvania Co. Ruddy complex., dark hair, hazel eyes '6''.

WARREN, GEORGE W.: Pvt.; Co. A 3/7/62 Kentuck; absent, sent to Richmond Hosp. 6/62-8/62. Returned 11/6/62. 11/13/62 Gen. Hosp., Danville, debilitas; 11/19/62 returned. POW and WIA Gettysburg 7/3/63. Gen. Hosp., Chester, Pa. 7/17/63, vulnus sclopet. Exchanged on or about 8/17/63; admitted Chimborazo #2 4/12/64 debility, to Farmville H 5/5/64, right thigh wound. Deserted 8/31/64; returned to be put on light duty on provost guard of Div. by Med. Ex. Board prior to 1/1/65 and thru 2/25/65. Paroled at Burkeville Junction 4/14-17/65.

WARREN, JAMES P.: Born 10/9/40. Sgt.; Co. B 6/4/61 Callands. Elected Jr. 2 Lieut. 5/1/62, promoted 2 Lieut. 12/22/62. Pres. til left sick at camp at Broad Run 9/23/61; present detached as a nurse 11/61; pres. til WIA slightly Crews Farm, Malvern Hill 7/1/62. Admitted Chimborazo #2 7/3/62 g.s. flesh wound of leg; admitted Danville Gen. Hosp. 7/12/62. Returned to duty 9/23/62. Present through to Appomattox Parole 4/9/65. Farmer and school teacher after war. Married Julia C. Fuller 12/10/67 and had 10 children. Married Fannie Dent in 1910 and had 2 children. Died 6/13/21. Buried in family cemetery, Sydnorsville in Franklin Co., Va.

WATERMAN, ABOLINA: Pvt.; 2nd Co. I. No further record.

WATKINS, GEORGE: Pvt.; 1st Co. I 6/20/61 Clarksville. Absent, sick in Chimborazo #4 10//28/61, pleurodyne. Returned 12/18/61, admitted Richmond Genl. Hosp. #18 4/13/62. Returned 4/22/62.

WATKINS, JAMES D.: 2 Lieut.; 1st Co. I apptd. 2nd Lt. 7/1/61. Pres. til failed to be elected as 2 Lieut. 4/29/62.

WATKINS, LINNAEUS D.: Born Pittsylvania Co. Corpl.; Co. E 6/8/61 Danville; 4th Corpl. to 3rd Corpl. by 4/62; 3 Corpl. to Pvt. prior to 6/30/63; Pvt. to Corpl. prior to 4/1/64; pres. til WIA severely Malvern Hill 7/1/62 carrying the colors. Present 6/30/63-4/1/64. MWIA at Drewry's Bluff 5/16/64. Died in Richmond Gen. Hosp. #9 5/21/64, g.s.w. through the hips, 20 years old.

WATSON, DAVID HARRIS: Born 10/21/30. Pvt.; Co. H 7/2/61 Pitts C.H.; pres. til Chimborazo #3 10/22/61. Honorably discharged from service 11/25/61, chronic rheumatism. 8/28/63, exempted from military duty by reason of being a shoemaker. 8/22/65, took oath of allegiance at Point Lookout, Md. Died 4/10/94. Buried Family cem. on south side Rt. 612 1.9 miles west of Chatham.

WATSON, JAMES H.: Pvt.; Co. H 3/16/63 Pittsylvania; pres. til deserted 6/63. Turned self in 11/63; held at Castle Thunder under sentence of death by court martial, to Richmond Gen. Hosp. #13 5/16/64 with diarrhoea. Pardon given and is returned to company prior to 12/31/64; pres. til POW Five Forks 4/1/65; City Point to Point Lookout 4/6/65; released there 6/22/65; res. Pitts. Co.; light complex., brown hair, light blue eyes, 5'6½", illiterate.

WATSON, JOAB: Pvt.; Co. H 7/2/61 Pitts C.H.; pres. til admitted Danville Hosp. 1/2/62; died in Richmond 2/62, exact date and cause not given.

WATSON, JOHN J.: Pvt.; Co. H 7/2/61 Pitts. C.H.; present until deserted 9/12/61 from camp on Broad Run. Absent through 2/62.

WATSON, JOHN W.: Musician; 2nd Co. I 3/16/63, Albemarle Co.; absent detached Brigade band; name on a list of prisoners in E.D.M. Prison who volunteered in Winder Legion for defense of Richmond against the Sheridan Raid in 1864 and pardoned by Pres. 8/3/64.

WATSON, WILLIAM E.: Pvt.; Co. H 7/2/61 Pitts. C.H.; died 9/27/61 near Centerville of typhoid fever.

WATTSON, JAMES: Pvt.; Co. H 3/9/no year listed, at Petersburg. Roll dated 4/1/64, Petersburg; absent, sentenced to be shot to death.

WEATHERFORD, HUGH N.: Corpl.; Co. G 5/18/61 Boydton; 2/2/62, home on furlough; 5/14/62, adm. Chimborazo #3, typhoid; 5/31/62 slightly wounded at Seven Pines. Pres. til admitted Chimborazo #4 6/23/62 chronic diarrhoea. Absent, detailed for ordinance duty 9/13/62 by order of Sec. of War through 8/31/64; present when resigned his corporalcy 12/31/64; absent, on detached services by order of Sec. War, skilled mech. as of 2/65. Bur. Boydton Town Cem., Park St., Boydton.

WELDON, H.: No rank or Co. listed. Deserted to the Federals 1/10/65.

WELLS, LABAN C.: Corpl.; Co. C 5/30/61 Laurel Grove; 1 Corpl. to Pvt. by 4/1/65; pres. til sent to hosp. in Richmond 5/62-7/62. Present, detailed extra duty in ambulance corps 1/63-1/64. Pres. through 2/25/65.

WELLS, ROLAND or ROBINS B.: Born in Henry. Pvt.; Co. K 2/28/62, Cascade. Admitted Chimborazo #2 3/30/62 colitis; transf. to Danville H. 5/7/62, acute diarrhea. Returned to duty 6/18/62; discharged 7/24/62, consumption. Age 23, 5'10", fair complex., grey eyes, light hair, farmer.

WEST, JAMES R.: Pvt.; 1st Co. I 6/20/61 Clarksville; present, only roll dated 7/17/62.

WEST, JOHN: Pvt.; Co. I, no date given. Died of typhoid fever 9/23/61.

WEST, JOHN: Pvt.; 2nd Co. I 3/11/62 Norfolk Co.; pres. til WIA 5/16/64 at Drewry's Bluff, admitted Chimborazo #5 5/16/64, wound right hand; returned to duty 9/13/64; deserted to Federals 12/15/64; captured 12/28/64, taken to Head Qts. of Provost Marshall at Bermuda Hundred to Wash. D.C. 1/3/65 and took oath. Transportation furnished to Norfolk, Va.

WESTBROOKS, JAMES S.: Pvt.; Co. E 6/8/61 Danville. Sick in Hosp. in July or Aug. 1864, returning by 8/31/64. Present through 2/25/65, last roll. Age 22. Bounty pay and receipt roll not dated.

WESTBROOKS, PASCHAL: Pvt.; Co. C 5/30/61 Laurel Grove. Sick at camp on Broad Run 10/61. Sent to hosp. 2/3/62; admitted Chimborazo #5 3/7/62 phthisis pulmonalis. Died there of phthisis pulmonalis 3/14/62. Bur. Oakwood Cem., Richmond.

WESTBROOKS, YANCY M.: Pvt.; Co. A, no date given. Died at Richmond 5/6/62.

WHITAKER, T. J.: Pvt.; Co. B, no date given; admitted Chimborazo #3 4/14/62. Transferred to Lynchburg 5/9/62; name appears on a Register of Claims of Deceased Soldiers filed 2/17/63. Date, place and cause of death not given.

WHITE, ABRAM: Pvt.; Co. C 5/30/61 Laurel Grove; sent to Chimborazo #1 3/14/62; furloughed 4/21/62 for 15 days. Pres. til WIA Seven Pines 5/31/62, severely through both legs. Absent through 9/62; returned prior to Gettysburg where WIA (both legs) and POW 7/3/63. Paroled from U.S.A. Genl. Hosp. West Bldgs, Baltimore, Md. 9/25/63 to be transferred to City Point for exchange; admitted Chimborazo #3 as nurse 9/28/63; furloughed 10/10/63, 20 days; returned to duty by 8/64; present through 2/25/65.

WHITE, DANIEL H.: Pvt.; Co. C 5/30/61 Laurel Grove; absent, left sick in camp at Winchester 7/8/61 unfit for duty on sick furlough 9/21/61 for 15 days. Sent to Chimborazo #4 12/2/61 pleurisy. Returned to duty 4/15/62; listed as deserter 9/62; but discharged 9/5/62, overage and having served his term, age 35.

WHITE, JERRIE or JERRY M.: Pvt.; Co. C 5/30/61 Laurel Grove; Pvt. to 2nd Corpl. prior to 4/1/64; 2 Corpl. to 1 Corpl. by 8/64. Present til WIA, g.s. right leg and left shoulder and back and POW 7/3/63 Gettysburg; from Gettysburg hospitals to Baltimore, Md., West Bldgs. Gen. Hosp., age 23. Paroled 9/25/63. Transferred to City Point to be exchanged, admitted Chimborazo #3 9/28/63 g.s.w. right leg. Furloughed 35 days 10/8/63. Returned to company 10/9/64, 30 day extension of furlough by Med. Examining Board due to suffering of unhealed wounds below knee. by 8/64. Pres. through 2/25/65. Alive at Malmaison on 5/29/82.

WHITE, JESSE M.: Pvt.; Co. C, no date given. Absent, sent to hosp. 5/62, there through 7/62. Died of typhoid fever at hosp., date not known but before 9/62.

WHITE, JOHN W.: Born Pitts Co. Pvt.; Co. C 5/30/61 Laurel Groves; pres. til admitted Chimborazo #5 3/30/62 bronchitis 4/14/62, furloughed 10 days Danville Hosp. with bronchitis 4/7/63; discharged from service 7/31/63 phthisis pulmonalis, physical disability. Age 32, 5'10", dark complex., blue eyes, black hair, farmer.

WHITE, THOMAS WISTAR: Asst. Surgeon; Co. C/F & S; 6/8/61, Richmond. Pvt. appointed Asst. Surg. at Camp Smith 11/8/61. Relieved command 2/63.

WHITEHURST, JAMES HENRY: Pvt.; 2nd Co. I 6/26/61 Norfolk Co.; pres. til POW Five Forks 4/1/65; City Point to Harts Island, N.Y. 4/7/65; took oath and released there 6/20/65; res. Norfolk Co. Dark complex., black hair, dark eyes, 5'2½". Died 5/12/93 Norfolk.

WHITEHURST, WILSON A.: Pvt.; 2nd Co. I 2/20/62 Norfolk Co. Pres. til deserted to Federals. Captured 10/2/64, confined Bermuda Hundred to go to Norfolk.

WHITLOCK, ACHILLES E.: Pvt.; Co. C 5/30/61 Laurel Grove. Pres. til admitted Chimborazo #4 10/25/61 rheumatism; returned 12/11/61; pres. til sent to Genl. Hosp. 2/27/62; died at Manassas Hosp. of typhoid fever 3/1/62. Also listed as dying of pnuemonia.

WHITTLE, POWHATAN BOLLING: Born 6/26/29 Mecklenburg Co., Va., 15th child in family. U.Va. graduate. About 6'6" tall. Commissed Lt. Col. 6/12/61 at Pittsylvania C.H. WIA (flesh wound of thigh) at Williamsburg on 5/5/62, while commanding regt. WIA (severely in left arm which was amputated) at Malvern Hill on 7/1/62, while carrying the colors. Returned to duty 4/29/63. WIA (severely in left thigh and flesh wound in right arm and shoulder) at Gettysburg on 7/3/63. Prom. to Colonel of the 38th on 7/2/63. Relieved from active duty and appointed Judge of military court of A. P. Hill's 3rd Corps on 11/15/63. Admitted Richmond Gen. Hosp. #4 on 4/20/64; and then to CSA Hosp. in Petersburg on 4/29/64. Furloughed 6/22/64. Lawyer, Legislator and Judge of Macon, Ga. Corporation Court after war.

WILES, ERASMUS A.: Pvt : Co. A 10/25/63 Danville; transferred to Co. from Danville arsenal 10/25/64. Present on extra duty as Brig. Teamster prior to 2/25/65; admitted to Chimborazo #5 3/10/65; POW near Farmville 4/6/65; City Point to Newport News 4/14/65; oath taken at Newport News 7/1/65; res. Pittsylvania. Fair complex., light hair, blue eyes, 5'5".

WILES, JAMES T.: Sgt.; Co. A 3/10/62 Kentuck; 5 Sgt. to 2 Corpl. prior to 4/1/64; back to 5 Sgt. by 12/31/64; present til admitted Chimborazo #3 4/24/62; returned to duty 6/16/62; admitted CSA Gen. Hosp., Danville 11/13/62; debilitas; deserted 1/13/63; returned to Co. prior to 2/25/63; pres. til admitted Farmville H. 3/11/65, eryesipelas. Returned 3/22/65; pres. til POW Petersburg 4/2/65; City Point to Point Lookout 4/4/65. Released there 6/22/65; res. Pitts Co.; fair complex., brown hair, blue eyes, 5'7¼".

WILES, ROBERT R.: Co. A. Post-war record only. Died at Sutherlin in 1870.

WILES, WILLIAM H.: Pvt.; Co. A, no date given. Pres. til admitted Chimborazo #4 5/31/62 acute diarrhea; transf. to Danville 6/9/62; returned to duty 8/13/62. Died at Quincy Station of fever 1/20/63.

WILKERSON, DAVID A.: Pvt.; Co. C 8/1/62 Falling Creek. Pres., detailed Ordnance guard 9/62. Present but WIA slightly 7/3/63 at Gettysburg. Pres. til deserted 3/3/65 to Federals; captured 3/4/65 Bermuda Hundred; to Wash. D.C. 3/8/65 where oath taken and trans. furnished to Boston, Mass.

WILKERSON, ROBERT W.: Pvt.; Co. C 5/30/61 Laurel Grove; pres. til admitted Chimborazo #4 10/25/61; measles and sequelae, jaundice. Returned to duty 4/19/62; present through 2/25/65. Paroled POW of Army of N. Va. Soldiers 4/25/65, list dated 4/27/65.

WILKERSON, WALTER S.: Pvt.; Co. C 5/30/61 Laurel Grove; pres. til admitted Danville Hosp. 9/1/62, debilitas. Returned duty 12/12/62; 6/19/64 admitted to Chimborazo #5 acute diarrhea. Trans. to Lynchburg 7/9/64. Pres. til POW, Dinwiddie C.H. 4/2/65; City Point to Point Lookout 4/13/65. Took oath and there released 6/21/65; res. Pitts Co.; dark complex., black hair, hazel eyes, 5'9½".

WILKES, CHARLES W.: No rank listed. Co G; same as a signature to a Power of Attorney authorizing Lieut. H. L. Lee to receive and receipt pay due to members of the organization for July and August 1861, dated 9/23/61, no other information.

WILKINS, J. H.: Pvt.; 1st Co. I 3/8/62 Clarksville; sent to Richmond Hosp. from Dam # 1 4/23/62.

WILKINS, WILLIAM ROBERT: Born 9/17,39. Pvt.; 1st Co. I 3/13/62; Clarksville; sent to Richmond Hosp. from Dam #1 4/23/62. Died 12/26/11.

WILKINSON, JOHN H.: Pvt.; 1st Co. I 3/5/62 Clarksville. Pres. til listed as MIA after Malvern Hill 7/1/62. May have later joined Co. G of 14th Va. Inf. and surrendered at Appox. 4/9/65.

WILKINSON, THOMAS C.: Pvt.; 1st Co. I 3/12/62 Clarksville. Sent to hosp. 4/27/62. Danville Hosp. 5/21/62, debilitas, deserted 10/21/62.

WILKINSON, WILLIAM: Pvt.; 1st Co. I 3/12/62, Clarksville; present, only roll dated 7/17/62.

WILLARD, BENJAMIN B.: Sgt.; Co. G 5/18/61 Boydton; 4 Corpl. appted. to 5 Sgt. 4/1/62; possibly prom. to 4th Lt. WIA seriously 5/31/62 Seven Pines; reported for duty 3/26/63; KIA at Gettysburg 7/3/63.

WILLIAMS, ALFRED B.: 2 Lieut.; Co. A 2 lieut. elected 2 Lieut. 8/1/62. Pres. til WIA at Drewry's Bluff and admitted Chimborazo #5 and 1 5/16/64 v.s.; returned to duty 7/16/64; 7/19/64 admitted Richmond Gen. Hosp. #4, v.s. amputated left leg; admitted Charlottesville 10/11/64 chronic cystitis. Retired 10/19/64; on a Register of Invalid Corps 4/28/65. Reported as paroled POW Richmond, Va.

WILLIAMS, DAVID L.: Pvt.; Co. C 5/30/61 Laurel Grove. Sick in camp prior to 8/30/61. Adm. Gen. Hosp. Orange CH 11/8/61. Returned to duty 11/23/61. Pres. til WIA 5/31/62 Seven Pines. Adm. Chimborazo #2 on 6/3/62 "shell of side" and furloughed for 15 days. WIA 7/1/62 Malvern Hill, adm. Chimborazo #2 on 7/4/62 gunshot flesh wound of arm; admitted 2/26/64 Chimborazo #3. g.s.w. abdomen. Returned 3/28/64; WIA 5/10/64 at Chester Station; admitted 5/12/64 Chimborazo #1, v.s. Furloughed 60 days 6/22/64. Adm. Chimborazo #1 9/16/64 for v.s. leg. Retired 12/17/64.

WILLIAMS, DAVID R.: Pvt.; Co. H 4/17/64; Danville conscript. Died of measles at Genl. Hosp. of Picketts Division 7/1/64. "Never has been paid."

WILLIAMS, EDWARD B.: 1 Lieut.; Co. A 5/30/61 Kentuck; appted. 1 Lieut 5/30/61 or sick furlough 6/23/61; resigned on or about 10/3/61.

WILLIAMS, THOMAS: 2 Lieut; Co. I; appted. 2 Lieut. 4/26/61. Dropped 3/9/62; failed to be reelected spring '62.

WILLIAMS, THOMAS M.: Born in Pitts. Co. Pvt.; Co. C 5/30/61 Laurel Grove; pres. til admitted Chimborazo #4 10/25/61 typhoid fever; returned to duty 11/27/61, pres. til sent to Richmond Gen. Hosp. #18 2/28/62; chronic diarrhea. Returned prior to WIA slightly 7/1/62 Crews Farm, Malvern Hill; died of typhoid fever either at home or at Chimborazo Hosp. 6/26/62.

WILLIAMS, WILLIAM C. G.: Born in Pitts. Co. Pvt.; Co. A 2/27/62 Kentuck. Adm. Chimborazo #3 4/14/62, furloughed 5/6/62. Pres. til WIA Seven Pines 5/31/62; returned by 8/62 when detailed extra duty as cook; pres. til killed Gettysburg 7/3/63. Wife: Sarah Williams.

WILLIAMSON, ABSALOM: Pvt.; 1st Co. I 6/20/61 Clarksville; present, detailed extra duty as Co. cook 6/62. Trans. to 2nd Co. G 14th Va. Inf. 6/27/62. Adm. Gen. Hosp. #21, Richmond, Va. 4/28/62 and sent to Lynchburg 5/5/62. Farmer. d. 8/30/88, bur. S.W. of Clarksville, Mecklenburg Co., Va.

WILLIAMSON, JOSHUA: Pvt.; Co. H 3/22/62 Orange. Pres. til detailed with Division Commissary Train prior to 1/64. Returned 12/31/64; present through 2/26/65.

WILLIAMSON, J. J.: Pvt.; Co. K, no date given; POW Five Forks 4/1/65; City Point to Hart's Island 4/7/65; took oath and released there 6/21/65; res. Pitts. Co.; dark complex., dark hair, blue eyes, 5'7½".

WILLIAMSON, M. W.: Pvt.; Co. H, no date given. Paroled at Lynchburg after Lee surrendered 4/15/65.

WILLIAMSON, NELSON: Pvt.; Co. H 4/25/64 Campbell; conscript. Adm. Chimborazo #5 5/23/64, diarrhoea. Sent to Lynchburg 5/27/64, admitted Chimborazo #1 11/24/64 pneumonia; furloughed 12/29/64; absent sick through 2/26/65.

WILLIAMSON, ROBERT: Pvt.; H & 1st Co. I 6/20/61 Clarksville; pres. til admitted Chimborazo #4 10/28/61 remittent fever; returned 11/12/61. Sick at Chimborazo #3 4/11/62; returned 4/25/62.

WILLIAMSON, WILLIAM: Pvt.; 1st Co. I 3/5/62 Clarksville. Died at Orange C.H. hosp. 3/28/62 meningitis.

WILLIS, JAMES M.: Pvt.; Co. D 5/24/61 Whitmell; absent sick 5 weeks prior to 8/30/61; discharged at camp near Orange C.H. 4/6/62 upon Surgeon's Cert.

WILLIS, JOEL L.: Cpl.; Co. E 6/8/61 Danville; Corpl. to 5th Sgt. 11/1/62; pres. til Chimborazo #4 10/28/61, mumps, returned 12/13/61. Pres. til killed in action 5/31/62, Seven Pines.

WILLIS, WILLIAM H.: Pvt.; Co. G 5/18/61 Boydton; pres. til discharged 3/8/62, disability. Reenlisted 10/14/64, Mecklenburg; AWOL 12/7/64, returned to Co. 12/29/64. Deserted 2/15/65 to Federals, Bermuda Hundred to Wash. D.C. 2/21/65; took oath there and trans. furnished to Moon Prairie, Jefferson Co., Ill.

WILMOUTH, JOHN A.: Pvt.; Co. G 5/18/61 Boydton; 2/12/62 on furlough at home for 30 days. Slightly WIA Seven Pines 5/31/62; WIA Malvern Hill 7/1/62. Adm. Chimborazo #2 9/27/62 v.s. of leg. WIA Gettysburg 7/3/63, admitted to Chimborazo #3 3/10/64 g.s.w. leg; admitted Gen. Hosp., Farmville 5/4/64 g.s.w. knee; admitted Chimborazo #2 12/22/64 old wound of tibia. Transf. to Farmville 2/1/65.

WILSON, JAMES: Pvt.; Co. G 1st Co. I 5/18/61, Boydton; transferred from Co. G 38th to 1st Co. I 38th Va. 6/1/62.

WILSON, LEE: Pvt. 1st Co. I 6/20/61 Clarksville; absent 10/61 sick furlough; absent 12/26/61 near Centerville, nurse of sick; sent to hosp. 2/27/62. WIA Crews Farm, Malvern Hill 7/1/62; Moore Hosp. #24, Richmond, 7/5/62.

WILSON, RICHARD: Pvt.; 1st Co. I 3/14/62 Clarksville. Present through last roll dated 7/17/62.

WILSON, ROBERT A.: Pvt. 1st Co. I. Co. A; 10/14/64, Danville. Present through 2/25/65.

WILSON, THOMAS: Pvt.; 1st Co. I 2/18/62 Clarksville. Present through only roll dated 7/17/62.

WILSON, WILLIAM C.: Pvt.; Co. K 6/2/61 Cascade. Admitted Hosp. #20, Richmond 12/28/62. Pres. til paroled Greensboro, NC 5/5/65. Pvt. 1 Sgt. prior to 2/25/65.

WINSTON, JOHN H. B.: Pvt.; Co. F 6/4/61. Republican Grove; pres. to Chimborazo #1 5/28/62 dysentery; returned 6/21/62. Died Halifax Co., at home 12/14/62, typhoid.

WOLF, I.: Co. A. Pvt. Killed at Saltville. Postwar record only.

WOOD, GEORGE T.: Pvt.; Co. C 5/30/61 Laurel Grove; absent, home on furlough 8/18/61 but too sick to return; sent to Chimborazo Hosp. #4 10/24/61, rheumatism and colic; returned 4/15/62; admitted to Chimborazo #3 4/28/62. Discharged 9/5/62 over age.

WOOD, JEREMIAH: Pvt.; Co. A 3/7/62, Kentuck. Died 4/24/62.

WOOD, JOHN S.: Capt.; 1st Co. I, appointed Capt. 7/1/61; sick on furlough 30 days from 9/26/61; present by 11/61; absent 12/20/62-3/62. Failed to be reelected 4/29/62.

WOOD, RICHARD T.: Pvt.; Co. C 3/10/62 Orange C.H. Absent in Richmond hosp. Died Chimborazo 4/30/62 of typhoid fever.

WOOD, WILLIAM B.: Pvt.; Co. A 10/14/64 Danville; Brigade Teamster prior to 12/31/64.

WOOD, W. W.: Capt.; 1st Co. I; elected Capt. 4/29/62. 6/7/62 requested transfer of his Co. to 14th Va. and Capt. Martin's Co. of 14th Va. to 38th, (100 members each Co.) Request to Sec. of War. WIA (slightly) 7/1/62 Malvern Hill at Crews Farm.

WOODALL, JAMES S.: Pvt.; Co. B 6/12/61 Callands; Danville Hosp. 6/29/62 typhoid fever; deserted 7/6/62, returned to Danville Hosp. 8/28/62; chronic diarrhea; deserted 11/22/62. Present til POW Gettysburg 7/3/63; Ft. McHenry, Md. 7/6/63 to Ft. Delaware, 7/12/63; paroled there, sent to Aikens Landing, Va. for exchange 9/30/64. Admitted Chimborazo #3 10/7/64 with debilitas, furloughed for 60 days 10/12/64. 26 yrs. old in 1862.

WOODALL, WILLIAM A.: Pvt.; Co. B 3/10/62 Callands. Pres. til admitted Chimborazo #3 4/14/62. Transferred to Lynchburg Hosp. 5/9/62. Transferred to Danville Hosp. 11/15/62 chronic diarrhea; deserted 2/18/63; but returned to company prior to 5/19/63.

WOODWARD, SAMUEL: Pvt.; 2 Co. I 2/22/62 Norfolk Co.; pres. til deserted, captured by Federals 10/2/64 Bermuda Hundred; to go to Norfolk.

WOODY, WILLIS H.: Pvt.; 2nd Co. I 3/6/62 Appomattox Co.; Pres. til AWOL 12/25/64; paroled Appomattox 4/9/65.

WORSHAM, WILLIAM B.: Pvt., Co. H 10/14/64 Pittsylvania. Pres. through 2/26/65. Post war record states: "killed by a Yankee in 1865 just after the surrender."

WRAY, W. W.: Pvt.; Co. B, no date given; absent, sent to hosp. 4/25/62.

WRIGHT, ANDREW J.: Pvt.; Co. K 6/2/61 Cascade; pres. til WIA Gettysburg 7/3/63; admitted Gen. Hosp. #9 Richmond 7/19/63. Danville H. 7/22/63; returned 11/8/63; but absent through 12/3/64. Retired 12/3/64 at age 32; member of Invalid Corps Danville Station.

WRIGHT, GEORGE W.: Pvt.; Co. D, no date given. Absent Orange C.H. Gen. Hosp. 4/6/62; died there of pneumonia 4/12/62.

WRIGHT, JAMES W.: Pvt.; Co. E, no date given. Paroled 5/20/65, Staunton, Va.

WRIGHT, MOSES G.: Pvt.; Co. H 4/26/64 Dublin; conscript, WIA 5/10/64 at Chester Station; Chimborazo #2 5/11/64. Furloughed 60 days 5/27/64 age 42, farmer. Absent through 2/26/65.

WRIGHT, STEPHEN: Pvt.; Co. B 7/10/61 Winchester; pres. til absent sick leave 2/2/62; returned to go back to hosp. latter part of April 62.

WYNN, ROBERT S.: Pvt.; Co. E 6/8/61 Danville. Listed as deserted 9/23/61. Returned by 4/62. Admitted 5/12/62 to Chimborazo #2 Richmond with debility. Transferred to Lynchburg 5/22/62 admitted Farmville Hosp. 5/23/62, pneumonia. Left as nurse for wounded at Gettysburg, POW there 7/5/63; Ft. McHenry 9/12/63; Point Lookout 9/15/63; exchanged 10/11/64; at Camp Lee by 11/26/64; returned to Company by 2/25/65; also lists POW, not paroled at Point Lookout til 2/18/65.

WYNNE, WILLIAM H.: Pvt.; Co. G 2/24/62 Boydton; pres. til admitted Richmond Hosp. about 5/1/62, camp fever. Transferred from Chimborazo #21 to Danville Hosp. 7/22/62. Remained there debilitas until returned to duty 5/21/63; POW Gettysburg 7/3/63; served as nurse in Gettysburg; Ft. McHenry 7/6/63 to Ft. Delaware 7/12/63; died there 8/5/63 chronic diarrhoea. Illiterate. Bur. Finn's Point National Cemetery, N.J.

YANCEY, EDWARD: Born 12/12/36 in Mecklenburg Co. Corpl.; 1st Co. I 3/8/62 Clarksville; present, prom. to Corpl. 5/1/62. Died 6/24/14.

YANCEY, JOSEPH S.: Sgt.; 1st Co. I 6/20/61, Clarksville; elected sgt. to 1st Lieut. 4/29/62. Absent chronic diarrhea, Richmond Genl. Hosp. #18 7/17/62, no leaving date.

YEAMAN, WILLIAM H.: Born Pitts. Co. Pvt.; Co. A 3/13/62 Pitts. Co. Pres. til WIA Seven Pines 5/31/62; absent through 7/62; returned by time killed at Gettysburg 7/3/63. No wife or children; son of John Yeaman.

YOUNG, JOHN: Pvt.; Co. C 5/30/6 ; Laurel Grove; pres. til detached by order of Sec. of War 10/7/61 to Ordnance Dept., Richmond. Detailed with Ordnance Dept. through 2/25/65. Absent at Danville on R&D R.R.

BIBLIOGRAPHY

Manuscripts

Moses Barker Letters. In possession of Mr. Stuart Welch, Richmond.
James Booker Letters. In possession of Freddie L. Hill, Danville.
John Booker Letters. In possession of Freddie L. Hill, Danville.
Col. George K. Griggs diary. Museum of the Confederacy, Richmond.
_____. Memorandum of the 38th's Service. Department of Military Affairs Papers, Virginia State Archives, Richmond.
Thomas J. Hines Letter. In possession of Miss Mayme Scearce, Danville.
Robert E. Lee Letter to Mary Custis Lee, April 12, 1863. R. E. Lee Papers, Virginia Historical Society, Richmond.
Andrew J. Leftwich Letter. In possession of Dr. James I. Robertson, Blacksburg.
Joseph T. Payne Letters. In possession of Mrs. Anna M. Day, Dry Fork.
"Roll of Honor," 345 volumes Confederate Memorial Literary Society, The Museum of the Confederacy, Richmond.
Thirty Eighth Virginia Infantry File, Department of Military Affairs Papers, Virginia State Archives, Richmond.
United Daughters of the Confederacy, Richmond. UDC application files.
Virginia-North Carolina Piedmont Genealogical Society (comp.), "List of Confederate Soldiers Who Died in the General Hospitals at Danville, 1862-1865," typescript, Danville Public Library.
_____. Records. Danville Public Library.
Col. John Wainwright Letters to the Adjutant General of Virginia. Dec. 18, 1906 and Jan. 3, 1907. 38th Va. Inf. File, Department of Military Affairs Papers, Virginia State Archives, Richmond.
Linnaeus D. Watkins Letter. In possession of Miss Mary B. Tinsley, Danville.
Col. Powhatan B. Whittle Letters. In possession H. George Carrison, Awendaw, S.C.
_____. Letter to Col. James McDonald May 12, 1884. 38th Va. Inf. File. Department of Miltitary Affairs Papers, Virginia State Archives, Richmond.

Published Primary Sources

Alexander, E. P. *Military Memoirs of a Confederate.* Ed. T. Harry Williams Bloomington, Ind., 1962.
Clement, Maud Carter (ed.). *War Recollections of the Confederate Veterans of Pittsylvania County, Virginia.* Danville, 1960.

Crocker, James Francis. *Colonel James Gregory Hodges - Confederate Hero of the 14th Virginia Infantry.* Address to Stonewall Camp, CV, Portsmouth. June 18, 1909.

———. *Gettysburg - Pickett's Charge.* Address to Stonewall Camp, CV, Portsmouth. November 7, 1894.

———. *My Capture at Gettysburg and Prison Reminiscences.* Address to Stonewall Camp, CV, Portsmouth. February 2, 1904.

———. *My Personal Experiences in Taking Up Arms and In the Battle of Malvern Hill.* Address to Stonewall Camp, CV, Portsmouth. February 6, 1889.

Early, Jubal Anderson. *War Memoirs.* Ed. Frank E. Vandiver. Bloomington, Ind. 1960.

Harrison, Walter. *Pickett's Men.* New York, 1870.

Johnson, R. U. and Buel, C.C. (eds.) *Battles and Leaders of the Civil War.* 4 vols. New York, 1884-1887.

Longstreet, James. *From Manassas to Appomattox.* Ed. Dr. James I. Robertson. Bloomington, Ind., 1960.

Poindexter, James Edward. *Lewis A. Armistead.* Address to Lee Camp, CV, Richmond, 1909.

Smith, James Power. *Stonewall Jackson and Chancellorsville.* Address to the Military Historical Society of Massachusetts. March 1, 1904.

United States War Department (comp.) *The War of the Rebellion: A Compilation of the Official Records of the Union and Confederate Armies.* 128 vols. Government Printing Office. 1880-1901.

Periodicals

Confederate Veteran, 1893-1932.
Richmond Dispatch, 1862-1864.
Southern Historical Society Papers, 1876-1959.

Other Sources

Amann, William F. *Personnel of the Civil War.* New York, 1961.

Barrett, John G. *The Civil War in North Carolina.* Chapel Hill, 1963.

Bearrs, Ed & Calkins, Chris. *The Battle of Five Forks.* Lynchburg, 1985.

Beitzell, Edwin W. *Point Lookout: Prison Camp for Confederates.* Abell, Md., 1972.

Boatner, Mark Mayo III. *The Civil War Dictionary.* New York, 1959.

Bracey, Susan. *Life by the Roaring Roanoke: A History of Mecklenburg County.* Mecklenburg Co., 1977.

Brandau, Kenneth. *The Oakes Family in the Civil War,* n.p., n.d.

Brock, R. A. *Virginia and Virginians.* 2 vols. Richmond, 1888.

Brown, Alexander. *The Cabells and Their Kin.* Boston, 1895.

Brown, Kent Masterson. "Pickett's Charge, and Numerous Countercharges," *Virginia Country's Civil War Magazine,* vol. 2, Middleburg, Va. 1984.

_____. "Trains of Misery," *Virginia Country's Civil War Magazine.* vol. 1, Middleburg, Va., 1983.

Bruce, Philip A. *A History of Virginia.* 6 vols. Chicago and New York, 1924.

_____. *Virginia.* 5 vols. Chicago and New York, 1929.

Calkins, Chris M. *The Battles of Appomattox Station and Appomattox Court House: April 8-9, 1865.* Lynchburg, 1987.

_____. *From Petersburg to Appomattox: April 2-9, 1865.* Farmville, 1983.

_____. *Thirty-Six Hours Before Appomattox.* Farmville, 1980.

Cauble, Frank P. *The Surrender Proceedings - April 9, 1865, Appomattox Court House.* Lynchburg, 1987.

Clement, Maud Carter. *The History of Pittsylvania County, Virginia.* Lynchburg, 1929.

Coddington, Edwin B. *The Gettysburg Campaign - A Study in Command.* New York, 1968.

List of Confederate Soldiers Buried in Pittsylvania County, Va. Unofficial records in Circuit Court Clerk's Office, Chatham, Va.

List of Confederate Veterans Buried in Hollywood Cemetery from Camp Lee Soldiers Home, 1894-1946. Privately printed by Garland-Rodes Camp, SCV, Lynchburg, 1968.

Dame, Geo. W., D.D. *Historical Sketch of Roman Eagle Lodge, No. 122, A.F. & A.M. 1820-1895.* Danville, N.D.

Davis, Burke. *To Appomattox: Nine April Days, 1865.* New York, 1959.

Evans, Gen. Clement A. (Ed.) *Confederate Military History.* 13 vols. Atlanta, 1899.

Fox, William. *Regimental Losses in the American Civil War, 1861-1865.* Albany, NY, 1889.

Freman, Douglas Southall. *R. E. Lee* 4 vols. New York, 1936.

_____. *Lee's Lieutenants - a Study in Command.* 3 vols. New York, 1942-1944.

Georg, Kathleen R. & Busey, John W. *Nothing But Glory - Pickett's Division at Gettysburg.* Hightstown, NJ (Longstreet House), 1987.

Hayes, Dr. Jack I. *The Thirty-Eighth Virginia Infantry Regiment.* N.P., N.D. copy in possession of the author.

Headspeth, W. Carroll. *Halifax Volunteers in the Confederate Army.* South Boxton, Va. N.D.

Herndon, John Goodwin, Ph.D. *The Herndons of the American Revolution. . . through the Seventh Generation.* Privately printed, 1952.

Hutchison, Scott W. (comp.) *List of 38th Virginia Infantry Soldiers Buried in Oakwood Cemetery, Richmond.* Copies in possession of the compiler and the author.

Jack, George S. *History of Roanoke County.* Roanoke, 1912.

Jordan, Weymouth T., Jr. *North Carolina Troops 1861-1865: A Roster.* Raleigh, 1983.

Krick, Robert K. *Lee's Colonels - A Biographical Register of the Field Officers of the Army of Northern Virginia.* Dayton, Ohio, 1979.

Maury, Col. Richard L. *The Battle of Williamsburg and the Charge of the 24th Virginia of Early's Brigade.* Richmond, 1880.

Miller, Joseph Lyon, M.D. *The Descendants of Capt. Thomas Carter 1652-1912.* Harrisonburg, 1972.

Moore, Munsey Adams. *Cemetery and Tombstone Records of Mecklenburg County, Va.* Chase City, Va., 1982.

Moore, Samuel J. T., Jr. *Civil War Guide to Richmond.* Richmond, 1978.

The Official Military Atlas of the Civil War. New York, 1978.

Osborne, Marvin L. (comp.) *Transcribed pension records of the 38th Va. Inf. Veterans.* Copies in possession of the compiler and the author.

Pickett, LaSalle Corbell. *Pickett and His Men.* Atlanta, 1900.

Stewart, George R. *Pickett's Charge.* Boston, 1959.

Sublett, Charles W. *57th Virginia Infantry.* Lynchburg, 1985.

Trask, Benjamin H. *9th Virginia Infantry.* Lynchburg, 1984.

Tucker, Glenn. *High Tide at Gettysburg,* New York, 1958.

Tyler, Lyon Gardiner, LL.D. *Encyclopedia of Virginia Biography.* 5 vols. New York, 1915.

Waldrep, George Calvin III. *Halifax County (Virginia) Cemeteries,* vol. 2. Greenville, S.C. 1986.

Walker, Charles D. *Biographical Sketches of the Undergraduates and Eleves of the Virginia Military Institute Who Fell During the War Between the States.* Philadelphia, 1875.

Walker, C. Irvine. *The Life of Lieutenant General Richard Heron Anderson of the Confederate States Army.* Charleston, S.C., 1917.

Wallace, Lee A., Jr. *3rd Virginia Infantry.* Lynchburg, 1986.

_____. *A Guide to Virginia Military Organizations: 1861-1865.* 2nd Edition. Lynchburg, 1986.

Watkins, Raymond W. (comp.) *List of Confederate Soldiers Who Died in the General Hospitals at Danville, Virginia 1862-1865.* Va.-N.C. Piedmont Genealogical Society, Danville, 1983.